AF545156

German Jihad

Columbia Studies in Terrorism and Irregular Warfare

Columbia Studies in Terrorism and Irregular Warfare

BRUCE HOFFMAN, SERIES EDITOR

This series seeks to fill a conspicuous gap in the burgeoning literature on terrorism, guerrilla warfare, and insurgency. The series adheres to the highest standards of scholarship and discourse and publishes books that elucidate the strategy, operations, means, motivations, and effects posed by terrorist, guerrilla, and insurgent organizations and movements. It thereby provides a solid and increasingly expanding foundation of knowledge on these subjects for students, established scholars, and informed reading audiences alike.

Ami Pedahzur, *The Israeli Secret Services and the Struggle Against Terrorism*

Ami Pedahzur and Arie Perliger, *Jewish Terrorism in Israel*

Lorenzo Vidino, *The New Muslim Brotherhood in the West*

Erica Chenoweth and Maria J. Stephan, *Why Civil Resistance Works: The Strategic Logic of Nonviolent Resistance*

William C. Banks, *New Battlefields/Old Laws: Critical Debates on Asymmetric Warfare*

Blake W. Mobley, *Terrorism and Counterintelligence: How Terrorist Groups Elude Detection*

Michael W. S. Ryan, *The Deep Battle: Decoding Al-Qaeda's Strategy Against America*

German Jihad

On the Internationalization of Islamist Terrorism

GUIDO W. STEINBERG

Columbia
University
Press
New York

Columbia University Press
Publishers Since 1893
New York Chichester, West Sussex
cup.columbia.edu

Library of Congress Cataloging-in-Publication Data
Steinberg, Guido, 1968–
German Jihad : on the internationalization of Islamist terrorism / Guido W. Steinberg
pages cm. — (Columbia studies in terrorism and irregular warfare)
Includes bibliographical references and index.
ISBN 978-0-231-15992-0 (cloth : alk. paper) — ISBN 978-0-231-50053-1 (ebook)
1. Terrorism—Germany. 2. Terrorism—Religious aspects—Islam.
3. Terrorists—Recruiting—Germany. 4. Qaida (Organization) I. Title.
HV6433.G3S727 2013
363.3250943—dc23

2012047653

Columbia University Press books are printed on permanent and durable acid-free paper.
This book is printed on paper with recycled content.
Printed in the United States of America
c 10 9 8 7 6 5 4 3 2 1

Cover design: Fifth Letter

In the memory of our dead soldiers at the Hindu Kush

Contents

Abbreviations

BfV	German Office for the Protection of the Constitution (Bundesamt für Verfassungsschutz)
BKA	German Federal Criminal Police (Bundeskriminalamt)
BND	German Federal Intelligence Service (Bundesnachrichtendienst)
CIA	US Central Intelligence Agency
EU	European Union
GIMF	Global Islamic Media Front
GSPC	Salafist Group for Preaching and Combat (Groupe Salafiste pour la Predicament et le Combat)
IBDA-C	Great East Islamic Raiders' Front (İslami Büyükdoğu Akıncılar Cephesi)
IED	improvised explosive device
IJU	Islamic Jihad Union
IMU	Islamic Movement of Uzbekistan
ISAF	International Security Assistance Force
LfV	State Office for the Protection of the Constitution (Landesamt für Verfassungsschutz)
LIFG	Libyan Islamic Fighting Group
NATO	North Atlantic Treaty Organization
PKK	Kurdistan Workers' Party (Partiya Karkerên Kurdistanê)
PRT	Provincial Reconstruction Team

Acknowledgments

Over the course of the past ten years, numerous people have helped me develop my thoughts about the international jihadist movement, and although not all of them can be named here, some deserve special mention. First, I thank Nils Wörmer and Yassin Musharbash for reading the manuscript. Nils's advice on military matters and his relentless quest for accuracy have been invaluable. Yassin has for nearly a decade been a tremendously knowledgeable and inspiring conversational partner about terrorism, the Middle East, and South Asia. Klaus Hummel and Raffaello Pantucci read parts of the manuscript, and I greatly appreciate their criticism and suggestions.

Special thanks go to my research assistants Ulrike Hoole and Michael McEvoy, who did an awesome job and suffered dearly while checking my text and doing all the greater and the lesser things that make the production of such a manuscript possible. Nicole Renvert knows how difficult their job has been because she read and corrected the proposal for this book. Without her constant support, I would never have finished it.

My thanks also go to Ahmet Senyurt, Florian Peil, Noman Benotman, Jeremy Binnie, Joanna Wright, Tim Pippard, Natasha Cohen, Stephen Tankel, Walter Posch, Holger Stark, Matthias Gebauer, Holger Schmidt, Souad Mekhennet, Marcel Häßler, Uwe Halbach, Ulrich Kraetzer, Eric Gujer, Wolf Schmidt, Aladdin Sarhan, Herbert L. Müller, Benno Köpfer, Wolfgang Würz, and Khalid Zoubairi. I am also grateful to my former colleagues in the German chancellery who taught me most of what I know about the inner workings of German politics and bureaucracy, but also about counterterrorism, the work of intelligence services, and the freeing of hostages. Among them, Hans Vorbeck can be named, but I am no less grateful to those whom I cannot mention here.

And last, I am especially thankful to all those friends, former colleagues, and interview partners who have to remain anonymous but who have contributed immensely to this book.

German Jihad

Prologue

Lone-Wolf Attacks and the Europlot

On March 2, 2011, Germany suffered its first terrorist attack since the days of the left-wing Red Army Fraction (1970–1998) and the very first attack perpetrated by a jihadist. A young Kosovar Muslim from Frankfurt killed two American soldiers and perilously injured two others at the Frankfurt airport. The twenty-one-year-old Arid Uka seems to have acted as a "lone wolf"—an appellation that security services sometimes use for terrorists who act on their own, independently of larger organizations. He had arrived in Germany with his family in 1994 and reportedly had not shown any jihadist inclinations prior to the attacks. Yet beginning in late summer 2010, Uka had radicalized in a very short period of time. As evidenced by his Facebook page under the pseudonym "Abu Reyyan" (*abu* means "father of"), he had established online contacts with many prominent Salafist preachers during the two to three weeks before his attack, leading specialists to conclude tentatively that his radicalization was not completed at the time of the attack. Most prominent among his contacts was the Moroccan preacher Abdallatif Rouali, known in Frankfurt as an adherent of jihadist ideology.[1] The preacher denied having come into contact with the killer. However, the police had searched Rouali's flat and those of several of his followers and contacts the week before the attack because he was suspected of having recruited volunteers for jihad. Because

Uka was reported as having tried to find a way to Afghanistan, there were widespread doubts concerning Rouali's possible role. Nevertheless, until late 2012, no evidence of a larger network had been unearthed.

Since January 2011, Uka had worked at the international letter-sorting office of the German postal service Deutsche Post at Frankfurt airport, so it was easy for him to find the terminal where US military buses commuted to and from Ramstein airbase, situated some 130 kilometers southwest of Frankfurt. He approached a bus in which members of an Air Force Security Forces team—a kind of military police—were waiting to be shuttled to Ramstein, asked an American soldier for a cigarette, and inquired whether the servicemen on the bus nearby were indeed on their way to Afghanistan.[2] When the soldier confirmed this, Uka drew his gun and shot another airman waiting to enter the bus twice in the back of the head. Uka then entered the bus, where he executed the driver and shot a third soldier in the head. The fourth victim received a bullet in the chest and was perilously wounded. When Uka tried to shoot the fifth airman in the head, his pistol jammed and failed twice, and when he tried to escape, he was chased by the airman and caught by German police. If the pistol had not jammed, Uka would have likely killed many more people because he carried a substantial amount of additional ammunition with him.

During his first interrogation, Uka tried to justify his actions as preventive self-defense. According to his statement, the night before the shootings he had watched a propaganda film produced by the Islamic Movement of Uzbekistan (IMU) that included alleged documentary material showing sexual assaults by Americans on Iraqi and Afghan women. The video had been produced for the German market and contained a longer German-language sequence featuring the German Moroccan Yassin Chouka (a.k.a. Abu Ibrahim al-Almani) calling on Muslims to defend Muslim women in Iraq and Afghanistan against American and allied rapists. Uka told his interrogators that a scene showing the rape of an Afghan girl by American soldiers had prompted him to act. What he did not know, however, was that the IMU had copied this scene from the film *Redacted* by Brian De Palma. Released in 2007, the film shows the so-called Mahmudiya killings of March 2006 in which a group of five American soldiers gang-raped a fourteen-year-old Iraqi girl and killed the girl and her whole family in a village close to the central Iraqi city Mahmudiya, south of Bagdad. The IMU propagandists had used the sequence to heighten the video's impact.

Uka claimed that, after a sleepless night, he went to the airport intending to kill American soldiers who were on their way to Afghanistan in order to prevent further atrocities like the ones shown in the video. That is why he asked one of the airmen whether he was going to Afghanistan. Indeed, Uka claimed that he would not have killed the Americans if they had been on the return journey. He had spent more than half an hour waiting in the terminal. When he had already decided to leave, he saw the bus driver entering the terminal hall, looking at the arrivals board. When the other soldiers arrived, Uka followed his victims outside to where the bus was waiting to leave for Ramstein.

A seemingly well-trained and lank young man five feet nine inches tall, Uka had dropped out of high school about a year before graduation. Although he had been a talented student, he entered a period of depression in the twelfth grade. He had difficulty getting up in the mornings and missed classes, which forced his school to expel him. Still living with his parents, Uka decided not to tell them of his expulsion and started working petty jobs, eventually ending up at the airport post office. Starting in late summer 2010, however, he turned increasingly to religion and changed his outward appearance according to the rules of Salafist Islam. He shunned ankle-length trousers because the Prophet had allegedly outlawed garments covering the ankles. He also made an effort to study Arabic in an online language school but was expelled because he did not do his homework. He seems to have been in the midst of a radicalization process that continued up until the attacks. Uka had difficulty, for example, accepting the ban on music, and only during the days before the attack did he switch to listening exclusively to jihad hymns (*nashid*, pl. *anashid*)—which are not prohibited by the Salafists.

Most important, Uka seems to have entered the world of jihadism exclusively through the Internet, where he followed the news of the jihadist battlefields, listened to jihadist sermons, and watched videos. He studied the ideology and politics of the jihadist movement intensively, but no ideological coaches, no religious authorities, and no masterminds were actively involved in his radicalization. After only a few months, Uka was ready to join the battle in Iraq or Afghanistan, but he later told his interrogators—to their surprise—that he did not have the necessary contacts.[3] Thus, after having watched the rape video, he decided to act alone and kill Americans on their way to Afghanistan.

The IMU propaganda seems to have had a decisive influence on Uka. Police later established that while going to the airport, he listened repeatedly to a German-language jihad hymn entitled "Mother, Remain Steadfast, I Have Joined the Jihad," sung by Yassin Chouka's brother Monir and released in September 2010.[4] The song seems to have had tremendous influence on the young Kosovar:

Mother, remain steadfast, I have joined the Jihad.
Do not mourn for me and know I have been awakened.
The umma has been blinded, but I have been honored.
Mother, remain steadfast, your son has joined the Jihad.
The umma has been blinded but I have been honored.
Mother, remain steadfast, your son has joined the Jihad.
The screams became louder, the injuries increased.
The unfulfilled duty, I could not find peace.
Today I must leave, tomorrow it is too late.
Mother, remain steadfast, your son has joined the Jihad.
Today I must leave, tomorrow it is too late.
Mother, remain steadfast, your son has joined the Jihad.
Relying upon my Lord I leave.
Fi sabili llah [In the path of God], wherever it will lead.
No matter how vast the desert, no matter how high the mountain
Mother, remain steadfast, your son has joined the Jihad.
No matter how vast the desert, no matter how high the mountain
Mother, remain steadfast, your son has joined the Jihad.
Mother, don't you see what is happening in Filastin?[5]
Mother, don't you hear the bombs in Iraq?
Our brothers and our sisters are imprisoned, and we are questioned.
Mother, remain steadfast, your son has joined the Jihad.
Mother, while your tears are flowing, blood is shed in Shishan.[6]
The Jews and the Christians are here in Khurasan.[7]
They insult the Prophet and tread on the Qur'an.
Mother, remain steadfast, your son has joined the Jihad.
They insult the Prophet and tread on the Qur'an.
Mother, remain steadfast, your son has joined the Jihad.
Mother, if I fall on the battlefield, do not think I am dead.
Rather, I am alive in a better place.

Flying in a green bird, my Lord looking after me.
Mother, remain steadfast, your son has joined the Jihad.
Flying in a green bird, my Lord looking after me.
Mother, remain steadfast, your son has joined the Jihad.
Mother, remain steadfast, I have joined the Jihad.
Do not mourn for me and know I have been awakened.
The umma has been blinded, but I have been honored.
Mother, remain steadfast, your son has joined the Jihad.
The umma has been blinded, but I have been honored.
Mother, remain steadfast, your son has joined the Jihad.

What is most striking is that this event made clear to what extent the Internet has gained significance in the radicalization of young Muslims during the past few years and how dangerous a lone wolf can be, giving security authorities no chance to thwart his plan. In addition, the role of IMU propaganda material produced for the German market hinted at the significance of the large number of German volunteers in the Pakistani camps of al-Qaeda and like-minded organizations.

In fact, this incident confirmed a trend. Germany in general and Americans in Germany in particular have become increasingly important targets for the jihadists. Only five months before the airport attack, on November 17, 2010, the German interior minister Thomas de Maizière warned with unprecedented candor of possible attacks in Germany. For the first time, he stated, there was concrete evidence of a planned attack in Germany that might be perpetrated before the end of November. Maizière also announced that he had already ordered the Federal Police (Bundespolizei) to increase its presence at airports and train stations.[8] During the next two months, heavily armed police became an integral feature of public life in the country.

The warning was based on two different observations. First and foremost, since 2007 al-Qaeda and other jihadist organizations had made clear on more than one occasion that attacking German targets in order to force the German government to withdraw its troops from Afghanistan was one of their priorities. At the same time, an ever-increasing number of young Germans of different origins had found their way to the training camps of al-Qaeda and other such groups in Pakistan, providing the jihadists with the recruits to embark on a terrorist campaign against Germany. In one case, the Uzbek organization Islamic Jihad Union (IJU, Ittihad al-Jihad al-Islami) had already sent a group of four German volunteers—the "Sauerland group"—back to Germany in 2006 in order to perpetrate an attack on American and Uzbek targets. German authorities with American help thwarted their plan, but the overall threat increased due to the rapidly rising number of German volunteers leaving for Pakistan since 2007.

In late summer 2010, information about a new terror plot emerged and became increasingly credible, with three threads of information decisively shaping the dramatic German assessment of the situation. The first individual to talk about the "Europlot," as it was later dubbed, was Ahmad Wali Sidiqi (b. 1974), a German Afghan from Hamburg who had first joined the IMU and then al-Qaeda in Pakistan and had been arrested in Kabul in July 2010 because of his connection to a terrorist organization (the reason for arrest in Afghanistan, Pakistan, or Turkey is in many cases unknown but is most likely alleged connection to a terrorist organization or illegal border crossing). Talking to his American interrogators in Bagram Prison north of Kabul, Sidiqi claimed to have been introduced to the midlevel al-Qaeda commander Yunus al-Muritani (Yunus the Mauritanian, Abd al-Rahman Wuld Muhammad al-Husain) in Mir Ali in the Pakistani tribal areas in early summer 2010. In what sounds like a recruitment effort, Muritani talked to Sidiqi about planned attacks in Europe, focusing on Germany, Great Britain, and France. The news jump-started American and European counterterrorism investigators, most of whom took the interrogation results seriously. Sidiqi's claims were then corroborated in the interrogation of a second German detainee, Rami Makanesi (b. 1985), a German Syrian, who had been arrested in Pakistan in June 2010 and subsequently deported to Germany.[9]

In a second thread of information, US security services provided the German government with intelligence about a group of terrorists who had already left the Afghan–Pakistani border and were heading toward Europe. A supposedly (but most likely not) Shiite Indian group called "Saif" (Arabic for "sword") had entered into an agreement with al-Qaeda and sent terrorists to Germany to perpetrate what has become known as a "Mumbai-style" attack—referring to the incident on November 26, 2008, in which ten members of the Pakistani terrorist organization Lashkar-e Tayyiba (Army of the Pure), armed with automatic rifles and hand grenades, spread throughout the center of the Indian metropolis, killing 166 people, injuring 304 others, and taking hostages in international hotels, restaurants, an important train station, a hospital, and a Jewish cultural center. In the aftermath of the attack, security specialists worldwide expressed fears that other terrorist groups would duplicate the Mumbai attack, which attracted worldwide media attention and paralyzed life in the economic capital of India. Ever since, the phrase *Mumbai-style attack* has referred to a commando action in which a heavily armed group carries out gun and grenade attacks, takes hostages in or around landmarks in a major city, and defends its positions while causing maximum damage.[10]

The third and final thread of information came from yet another dubious source. In October 2010, a German jihadist based in Pakistan contacted the German authorities by phone and gave a detailed warning of an attack similar to the one in Mumbai that was planned for February or March 2011. According to this witness, two people had already arrived in Germany and gone underground in Berlin. Four others were awaiting their travel orders in Pakistan.[11] The informant was Emrah Erdoğan (b. 1988), a jihadist from Wuppertal, near Cologne, who might have been a member of the group German Taliban Mujahideen (Deutsche Taliban Mujahideen) until June 2010. After this group disbanded, he joined al-Qaeda.[12]

The terror warnings triggered a heated debate among security specialists and led to interagency tensions with—as is so often the case in the years since the attacks on September 11, 2001 (9/11)—the Federal Criminal Police (Bundeskriminalamt, BKA) on one side and the intelligence services on the other. Whereas most police officials argued that the warnings were so specific that they had to be taken seriously, the spy agencies tended to belittle the value of the evidence.[13] No one disputed, however, that Germany (including American targets in Germany) had been a high-value target for the jihadists for some years already, and since 2007 the German jihadist scene—although still small—had become the most dynamic in Europe.

Chapter 1, "Unlikely Internationalists: Putting German Jihadism into Perspective," puts the growth of jihadism in Germany within its larger context—namely, the development of global jihadism since 2001 and the internationalization of jihadist ideology, strategies, and social base. Chapter 2, "Two Hamburg Cells: A History of Jihadist Terrorism in Germany," provides a detailed analysis of the history of the German community, highlighting continuities and changes between the first Hamburg cell—which provided three of the four pilots for the September 11 attacks—and the travel groups who, since 2006, have been leaving Germany in order to join al-Qaeda and other jihadist organizations in Pakistan. Chapter 3, " 'A Second 9/11': The Sauerland Plot," deals with the most important terrorist plot hatched in Germany after 2001.The so-called Sauerland plot of 2007 became a milestone for German jihadism in several ways, most notably for how the Sauerland group paved the way for dozens of new recruits traveling to Pakistan in subsequent years. Most of them joined the IJU, which is the subject of chapter 4.

Turkey is the most important way station and logistics hub for most German jihadists, many of whom are ethnic Turks or Kurds, so chapter 5, "The Turkish Dimension," gives an overview of the situation in Turkey, the role of Turks in Bosnia, Chechnya, and Afghanistan, and their connections to Germany. Chapter 6, " 'Leaving Kuffaristan': Radicalization and Recruitment in Germany," focuses on modes of radicalization and recruitment in Germany and why increasing numbers of jihadists are leaving the country to go to Pakistan. Chapter 7, "The German Taliban Mujahideen," deals with the first exclusively German jihadist group, formed in Pakistan in 2009 as a result of the influx of German recruits. The internationalization processes analyzed in chapter 1 also affected organizations such as the IMU, which in turn integrated about a dozen Germans into its ranks starting in 2008 and developed an increasingly anti-German ideology, a development that is depicted in chapter 8, " 'The Worst Enemy of Islam': The Islamic Movement of Uzbekistan Against Germany." The effects of this internationalization process became most palpable in the German area of operations in northern Afghanistan, where the German army, the Bundeswehr, was confronted not only with Afghan insurgents, but also with an increasing threat posed by IMU fighters, among them the first Germans in 2010. This is the topic of chapter 9, "Germans in the Taliban Stalingrad: Fighting the Kunduz Insurgency," which is followed by concluding remarks in " 'This Is the Last Year America': Threats and Prospects" about the threat to Germany in particular, the future of the jihadist movement in general, and some suggestions for possible strategies for countering the threat.

1

Unlikely Internationalists

Putting German Jihadism into Perspective

In March 2010, Germany's most publicized Islamist terrorism trial to date ended with the sentencing of the four defendants to between five and twelve years in prison. Led by the German convert to Islam Fritz Gelowicz, the group had been arrested in September 2007 while its members were attempting to assemble homemade bombs. Dubbed the "Sauerland cell" by the German media (after the region in western Germany where they were caught), the four had planned to attack nightclubs frequented by American military personnel and possibly the Ramstein Airbase, the largest US military facility in Germany. Although Arid Uka carried out the only successful jihadist attack in Germany up to 2011, the Sauerland plot was potentially the most dangerous terrorist plot hatched in Germany since the days of the Hamburg cell of pilots involved in the 9/11 attacks.

Gelowicz and his friends Adem Yilmaz, Daniel Schneider, and Atilla Selek had come a long way from their life in provincial German towns to careers as the most prominent terrorist suspects in recent German history. Between 2004 and 2007, the plotters undertook a long jihadist journey that led them to Turkey, the jihadist logistics hub and way station between Europe, the Middle East, and South Asia; then to Arabic-language schools in Syria and Egypt; to Iran; and finally from there smuggled into the Pakistani tribal areas—the epicenter of jihadism ever since the withdrawal of al-Qaeda and its allies from Afghanistan to the Pakistani side of the border.

The plot began shortly after September 11, 2001, in the twin cities of Ulm and Neu-Ulm in southern Germany. The future ringleader Fritz Gelowicz and Atilla Selek were part of a small network of young Germans, Turks, and Arabs radicalized in a local Salafist center, the Multicultural House (Multikulturhaus) in Neu-Ulm. The figurehead of the Ulm scene was an Egyptian imam who had been rising to prominence in Islamist circles in Germany since the early 1990s and who was known to have extensive contact with jihadists worldwide. In 2004, Gelowicz tried to find a way to join the rebels in Chechnya, following in the footsteps of some of his friends, who had already left the twin cities for the Caucasus in April 2002. When Gelowicz's contacts in Istanbul told him that it would be impossible to reach Chechnya, he and the future perpetrators first went on a pilgrimage to Mecca in January 2005 before they traveled to Syria and Egypt in order to study Arabic and to look for possible ways to join the insurgents in Iraq.

It was in the Syrian capital Damascus that, according to the four young men's later confessions, a small group of jihadists from Azerbaijan approached Gelowicz and Yilmaz and offered to take them to Chechnya. Their new friends insisted, however, that in order to join the Chechen rebels they would first need to undergo military training. To this end, the Azeris sent them to Pakistan, where they would be trained in the camp of a small organization from Uzbekistan, the IJU. Starting in April 2006, the four volunteers traveled via Turkey and Iran to Pakistan. They reached the tribal area of North-Waziristan, close to the Afghan border, where they joined the IJU. The organization's leadership soon sent the young men back home to Germany, however, where they were supposed to carry out attacks on American targets.

Their itineraries and contacts identified the Sauerland four as true internationalists, in spite of the fact that the two German converts to Islam and the two ethnic Turks seemed ill prepared for the journey they were to undertake as global jihadists—from Germany to the Middle East and South Asia—where they would join a Central Asian organization. None of the young men spoke English or any other foreign language except Turkish, their educational records were poor, and prior to 2005 their international experience had been restricted by and large to short stays in Turkey. It was not their upbringing and education that set them on the path they were to follow. Rather, it was the Salafist milieu in which the young men immersed themselves, combined with their increasingly internationalist jihadist ideology and the militant networks' readiness to integrate the German and Turkish newcomers, that led the members of this small group to become internationalist jihadists, travel half the globe to join the jihad, and devise the most dangerous terrorist plot in German history.

A Not so Global Jihad

It is this book's central hypothesis that the internationalist scene and ideology we witness today developed only after September 11, 2001, and that the jihadist movement has been going through an internationalization process ever since, which has profoundly changed its characteristics. Whereas in 2001 there was no such thing as global jihad, in 2012 one might be justified in using that term. This claim might surprise those readers who have grown accustomed to politicians, academics, and journalists describing al-Qaeda as a global phenomenon as early as the bombing of the twin towers in the United States. But the fact is that two distinct schools of thought have offered two competing ways of explaining the motivation of al-Qaeda and its leadership.

The first globalist school of thought primarily saw al-Qaeda as an anti-Western and anti-American force that in late summer 2001 had transcended its former orientation toward its leaders' and members' home countries in the Arab Middle East. Among adherents of this school and the wider public, terms and notions such as *global jihad*, *transnational*, *new terrorism*, and later on *radical Islam* gained currency. Under the influence of the events of September 2001, those who did not have any prior relation to or knowledge of the Middle East stressed the fact that al-Qaeda had attacked the United States following a global rather than a regional agenda. Some adherents to this school interpreted the events in a culturalist way, seeing evidence for a civilizational conflict between the Muslim and the Western worlds. Others highlighted al-Qaeda's nihilistic character, basing this argument on, inter alia, the absurdity of al-Qaeda's efforts to defeat the only remaining superpower and its numerous allies worldwide.

According to this reading, al-Qaeda did not have any concrete political goals but rather stuck to terrorist violence as an end in itself.[1]

However, for those observers who took an interest in al-Qaeda on the basis of their prior knowledge of the Middle East, the first school of thought did not offer any convincing explanation. For this second, regionalist school, it seemed obvious that the jihadist movement was rather one faction in a much greater civil war within Arab and Muslim countries and that the attacks on Western targets were a side effect and a reaction to Western and American Middle East policies. Although some of these pundits focused on the Israeli–Palestinian conflict as a prime motivating factor, other adherents of this school stressed that the al-Qaeda leadership in its majority hailed from Egypt and Saudi Arabia and that the root causes of 9/11 could be found in these countries. The roots of al-Qaeda's decision to carry out terrorist attacks at home and abroad could be found in the West's support of oppressive regimes in the Arab world. For proponents of these theories, it seemed obvious that al-Qaeda attacked the United States in order to force its withdrawal from the Arab Middle East, especially Saudi Arabia and Egypt. The message of the 9/11 masterminds was, "Withdraw your troops from Saudi Arabia and your financial and military support from Egypt; otherwise we will attack you time and again in the United States and elsewhere." According to this interpretation, the jihadist movement in general and al-Qaeda in particular were firmly rooted in their home countries, and anyone who wanted to understand the tragic events in New York and Washington had to take a closer look at al-Qaeda's domestic environment and the Middle East as a whole.[2]

In 2001, the proponents of the regionalist school were much closer to the truth than the globalists. In spite of the prominence of globalization theories, adherents of the jihadist movement in general and of al-Qaeda in particular remained firmly rooted in their respective national political cultures. This conclusion becomes clear when one looks at al-Qaeda's membership structure shortly before it lost its safe haven in Afghanistan ı 2001. First and foremost, al-Qaeda was a multinational, not a multieth-:, organization. With few exceptions, it consisted of Arabs of different ionalities. The most prominent exception was Khalid Sheikh Moham- (commonly dubbed "KSM" by the security specialists), the chief ect of the 9/11 attacks. He was born in Kuwait in 1964, and his father hailed from the Pakistani province of Baluchistan. Sheikh Mohammed was integrated well into Kuwaiti society, however, and his thinking in his youth seems to have been shaped deeply by the local form of Islamism prevalent in the small sheikhdom, so he might well be considered sociologically Kuwaiti.[3]

At the time of the 9/11 attacks, al-Qaeda was an exclusively Arab organization, made up of Egyptian and Saudi nationals, with some Kuwaitis and Yemenis. Its core constituency consisted of Arabs from the states of the Arabian Peninsula, primarily Saudi citizens such as Osama Bin Laden, Yemenis from Bin Laden's ancestral home country, and some Kuwaitis. All of these nationalities shared common religious, ideological, cultural, and even tribal and family bonds, which assisted the foundation of a relatively cohesive core group. This Saudi–Yemeni–Kuwaiti cluster had become the most dynamic force in international terrorism since the early 1990s, and among the different groupings that formed al-Qaeda it was the most internationalist in outlook because its radicalization went back to the Gulf War in Kuwait in 1991 and the protests against the American presence on Saudi and Kuwaiti soil. Al-Qaeda's Saudi factions were the militant wing of an Islamist opposition movement that developed after the kingdom asked the United States to deploy troops on its territory in order to defend Saudi Arabia from a possible Iraqi invasion in August 1990. As a consequence, anti-Americanism was a particularly important motive for the jihadists from the Arabian Peninsula.[4]

In the mid-1990s, Bin Laden and his followers entered an alliance with a group of Egyptians under the leadership of Aiman al-Zawahiri, who became number two in the al-Qaeda-hierarchy and in 2011 Bin Laden's successor. Prior to that, Zawahiri and his followers in the Egyptian Jihad Organization (Tanzim al-Jihad) had been more nationalist in outlook than their brethren from the peninsula.[5] Since the early 1980s, their sole aim had been to topple the regime of Egyptian president Hosni Mubarak, and all of their activities in Afghanistan and Sudan were oriented toward this goal. This goal changed when in the mid-1990s they realized that an Islamist insurgency that erupted in their home country in 1992 had failed. Aiman al-Zawahiri came to the conclusion that if the Jihad Organization wanted to continue its armed struggle, it would require a shift in strategy, so he decided to attack the "far enemy" (the United States) in order to weaken the "near enemy" (the Mubarak regime).[6]

The alliance between Zawahiri and Bin Laden, between the Egyptians and the Saudi Arabians, formed the ideological and strategic basis for the new organization. By attacking the United States and their allies, they intended to force an American withdrawal from the Arab and Muslim worlds. After having achieved this, they planned to topple the regimes in their own home countries and their followers' home countries. Rather than an outright global strategy, the strategy was one in which local and global aims were closely intertwined. It is noteworthy in this context that in order to become an organization with global reach (and if only for the one attack in the United States), al-Qaeda needed the help of a third group, which was responsible for the professionalization of its terrorist activity. In 1996, Khalid Sheikh Mohammed, bringing with him several years of terrorist experience, joined al-Qaeda in Afghanistan. He had already been involved in the first bombing of the World Trade Center in 1993, and in 1994–1995 he planned to detonate bombs on airplanes traveling from East and Southeast Asia to the United States. He joined al-Qaeda as a sort of "terrorist contractor," with a high degree of operational independence. He did not fit well into any of the national groups that made up al-Qaeda at that time but instead resembled the profit-oriented terrorist embodied most prominently by the Venezuelan Illich Ramírez Sánchez. Under the alias "Carlos, the Jackal," Ramírez had been Osama Bin Laden's predecessor as the most wanted international terrorist until his arrest in 1994.[7] It was not until Khalid Sheikh Mohammed took over parts of al-Qaeda's operational planning that the organization developed the capabilities to plan and organize the attacks on September 11, 2001.[8]

Only after all of these elements were put together was al-Qaeda able to develop a more transnational character. Especially after the bombings of two US embassies in Nairobi and Dar es Salaam in August 1998, al-Qaeda and its leader became world famous, and new recruits from all over the world flocked to Afghanistan to join Osama Bin Laden's anti-American jihad. Nevertheless, Arabs remained the overwhelming majority within the organization, and the leaders were primarily Egyptians and Saudi Arabians. Calling this phenomenon "global jihad" in late 2001 was therefore misleading. Rather, al-Qaeda had exported the civil wars in the Arab world to the United States and had never lost its focus on its home countries. It would take several more years and severe mistakes by al-Qaeda's adversaries to further internationalize the jihadist movement.

Internationalizing Jihadist Terrorism

More than a decade after 9/11, the situation has changed. Al-Qaeda and the jihadist movement in general have gone through a profound process of "internationalization." This means that national, regional, and ethnic dividing lines have lost their former importance and are giving way to a more truly global movement. Although the organization was an exclusively Arab phenomenon in 2001, in subsequent years it increasingly attracted Pakistanis, Afghans, Turks, Kurds, and European converts of different nationalities. And from being dominated by Egyptians and Gulf Arabs and being seen by other Arabs as an exclusively Egyptian–Saudi endeavor in 2001, it became an organization in which North Africans, Jordanians, Palestinians, and Iraqis have gained importance owing to the emergence of regional affiliates in Iraq, Algeria, and Yemen. This internationalization process—which becomes so obvious in the biographies and itineraries of the Sauerland four and numerous other German jihadists—began before 9/11 and has continued ever since. The process is most obvious with regard to the national and ethnic base of the jihadist movement, but it has ideological and strategic dimensions as well.

INTERNATIONALIST IDEOLOGY AND IDEOLOGUES

Back in 2001, the "near enemy" paradigm still held sway in the jihadist movement, but even before then al-Qaeda's spectacular attacks on the US embassies in East Africa in 1998 and on the destroyer USS *Cole* in Aden harbor in October 2000 had catapulted Bin Laden and his followers to the forefront of the jihadist movement. Bin Laden and Aiman al-Zawahiri's strategy was subject to a heated debate in militant circles because many fellow jihadists still stuck to the "near enemy" strategy, with the goal of spurring national revolutions in their home countries. The Egyptians especially had been preparing themselves for the fight against the regime of President Hosni Mubarak since the early 1980s. Many of them were not ready to put aside their priorities in favor of a fight against the United States and their allies, which some of them deemed to be an unrealistic undertaking. This branch of the jihadist movement lost influence after September 11, 2001, however, when the US "war on terror" targeted not only the internationalists responsible for the 9/11 attacks, but also the nationalist revolutionaries who had not sought to attack the far enemy. For the latter, it became increasingly difficult to argue convincingly that the fight against the home regimes could be isolated from the larger struggle taking place.

Furthermore, after 9/11 many leading adherents of the Islamonationalist strand within the movement, among them some Egyptians and Libyans, were killed or arrested, or they renounced violence.[9] The leading intellectual figures had to give way to a new generation of ideologues and religious thinkers who increasingly propagated an internationalist line of argumentation. The rise of the Libyan Hasan Muhammad Qaid (a.k.a. Abu Yahia al-Libi) exemplifies this trend. From 2006 until his death in June 2012, Libi established himself as the most important internationalist ideologue in the jihadist movement and the most influential religious authority within the al-Qaeda senior leadership in Pakistan.

Libi's career is paradigmatic because he started off as a member of one of the most staunchly nationalist jihadist organizations, the Libyan Islamic Fighting Group (LIFG, al-Jamaʿa al-Islamiya al-Muqatila bi-Libiya). From its inception in the early 1990s, the LIFG worked exclusively toward toppling the regime of Muammar al-Gaddafi. Between 1995 and 1998, the LIFG fought a small-scale insurgency in eastern Libya but had to give up after three years of tough fighting due to the overwhelming strength of the Libyan security apparatus. As a consequence of its Islamonationalist orientation, the organization kept its distance from al-Qaeda, although in the 1990s many of its members stayed in close proximity to Bin Laden, Zawahiri, and their followers in Sudan, Afghanistan, and Pakistan. Like the other national groupings, the Libyans profited enormously from the protection granted to them by the Taliban state in Afghanistan. In contrast to al-Qaeda and the internationalists, however, they sought closer relations to their (equally nationalist-minded) Afghan hosts than to fellow Arabs. Many LIFG leaders were even openly critical of al-Qaeda because its attacks on American targets had provoked the US invasion of Afghanistan, which led to the downfall of the Taliban state in late 2001.[10]

Born in southern Libya sometime between 1963 and the late 1960s, Abu Yahia al-Libi, the younger brother of a leading LIFG functionary, first arrived in Afghanistan around 1990. Shortly afterward, the LIFG leadership picked Libi from its ranks when looking for promising young members in Pakistan and Afghanistan to undergo religious training courses in Mauritania.[11] This strategy shows that the LIFG developed a profound awareness early on of the importance of religious authority for the future of the jihadist movement. Jihadist organizations have to provide their followers with a convincing ideology propagated by religiously educated, charismatic, and credible thinkers. Only with the help of such personalities and the religious, ideological, and strategic training they offer can jihadist organizations hope to motivate their personnel sufficiently and produce cohesive and durable organizational structures with a common purpose and strategy. Focused ideological training can help these groups survive even in extremely hostile environments.[12]

After about two years of study in Mauritania, Libi returned to Afghanistan, where the Taliban had taken over the country and provided a safe haven for the Arab militants. Libi traveled around the Arab volunteers' training camps, started preaching to them, and was from then on considered a religious scholar among his comrades. Although his religious knowledge was far from profound, it was sufficiently erudite to convince his fellow fighters that his sermons and lessons were worth listening to. In fact, in light of his publications after 2005, his understanding of jihadist thought was acceptable even when compared to the more well-known religious authorities of the movement, such as the Jordanian Palestinians Abu Qutada al-Filastini and Abu Muhammad al-Maqdisi, whose academic credentials are without exception deficient.[13] Although Libi became well known among the Arabs in Afghanistan and Pakistan, he remained a mid-ranking member of the LIFG and had to stick to the ideological guidelines defined by the movement's paramount religious thinker, Sami Mustafa as-Saidi (a.k.a. Abu l-Mundhir as-Saidi). Most important, he continued promoting the LIFG's Islamonationalist ideology.

Libi's evolution from follower of a staunchly nationalist organization to proponent of jihadist internationalism occurred sometime between 2001 and 2005. In 2002, he was arrested by Pakistani authorities in Karachi and handed over to the United States. He spent the next three years in Bagram Prison in Afghanistan, suffering—if one believes his testimony—from a whole range of torture and degradation inflicted on him by his American captors. On July 10, 2005, Libi and three other high-profile jihadists managed to escape from the prison.[14] The breakout was highly embarrassing for the US government not only because important al-Qaeda members had managed to escape from one of the three most infamous American detention facilities worldwide (Guantánamo and Abu Ghraib being the other two), but because shortly afterward in September 2005 Libi published an account of his stay in Bagram on jihadist Web sites that in jihadist circles became standard reading on the American treatment of prisoners.[15] Libi made his way to the Pakistani mountains, where he joined the insurgents and al-Qaeda. His first propaganda video was published by the Arabic satellite TV chain al-Arabiya in November 2005.[16]

Starting in late 2005, Libi quickly established himself as the leading internationalist propagandist of the jihadist movement and made a clear break with the LIFG's ideology. Videos of his speeches were published on the Internet and widely spread among a growing internationalist audience worldwide. Libi now targeted the United States and its allies, the "far enemy." Echoing Osama Bin Laden's and Aiman al-Zawahiri's well-known messages, he called on fellow Muslims to fight the "unbelievers" (i.e., the United States and its Western allies) and "apostates" (i.e., nominally Muslim regimes) in Afghanistan and Pakistan. Furthermore, he became an important voice in debates over the legitimacy and scope of violence against Shiite and Sunni civilians in Iraq and successfully tried to establish himself as an authority for jihadists in Somalia, Yemen, North Africa, Central Asia, and Europe. Believed to have been fluent in Pashtu and Urdu in addition to his mother tongue, Arabic, Libi made tremendous efforts to transcend the ethnic and national dividing lines that still kept the jihadist movement from becoming a truly global force. Perhaps most important for this book's subject, he has been accepted as a religious authority by the Uzbek IJU, the very group that hosted most German jihadists between 2006 and 2009 (see chapter 4 for more detail on the IJU). In an IJU video that appeared in early June 2009, Libi gave a speech exhorting his listeners to continue the jihad and search for martyrdom. The video shows him sitting in a closed room most likely situated in a village in the Pakistani tribal region of North Waziristan, surrounded by IJU personnel. Next to him sits the military leader and, later, overall IJU commander Abdallah Fatih, listening carefully.[17] Among Germans and other nationalities, Abu Yahia al-Libi had become, in effect, the most important voice calling for the globalization of jihadist ideology.

It is important to understand the underlying reasons for Libi's conversion to jihadist internationalism and his increasing anti-Americanism. One reason might be that the US government had captured the LIFG leader

Abdallah Sadiq (a.k.a. Abdalhakim Belhajj) and the organization's religious head Abu l-Mundhir as-Saidi while they were on the run in Bangkok and Hong Kong, respectively, and extradited them to Libya in 2004—exposing them to potentially draconian revenge by the Libyan regime.[18] More important, however, Libi seems to have adopted jihadist internationalism as a result of his treatment in jail and his subsequent life on the battlefield in the Pakistani tribal areas under constant American pressure.[19] (It was in fact erroneously reported in December 2009 that he was killed by an American drone strike.) Libi has become one of the most important representatives of a younger generation of jihadist leaders who have risen to prominence in the long years of war in Afghanistan and who—due to their experiences since 2001—see the United States as their most dangerous enemy.

Libi's rise had organizational consequences as well. With the former (Islamonationalist) leaders in jail, the remaining Libyans in Pakistan and Afghanistan prepared to merge the vestiges of the LIFG with al-Qaeda in November 2007. While Abu Yahia al-Libi laid the theoretical ground for this step, his fellow Libyan Ali Ammar al-Ruqayi (Abu Laith al-Libi) served as acting leader of the LIFG contingent in the merger.[20] Like the change in Abu Yahia's career, the merger of the LIFG with its former competitors was evidence of the growing trend toward internationalization.

INTERNATIONALIST STRATEGIES

When the LIFG joined al-Qaeda in late 2007, the move did not have a huge effect on the jihadist scene because the LIFG seemed at the time to be a spent force. Its failed uprising in the 1990s had clearly shown that the organization lacked sufficient public support in its home country, and it never came close to threatening the Gaddafi regime. With the loss of its refuge in Afghanistan and its leadership arrested, the organization virtually ceased to exist, making the merger with al-Qaeda more of a propaganda coup than the union of two partners. According to rough estimates, the number of Libyans in Pakistan and Afghanistan at the time did not exceed two dozen.[21] Other, more dangerous organizations adopted an internationalist strategy after 2001, however, and in doing so changed the balance of power within the jihadist movement. The most important group was the Algerian Salafist Group for Preaching and Combat (GSPC, Groupe Salafiste pour la Predicament et le Combat or al-Jamaʿa al-Salafiya li-l-Daʿwa wa-l-Qital), which joined al-Qaeda in January 2007.

Algeria had been one of the main battlefields for militant Islamists since the early 1990s, when a bloody civil war broke out that did not subside until after 1995. Although many Algerians fought in Afghanistan during the 1980s, the Algerian jihadist scene remained strongly oriented toward regime change at home, even if it had long become clear to impartial observers that the Islamists would not be able to overthrow the regime. The resilience of the Algerian struggle was in part due to the fact that jihadist groups were able to continue their fight in Algeria even after the civil war ended. These groups withdrew to the rugged mountains east, southeast, and west of the capital Algiers, where they continue to fight the Algerian security forces to this day.

The continuing jihadist presence at home is what largely differentiates the Algerian scene from the Egyptian, where the militant underground was virtually wiped out by the security forces after the breakdown of the insurgency in 1997. As a consequence of this decimation, the Egyptian jihadists could only hope to reorganize abroad and join forces with their brethren from other countries. Aiman al-Zawahiri's alliance with Osama Bin Laden and the emergence of al-Qaeda were a direct result of this development. In Algeria, the jihadists retained the opportunity to fight on Algerian soil, and in 1998 the GSPC became the strongest local organization. It was founded the same year as a splinter group of the older Armed Islamic Group (Groupe Islamique Armée or al-Jamaʿa al-Islamiya al-Musallaha), which lost public support because of its indiscriminate use of violence against civilians. Jihadist internationalism was alien to the GSPC, and until 2003 its only aim was to topple the regime in Algiers and establish an Islamic state in the country.

In October 2003, though, the situation changed when the GSPC's then leader Nabil Sahraoui (d. 2004), announced that the GSPC had subordinated itself to Osama Bin Laden and the Taliban leader Mullah Omar.[22] In the following years, the group strengthened its ties to the al-Qaeda affiliate in Iraq and to the organization's senior leadership in Pakistan. Finally, in January 2007, the GSPC declared its merger with al-Qaeda and changed its name to "al-Qaeda in the Islamic Maghreb" ("Maghreb" is the Arabic name used for the western regions of the Arab world—Mauretania, Morocco, Algeria, Tunisia, and Libya). This move was followed by a revision of the group's strategy. In December 2007, the GSPC attacked the United Nations headquarters and the building of the constitutional court in Algiers, killing 41 people and injuring 170 others.[23]

The merger with al-Qaeda and the attacks on international targets convinced many young North Africans that the Algerian jihadists had effectively adopted jihadist internationalism. So the Algerian al-Qaeda increasingly recruited non-Algerian North Africans as well as fighters from Mali and Nigeria—kick-starting a process of "pan-Maghrebization" in North African jihadist circles, which has led primarily to intensified terrorist activity in Mauritania and affected the security situation in Morocco, Tunisia, and the states bordering southern Algeria in the Sahel.[24] In many cases, French and Spanish citizens were the victims of sporadic attacks and kidnappings. Following the logic of jihadist internationalism, attacks on the soil of the most important state supporters of the Algerian regime should have followed. The Algerian al-Qaeda supported this tactic, and in 2009 its emir threatened France with attacks in French territory.

France ruled over Algeria for 132 years and accepted the colony's independence only after a protracted war that ended in 1962. Their shared history has engendered frequent tensions, yet the two countries remain closely connected—militarily, politically, economically, and culturally. Of the approximate 3 to 3.5 million people of North African origin living in France today, for example, about 1.5 million are of Algerian descent.[25] Most important for the Islamist opposition, France steadfastly supported the ruling regime's fight against militant groups during the civil war. As a result, France fell victim to the first wave of Islamist terrorist attacks between 1994 and 1996. On Christmas Eve 1994, in a dramatic event foreshadowing of the 9/11 attacks in New York, Algerian terrorists hijacked an Air France flight bound for Paris from Algiers, planning to use the plane as a missile against the Eiffel Tower. French security forces were fortunately able to storm the plane and kill the terrorists during a stop in the southern French city of Marseille.[26]

Since 2003, French security authorities have been increasingly alarmed by the events in and around Algeria and prepared for the worst. Their concern was shared by Spain, which since 2001 has become an ever more important target for North African terrorists. In March 2004, a cell composed of North Africans detonated bombs in five commuter trains in the Spanish capital of Madrid, leaving 192 people dead and hundreds of others wounded. The number of North African, especially Moroccan, immigrants in Spain has risen sharply since 2000 and has reached roughly one million today. The Belgian and Dutch governments also were worried. Even in Germany, where the number of North African immigrants (between 260,000 and 300,000)[27] is considerably lower when compared to the number in western Europe, high-ranking officials in 2007–2008 feared that the new Algerian al-Qaeda branch constituted the biggest short-term threat to all countries hosting substantial North African migrant communities.[28]

The internationalization of the GSPC was prompted by two factors: the Iraq War and intensified American and European intervention on the side of the Algerian security forces against the terrorist group. After 2001 and especially 2003, the GSPC had come under pressure from inside and outside Algeria. The Iraq War threatened it with the loss of recruits to a far-away jihad theater, which was especially serious because the GSPC had already been on the defensive for several years. Highlighting the enormous appeal of internationalism among the jihadist rank and file, in 2003 a growing number of Algerian jihadists decided to travel to Iraq and join the insurgents there.[29] In order to prevent these potential recruits from leaving Algeria, the GSPC decided to bolster its jihadist credentials by internationalizing its strategy and propaganda work. Indeed, the new al-Qaeda label seems to have prompted a new, more internationalist-minded, and more radical generation of young jihadists to fight Americans and their allies on Algerian soil.

The second and arguably more important cause for the strategic shift was that, with the assistance of the United States and its European allies, the Algerian government had improved its counterterrorism capabilities. This assistance became especially obvious following the February 2003 kidnapping of thirty-two European tourists—mostly Germans, Swiss, and Austrians—in southern Algeria. One German woman died of heatstroke before ransom was paid and the hostages were released. During and after the incident, the Algerian government received even more counterterrorism aid from the United States, France, and Germany, including training, equipment, and money. Thus, as in Egypt and Saudi Arabia, the United States became a target of the jihadist group in Algeria because of its alliance with the ruling regime. The difference in Algeria's case was that France also played an important role in the situation. The GSPC's emir, Abd al-Malik Drukdal (a.k.a. Abu Musab Abd al-Wudud), explained in a 2008 interview with the *New York Times* that US intervention on the side of the Algerian government was the main reason for the GSPC's merger with al-Qaeda:

> When we carried arms we declared that we are fighting the crusaders' agents among those rulers who came out against Islam and committed crimes of corruption and tyranny and treason against the religion and the nation. And we said that we want to bring back the place of Islam in the country and the ruling of the Koran over the people, and bring to the nation its rights that were taken. But what happened later on is the West. They provided it [the Algerian government] with all kind of support and encouraged it and supported it in the forums. It did not stop there, it even went further to a direct intervention. Then we found ourselves on the black list of the U.S. administration, tagged with terrorism. Then we found America building military bases in the south of our country and conducting military exercises, and plundering our oil and planning to get our gas. Also, opening an F.B.I. branch in our capital city, and starting an unusual Christian conversion campaign among our youths to change their religion in order to create religious minorities among us.
>
> Its [America's] embassy in Algeria began playing almost the same role as the American Embassies in Baghdad or Kabul. It intervenes in the internal policy by planning, instructing and controlling. All of that just to kill the spirit of jihad and resistance among the Muslims so that it can put its hand on the energy stock that we have. So did America leave us any choice with this flagrant aggression? No doubt that the answer is going to be no. Therefore, it became our right and our duty to push away with all our strength this crusade campaign and declare clearly that the American interests are legitimate targets to us.[30]

The episode shows quite strikingly that US policies remain an important factor in fueling internationalist ideologies and strategies. The war in Iraq and US cooperation with the authoritarian regimes of the terrorists' home countries have been among the most important motives for the radicalization of young jihadists since 2001.

INTERNATIONALIZING THE JIHADISTS' SOCIAL BASE

The broadening of the jihadist movement's social base was perhaps the most important dimension of the internationalization process depicted here. It involved the recruitment of a more varied cluster of Arab nationalities, such as Syrians, Palestinians, and Jordanians, but also the increasing attraction of Pakistanis, Afghans, Turks, Kurds, and European converts. The globalization of Islamist terrorism gained traction, and the European diaspora was among the drivers of this development. Before al-Qaeda was to go truly global, however, it first had to become truly pan-Arab by increasing its attractiveness among young militants in the heart of the Arab world—the countries of the northern fertile crescent. Until 2001, Syrians, Palestinians, and Jordanians were grossly underrepresented within al-Qaeda. Among Arab militants, the organization had the reputation of overstressing the aims of its Egyptian and Gulf Arab core. According to a widespread view, Osama Bin Laden and his entourage were not particularly interested in the Palestinians' plight. So jihadists hailing from Israel's neighboring states had always kept their distance from al-Qaeda. Although at first they lacked alternative organizations to which they could turn, in 2000 the Jordanian Abu Musab al-Zarqawi founded an organization called al-Tawhid (Monotheism), which became the rallying point for many disgruntled jihadists who instead opted for a strategy whose goal was to destroy Israel and fight against the regimes in its neighboring countries.

Zarqawi (b. 1966) had spent most of the 1990s in a Jordanian jail and had traveled to Afghanistan after he was given amnesty in 1999. Once there, he built contacts with al-Qaeda but refrained from joining. He instead obtained permission to establish his own training camp in the western city of Herat, close to the Iranian border and far away from al-Qaeda's headquarters in Kandahar. His small organization consisted exclusively of Jordanians, Palestinians, Syrians, and Lebanese who shared his priority goals of toppling the monarchy in Jordan, destroying Israel, and, as a result, "liberating" Palestine.

When al-Qaeda and its allies lost their base in Afghanistan in late 2001, Zarqawi and his followers were forced to escape via Iran back to the Arab East. Zarqawi seems to have spent most of 2002 in Iran and in the enclave of a small jihadist organization in Iraqi Kurdistan. His rise to prominence in the coming years was made possible by the American invasion of Iraq in spring 2003. When during 2002 it became clear that the United States would attack Iraq, Zarqawi took the chance to reorganize his network and redirect it for the fight against the United States. In 2003, he began to rely on a growing number of Iraqis to join his group. Most important, with regard to the internationalization processes analyzed here, the war in Iraq opened new recruiting pools in Iraq's neighboring countries: large numbers of young men arrived from Syria, Jordan, Saudi Arabia, and Kuwait in order to fight the Americans.[31]

As a consequence, Zarqawi adapted his strategy to the new circumstances. He could not restrict himself to his former agenda, which focused first and foremost on Jordanian and Israeli targets, because he now heavily relied on Iraqi personnel—who wanted to fight the Americans and the new Iraqi state. So as of 2004 Zarqawi declared that his organization would first expel the Americans from Iraq and establish an Islamic state there. It would then extend its "holy war" to the neighboring countries, with the final goal of "liberating" Jerusalem.[32] It was obvious that Zarqawi's pragmatic approach to integrating new elements into his strategy stemmed from the need to take both the Iraqis' and the foreign volunteers' interests into account.

This development was momentous for the jihadist movement in general and for al-Qaeda in particular because thousands of young fighters heeded Zarqawi's call to arms and flocked to Iraq to fight the American invaders. This increase in the number of jihadists affected al-Qaeda proper insofar as Zarqawi subsequently joined the organization. In October 2004, he publicly declared his allegiance to Osama Bin Laden and afterward changed the name of his organization to Qaedat al-Jihad in Mesopotamia (Qaᶜidat al-Jihad fi Bilad al-Rafidain). Although Zarqawi sought primarily to tap into al-Qaeda's support networks in the Gulf, gaining access to new funds and recruits, he effectively integrated many Syrians, Jordanians, Palestinians, and even Iraqis into al-Qaeda's more global campaign. The Iraq War and the insurgency had presented al-Qaeda with a golden opportunity to win over jihadists from areas where it had never commanded a following.

The second wave of internationalization started in 2005, when it became more and more obvious that the old national and ethnic boundaries within the jihadist movement were losing importance. Al-Qaeda and other organizations were increasingly able to recruit non-Arabs, especially young members of the Western Muslim diaspora, with many young Pakistanis, Afghans, Kurds, Turks, and European converts heeding the call to join the jihadist caravan. First, a growing number of Pakistanis, many of them from the Pakistani diaspora in Great Britain traveled to the training camps in the Pashtun areas of Pakistan and joined al-Qaeda and other groups. The British government received early warnings of this trend toward radicalization among British Muslims in March 2004, when security authorities thwarted the so-called fertilizer bomb plot by a cell of Pakistani-origin jihadists. Most important, however, the attacks on the London transport system on July 7, 2005, which killed fifty-two and wounded more than seven hundred, were a direct result of this development. The perpetrators had been trained in an al-Qaeda camp on the Pakistani side of the Afghan–Pakistani border region. Although this trend came as a shock to the British government and public, it was not that surprising in light of the long tradition of militant Islamism in Pakistan and the activism of different Pakistani jihadist organizations since the 1980s. It should have been expected that the Pakistani diaspora would in one way or another be affected by the growth of jihadist sentiment in South Asia.

Yet the case for Turks was somewhat different. The number of ethnic Turks and ethnic Kurds originating from Turkey joining the jihadist movement has increased rapidly since 2001. This increase holds true for those coming from within Turkey but has been most visible among the Turkish diaspora in Europe—especially Germany, which is home to some 2.5 million ethnic Turks and ethnic Kurds from Turkey, the largest Turkish community in Europe.[33] The "Ulm–Sauerland network" of plotters in Germany seems to have been the nucleus of the Turkish jihadist scene there. Since the time when the four conspirators went to Pakistan, an increasing number of Turks and Kurds have joined the jihadist movement by traveling to Pakistan and training with different organizations, especially the IJU and the IMU. It was this integration of the Turks and Kurds that made the German jihadist scene perhaps the most dynamic in Europe after 2006.

Causes for Internationalization

At first glance, it might seem to be purely an academic question whether the jihadist movement was already a global phenomenon in 2001 or became internationalized in the years after 2001. If one assumes, however, that the internationalization of jihadism gained a new impetus after 2001, then the question must be asked: To what extent have Western reactions to the events in New York and Washington featured in this process? Indeed, there is ample evidence that the invasions of Afghanistan and Iraq by the United States and its allies have undoubtedly played an important role. But Western intervention is only one part of the story. Rather, the internationalization of jihadism is the result of a complex interplay of causes both exogenous and endogenous to the jihadist movement or, in simpler terms, between Western intervention in Muslim states and the increasing attractiveness of internationalist ideology among young Muslims themselves.

WESTERN INTERVENTION IN MUSLIM COUNTRIES

The German experience might serve as evidence of the consequences of Western intervention in Muslim countries because Germany became a terrorism target owing mainly to its presence in Afghanistan. On the one hand, Germany's intervention prompted international jihadist organizations to target it in order to force a withdrawal of German troops. On the other hand and more important for this book, the presence of German and other Western troops in the Hindu Kush was a forceful radicalizing factor for would-be jihadists from within Germany. Many stated that the suffering of Afghan Muslims at the hand of Western forces was one of their prime motives for joining the jihadist caravan.[34]

Germany sent troops to support the United States in Afghanistan in late 2001 but refused to take part in the Iraq invasion in 2003. As a result of the second decision, many Germans thought that al-Qaeda would spare their country attacks like those in Madrid in March 2004 or in London in July 2005. Although countries providing troops for the invasion of Iraq and the stabilization effort afterward were more important targets than Germany, France, or Belgium, the belief that opponents of the American Iraq adventure would be spared quickly proved to be erroneous. When the Taliban insurgency in Afghanistan gained momentum beginning in 2005–2006, the attention of the jihadist movement turned once more to Germany. The presence of German troops in north Afghanistan suddenly became an important subject on the Internet and among militants, supporters, and sympathizers in Germany. Finally, the Sauerland plot provided ample evidence that jihadist organizations had singled out Germany as a potential target for attacks and that a new generation of German jihadists was sufficiently radicalized to be recruited by al-Qaeda and its allies.

The strategic decision to attack Germany was not made solely because Germany was an important source of troops in Afghanistan. In summer 2012, the 5,000 German troops there represented the third largest contingent behind those of the United States and Britain and ahead of those of France and Canada. In addition, the jihadists identified Germany as the weakest link in the chain of countries providing military reinforcements. The German case seemed to resemble Spain in 2004: the masterminds of the Madrid bombings in March 2004 had singled out Spain because they thought that a large-scale attack might foster public opposition to the Spanish troop presence in Iraq and prompt the government to withdraw its military. And indeed, three days after the attacks, the socialist opposition won the Spanish parliamentary elections and made good on its promise to withdraw Spanish troops from Iraq as soon as possible.

The Uzbek masterminds of the Sauerland plot had a similar scenario in mind. They wanted the attacks to take place during the German debate over extending the Afghanistan mandates to participate in the International Security Assistance Force (ISAF) and Operation Enduring Freedom. The German military presence in Afghanistan had never been popular in Germany. In the first half of 2007, opposition was again mounting within the Social Democratic Party, which at that time was the junior partner in a grand coalition with Chancellor Angela Merkel's conservative Christian Democratic Union. The IJU leaders evidently calculated that attacks just before the Bundestag (the Parliament's lower house) votes in October and November 2007 could prevent an extension and force the withdrawal of German troops.[35]

The decision made by the IJU, al-Qaeda, and other jihadists to attack Germany could become consequential, however, because they commanded an increasing number of German recruits, who were enthusiastic about joining the Afghan jihad. The Sauerland group apparently opened the gate for the jihad enthusiasts who flocked to Pakistan from Germany in 2007. First, while plotting the attacks during 2007, the group recruited friends and acquaintances to follow in their footsteps and join the IJU in its Pakistani hideout. A small number of recruits consequently traveled to Pakistan and established what would become the nucleus of the German presence in the tribal areas. Once a number of German recruits had found the way to Waziristan, young people from other cities and regions followed. Dubbed "travel groups" by the German authorities, several dozen young men and women from Bonn, Hamburg, Berlin, and other German cities went to join the jihad in Afghanistan between 2007 and 2010. In 2009, they even founded the first exclusively German jihadist group, the German

Taliban Mujahideen (for more on this group, see chapter 7). Thus, an identifiable German jihadist community developed in the Pashtun mountain areas. The young men's motives varied, including a lust for adventure, the wish to leave their allegedly corrupted home society, the prospect of imitating the life of the first Muslims in Mecca and Medina in the seventh century, and hatred of the United States, Germany, and their allies. In all cases in which the course of their radicalization has been established, however, non-Muslim interventions in Muslim countries played an important role.

Many young Germans were radicalized following the US–British invasion of Iraq. Beginning in 2002–2003, the national and ethnic composition of active jihadists in Germany changed. For the first time, many Iraqi Kurds, about 50,000 to 80,000 of which live in Germany, started to lend financial and logistical support to the Iraqi Kurdish organization Supporters of Islam (Ansar al-Islam).[36] It was not only Iraqis, however, who were mobilized by the events in Mesopotamia. In Hamburg, a group of four, mostly North African men formerly connected to the 9/11 Hamburg cell traveled to Syria in 2003 in order to join the Iraqi insurgency.[37] They were arrested by the Syrian authorities, however, and sent back to Europe. The Sauerland four were also deeply affected by the Iraq War, but when they arrived in Syria, they realized that they could not enter Iraq and changed their plans.

Beginning in 2005–2006, the situation again changed. Although the war in Iraq and the non-Muslim presence in the country remained a powerful mobilizing factor among German jihadists, Afghanistan gained importance. This shift might have been due to a redefinition of priorities on the part of al-Qaeda's senior leadership. In 2005, the Afghan insurgency gained ground, and in 2006 the Taliban and its allies began to put their adversaries on the defensive. At about the same time, al-Qaeda reestablished its former alliance with the Taliban and was therefore able to profit immensely from the successes of the Afghan insurgents. Although the group was believed to command no more than four to five hundred men in Pakistan and Afghanistan, and although it was restricted to a supporting role for the insurgents and worked primarily to transfer terrorist knowhow, al-Qaeda was able to convey the impression that it was a big player in the Afghan theater of war. This perception was widespread among the public in the West, but also among potential recruits in these countries. As a result, the jihadists active in Pakistan and Afghanistan were able to tap into new recruitment pools in Western countries, where "Afghanistan enthusiasm" spread among young Salafists.

At the same time, al-Qaeda profited from the decay of insurgencies in other areas of conflict. This was perhaps primarily due to the difficulties of reaching the battlefields of the Caucasus, most notably Chechnya. Until 2004–2005, most foreign fighters reached Dagestan and thus Chechnya by way of Turkey. Because of improved relations between the Turkish and Russian governments, however, the route for fighters through Turkey was apparently closed after that. The conflict in Chechnya also died down, and the operating climate for the jihadists became even more difficult. The country consequently lost most of its former attraction for Arab, Turkish, and European volunteers.

The end of the insurgency in Iraq played a major role as well. From 2002, foreign jihadists traveled to Iraq mainly by way of Syria. The flow of volunteers slowly died down, however, due to a combination of factors. Significantly, the American surge in Iraq, divisions among the insurgents, and the Sunnis' fear of a Shiite takeover led to the defeat of the insurgency and the end of the Iraqi civil war in 2007–2008. As a consequence, the operating environment for the al-Qaeda jihadists in Iraq thus became ever more difficult, so that the Iraqi theater of war lost its attractiveness for many potential recruits from the Arab world and Europe. Those who had formerly gone to the Caucasus and Iraq now increasingly headed to South Asia (see chapter 7 for more on this topic).

CONTINUING ATTRACTIVENESS OF CLASSICAL INTERNATIONALIST THOUGHT

It would be much too simple to attribute the trend toward internationalization solely to the foreign policies of the United States and its allies. Rather, these policies clashed with religious-ideological currents in the Muslim world that provided the jihadists with the fertile ground they needed in order to recruit young volunteers for their campaigns in Afghanistan, Iraq, and the Caucasus. The most serious mistake made by the United States seems to have been that it did not identify these currents in advance of its invasions of Afghanistan and Iraq. The most important of these strains of thought might be called "classical jihadist internationalism," which describes the conviction that every individual Muslim, no matter where he or she lives, is obliged to fight non-Muslims who occupy Muslim territory.

Three main currents of thought inform contemporary jihadist thinking: revolutionary nationalism, modern internationalism, and classical internationalism. For most of the 1990s and the 2000s, militancy debates focused on whether to fight the "near enemy" or the "far enemy." Until the mid-1990s, the revolutionary nationalists represented the strongest trend in the jihadist movement and are still strong today. They primarily fought the "near enemy"—that is, the regimes in their respective home countries, where they sought to establish Islamic states. This current lost its dominance after it became clear that the militants were not able to overthrow the regimes in their countries—for example, in Egypt and Algeria in the early 1990s. Nevertheless, many jihadists stuck to the notion that only the fight against the oppressive rulers of their home countries was legitimate and worthwhile.

On the contrary, the modern internationalists—or "global jihadists" as they are often called—tried to combine the fights against the near enemy and the far enemy. In order to regain the initiative in the fight against their home regimes in the Arab world, they decided to enter into battle against the latter's most important foreign supporters. Forcing the United States to withdraw from the Middle East, they argued, would pave the way toward successful attacks on the regimes in Cairo, Algiers, and Riyadh again. The internationalist jihadists' rise to prominence began in the 1990s, when Aiman al-Zawahiri and his Egyptian followers decided to adopt an anti-American strategy. Only when these Egyptians joined Osama Bin Laden in Afghanistan in 1997 was al-Qaeda born. And although this current gained the most attention from the events of 2001, its success in recruiting new followers after 2001 must be attributed primarily to the overwhelming attractiveness of classical internationalist thought.

Events in recent years have shown that classical internationalism is much more influential than modern jihadist internationalism mainly because classical internationalists can argue that their beliefs are firmly rooted in the classical Muslim law of nations. As a result, it has proved to be much easier to recruit young Muslims in order to fight the Americans in Iraq and Afghanistan, the Russians in Chechnya, the Ethiopians in Somalia, the Israelis in Palestine, and the Indians in Kashmir than to convince people to attack the United States on their own soil or to fight their own home regimes.

The classical internationalist current in the jihadist movement has its roots in the Soviet–Afghanistan War in the 1980s and in the writings of the Palestinian Abdallah Azzam (1941–1989), its most famous theoretician. How powerful a mobilizing factor it was, however, became clear with the beginning of the Iraqi insurgency in 2003. Thousands of young Arabs who would have nothing to do with al-Qaeda decided nevertheless to fight in Iraq because the United States had attacked and occupied a Muslim territory and core country of the Arab world. The classical internationalists profited from Sunni religious scholars' arguments that jihad against the Americans in Iraq was lawful or even obligatory even when the scholars were generally hostile to al-Qaeda. Because of such arguments, many volunteers who followed the classical internationalist position thus did not join al-Qaeda in Iraq, but rather the more Islamonationalist-inclined Iraqi groups.[38] At the same time, al-Qaeda claimed to follow at least in part the classical internationalist paradigm and could use its own presence in Iraq and Afghanistan as a powerful argument. It is now apparent that the United States and its allies had not taken into account the danger inherent in these ideological preferences before they went to war. Giving al-Qaeda the opportunity to base its argumentation on classical internationalist thought most likely saved the organization from demise after 2001.

Among the new recruits were an increasing number of young Muslims from the Western diaspora, especially Europe. Their greater presence was only logical because European jihadists had always tended to think internationalist; most of them (with the exception of some converts) were by definition rooted in more than one society and were not so inclined to exclusively fight regimes in the Middle East, a place where they had not spent their lives. It took the jihadist movement some years to tap into these recruitment pools. One reason for this delay was a lack of communication between the jihadist movement and the diaspora. Al-Qaeda's propaganda was tailored to suit its needs in its home countries in the Arab world, from where it drew its finances and recruits. Only with the advent and spread of the Internet did it become possible to address young Muslims worldwide. The organization thus began to disseminate translations of religious, ideological, and strategic materials, catering to the needs of a growing community of sympathizers among non-Arabic speakers. Today, all relevant materials and forums are available in a range of languages, including Turkish, Uzbek, Urdu, German, English, French, and others. And more Turks, Uzbeks, Pakistanis, Germans, Brits, Americans, and French have joined the jihadist caravan.

2

Two Hamburg Cells

A History of Jihadist Terrorism in Germany

In the summer of 2010, news from Bagram Airbase, Afghanistan, electrified German and American counterterrorism investigators. The detained Ahmad Wali Sidiqi (b. 1974), a German Afghan from Hamburg who had spent more than a year in Pakistan and Afghanistan, told his American interrogators not only about the "Europlot" that was being hatched by al-Qaeda against Germany, Britain, and France, but also that he had met the al-Qaeda operative Said Bahaji (a.k.a. Abu Zuhair, b. 1975) in Waziristan. A member of the Hamburg cell including Mohammed Atta and the other pilots involved in the 9/11 attacks and a fugitive since September 2001, Bahaji has been one of the most wanted al-Qaeda terrorists ever since.

Son of a German mother and a Moroccan father and himself a German citizen, Bahaji grew up in a small town in Lower Saxonia and was then educated in Morocco. In 1995, he moved to Hamburg in order to study electrical engineering. Some time in the following years, he befriended Mohammed Atta and joined the group of young jihadists that formed around the infamous al-Quds (Jerusalem) Mosque in Hamburg. In November 1998, Bahaji moved into Marienstraße 54 with Mohammed Atta and Ramzi Binalshibh, the two leaders of the cell. The flat soon became the headquarters of the small group that Atta named "Dar al-Ansar" (House of Followers).[1] Bahaji was an intimate friend of the future hijackers and many of their associates, most of whom attended his wedding in October 1999. He assisted with handling his comrades' affairs while they were training in Afghanistan from December 1999 to January 2000, thereby helping to keep their absence secret.[2] Although he seems to have been assigned only a minor logistical role, he left Germany for Pakistan a week before the attacks in September 2001.

Sometime in the next few years, Bahaji sent messages to his wife, Nese, who had stayed behind in Hamburg, but not much is known of his career. His leg was injured during fighting in late 2001, when the Taliban and al-Qaeda retreated to Pakistan, and he apparently never fully recovered, several sources who met him in 2010 reporting that he was walking with a limp. In the following years, he worked as a propagandist for al-Sahab (the Clouds), the al-Qaeda media production company.[3] It is likely that Bahaji spent most of these years in the Pakistani tribal areas because during an offensive in October 2009 Pakistani troops found his German passport in a small village northeast of Wana, the capital of South Waziristan, one of the tribal agencies where al-Qaeda and other jihadist organizations found refuge after the downfall of the Taliban emirate in Afghanistan in late 2001. But it was in Mir Ali, a jihadist stronghold in the neighboring agency of North Waziristan, that Sidiqi claimed to have met Bahaji. In May or June 2010, Bahaji met with Sidiqi and Naamen Meziche, another old acquaintance from Hamburg. "If one believes the descriptions, it must have been a joyous reunion of the veterans," commented the German weekly *Der Spiegel*.[4]

Meziche, a French Algerian citizen born in 1970, had been an associate of the Hamburg cell members until 2001, but the German authorities had never charged him with any crime. He had been under surveillance since August 2003 and had been in the highest possible category on an internal watch list since April 2003.[5] Nevertheless, he found a way to leave Germany in March 2009 in order to join al-Qaeda in Pakistan, traveling with a group of eleven young jihadists from Hamburg.

The "Hamburg reunion" in remote Waziristan hinted at a certain continuity of German jihadism between 2001 and 2010. Less important members of the first Hamburg cell and their like-minded acquaintances successfully avoided prosecution and arrest and were therefore able to play a role within al-Qaeda once more. Nevertheless, Germany's role in the jihadist movement had changed. Perhaps most important, it had developed from being a safe haven and logistics base to becoming an important target for al-Qaeda and other organizations due mainly to the emergence of a new current among German jihadists—the new internationalists, who made their way to Pakistan in 2006.

The First Hamburg Cell

Before al-Qaeda attacked the United States on September 11, 2001, Germany had for years been a logistics base for the organization. Just as in Britain and Spain, veterans of the Soviet–Afghanistan War, of the conflict in Bosnia, and of the insurgencies in Syria, Algeria, and Egypt built an extensive network in Germany, providing al-Qaeda with money, passports, and recruits for its training camps in Afghanistan. The German authorities, like those of other countries, did not grasp the significance and danger of these networks, although there were warnings that al-Qaeda was active on German soil as well.

AN EARLY WARNING

Al-Qaeda's presence in Germany became most obvious back in 1998, when Mahmud Mamduh Salim (a.k.a. Abu Hajir al-Iraqi), a leading al-Qaeda operative, was arrested in Freising near the Bavarian capital Munich on the basis of an American extradition request. Salim was a close confidant of Osama Bin Laden as well as a chief logistician and procurement officer for al-Qaeda. He was wanted by the United States in connection with the bombings that had targeted the US embassies in Nairobi and Dar es Salaam in 1998, and in November that year a Munich court approved his extradition to the United States. His arrest by the Bavarian police in September left the German press and probably most politicians puzzled. Journalist Hans Leyendecker of the renowned *Süddeutsche Zeitung* (the German equivalent of the *New York Times*) revealed serious doubts as to the reliability of the American information on Salim and added: "Even days after his arrest it is totally unclear what Salim planned to do in Germany. All his contacts were harmless."[6] The German security establishment shared Leyendecker's assessment, thinking that with Salim's extradition the problem was solved.

The Germans unfortunately missed several factors, among them the significance of Salim and the organization he worked for and the importance of some of his contacts in the country. In 1998, al-Qaeda was virtually unknown even among German security specialists. Although the events in East Africa had been registered in security agencies' headquarters, most politicians and intelligence officials did not grasp the transnational nature of al-Qaeda and its network. As a government official already dealing with counterterrorism in 1998 recollects, "They [the Office for the Protection of the Constitution (Bundesamt für Verfassungsschutz, BfV), Germany's domestic intelligence service] used to say, 'Those guys that we have around here, they don't do anything. We have a strong grip on the issue.' "[7] Perhaps more important, Bin Laden's organization was considered to be an American rather than a European problem—if it was perceived as a threat at all. As the same official recounts, "The federal government [in Germany] did not take the Americans seriously. Many said that they [the Americans] simply needed a new enemy, and that is why they pester us with these Arabs."[8] If it had not been for this peculiar mixture of ignorance and arrogance, it is inconceivable that the arrest of such a prominent operative as Mahmud Mamduh Salim would not have set off alarm bells in Bonn, then the seat of the German government.

Salim is considered to be one of the founding fathers of al-Qaeda. Born to Iraqi Kurdish parents in Sudan in 1958, he first studied electrical engineering in Iraq. From 1981 to 1983, he served as a communications officer at the rank of colonel in the Iraqi army before deserting and traveling to Iran and then to Pakistan, where he joined the Afghan Arabs. He seems to have met Bin Laden in 1986 and quickly became a close friend of and religious adviser to the Saudi. As Lawrence Wright writes, their relationship was exceptionally close: "They had worked together in the Services Bureau in Peshawar and fought together in Afghanistan, forging such powerful bonds that no one could get between them. Unlike nearly everyone around Bin Laden in Sudan, Abu Hajer [i.e., Salim] had never sworn fealty to him; he saw himself as an equal, and Bin Laden treated him as such. Because of his piety and learning, Abu Hajer led the prayers; his voice, singing the verses of the Quran in a melancholy Iraqi style, was so lyrical that it made Bin Laden weep."[9]

One of the few non-Egyptians in the inner circle of power around Bin Laden, Salim took part in discussions leading to the foundation of al-Qaeda in 1988.[10] He first became head of Bin Laden's fatwa committee, but in the 1990s he acted primarily as a finance and logistics officer, traveling the globe from his base in Sudan.[11] Commenting on his arrest in 1998, the US National Commission on Terrorist Attacks upon the United States (9/11 Commission) called Salim "the most important of Bin Laden's lieutenants captured thus far."[12]

Salim's contacts in Germany were equally important, although this importance did not become clear until after the 9/11 attacks. Most strikingly, Salim had visited Mamoun Darkazanli, a key suspect in the events of 9/11, at least five times in Hamburg, and Darkazanli at one point had power of attorney over Salim's account in a Hamburg branch of the Deutsche Bank.[13] Darkazanli (b. 1958) maintained contact with a number of important al-Qaeda logistics officials all over Europe, most of them Syrians from Aleppo who as young men in the late 1970s and early 1980s had taken part in the Islamist insurgency against the regime of Hafiz al-Asad in their home country. The common experience seems to have formed the basis for their cooperation on behalf of al-Qaeda in Europe. The center of this Syrian network was Madrid, where Imad al-Din Barakat Jarkas (a.k.a. Abu Dahdah) served as one of al-Qaeda's most important proconsuls in Europe.[14]

Most important for the sequence of events, Darkazanli was a regular visitor to the al-Quds Mosque in Hamburg and stayed in close contact with the members of the Hamburg cell, so he might well have played a role in the actual 9/11 plot. When German authorities discovered a video of Said Bahaji's wedding just after 9/11, it became evident just how close his connections were to the pilots' cell. The ceremony had taken place in the Quds Mosque in October 1999, and the video shows a "who's who" of the Hamburg al-Qaeda cell, among them the future pilots Mohammed Atta, Marwan al-Shehhi, and Ziad Jarrah. The hijackers-to-be and their friends and helpers gave militant speeches and sang songs celebrating jihad and martyrdom. Mamoun Darkazanli featured prominently among the two dozen participants.

THE HAMBURG CELL

The so-called Hamburg cell consisted of a group of about a dozen young men, most of whom were students at the University of Applied Sciences in Hamburg-Harburg, where they studied technical disciplines. The cell's main contact to the al-Qaeda leadership and the most senior al-Qaeda-member in the group was the Yemeni Ramzi Binalshibh (b. 1972). Having arrived in Hamburg in 1995, Binalshibh served as trusted lieutenant to 9/11 chief planner Khalid Sheikh Mohammed in Hamburg. He registered as a student at the University of Applied Sciences but soon quit because of his miserable academic record. He had planned to join the pilots in the United States but failed to obtain a visa and so took over a coordinating function for the operation in Hamburg while his comrades were preparing for the attacks in the United States. Together with Binalshibh, the future pilots Mohammed Atta from Egypt, Marwan al-Shehhi from the United Arab Emirates, and Ziad Jarrah from Lebanon formed the inner circle of the Hamburg cell. The dogmatic and fanatical Mohammed Atta (b. 1968) seems to have become its commander after they entered the United States and when Ramzi Binalshibh had to remain in Germany.

In a second circle, close friends of the hijackers—Said Bahaji, the Moroccans Zakariya Essabar and Mounir al-Motasaddeq, and possibly others—took over logistical functions. Bahaji seems to have been the closest to the hijackers because their plans to train with al-Qaeda in Afghanistan began to take shape when Atta, Shehhi, and Bahaji moved into the Dar al-Ansar 1998. Motasaddeq joined the future hijackers on their trip to Afghanistan in late 1999.[15] Shortly before the 9/11 attacks, the members of the second circle had to choose whether to remain in Germany and possibly face prosecution or leave the country. Motasaddeq decided to stay in Hamburg and was later convicted and sentenced to fifteen years in jail, but Said Bahaji and Zakariya Essabar fled to Pakistan shortly before the attacks in New York and Washington. Once they joined al-Qaeda in its Pakistani hideouts, they formed a potential nucleus for the future German presence in South Asia.[16]

In addition, there was a third layer of friends and acquaintances who sympathized with the terrorists but did not commit any crimes—or because of a lack of evidence could not be convicted of any crimes they may have committed. Among them were Ahmad Wali Sidiqi and Naamen Meziche. Both befriended Mounir al-Motasaddeq in the second half of the 1990s. When Motasaddeq was later imprisoned in Hamburg in 2002, Sidiqi helped his father, who had come to Germany from Morocco. In July 2002, Sidiqi and Meziche spent time with Motasaddeq's family in Morocco.[17] But it was only in 2009, when both men traveled to Pakistan, that they met Bahaji in North Waziristan.[18]

Preparations for the 9/11 attacks began shortly after Bahaji's wedding in November 1999, when Atta, Binalshibh, Jarrah, and Shehhi traveled to

Afghanistan in order to join al-Qaeda and attend a terrorist training course. The German contingent solved a serious problem for al-Qaeda. Before Atta and his comrades arrived, Khalid Sheikh Mohammed had already spent the better part of 1999 drawing up a list of candidates for the pilot roles in the attacks. But the Yemeni and Saudi Arabian volunteers lacked the necessary fluency in English and basic technical knowledge to enroll in flight school. And in order to move around the United States undetected, the candidates would need to demonstrate a profound knowledge of life in the Western world. Most volunteers ready to take part in the attacks could be used as foot soldiers, but not as pilots. The Yemenis also had problems obtaining visas for entrance into the United States. When the German contingent appeared in Afghanistan, it soon became clear to Khalid Sheikh Mohammed and al-Qaeda that they would be ideal candidates for the more sophisticated tasks in the plot.[19]

In fact, the Hamburg cell highlights two main characteristics of al-Qaeda in 2001—namely, its predominantly Arab recruitment base and its desire to command and control its operations centrally. All members of the Hamburg cell were Arabs, mirroring the exclusively Arab character of Bin Laden's organization at that time. The group was formed by a Yemeni, an Egyptian, a Lebanese, an Emirati, and several North Africans, most of them Moroccans. In preparation for the attacks in New York and Washington, they cooperated with fifteen Saudi Arabians who formed the rank and file of the actual cells that hijacked the planes. This large number of Arabs from the Arabian Peninsula mirrored the structure of al-Qaeda, which was still very much an Egyptian–Saudi Arabian joint venture in 2001. Since the attacks on the American embassies in 1998, Osama Bin Laden had become front-page news around the world. With his growing popularity, though, al-Qaeda began to attract an increasing number of volunteers from countries that had not previously provided it with large numbers of recruits. More North Africans and European diaspora members traveled to Afghanistan, and the travels of the Hamburg jihadists were but one result of this development.

Second, al-Qaeda took sole responsibility for the command and control of the group of recruits, leaving virtually no room for individual initiative except when absolutely necessary. In spite of its use of networks, al-Qaeda in its early years showed a pronounced inclination toward a bureaucratic structure. Its leaders commanded the organization in an authoritarian manner and tried to discipline their followers by establishing strict hierarchies. Only after the loss of their base in Afghanistan did Osama Bin Laden and his followers begin to think about alternative ways of leading the jihadist movement. In the planning process leading up to the 9/11 attacks, however, the al-Qaeda leadership insisted on controlling almost every minute detail of the operation. Khalid Sheikh Mohammed led the Hamburg cell through Ramzi Binalshibh, who made sure that all activities on the ground would be in line with the orders given from Afghanistan. There are even unconfirmed reports that Khalid Sheikh Mohammed himself flew to Germany more than once before September 2001;[20] these reports would fit the picture of a cell tightly restrained by al-Qaeda's autocratic command-and-control structures. These rather traditional preparation methods should have given German authorities numerous opportunities to disrupt the organization while it was still making plans in Germany.

But the German government failed to see the writing on the wall. Looking back at the workings of the German authorities before September 2001, a high-ranking German police official stated: "Decision makers before 2001 were blind, fixed on everything but the actual threat."[21] Darkazanli for his part seems to have acted behind the scenes, providing al-Qaeda and the Hamburg cell with a dense web of relations all over Europe. Although the discovery of Mahmud Mamduh Salim's network in 1998 could have led the German authorities directly to the trail of Mamoun Darkazanli and his young comrades, they failed to make the connection. From 2001 on, fighting terrorists in Germany would never again be so easy.

From the Hamburg Cell to the Sauerland Group

It was only after al-Qaeda lost its base of operations in Afghanistan in late 2001 and had to withdraw to its current hideouts in the Pakistani mountains that it also lost most of its capacity to control its terrorist cells worldwide. At the same time, both the demographics and size of the jihadist recruitment pool developed significantly. Terrorist cells today are less homogenous ethnically and nationally than they were ten years ago. Although Arabs are still prominent in them, non-Arabs such as Pakistanis, Afghans, Central Asians, Turks, and Kurds have gained importance in the jihadist movement and pose new problems for European societies.

This process goes hand in hand with al-Qaeda's loss of influence relative to that of other jihadist organizations; joining it is no longer the only goal of jihadists from Europe and the Middle East. Because of enormous pressure exerted by the United States and its allies, terrorist organizations generally have problems planning attacks across continents, and as a result conspirators enjoy greater leeway on the spot. The downside of this trend (for jihadists, of course) is that many of the current plans are drafted with less precision and professionalism than they were some years ago. Indeed, most terrorist plots in Europe in recent years have failed or been thwarted.

For Germany's part, this development meant the growth of a distinct local or "homegrown" scene. The Hamburg cell was still very much a phenomenon isolated from German society. The actual 9/11 plot originated abroad in Afghanistan, and the nucleus of the cell was made up of Arab students who had arrived in Germany between 1993 and 1996 and thus had not struck deep roots in German society. Said Bahaji might have been the only exception, but even though a German citizen he had spent most of his childhood and youth in Morocco. After 2001, however, young Muslims who had lived most or all of their lives in Germany began to enter the jihadist scene. Due to the increasing "German" character of this phenomenon, the Arabs lost their former dominance. Rather, Turks and Kurds—who form the majority of the German Muslim population—now joined the movement in larger numbers. Furthermore, German converts to Islam began to discover the attractiveness of jihadism. They and others looked for ways to connect with networks abroad and found an increasingly varied pool of organizations ready to recruit them. Although some German recruits still opted to join al-Qaeda, many found Uzbek and Turkish organizations more attractive due to shared ethnic and linguistic ties.

As the characteristics of the groups that mushroomed after 2002 became more varied, so too did their organizational structure. First, Palestinians and Iraqi Kurds affiliated with larger organizations abroad moved to the forefront, attempting to perpetrate attacks in Germany. Second, independent-minded jihadists of different origins attempted their own attacks without referring to al-Qaeda and its allies. Third, young Turks, Kurds, and Germans radicalized in growing numbers and moved to the Pakistani tribal areas in order to join the jihadists in their fight in Afghanistan and Pakistan. One might analytically differentiate between three different organizational forms of jihadist groups that dominated the jihad theater in Germany after 2001: the organized jihadists, the independent jihadists, and the new internationalists. Organized jihadists are those who act as integral parts of larger organizations such as al-Qaeda, whereas the independent jihadists act without support. New internationalists are a hybrid variant, combining the advantages of both organized and independent forms of organization and modes of action. Although they radicalize independently of larger organizations, they subsequently travel to the Middle East or South Asia to gain access to the logistics and training infrastructure of a larger organization such as al-Qaeda and its allies. All three forms of jihadists have been dominant at various times in Germany.[22]

THE ORGANIZED JIHADISTS

In the first years after the events of 9/11 until about 2005, the organized jihadists were at the forefront of the jihadist movement in Germany. They were affiliated mostly with larger foreign organizations such as al-Qaeda, Zarqawi's Tawhid, and the Iraqi Kurdish Supporters of Islam and were acting on the orders of their superiors in Pakistan or Iraq. These groups were still by and large nationally homogenous and consisted primarily of Palestinians and Iraqi Kurds. The terrorist cells grew out of groups that used Germany mainly as a refuge and support base, but, following developing events in Afghanistan, the Palestinian territories and Iraq moved on to hatch their own terrorist plots as well.

The most dangerous of these groups was the "Abu Ali or Tawhid group," which was made up of four Palestinians, based mainly in the western German industrial city of Essen, and operated as part of Jordanian terrorist Abu Musab al-Zarqawi's Tawhid organization. It had formed around the ringleader Mohammed Abu Dhess (a.k.a. Abu Ali) in 2001, who was already in contact with Zarqawi when another group member, Shadi Abdallah, returned from Afghanistan, and two other young Palestinians joined them. At first, the group's main task seems to have been logistics: Abu Ali and his followers gathered donations and transferred them to Afghanistan and Iran. They helped smuggle volunteers to join Zarqawi's organization—including one of the cell's members—and they forged and procured travel documents. These services became especially important when Zarqawi and his followers fled to Iran beginning in October 2001. At that time, the group provided the Tawhid organization with dozens of forged passports, allowing a considerable number of Zarqawi's fighters to move on to the Arab Middle East.[23]

In October 2001, the German BfV intercepted a phone conversation between a Palestinian living in Essen and the terrorist leader Zarqawi in Iran. In the talk with Zarqawi, Abu Ali excitedly pledged his willingness to execute a terrorist attack and eventually die for their cause: "By God, Sheikh, I swear by God, I swear, if you ordered me to die, with God Almighty's permission, I would do it. I swear by God that I am not afraid, not afraid. . . . The day before yesterday or some days ago, I have contacted my mother and bade her to pray for me to die as a martyr."[24]

The Federal Intelligence Service (Bundesnachrichtendienst, BND) informed the BKA, and from that moment on the investigators were on high alert. Abu Ali had been under scrutiny since before September 2001, but only after the attacks in New York and Washington, DC, did the German authorities realize the potential danger posed by individuals like him and consequently intensify their scrutiny of his activities. How important his activities were and how close his relationship was to the Jordanian terrorist leader Zarqawi—widely unknown even in security circles—only became clear after this phone conversation was intercepted. However, Abu Ali's death wish—if it had in fact been meant seriously—seems not to have pleased his superior. The more strategic-minded Zarqawi calmed down his follower and made clear that Abu Ali was needed as his trusted lieutenant in Germany.[25]

During the following investigations, it became clear, however, that Abu Ali had already been ordered to prepare for an attack in Germany. Just before the New York and Washington attacks, Abu Ali had traveled to Tehran on September 7, 2001, where he met Zarqawi and was given orders to attack Jewish or Israeli targets in Germany. After his return to Essen five days later, he informed his co-conspirators of an impending "wedding" that would take place in Germany soon.[26] Although Abu Ali had confirmed his willingness to carry out an attack in the phone conversation with Zarqawi, he and his comrades soon realized that they were being observed by the German police. Abu Ali consequently proposed to Zarqawi that the preparations for such an attack be put on hold for another three to four months in order not to endanger the plot and the cell.[27]

Despite this proposal, the other cell members had already received orders from both Abu Ali and Abu Musab al-Zarqawi and so continued their preparations. A young Palestinian, Shadi Abdallah, who had spent nearly two years with al-Qaeda and Zarqawi in Afghanistan between 1999 and 2001, had been tasked with identifying possible targets and procuring the necessary weapons. Abdallah preliminarily proposed to target a well-known Jewish community center in Berlin as well as a nightclub and a bar in Düsseldorf.[28] The latter two sites were chosen because Abdallah erroneously thought they were owned or frequented by Jews or both.

Procuring the weapons proved to be more difficult. Abdallah's main contact for this task was the Algerian Djamel Moustafa, a close associate of Abu Ali who was known in criminal circles as someone who made a living by forging passports. Weapons were obviously not his specialty: when the group was arrested on April 23, 2002, Abdallah had still not managed to buy a pistol with a silencer and hand grenades, which the conspirators called "the mute" and "Lebanese apples," respectively, in their communications. In the meantime, their superior in Iran grew increasingly impatient with the German cell. He frequently called its members personally and pressured them to follow through with the attacks as soon as possible. After Zarqawi threatened Abdallah with unknown consequences if he did not proceed according to plan and execute the attack in early April, the German authorities, watching the group all the while, decided to intervene and so arrested the conspirators.

After court proceedings of more than three years, four of the five plotters were given jail sentences between five and eight years. Shadi Abdallah had decided to serve as a star witness and was sentenced to four years in jail but was released in 2004. The presiding judge spoke in his concluding remarks at the second trial of the "special danger" emanating from this group of "fanatic persons."[29]

If one excludes the Algerian passport forger Djamel Moustafa, who knew of the plot but was not directly involved in it, all of the group members were Palestinians. Their hatred of Jews and Israelis was the main reason they set out to attack Jewish targets. The ringleader, Mohammed Abu Dhess (Abu Ali), had already been a Zarqawi associate before 2001, although it could not be established when the two first met. Abu Ali (b. 1964) hailed from a Palestinian refugee camp in Irbid, Jordan, a stronghold of Jordanian jihadists since the 1990s. Although he had studied economics, he seems not to have found an adequate job and so performed as a singer in a band and played basketball in the Jordanian national team. In 1992, he left Jordan for Germany, where he unsuccessfully applied for asylum. He first went into hiding but then returned to his native Jordan, where he now displayed signs of a turn toward conservative Islam. He gave up music and sport, grew a beard, and worked as a muezzin in different mosques in Irbid. He also studied religious texts and was soon accepted as a religious authority by his friends. In 1995, he entered Germany again and applied for asylum, posing as an Iraqi refugee. Although his application was rejected again, he was not deported. Living in Essen, he received social benefits and started his career as a jihadist logistics official.[30]

The future star witness Shadi Abdallah (b. 1976) had been the drummer in Abu Ali's band in Irbid and had joined him when he traveled to Germany in 1995. Rather than following his mentor's religious turn, however, he started consuming drugs and alcohol and frequenting bars catering to homosexuals in the Ruhr region. It was not until 1998–1999 that Abdallah became more religious after he came into contact with members of the preacher's movement Tablighi Jamaat (Missionary Society)—an organization often suspected of serving as a way station and catalyst for jihadist radicalization.[31] His newfound friends took him to Mecca, from where they planned to join al-Qaeda in Afghanistan. After arriving in Karachi, Abdallah traveled to Kandahar, where he joined al-Qaeda and met several of the 9/11 conspirators, including Ramzi Binalshibh. In March 2001, however, he met his fellow countryman Zarqawi and joined Zarqawi's organization. He was then sent back to Germany, where he arrived in July or August 2001 in order to join Abu Ali's team.[32] After the group's arrest, Abdallah offered to confess and became the most important source of information for the prosecution.

The two other collaborators, Ashraf Al Dagma, a stateless Palestinian who was born in the Gaza strip in 1969, and Ismail Shalabi, a Jordanian citizen of Palestinian origin born in 1973, shared similarly miserable biographies. Dagma had finished high school and left his native Gaza Strip for Libya in 1987–1988, where he attended and then dropped out of university. After he arrived in Germany in 1994, his asylum application was rejected, but he was not deported. Before moving to Beckum close to Essen in 2000, Dagma earned a living by dealing cocaine and heroin in Berlin. After he moved, however, he became a pious Muslim and met Abu Ali, who recruited him for the cell. In September 2001, he traveled to Tehran with Abu Ali and joined Zarqawi there, receiving some kind of military training in an unknown location.[33] Shalabi had grown up in Germany and the Palestinian territories. Without a high school degree, he was unemployed and worked occasional jobs.[34] He was supposed to join Dagma on his planned trip to Afghanistan but opted out because he had to take care of his family at home.

This small group's social base was quite different from the Hamburg cell's. Most of its members were petty criminals rather than students and had arrived in Germany during the 1990s, profiting from the lax application of German asylum laws. In fact, the judge in the Tawhid group trial, Ottmar Breidling, severely criticized the German immigration authorities and emphasized that both Abu Dhess and Shadi Abdallah should have been deported to Jordan long before the attacks were planned: "Both al-Tawhid cases need not have happened if immigration law had been properly enforced."[35]

THE INDEPENDENT JIHADISTS

Beginning in 2005–2006, a growing trend toward independent, "leaderless" terrorist action became evident in Germany. Its protagonists were sometimes students from Arab or Muslim countries, but increasingly they were also young Muslims who were born in or had grown up in Germany. Most important, this new generation of activists lacked the larger organizations' professional terrorist training and sophisticated support networks. In some cases, there were hints that they had contacts with larger organizations in the Middle East and South Asia, but these hints could not be substantiated by any concrete evidence. Until Arid Uka perpetrated his lethal attack on American soldiers at Frankfurt airport on March 2, 2011, as recounted in the prologue, all of the independents' plots were thwarted in time, although some of them came dangerously close to carrying out successful attacks in Germany. Their failure, however, made clear to their successors that those wishing to strike their enemies effectively needed the terrorist training and logistics that only the larger organizations could provide.

The "Lone-Wolf Nightmare"

On March 20, 2006, the twenty-eight-year-old Pakistani student Amir Cheema appeared in the lobby of the Axel-Springer publishing house in

Berlin. (Axel-Springer's influence in German media is comparable to that of Rupert Murdoch's News Corporation in the United States—albeit on a smaller scale.) When security guards refused to let him enter the building and see the editor in chief of the conservative daily *Die Welt*, he drew a kitchen knife and threatened the guards. He was quickly overpowered and arrested. During the interrogations of him, he claimed to have planned to stab the Swiss editor in chief Roger Köppel because *Die Welt* had reprinted some of the Danish cartoons of the prophet Muhammad, which he deemed insulting and provocative.

German security officials were extremely worried by this event. *Spiegel Online* entitled an article on the case "Lone-Wolf Nightmare" and quoted a Berlin police official: "If the perpetrator had been a bit more lucky, we would have seen the second van Gogh case."[36] The Dutch Moroccan Mohammed Bouyeiri had stabbed the Dutch filmmaker Theo van Gogh to death in Rotterdam in November 2004 because of a film Bouyeiri deemed to be insulting to Islam. And although there was ample evidence that Bouyeiri had acted as part of a larger group of terrorists from North Africa, the case became the most prominent example of leaderless terrorism by European Muslims. European security authorities became increasingly concerned that individuals would initiate terrorist plots independently—that is, without the influence of an organization. The lone terrorist was considered especially dangerous because European police and intelligence services' counterterrorism measures depended heavily on intensified control of jihadist communication lines. Where there was no larger organization involved, communication was less important, and so thwarting the plot became increasingly difficult.

Amir Cheema's actions were a case in point. Hailing from the garrison city of Rawalpindi, he had moved together with other Pakistanis to the western German city of Mönchengladbach, studying textile management at the local University of Applied Sciences. While visiting relatives in Berlin, he took the knife from their kitchen, got on the subway, and tried to enter the Axel-Springer headquarters. After his arrest, police interrogated his friends, but there was no evidence that anyone had known of Cheema's plans in advance. They had taken note of the fact that Cheema had been outraged by news of the Muhammad cartoons, but they had not expected him to take action.[37] While still in pretrial confinement, Cheema committed suicide.

The Cheema case was the first hint that the Danish cartoons and their reprint by several German newspapers had the potential to trigger terrorist action in Germany. Twelve editorial cartoons had been published in the Danish newspaper *Jyllands-Posten* on September 30, 2005, most of which depicted the prophet Muhammad. When news of the cartoons spread, it sent shockwaves throughout the Muslim world and sparked international controversy. According to the newspaper, the publication was an attempt to contribute to the debate regarding criticism of Islam and self-censorship and followed the editor's reaction to the fact that author Kåre Bluitgen had difficulty finding illustrators to draw Muhammad for his children's book *The Quran and the Life of the Prophet*. The most famous of the caricatures, drawn by Kurt Westergaard, portrayed Muhammad with a bomb in his turban.

Following protests by Danish Muslims, the cartoons were soon reprinted in more than fifty other countries, leading to outrage across the Muslim world—some of which escalated into violent protests, reportedly causing more than one hundred deaths. The publishing of the cartoons was deplored on hundreds of jihadist Web sites and used as fuel for propaganda. The most famous incidents cited as direct reactions to the caricatures include two assassination attempts on Kurt Westergaard in 2008 and 2010; a letter bomb that exploded at the Hotel Jørgensen in Copenhagen, supposedly intended for *Jyllands-Posten*; and two other failed attacks at the newspaper's offices, all in 2010. Some of these activities were reportedly connected to plans hatched by Ilyas Kashmiri (1964–2011), a midlevel commander in al-Qaeda who became prominent because of his planning activities in 2010.[38]

During the course of 2006, it became clear that Amir Cheema was not the only person motivated to take action against German targets because of the cartoon crisis. To this day, the jihadists have never come as close to a successful attack in Germany as the "suitcase bombers" did.

The Suitcase Bombers

On July 31, 2006, German rail employees found two suitcases left in two regional trains commuting between big population centers in North Rhine–Westphalia. When they routinely opened the suitcases the next day, they immediately called for the police. Specialists quickly established that the homemade bombs consisted of propane gas, with additional bottles filled with gasoline, diesel fuel, and nails in order to heighten the devices' deadliness. It was only because of a technical error that the bombs did not explode. Had they detonated according to plan, up to seventy-five people would have died. German authorities immediately began a frenzied search for the perpetrators, fearing that a second attack might be imminent.

The Lebanese military intelligence service provided the decisive hint as to the plotters' identity. One of the men, the Lebanese student Yusuf al-Hajj Dib, had panicked and hastily called his father in Tripoli after German TV aired surveillance camera footage showing him on the platform of the Cologne central station carrying one of the two suitcases into the train to Dortmund.[39] What Dib did not know was that the family phone was bugged because his father and several of his brothers were known members of different Islamist organizations, which is how Lebanese intelligence gained the information it provided to German police. Now that the German authorities knew about the identity of the first perpetrator, it was only a matter of time before the Lebanese police would make an arrest.

Dib and his co-conspirator, Jihad Hamad, had taken flights to Istanbul just after they had planted the bombs, and from there they had traveled to Damascus and their homes in North Lebanon. Jihad Hamad gave himself up to Lebanese authorities in Tripoli, but Dib for some reason had returned to Germany only a few days after his flight from the country and was arrested there on August 19. During their interrogations and trial, the young men incriminated each other as having been the mastermind of the plot. Lebanese authorities refused to extradite Hamad but allowed German police to interrogate him in Beirut. A Lebanese court then sentenced him to twelve years in jail and convicted Dib in absentia to life imprisonment. Dib had to stand trial in Germany, where he was convicted and received the same sentence.

Both plotters had arrived in Germany only a short time before the attacks (Dib two years and Hamad a mere six months) and so had not laid down roots there. Both had attended a German-language school in their hometown, but at different times. Dib (b. 1985) grew up in a poor section of Tripoli, where extremist groups jockey for members and speak freely of holy war. He left his native Lebanon in autumn 2004 in order to study information technology in Germany. In 2006, he was just about to start university in Kiel, a city close to the Danish border in northern Germany, after he had successfully finished obligatory German-language classes. Jihad Hamad (b. 1985) came from a different part of Tripoli and a struggling middle-class family aspiring to economic and social mobility. He had arrived in Germany in February 2006 in order to study mechanical engineering in Cologne. Although both hailed from the same city in their home country, there is no evidence that they knew each other before arriving in Germany. Rather, Khalid al-Hajj Dib, Yusuf's older brother, is said to have established the contact between Jihad and Yusuf shortly after the former arrived in Germany.[40]

Of greatest concern for the German authorities was that they had not received the slightest hint that the two individuals were radicalized and preparing an attack.[41] Their worst fear was that Germany might be confronted with many more similar cells or small groups that would go through the whole process from radicalization to perpetrating an attack without establishing any links to known organizations. In the case of the suitcase bombers, the German police searched for months for a possible affiliation to a larger organization. The most convincing track was Dib's family.[42] His father, Yusuf al-Hajj Dib, was reported to be a member of the Islamic Liberation Party (Hizb al-Tahrir), a nonviolent but extremely anti-Israeli organization that aims at reestablishing the caliphate in the Muslim world. Perhaps even more important, Yusuf's older brother Saddam (b. 1984) was a high-ranking member of the Lebanese Jihadist organization Fatah al-Islam (Conquest of Islam). The latter outfit became famous in 2007 when militants in it occupied parts of the Palestinian refugee camp Nahr al-Barid next to Tripoli and were evicted only after a protracted siege and bloody battles that lasted from May to early September 2007. The conflict ended with most of the camp in ruins and many of its inhabitants as well as some 130 jihadist fighters and more than 150 government forces dead.[43] Saddam al-Hajj Dib was killed in an engagement with Lebanese security forces in Tripoli in May. Although a connection to the events in Lebanon might have played a role in the suitcase plot, the available evidence suggested otherwise, and Yusuf al-Hajj Dib was in the end not even accused, let alone convicted, of being a member of a terrorist organization, which according to German law has to consist of a minimum of three persons.

All available information pointed to the publication of the Muhammad cartoons in 2005 as the key motivation for the pair's decision to perpetrate an attack. After Yusuf al-Hajj Dib's arrest, pictures of him appeared in the press showing him marching in a protest rally against the publication of the cartoons in Kiel in February 2006. In court, he stated that the cartoon crisis had prompted him to take action but denied that he had planned to kill anyone: "We did not want to kill good people."[44] During his interrogations in Beirut, Dib's accomplice, Jihad Hamad, confirmed that they had been motivated by the cartoon crisis.[45] For the German public, the failed attacks were a wake-up call. It suddenly became clear that Germany was also a target even though the country's government had rejected the Iraq War.

The Need for Organizational Support

Jihadists did not fail to notice that all terrorist plots hatched by independents either failed through incompetence or were thwarted by the authorities. Some independent jihadists became increasingly aware of the need for terrorist training and logistical support in order to plan, organize, and execute terrorist attacks effectively. A striking example of this awareness was the case of the Moroccan student Radwan al-Habhab, who was arrested in Hamburg in July 2006. Habhab conveniently owned an Internet café in the northern German city of Kiel, where he first became a jihadist Web activist before he began organizing the travels of young Moroccan volunteers to Iraq via Syria. He realized, however, that the trust he needed in order to work effectively could not be won over Internet forums and chat rooms, but only by meeting members of a jihadist organization personally. Habhab therefore decided to travel to Syria and later to Algeria, allegedly in order to receive terrorist training in a camp of the GSPC. Together with some friends, he had decided that in order to build a cell he needed specialized terrorist training. But all his plans to establish a terrorist group were thwarted when he was arrested because of his propaganda and recruitment activities and in January 2008 sentenced to five years and nine months in prison.[46] That Habhab was not an isolated phenomenon became clear in the following years, when more German jihadists began to travel to the Pakistani training camps sponsored by different organizations.

THE NEW INTERNATIONALISTS

After 2006, a distinct German scene developed that transcended some of the important dividing lines between national and ethnic affiliations and that consisted of individuals who had either grown up in Germany or had spent most of their lives in the country. Groups of German volunteers became increasingly integrated into transnational networks quite different from what Germany had witnessed until then—which is the main reason why they are labeled the "new internationalists" here. Between 2006 and 2008, the emergence of these groups apparently heralded the entry of Turks and Kurds into the global jihadist scene. As the groups became more German in character, it was only logical that an increasing number of members of the two biggest Muslim communities in Germany would join them. As of 2009, however, it became clear that these groups' membership base had lost most of its ethnic and national characteristics. The second Hamburg cell of young Muslims from various backgrounds, which left Germany for Pakistan in March 2009, was one of the main examples of this trend. Despite the differences between their members, these groups had one thing in common: they all adopted "hybrid" forms of jihadist organization. The Sauerland group paradigmatically combined the strengths of both hierarchically structured and more independent forms of organization. The group was formed independently of any larger terrorist organization, so its activities—at least in its early stages—were difficult for the security services to detect. Its members then traveled to Pakistan, joined a terrorist organization, and acquired the necessary terrorist know-how in order to effectively carry out an attack in Europe. They thus posed a new threat to European societies quite unlike the threat offered by either the organized or the independent jihadists.

Turks, Kurds, and the Sauerland Cell

The Sauerland cell consisted of two Turks and two German converts to Islam. Three of its members, the two converts Fritz Gelowicz and Daniel Schneider and the Turk Adem Yilmaz, were arrested in a small town in the Sauerland region in the western state of North Rhine–Westphalia in early September 2007. After the plot was thwarted, it became clear that those arrested were part of a larger group of around two dozen people, most of whom were of either Turkish or Turkish Kurdish origin. They had become radicalized in Germany and had formed a group of like-minded young men around a Muslim cultural center in Ulm in southern Germany and in the Frankfurt and Saarland regions. They then established contacts with a Turkic jihadist network that ranged from Turkey to Azerbaijan, Pakistan, and Central Asia. Adem Yilmaz and a group of Azerbaijani jihadists in Damascus who were connected to the Uzbeks of the IJU seem to have made the first contact. The German group did not speak passable Arabic or Pashto, which made training with the Arabs of al-Qaeda and the Pashtun Taliban difficult. Turkish and Azeri, however, are closely related, and Uzbek is a Turkic language, which makes communication between Uzbek and Turkish speakers relatively easy. Therefore, the camps established by Uzbek fighters were an ideal training location for the volunteers from Germany, so it is no coincidence that most German volunteers to the jihadist movement joined Uzbek organizations in Pakistan.

"We Wanted to Fight": The Second Hamburg Cell

It soon became clear, though, that the internationalization would not stop with the Turks and Kurds suddenly flocking to join the jihad. After 2008, the German jihadist scene grew exponentially. The recruits now came from a variety of towns and cities, among them Bonn, Hamburg, and Berlin, and the volunteers' national and ethnic background was more varied than in the past. In this way, the youngest generation of jihadist recruits went farther down the road that the Sauerland four and their wider network had paved. No longer is a single nationality or ethnic background prevalent in the groups leaving Germany for Pakistan. Most striking in this regard was a group of ten Hamburg citizens, the majority of whom left the city in March 2009, consisting of young Muslims from widely differing origins, including

- An ethnic Algerian with French nationality, Naamen Meziche (born in 1970 in Paris), the son-in-law of the famous Moroccan jihadist preacher Mohammed Fazazi and a veteran jihadist with connections to the Hamburg cell of 2001, who took part in the meeting with Said Bahaji in Waziristan in May or June 2010[47]
- Three Afghans, among them Ahmad Wali Sidiqi (born in 1974 in Kabul), who was in close contact with the first Hamburg cell in 2001 and met Said Bahaji together with Meziche in 2010; his brother Sulaiman Sidiqi (born in 1986 in Kabul); and Assadullah Muslih (born in 1953 in Kabul), who had been suspected of terrorist activities since 2002

- Two Iranians, Shahab Dashti (born in 1983 in Teheran and died in 2010) and Mohammad Mohammadi (born in 1985 in Teheran), both of whom had converted from Shiism to Sunnism[48]
- The German Syrian Rami Makanesi (born in 1985 in Frankfurt), who had an extensive network of jihadist contacts all over Germany and who was deported to Germany after his arrest in Pakistan in June 2010, the interrogation of whom contributed to the heightened alert in Germany beginning in November 2010
- Two German converts to Islam, Alexander Janzen (born in 1980 in Prokhladny, Kabardino-Balkaria, USSR) and Michael Wallinger (born in 1985 in Alma-Ata, Kazakhstan, USSR), both resettled in Germany from the former Soviet Union
- Two women, among them Ahmad Sidiqi's wife, the Indonesian Shinta Parlina (born in 1974 in Jakarta), and Dashti's partner Seynabu Sow (born in 1987 in Hamburg), a German of Senegalese origin.

The group was led by Naamen Meziche, who—according to his comrade Ahmad Wali Sidiqi—had already been to an al-Qaeda training camp in Afghanistan in the 1990s and was reported to have played soccer with Osama Bin Laden while there. Assadullah Muslih seems to have had a recruiting function. He had lived in Hamburg in the past but now resided in Peshawar, where he prepared for the arrival of those group members who traveled to Pakistan by plane. Rami Makanesi, although reputed to be "a big baby, immature, mercurial and chatty," helped to motivate the other group members because of his enthusiastic wish to fight in Afghanistan.[49] Although most of the group members traveled directly to Peshawar and from there to Waziristan, the Arabs traveled via Iran because they feared arrest upon arrival at a Pakistani airport. Based on the interrogations of Makanesi and Sidiqi, it is believed that most of the group members apparently had no idea where exactly they were going and which organization they were to join in the tribal areas. Although most of them at first joined the IMU, they later left that group, seeking to fight with al-Qaeda.

With the exception of the striking lack of any Turks, the composition of the group was paradigmatic for the development of German jihadism after 2001. First and foremost, the group no longer had an ethnic or national profile. The Hamburg scene had been dominated by North Africans since the 1990s, who continue to remain a force among Hamburg jihadists, but in this travel group the North Africans were represented only by the already well-known Naamen Meziche. Nonetheless, as a veteran of the first Hamburg cell with good contacts in the international jihadist scene, Meziche seems to have been the group's natural leader. Second, for the first time ever, Afghans appeared in a German jihadist group, despite not playing any role in these networks previously and having hardly any representation in al-Qaeda. Third, converts to Islam and—in two cases from Shiism—began to be overrepresented among German recruits starting in 2006, giving the jihadist scene an increasingly local character. Fourth, young women were now joining their boyfriends or husbands and sometimes even bringing children to Pakistan, which might have been a result of increased Internet propaganda, with German jihadists in Pakistan calling upon their comrades in Germany to bring their families with them. Fifth, four of the eleven persons mentioned here had criminal backgrounds, and most lived on social benefits while still in Germany, hinting at a precarious social and economic status that has become more common among German jihadists in recent years. This characteristic seems to be evident even to many jihadists themselves, with, for instance, Sidiqi calling his comrade Alexander Janzen "a typical Russian drunkard" during his interrogation.[50]

From a historical point of view, however, the continuity between 2001 and 2009 is one of the most striking features of the Hamburg scene. Most notably, the al-Quds Mosque played a central role in the radicalization process of the second Hamburg group. According to Sidiqi, the group members regularly met in the mosque in the months prior to their departure, utilizing the time after the morning prayers, when no worshippers and officials were present, to prepare themselves physically by jogging and boxing. Their aim was to prepare for the physical hardships in Afghanistan, as Sidiqi explicitly stated: "We wanted to fight."[51] There is no conclusive evidence of the involvement of any mosque officials in the recruitment of the group, but the group members' activities cannot have gone unnoticed. It is therefore noteworthy that Mamoun Darkazanli started to officiate as an imam in the mosque beginning in 2008, hardly making an effort to hide his jihadist views. His reappearance at this time shows another striking and continual feature of German jihadism: many activists who played a role in jihadist organizations in the past return to their activities at one point or another. As a German security official commented, “Even if they disappear from our radar screens for a while, they all show up again.”[52] Darkazanli, Meziche, and Sidiqi were linked to the events in the run-up to 9/11, and their careers provide ample evidence for the continuity in German jihadism. Nonetheless, after 2006 they operated in a rapidly internationalizing environment. The first steps toward the internationalization of German jihadism were taken by the Sauerland group.

3

"A Second 9/11"

The Sauerland Plot

In early September 2007, the citizens of the remote village of Oberschledorn in the hilly Sauerland region in the western part of Germany witnessed dramatic events. The three young men who later became known as the "Sauerland group" had rented a holiday home in this area in order to organize their plot undisturbed. When they began to assemble homemade explosives based on highly concentrated hydrogen peroxide, the police stormed the one-family house. Whereas Fritz Gelowicz and Adem Yilmaz were so perplexed that they did not resist, Daniel Schneider, the only member of the group with military training, managed to escape through the bathroom window and was caught only after he had unsuccessfully tried to shoot one of the police officers chasing him through the yards in the neighborhood. In the course of the investigations, it was established that the group had received their training with the Uzbek IJU in North Waziristan in the Pakistani tribal areas and that the organization had sent them back to Germany to execute attacks on American and Uzbek targets. The three seem to have settled on attacking the entrance to the US airbase in Ramstein in the German state of Rhineland-Palatinate as well as off-base facilities and nightclubs frequented by American military personnel in the area.

The Cell

The ringleader, Fritz Gelowicz, was born in the Bavarian capital of Munich in 1979 but spent most of his life in Ulm, where his father owned a small company distributing solar panels, and his mother was a practicing physician in a local hospital. He converted to Islam at age fifteen, encouraged by Tolga Dürbin (b. 1978), one of his father's employees. Dürbin, who was later arrested at the Pakistani border in summer 2007 (probably for crossing the border illegally), invited the young man to visit his conservative Muslim family, where Gelowicz seems to have found the safety and home that his parents' early divorce had taken from him.[1] It was Dürbin who soon introduced him to the world of Salafist Islam by taking him to the Multicultural House, a cultural center in neighboring Neu-Ulm. In 2000, both young men came under the influence of the Egyptian preacher Yahia Yusuf, the godfather of German jihadism. Although Gelowicz came from a middle-class background and his teachers remember him as an intelligent boy, he was an unsuccessful student. According to his own statement in court, he suffered from a certain degree of text blindness and dyslexia and was weak at foreign languages. He did not finish school, dropping out at age eighteen, and only managed to get his high school diploma at evening classes some years later, albeit with below-average grades. In 2003, he began studying economic engineering at university but soon lost interest. In spite of these failures, during his terrorist career Gelowicz proved to be by far the most intelligent member of the cell, and so the IJU leadership chose him as the ringleader of the plot. He was the only member of the group who spoke some Arabic, and he also developed an interest in the Turkish language.[2]

Adem Yilmaz had aspired to more but ended up as the number two of the group after arrival in Pakistan. A Turkish national born in Bayburt in northeastern Turkey in 1978, Yilmaz moved with his family to Langen, a small town south of Frankfurt, when he was eight years old to join his father, who already lived and worked in Germany. Like most Turkish migrants of his generation, Yilmaz went to a secondary school of inferior quality and left it with only a rudimentary education and deficient knowledge of both German and Turkish. He later worked as a ticket inspector for the state-owned Deutsche Bahn (German Railways) but quit his job in 2002. With minor exceptions (he quit a job as a department store detective after a month because, as he put it, he had "had enough of it"), he lived on unemployment benefits and looked for guidance in Islamist circles in Frankfurt and the surrounding towns. He frequented the notorious Bilal Mosque in Frankfurt and seems to have come into contact with like-minded Salafists in a so-called Islam seminary in Bonn, where he first met his future co-conspirator Atilla Selek (on the importance of the Bilal Mosque, see chapter 6). These seminary courses, organized sporadically by Salafist preachers, have become the main meeting points for the growing Salafist scene in Germany since 2001. Yilmaz apparently first came into contact with Gelowicz during a pilgrimage to Mecca in January 2005. Casting himself as the hardliner and militant loudmouth in the small cell, he openly claimed a leadership position, which he lost to Gelowicz when the IJU leadership named the latter the cell's emir.[3]

Daniel Schneider, the second German convert in the group, was born in 1985 in Neunkirchen in the Saarland region close to the French–German border. Like Gelowicz, he dropped out of high school with more than a year still to go. Again, this decision was not due to a lack of intelligence; his marks were good until grade 11. According to the testimony of the forensic psychiatrist in court, he had lost focus due to a long and messy divorce battle between his parents.[4] For years, Schneider desperately searched for meaning in his life. He started misbehaving at school, drinking alcohol, and smoking marijuana. He was convicted of robbery and violent assault. He finally found the direction he was looking for with Muslim friends who introduced him to Salafist Islam in 2003. He started out working petty jobs to earn a living and was subsequently drafted into military service with an airborne combat engineer unit in Saarlouis in 2004.[5] Remaining in service was impossible, however, because he lacked a high school diploma and had health problems.

The second youngest of the four plotters, Attila Selek was born in Ulm in 1985 and was the closest of all the cell members to Fritz Gelowicz. His father owned a small transport business and was a member of a Turkish right-wing nationalist group called the Gray Wolves. His mother, in contrast, was a devout and conservative Muslim. After six depressingly unsuccessful years in secondary school, he became an apprentice in putting high-gloss paint on cars. Here, he seems to have managed well but stopped showing up after his boss took on a girl as an apprentice. Selek firmly believed in the necessity of a strict separation of the sexes; had he stayed on, he would have been required to work with a woman to whom he felt attracted. Fearing that he would not be able to resist the temptation, he chose to quit his job. During the next few years, Selek lived on social benefits, and his Salafist networks gave him the direction he had been longing for. In winter 2003, he became an active member of the Multicultural House in Neu-Ulm, taking part in its publishing activities. He quickly developed a strong relationship with Fritz Gelowicz, who became his mentor.[6]

Difficult Choices

The plot originated in the southwestern twin cities of Ulm and Neu-Ulm, where Gelowicz and Selek lived. As previously mentioned, Neu-Ulm was home to the Multicultural House, a highly popular Salafist cultural center, which after 2001 became the nucleus of the new internationalist stream of German jihadism. It is where Gelowicz and Selek were introduced to Salafist Islam (for more on Salafism, see chapter 6).

Although the physician and Salafist preacher Yahia Yusuf (a.k.a. Abu Omar, b. 1958) never held an official position at the Multicultural House, he was its head. Trained as a physician, Yusuf had been an activist in the Egyptian Islamic Group (al-Gamaʿa al-Islamiya) before leaving for Freiburg, a university town in southwestern Germany, in 1988. He soon became a prominent figure called "Sheikh" in the local scene, preaching in the small backyard Servants of the Merciful (Ibad al-Rahman) Mosque. The mosque was frequented mainly by Arabs who had left the local mosque of the Turkish Islamist Milli Görüş movement because their more radical views were incompatible with their hosts'. Instead, Yusuf and his comrades maintained contacts with Algerian militant groups and soon became deeply immersed in the struggle in Bosnia. The Freiburg group supported the armed struggle of the Bosnian Muslims against Serbs and Croats and were joined by like-minded friends, including the Egyptian Reda Seyam (b. 1960), a propagandist who was later suspected of being involved in the planning of the Bali bombings in 2002; Aleem Nasir (b. 1962), who became a recruiter for the Pakistani Lashkar-e Tayyiba and al-Qaeda; and the Turk Muhammad Çiftçi (b. 1973), who subsequently turned into the most prominent Turkish Salafist preacher in Germany. To this end, they helped bring humanitarian aid to the Balkans. Some visitors of the Ibad al-Rahman Mosque even took part in actual fighting.[7]

Meanwhile, Yusuf held a research position at the University of Freiburg, working on pharmacological studies, for which he even won a prize sponsored by the German pharmaceutical giant Boehringer. He had to leave the university, however, when his temporary contract ended in 1998. Although he spent some time in a retraining program in Cologne and founded a dubious import–export company, the loss of his job meant considerable social decline.[8]

In 2000, Yusuf moved to Neu-Ulm and quickly became the most prominent teacher in the Multicultural House, attracting young Muslims of different national and ethnic backgrounds. By 2002, it was obvious to at least one observer that Yahia Yusuf's teachings attracted an increasingly radicalized audience that quickly transcended the national and ethnic dividing lines between Turks, Kurds, Arabs, and German converts.[9] One important reason for the center's popularity seems to have been that lessons were given in German at a time when Salafism was still very much a phenomenon in which Arabic-speaking preachers dominated. Besides gaining fame through his position at the Multicultural House, Yusuf built a small circle of dedicated young followers and taught them his version of Salafist Islam. As a state intelligence official had it, "Yusuf drew people to his small circle of followers, watched videos with them, and riled them up."[10] The war in Chechnya seems to have been the dominant theme of the sessions, with most of the young men close to Yusuf developing an obsession with the plight of Muslims there.

Yahia Yusuf and the Multicultural House also gained fame in other areas of Germany in part because he and his followers published the small but popular magazine *Think Islamic* (*Denk mal islamisch*). It appeared in September 2003 and remained the only German jihadist publication available for a number of years. The small pamphlet was officially published by the Islamic Information Center (Islamisches Informations Zentrum) in Ulm, where the jihadist-minded members of the Multicultural House assembled. In 2004, the future Sauerland plotters Fritz Gelowicz and Atilla Selek belonged to the publishing team, along with Yahia Yusuf's son Omar and Gelowicz's friend Tolga Dürbin.[11] The magazine had its last run in February 2006 because most members of the publishing team either had been arrested or had left Germany for Alexandria, Egypt, where some members of the Ulm jihadist scene had assembled because of the pressure exerted on them by the German authorities in previous years.[12]

Readers of the magazine were more than once reminded that the only way to avoid the torments of hell, which were vividly depicted, was to join the jihad against the enemies of Islam. Sermons and other texts written by Yahia Yusuf figured prominently in *Think Islamic*, which became a powerful radicalization tool and raised awareness among young Salafists that jihad constitutes the highest form of worship to God.[13] The small magazine spread far beyond jihadist circles in southwestern Germany to other parts of the country and became an important instrument linking the emerging jihadist scenes in different cities. Many future jihadists are said to have been influenced by *Think Islamic*.[14]

The Multicultural House became known to a wider public in 2003–2004 when news emerged of a group of German volunteers fighting in the war in Chechnya. In spring 2002, four young men traveled from Germany to Istanbul and then to Chechnya. Mevlüt Polat, a German Turk, and Tarek Boughdir, a German Tunisian, were killed in October 2002. Another young German Turk disappeared. In November, the remaining member of the group, the German Muslim convert Thomas "Hamza" Fischer (b. 1978), was killed by Russian Special Forces when they attacked a group of rebels in the forests of Serzhen-Yurt some fifteen miles south of Grosny. Fischer was one of twenty-two dead fighters, but it was only after the first ethnic German was killed in Chechnya that the German public began to pay some attention to the rebellion there. Fischer had converted to Islam in 1998 and changed his name to "Hamza" after he started to adopt militant ideologies in the Multicultural House, where watching videos of the Chechen wars was a popular pastime and enthusiasm for the Chechen jihad was widespread.[15] After his conversion, Fischer had completed his German military service, which provided him with the basic training he needed in order to be accepted by the Chechen rebels and join the fight against the Russians. To date, it is not known who recruited him to go to the Caucasus.

The enthusiasm in Ulm for the Chechen cause has become nearly as typical for German jihadism as it is for the Turkish members of the jihadist movement. Most notably, the first Hamburg cell had originally planned to travel to the Caucasus and join the rebels in their jihad against the Russians in the late 1990s. However, one of their contacts in Germany convinced them that it would be difficult to reach Chechnya at that time and that they should go to Afghanistan first, where they could complete military training with al-Qaeda before traveling on to Chechnya.[16] As happened to so many others, once the members of the Hamburg cell arrived in Afghanistan, they gave up their plans to travel to the Caucasus and joined al-Qaeda.

Enthusiasm for the Chechen cause was in part the result of the rebels' propaganda efforts. In the mid-1990s, they began publishing videos of their fight against the Russians, which influenced a whole generation of young jihadists in the Muslim world and Europe. Among the most influential of these videos was the German version of *The Gate of Grief* (*Das Tor der Trauer*), which was produced by two members of the Multicultural House, Tolga Dürbin and Omar Yusuf, and became widespread among jihadist circles in Germany in the early 2000s.[17] The video starts as a jihadist country study, presenting basic information on Chechnya and its history from a jihadist viewpoint, with a focus on the history of the Chechen wars between 1994 and 2000. The second Chechen war, which started in 1999, is described as "one of the bloodiest catastrophes our time has witnessed" and is characterized as a campaign by the Russian state to annihilate the entire Chechen population. Celebrating the Chechen resistance against the superior Russian army, the film contains sections of different jihadist videos from Chechnya, showing insurgent operations. It depicts the war as the bloodiest and most horrible episode of a wider war waged by Christians and Jews against Islam and calls for the support of German sympathizers. (For more on this video, see chapter 6.)

In a plethora of testimonies, jihadists from the Middle East and Europe have reported on the radicalizing influence of the videos produced by the Chechen rebels. In the late 1990s, many Saudi and Jordanian citizens went to join the Arab contingent that assisted the Chechens under the charismatic leadership of the now legendary Saudi field commander Samir al-Suwailim (a.k.a. Khattab or Ibn al-Khattab, killed in 2002). The videos, watched with friends in mosques, prompted many of them to leave their home countries. It was next to impossible, however, to join the Chechen rebels without having first completed some military training because the recruits would become burdens rather than reinforcements and could not expect to survive long. Thus, many volunteers were either rejected or sent to Afghanistan, where they could acquire the necessary experience to join the fight against the Russian army.[18]

The German jihadists' desire to fight in Chechnya also reflected the preferences of their counterparts in Turkey, who have long preferred to fight in the Caucasus rather than in Pakistan and Afghanistan. Turkish jihadists have by and large adopted a different perspective on the diverse zones of conflict: they have generally shown a more marked interest in the situation of Muslims in the Balkans and the Caucasus. The young Turks and Europeans' trips to the Caucasus were greatly aided by the ambivalence of the Turkish state, which turned a blind eye to the channeling of recruits via Istanbul to the Caucasus. This indifference changed around 2004–2005, when a substantial rapprochement between the Turkish and Russian governments prompted the former to stop the flow of recruits and support to the Chechen rebels, so that it became increasingly difficult for jihadist recruits to enter the war zone in the Caucasus.

This difficulty became a serious problem for the ambitions of the Sauerland group in its formative period. The future conspirators sought mainly to join the Chechen rebels in their fight against the Russians. Gelowicz and Selek seem to have been motivated by the popularity of the Chechen jihad among their friends in the Multicultural House.[19] Gelowicz had known Thomas "Hamza" Fischer. They were the same age, and Gelowicz might even have befriended Fischer. By traveling to the Caucasus and joining the Chechen rebels, Fischer had become a celebrity in the Multicultural House, where, along with Mevlüt Polat, he was celebrated as a martyr.[20] Gelowicz seems to have considered the dead convert a kind of role model and decided to follow in his footsteps. In Gelowicz's words, "The fact that Mr. Fischer joined the jihad showed me that it is also possible for someone like me to join the jihad. Until then the jihad was for me something unreachable."[21]

In summer 2004, Gelowicz traveled to Istanbul and contacted Chechen fighters in a mosque. He was told, however, that it was already too late in the year to start the long journey to the Caucasian battlefields.[22] Perhaps Gelowicz's lack of military training also played a role in the delay. From the beginning, however, the Sauerland four had mulled over another alternative. Adem Yilmaz had thought about going to Chechnya, but in October 2003, when he decided that he wanted to leave Germany, he chose to join the fight in Iraq. Although the difficult climatic and military conditions in Chechnya were important factors in his decision, Yilmaz was motivated primarily by an extreme hatred of the Americans, whom he considered "the main enemy of Islam." Joining the insurgents in Iraq seemed only logical to him because the country had just been invaded and occupied by American troops in spring 2003. When Gelowicz and Yilmaz first met in

2005 and started discussing a journey to the battlefield of jihad, they had initially settled on going to Iraq in order to fight the Americans.[23]

In August 2005, Gelowicz, Yilmaz, and Selek traveled to the Syrian capital Damascus. Because none of them spoke Arabic, a necessary precondition for joining any Iraqi insurgent organization, they enrolled in a local language school.[24] They did not manage to make connections with human traffickers to take them to Iraq, as they had expected. Rather, Adem Yilmaz made friends with a group of jihadists from Azerbaijan, who promised to find a way to Chechnya via Turkey. But when Yilmaz arrived in Istanbul in April 2006, he was told that he and his friends needed military training before they could join the Chechen rebels. Yilmaz's Azeri contact proposed to send the group to Pakistan, where they would be trained by a group that fought against the Pakistani army. After they completed this training, they would have the opportunity to join the fight in Chechnya. Yilmaz and Gelowicz—when he arrived separately in Istanbul from Damascus—agreed, in part because they did not care that much about which country they fought in.[25]

In Waziristan

The Azeris made good on their promise. They first sent Yilmaz and Gelowicz to Waziristan in April 2006 and then Selek and Schneider in June 2006. The friends took a route that later became the standard journey for German jihadists heading to Pakistan: after flying from Turkey to Mashhad in northeastern Iran, they went to Zahedan, a frontier Iranian town at the nexus of Iran, Afghanistan, and Pakistan.

A city of some 600,000, Zahedan has been an important center on the drug-smuggling route from Afghanistan into Iran for decades. In the 1980s, tens of thousands of Afghan refugees flooded the city. Its inhabitants belong mainly to the Sunni Baluch minority, who are on bad terms with the government of the Shiite Islamic republic. After the fall of the Taliban regime, al-Qaeda and other jihadist groups began to exploit the local population's sympathies and build an important way station for fighters, volunteers, and couriers either to or from Pakistan.[26] The Makki Mosque—the largest Sunni house of worship in Iran and the spiritual center for the Sunnis of eastern Iran—has become notorious as a meeting point for European volunteers seeking to enter Pakistan illegally. It was there that the Sauerland four were received by the Uzbek Gofir Salimov, a logistics officer facilitating the travel of IJU volunteers to Pakistan and a central figure in the organization.[27] After crossing the border, the young Germans took a bus to the Baluch capital of Quetta and continued on to Bannu in southern Khyber Pakhtunkhwa, where they were then brought to the IJU headquarters close to Mir Ali in North Waziristan.

North Waziristan, with its capital Miranshah, is part of the Federally Administered Tribal Areas, a territory that was created in 1947 and comprises seven tribal agencies (Bajaur, Khyber, Kurram, Mohmand, North Waziristan, Orakzai, and South Waziristan). This territory is inhabited by Pashtun tribes who have hosted a plethora of Afghan insurgent groups and Arab, Central Asian, and Pakistani jihadists since the downfall of the Taliban in late 2001. The Pakistani state has never been able to control this area effectively and has only recently made some hesitant and largely unsuccessful attempts to reassert the control that the Pakistani army had lost when militants from the tribal areas began to threaten Pakistan itself in 2007. Exerting effective control over this area is so difficult because the Pashtun tribes living here entertain much closer socioeconomic, cultural, and tribal relations to their relatives on the Afghan side of the border than to the Pakistani mainland. In fact, the Pashtuns on both sides of the border have never recognized the Durand line of 1893, which demarcated the border between Afghanistan and Pakistan. In addition, the mainly mountainous terrain is ideally suited to guerrilla warfare, a fact amply exploited by the Afghan insurgents in their quest for a safe haven.

As a result of the Taliban withdrawal from Afghanistan in 2001 and its subsequent presence in Pakistan, its supporters in the tribal areas have effectively managed to prevail over the Taliban's local competitors and have triggered a process of "Talibanization," which has affected all the tribal agencies but seems to have been particularly effective in Waziristan. And although the Pakistani government started a large-scale offensive against insurgents in South Waziristan in October 2009, it has refrained from doing so in North Waziristan, where Pashtun and foreign militants have lived by and large unhindered by the Pakistani government since 2001. The government chose South Waziristan for its offensive mainly because this agency was and still is a center for groups primarily fighting the Pakistani state, whereas the Pashtun scene in North Waziristan is dominated by organizations fighting in Afghanistan and so in this way serving the interests of the Pakistani army, which has tolerated the Afghan insurgents' use of its territory as a safe haven. As a result, Pashtun groups, Arabs, and Central Asians have made this remote tribal agency the epicenter of Islamist terrorism worldwide.

When the German group arrived in Mir Ali, they apparently knew nothing of North Waziristan's legal and political status. In fact, if one believes their confessions, they did not even know exactly where they were going. Only Gelowicz claimed that he had heard of Waziristan before 2006, but no member of the group had any prior information about the Uzbek organization they were about to join. Even after the four arrived, they knew it only as the "Uzbek" or "Ahmad" group, named after an alias used by its leader Najmiddin Jalolov. Only later was Gelowicz told that the group's official name was "Islamic Jihad Union."[28] The others only seemed to have realized that this was the group's name when the German press first reported on the group's own activities in April 2007, several months after they had returned to Germany.[29]

Moreover, it soon turned out that the young Germans were not prepared for the harsh living conditions in the mountains of Pashtunistan. Food was scarce and, in any case, bad; they had to content themselves with a miserable diet of rice, potatoes, bread, and tea.[30] The water, too, was of the worst imaginable quality and often undrinkable for Westerners. Shortly after their respective arrivals, the recruits caught different diseases and remained seriously ill for the rest of their stay. Yilmaz and Gelowicz suffered from vomiting, high fever, and ague, the symptoms of malaria.[31] Schneider developed diarrhea, and Selek suffered from an ill-defined gastrointestinal disease, forcing him to check into a hospital after his return to Germany, where he was diagnosed with Hepatitis A.[32] Under these circumstances, the training in the mountains became a tough experience for the four. Only Schneider seems to have done better than the other Germans, probably due to his prior military experience. Gelowicz and his friends were obviously ill prepared to join the Afghan insurgents, which is possibly why the IJU—at that time focusing its activities on supporting the fight in Afghanistan—sent the young men back to Germany and instead planned to have them carry out an attack there.

The four had planned to finish training, join the fight in Afghanistan, and—if they survived—join the rebels in Chechnya. After they went through basic military training, though, Gelowicz soon realized that Jalolov had decided to send them to carry out an attack in Germany. The basic-training course was similar to most courses offered by al-Qaeda and its allies since the 1980s. It consisted of basic weapons training with different types of Kalashnikov assault rifles, hand grenades, pistols, an RPG 7, and the PK machine gun (a heavier version of the AK 47). The course that the Sauerland group experienced seems to have been more professional, varied, and demanding than training courses that other German volunteers subsequently underwent in the tribal areas. And it was followed by a more specialized explosives course during which the volunteers were taught how to use different kinds of industrial detonators and how to handle different sorts of explosives, including TNT, C4, and dynamite. During an electronics course, Gelowicz and his friends learned how to cause a detonation with a digital wrist watch or a mobile phone. This course was followed by one on how to produce unconventional explosives, including a mixture consisting of highly concentrated hydrogen peroxide, flour, sugar, and coffee.[33]

Gelowicz and Yilmaz decided that a homemade bomb based on hydrogen peroxide would suit their purposes best in part because its ingredients would be easiest to procure in Germany. The IJU specialists taught both of them how to produce highly concentrated hydrogen peroxide (i.e., a 60–70 percent solution) by cooking a low-concentrate solution of 35 percent. By adding flour, they managed to produce a powerful explosive, which they tested using industrial detonators.

In an early phase of their stay with the IJU, Jalolov's right-hand man Suhail Buranov (a.k.a. "Sulaiman") approached Gelowicz and asked him about the possibility of the Germans perpetrating an attack in Europe. He talked at length about a grandiose scheme "something like September 11," a "huge blow against the unbelievers." At first, both Gelowicz and Yilmaz voiced reservations. Gelowicz reminded his host that their goal was to join the fight in Afghanistan, and Yilmaz declared that his Azeri friends had promised that the Germans would have the chance to join the fight in Chechnya after having completed training. Finally, however, all the recruits agreed to take part in the operation. Gelowicz and Yilmaz were given the opportunity to take part in an operation in Afghanistan, and Jalolov and Buranov told the volunteers that they could return to Waziristan and join the IJU for good after they had executed the bombings.[34] Interestingly, there does not seem to have been any discussion of suicide attacks.

After the conspirators agreed to perpetrate attacks, the debate focused on possible targets. From the beginning, the IJU leaders made it clear that American installations were a priority because, as they argued, it was easier to attack them in Germany than in Pakistan, especially if the plotters knew the terrain. The aim was to kill as many American soldiers as possible and to attack one American target of political significance, such as a consulate. They already had talked about an attack on Ramstein Airbase. Furthermore, Jalolov and Buranov asked the Germans to attack the Uzbek embassy or other Uzbek targets if possible and to select a target of symbolic importance that would send a "warning" to all Germans.[35] Within these parameters, the group enjoyed a wide berth to maneuver. In fact, the lack of concrete orders led to lengthy discussions between Gelowicz, Yilmaz, and Schneider about potential targets.

Before the Germans were sent back to their home country, one last problem had to be solved: the group had no leader. Yilmaz had established contact with the Azeris in Syria and seems to have led the group while it traveled from Turkey to Waziristan. His knowledge of Turkish might have played a role in this context, Turkish and Azeri being closely related languages and mutually intelligible. Gelowicz, however, was by far the most able group member intellectually, organizationally, and otherwise. Thus, the IJU leadership named Gelowicz rather than Yilmaz the "emir" of the Sauerland cell.[36] The somewhat amusing but nevertheless fierce cockfight that ensued between the two continued right up to their trial, with Yilmaz playing the militant loudmouth, defying the judge's orders and obstructing the first weeks of the trial proceedings.[37] These disagreements might have contributed to the erosion of the cell members' resistance to interrogation and, finally, to their decision to confess.

Jihad in Germany

Each of the four cell members began his separate journey back to Germany starting in late August 2006, arriving there sometime between September 2006 and February 2007.[38] In October 2006, those members of the group who were in Germany started preparations for the plot and duly applied what they had learned in Waziristan. Their plan was to assemble homemade bombs based on highly concentrated hydrogen peroxide, and their preparations consisted mainly of efforts to procure a sufficient amount of hydrogen peroxide and functioning industrial detonators.[39]

In 2006, low-concentrated hydrogen peroxide in a solution of up to 49.9 percent was readily available in specialized chemical suppliers in Germany. It is a colorless liquid, and its strong oxidizing qualities mean it is commonly used as a bleaching agent, disinfectant, and ingredient in cleaning agents. The purchaser had only to present a valid identity card. Between December 2006 and July 2007, Gelowicz obtained twelve canisters of hydrogen peroxide using fake identities and disguising his appearance. In order to store the canisters, he rented a garage in the small town Freudenstadt in the northern Black Forest region in southwestern Germany.

In the meantime, the IJU leadership pressured the Germans to take action. They communicated through email messages stored in draft folders, believing that in this way the messages could not be tracked by the authorities. They proposed late in 2006, however, that in order to carry out the attack quickly, the plotters should reduce its scope.[40] They did not, however, revoke an order given to Gelowicz while he was still in Waziristan to wait for detonators to be sent by the organization via Turkey. When obtaining the detonators took more time than expected, the cell decided to continue collecting hydrogen peroxide until the devices arrived and to stick to the original plan of detonating a large bomb. In January 2007, Gelowicz sent Selek to Turkey in order to organize the transport of the detonators and facilitate the group's escape after the attack. When Selek arrived in Istanbul, he contacted Mevlüt Kar, a German Turk trafficker of volunteers for the fight in Chechnya, whom both Selek and Gelowicz had known for some years.[41] Meanwhile, the IJU made good on its promise and informed Gelowicz that a contact person in Turkey was waiting for Selek to retrieve the detonators, which were hidden in the soles of a pair of shoes. When Selek was unable to establish contact with the courier but instead was told to meet with a second person involved in the operation in an Istanbul mosque, he asked the well-connected Kar for help (see chapter 5 for more on Selek and Kar's encounters).

In April 2007, Kar informed Selek that he had been given the shoes carrying the detonators. He argued, however, that they should wait to transport them to Germany because the network in Turkey through which he procured materials was under surveillance. In July, Selek—staying with relatives in the Central Anatolian city of Konya—went back to Istanbul in order to prepare for the transport of the shoes. At that time, Kar told Selek that he had used other contacts to send six detonators directly to Germany. Having maintained a strong Balkan connection as well, Kar had apparently procured Serbian and Bulgarian detonators from a source in Kosovo.[42] These detonators arrived in Germany in early August. Gelowicz picked them up from a contact person in a mosque in Mannheim in southwestern Germany but concluded that six were not sufficient. Still in Istanbul, Selek then checked the shoes. They contained twenty industrial detonators produced in the Czech Republic and probably originating in Syria. Kar decided to send someone previously unknown as a courier: the fifteen-year-old German Tunisian Alaeddine Taieb, who was temporarily in Istanbul and who—although he was well connected in jihadist circles—allegedly did not know that the shoes contained detonators.[43] When Taieb returned to Germany in late August, he met up with Gelowicz in a mosque in Brunswick, and they arranged for Gelowicz to collect the shoes from Taieb's flat in Wolfsburg. Now the preparations for the attack would enter their final phase.

In mid-August 2007, Gelowicz and Yilmaz met in Stuttgart in order to organize final preparations for the plot. Meanwhile, the IJU leadership had grown increasingly dissatisfied with the delay of the plan and issued an ultimatum: if the Germans had not carried out the attacks within two weeks time, the plan would be canceled and the four young men ordered back to Waziristan.[44] The IJU wanted the attacks to take place during the German debate over the extension of the Afghanistan mandates for participation in the ISAF and Operation Enduring Freedom and seems to have calculated that attacks just before the Bundestag votes in October and November 2007 could prevent an extension and ideally force the withdrawal of German troops.[45] In response, Gelowicz and Yilmaz informed their superiors that they would continue the preparations, but they needed a little more time.[46] On August 31, they moved into a holiday home that they rented in Oberschledorn in Sauerland in order to assemble the bombs.

The three plotters agreed to choose the final targets shortly before the attacks. In fact, they discussed possible targets during car rides in the days before their arrest. By this time, though, the police had bugged the car they used and could follow their conversation about the Frankfurt and Ramstein airports and American pubs and night clubs (see the next section on how the police dealt with the Sauerland cell and their plan).

The plotters seem to have agreed that the attack should achieve the most casualties possible, with Yilmaz boasting that they should aim at a "second 9/11" with at least 150 victims.[47] It is also clear that the group had settled on three American targets, but that they had not made their final decision. In order to make their homemade bombs even more lethal, they talked about adding nuts and bolts, which would kill more distant bystanders, and gas canisters, which would fuel the fire resulting from the explosions. Following the model of the Bali nightclub bombings in October 2002, they also considered causing a small explosion inside a nightclub in order to cause panic and then detonating the large bomb outside as people rushed to leave the location. Each of the three plotters was supposed to park a car filled with explosives in front of the target and the three devices would go off at about the same time.[48]

Thwarting the Plot

German police eventually decided to take action when they discovered the group's rented garage in Freudenstadt containing the bomb materials. In a clandestine operation, officers substituted the group's higher-concentrated 35 percent hydrogen peroxide solution with a much weaker 3 percent solution that looked the same but was in effect useless for the purposes of making a bomb.[49] It was only when the plotters began to boil the hydrogen peroxide in large pots in order to produce a higher-concentrated solution that the police finally decided to storm the holiday home they had rented and arrest Gelowicz, Yilmaz, and Schneider before the plotters realized they had been fooled.

In the years and months before the Sauerland plot, the performance of the German security authorities had been much less impressive. In fact, rather than successful surveillance of the jihadist scene in Germany, it was help from the United States that saved Germany from what could have been the most devastating terrorist attack in the country's history. In this case specifically, the German authorities first received information about the Sauerland group in October 2006 when the US government informed them about email exchanges between Pakistan and Germany that the US National Security Agency had monitored. After following up on this initial lead, the German security services and police started a huge counterterrorism operation, code-named Operation Alberich, and monitored the group throughout the coming months.[50]

The plot and how the German authorities handled it did indeed uncover severe weaknesses in the German security services apparatus. Although Gelowicz and Selek had been known to the authorities for years, and although they regularly frequented a known center of German jihadists, details about their radicalization, their travels to Syria and Pakistan, and their return to Germany remained undiscovered. If the United States had not provided the German authorities with information about the four and their plans, it is very likely that the attacks would have been carried out. In this and other cases, it was more than obvious that the German police and intelligence services had only superficial insight into the radicalization and recruitment of young Germans by jihadist groups. The country's growing jihadist scene made it ever more difficult to identify those who were planning to leave for Pakistan, and the lack of qualified security personnel as well as legal and political restrictions on monitoring mosques and cultural centers hampered the effectiveness of security efforts.

At several points in the investigation, the plotters realized that they were under surveillance. In each instance in which they thought they were being watched, however, they must have eventually concluded that the security authorities had stopped following them, and so they carried on with their plans. It is remarkable that they did not cancel their preparations even when the German weekly magazine *Der Spiegel* reported in April 2007 that a cell belonging to the IJU was on its way from Turkey to Germany and was planning terrorist attacks in Germany. The report included information about intercepted emails from Germany containing suspicious code words.[51] Although the plotters read the article and realized that the journalists were describing their own activities, they nevertheless continued undeterred. Their relentless pursuit of their goal did not change even when ever more detailed articles about the plot were published in May and June 2007. The weekly magazine *Focus*, for instance, reported that the cell consisted of five people—two German converts to Islam and three ethnic Turks. The article also mentioned that they were IJU members and that the police had searched group members' apartments in January.[52] In June, there were additional reports about US warnings that a terrorist attack in Germany might be imminent.[53] The German press explicitly connected these warnings to previously published information on the IJU and its cell in Germany, but, again, the plotters surprisingly did not stop their preparations. It seems as if Gelowicz and his friends simply believed that they had managed to shake their observers off and that their preparations remained undiscovered. They do not seem to have thought highly of their adversaries. This lack of respect became especially obvious in Ulm in January 2007 when Selek noticed that he was being followed. Realizing that it was a surveillance team, he simply got out of his vehicle, drew his knife, and slashed a tire of the car in which the team was following him. The vehicle occupants, employees of the domestic intelligence service BfV, did not react.[54]

Nevertheless, once the danger was known to the authorities, they did their utmost to thwart the plot. Operation Alberich became known as the largest counterterrorism operation by the German security authorities to date. For months, several hundred police officers tracked the plotters. The ensuing trial in Düsseldorf was of similar dimensions: with hundreds of witnesses and experts, it was the largest and most publicized terrorism trial since the 1970s, when the left-wing Red Army Fraction put the whole country on high alert. The case was initially expected to last around two years, but the group's confessions allowed judges to pass sentences in March 2010, one year after the perpetrators first appeared in court. These confessions also allowed the court to paint a reasonably comprehensive picture of the biggest terror plot in German history. Fritz Gelowicz, the ringleader, and Daniel Schneider were sentenced to twelve years in prison. In Schneider's case, the attempted murder of a police officer during his escape from the rented holiday home in the Sauerland where the group was assembling the homemade bombs counted heavily against him. Yilmaz was sentenced to eleven years, and Selek to five years. Although the young men had organized the most serious terrorist plot hatched in Germany since 9/11, they had all in all acted quite amateurishly, so that it is hardly conceivable that they would have been able to detonate a bomb close to Ramstein Airbase. Nevertheless, if they had attacked softer targets such as nightclubs, they might have killed a substantial number of civilians.

4

The Islamic Jihad Union

On March 3, 2008, Cüneyt Çiftçi, "the first German suicide bomber," as he was called by some media outlets, carried out a suicide attack on the Zabari District Center in the Afghan province of Khost, killing two American and two Afghan soldiers. A Turkish citizen born in Germany in 1980, Çiftçi lived in the Bavarian town of Ansbach and had been recruited by the Sauerland group member Adem Yilmaz, whom he had met at a Salafist seminary in Brussels. Although Çiftçi had brought his wife and small child with him to Pakistan, he decided to carry out a suicide attack on behalf of the IJU. The fact that a jihadist from Germany killed American soldiers in Afghanistan shocked many transatlanticists in the United States and Germany and confirmed the impression from the Sauerland case that many German militants aimed specifically at American targets. Moreover, the attack highlighted the threat posed by the IJU, which until 2007 had been unknown.

The Sauerland plot catapulted the IJU to the center stage of public attention. Some six days after Gelowicz and his accomplices were arrested, the organization published a Turkish-language "press statement" in which it claimed responsibility for the attack plan:

> On 5 September 2007 in the German state [*sic*] of Oberschledorn, three of our brothers were arrested by German intelligence. They were preparing

> to conduct operations against the American military airbase at Ramstein in Germany, and against the American and Uzbek Consulates General in Germany. Our goal in these operations was to express, in a drastic and intensive way, that we are against the oppression of the two states, the United States and Uzbekistan, that have adopted leadership roles in the policy of savagery against Islam and the Muslims, and to be a warning that the Germans withdraw their military airbase from Termez in the state of Uzbekistan. These two states already proved a long time ago by their actions that they do not understand words. Consequently, even if they should conceal, with various sorts of lies, the inhuman actions that these states and their supporters have committed, which are waging a treacherous struggle against Islam and Muslims, they should be aware that there are Muslims who do not believe these lies, and they should also be aware that if they do not abandon this behavior, they will be the targets of such actions.[1]

The statement was signed by the "political leadership of the Islamic Jihad Union." Although there were some doubts as to its authenticity after it was first published, Fritz Gelowicz later confirmed that he had agreed with the IJU leadership on a draft of the document when the Sauerland group was still in Pakistan.

Yet when German authorities announced in September 2007 that they had successfully thwarted the terrorist plot hatched by the Sauerland group and that it had been ordered and planned by the IJU, even many specialists had not heard about this small Uzbek organization. It had been active in Pakistan and Central Asia for about half a decade after it split from its "mother organization," the older, better-known, and far stronger IMU. From 2006 until 2009, the IJU became the most important destination for German jihadists in Pakistan mainly because of the IJU's internationalist ideology: Najmiddin Jalolov and his supporters followed a strategy like al-Qaeda's, targeting simultaneously both the near enemy (i.e., their home governments) and the far enemy (i.e., the United States and countries in the West) and in 2002 had therefore left the IMU, which remained staunchly nationalist until 2007. In North Waziristan, the IJU had entered into a close alliance with al-Qaeda and found shelter with a local insurgent network and took part in fighting the international coalition and their local allies in neighboring Afghanistan. In this setting, the Uzbek organization warmly welcomed the German recruits.

A New Base in North Waziristan

The IJU's history is closely connected to the career of its leader, Najmiddin Jalolov (1972–2009), an Uzbek citizen and former member of the IMU. His name was first heard in the international media after a string of car bomb attacks hit the Uzbek capital Tashkent on February 16, 1999. In this failed attempt to kill President Islam Karimov, thirteen people died, and more than one hundred were wounded. In one of the attacks, working with a second IMU fighter, Jalolov placed an explosive-laden car in front of the National Bank. The subsequent detonation caused the death of nine people and wounded dozens. Jalolov and the other perpetrator fled to Shimkent in southern Kazakhstan.[2] He seems then to have traveled to Chechnya—where he had already stayed before 1999—and joined the rebels there before he went to Afghanistan and Pakistan, where he founded the new organization IJU in 2002.

The IMU seems to have experienced a severe crisis in 2001. Based in Afghanistan and allied with the Taliban, who still ruled the country at that time, many IMU members and some leading figures demanded an internationalization of the group's strategy in line with al-Qaeda's more global approach. Although the Islamonationalists within the IMU prevailed, their opponents did not give in. The crisis came to a head after the fall of the Taliban in late 2001. The IMU had suffered heavy losses in its bases in northern Afghanistan in general and in Kunduz in particular and had to withdraw to the Pakistani tribal areas. In late 2001 or early 2002, Jalolov and his followers split from the IMU and formed the IJU. There is hardly any information on this phase except that the IJU consisted of no more than ten to fifteen members, all of whom left the IMU in order to follow Jalolov.

For Jalolov, personal motives seem to have played a role in the decision to form a splinter group. The charismatic Tahir Yoldashev (1968–2009) led the IMU in an authoritarian way, leaving hardly any space for ambitious personalities such as Jalolov and trying to suppress dissenting voices in the organization. However, concrete information about this clash of personalities is scarce. The ideological divide between Jalolov and Yoldashev is easier to identify because the IMU remained clearly committed to its rather nationalist Central Asian agenda in the years following the split. In winter 2001–2002, the parent group retreated to Wana, the capital of South Waziristan, and built its headquarters and camps in several smaller villages west of the city.[3] It is striking that the IMU refrained from joining the Taliban's fight in Afghanistan at this time; rather, the organization allied itself with local Pashtun groups, which after 2007 increasingly targeted the Pakistani state. With this choice, it drew the ire not only of Afghan Taliban factions and al-Qaeda, but also of the Pakistani military establishment. After 2004, the IMU frequently became a target of Pakistani military operations, the most recent being a military offensive in October 2009, when parts of the organization had to flee South Waziristan.

The IJU, in contrast, built its headquarters close to Mir Ali, the second most important city of North Waziristan, which after 2002 became a safe haven for al-Qaeda and other militant groups and as of 2006 for the growing German jihadist community. The IJU's main local ally was the so-called Haqqani network, named after Jalaluddin Haqqani (born probably between 1930 and 1938).[4] This network is the dominant Afghan insurgent faction in the Mir Ali area and in North Waziristan and, as such, hosts most German recruits in Pakistan. Since 2005, it has established itself as one of the three dominant insurgent groups in Afghanistan—all of whom consist mostly of Pashtuns—besides the (Quetta Shura) Taliban and the Islamic Party (Hezb-e Islami) of Gulbuddin Hekmatyar.

The remnants of those Taliban who once ruled the Islamic Emirate of Afghanistan between 1996 and 2001 are also called Quetta Shura Taliban because the group's main decision-making body, the consultative council Rahbari Shura, was reported to have been based in Quetta, the capital of the Pakistani province of Beluchistan.[5] The Taliban dominates the insurgency in the southern and southeastern Afghan provinces of Helmand, Kandahar, Oruzgan, and Zabol and withdraws to its safe havens in Baluchistan, which in its northern parts is heavily populated by ethnic Pashtuns and since the 1980s has hosted a considerable Afghan refugee population. The Taliban's leader remains the enigmatic Mullah Omar, who had been the Islamic Emirate's head of state until its demise in 2001 and whose whereabouts are unknown.[6]

In the eastern and northeastern part of the "front," the Islamic Party plays an important role in addition to the Taliban. In the 1980s, its leader, Gulbuddin Hekmatyar (b. 1947), had become known as commander of one of the strongest insurgent organizations in the fight against the Soviet occupation of Afghanistan. He and his followers maintain their rear bases in the northern part of the former Northwest Frontier Province, now called Khyber Pakhtunkhwa, in Pakistan and around its capital Peshawar. His units operate primarily in the adjacent provinces of Nuristan, Kunar, Nangarhar, Laghman, and Kapisa but are also present in Kabul and especially in the areas east of the city.

The Haqqani network has built its headquarters in North Waziristan and has enjoyed—even more than the Quetta Shura Taliban—virtual immunity from the Pakistani government's countermeasures against the use of Pakistani territory as a safe haven. From its bases around the North Waziristan capital of Miranshah, the organization dominates the fight in the eastern Afghan provinces of Khost, Paktia, and Paktika. Since 2008, Haqqani and his followers have broadened their area of operations to include Kabul, Logar, and Wardak and have claimed responsibility for several high-profile terrorist attacks in the Afghan capital, among them the assault on the Serena Hotel in January, the attempted assassination of President Hamid Karzai in April, and the attack on the Indian embassy in July 2008.

The first major attack attributed to the Haqqani network took place on January 14, 2008, when a team of fighters stormed the Serena Hotel in central Kabul, which is popular with Western expatriates. The attackers used a combination of small arms, grenades, suicide vests, and a car bomb. Eight people were killed, among them a contractor for the US Agency for International Development and a Norwegian journalist.[7] The attack left expatriates in Kabul and many inhabitants of the city with a profound feeling of insecurity.

In an even more daring and spectacular attack, Haqqani fighters using automatic weapons and rocket-propelled grenades attempted to assassinate Afghan president Hamid Karzai during a military parade on Mujahideen Day, April 27, 2008. The event was held to mark the sixteenth anniversary of the fall of the Afghan Communist government to the mujahideen in 1992. Although Karzai was safe, three people—among them an Afghan parliamentarian—were killed, and ten were injured. Perhaps most striking, the assault resembled the assassination of Egyptian president Anwar al-Sadat by members of the Egyptian Jihad Organization on October 6, 1981, one of the greatest successes in the history of the jihadist movement. Finally, on July 7, 2008, the Haqqani network targeted the Indian embassy in Kabul in a suicide car bombing that killed more than sixty people, including the Indian defense attaché and many Afghan civilians lined up seeking visas to India. Similar attacks followed in 2009 and 2010, showing the Haqqani network's enormous terrorist capabilities.[8]

The danger emanating from the Haqqani network was perhaps most clearly evidenced by yet another attack on Forward Operating Base Chapman near Khost on December 30, 2009. A Jordanian jihadist and trusted informant of the US Central Intelligence Agency (CIA) named Humam al-Balawi (a.k.a. Abu Dujana al-Khurasani, b. 1977) entered the base and detonated his suicide vest, killing seven CIA officials and one Jordanian official. Although Balawi acted primarily on behalf of the Pakistani Taliban and their leader Hakimullah Mehsud, the attack was executed on Haqqani territory, so the network's participation can be taken for granted.[9]

Jalaluddin Haqqani is a member of the Pashtun Zadran tribe, which resides in the Afghan border provinces of Paktia, Paktika, and Khost. In the mid-1970s, he left his native Khost Province and settled in Miranshah in North Waziristan. During the 1980s, he had become one of the most famous Mujahidin commanders, fighting the Soviet troops and their local allies in neighboring Afghanistan from his safe haven in North Waziristan. It was in these years that he established close contacts with Arab volunteers, among them Osama Bin Laden.[10] He celebrated his biggest military victory in 1991, when he took the city of Khost from the troops of the Najibullah regime that the Soviets had installed and had left in Kabul after their withdrawal.

Haqqani's relationship with the Taliban has always been ambivalent. When the Taliban swept the Afghan countryside in the mid-1990s, Haqqani initially resisted its advance into his strongholds in Paktia, Paktika, and Khost but was then persuaded to accept Taliban rule.[11] After the Taliban took Kabul in September 1996 and established its own government, Haqqani took a position as minister for borders and tribal affairs but did not spend much time in the capital. Rather, he seems to have seen his post as one way of effectively securing his control over Paktia, Paktika, and Khost. Although in principle loyal to the Taliban leadership, Haqqani asserted his independence in these provinces.

When the Taliban regime fell in late 2001, Haqqani withdrew to Miranshah again, profiting from an infrastructure he had built in the 1980s, including mosques and religious schools that also served as fertile recruitment ground for his troops. Since then, his organization has remained autonomous, with a command-and-control structure independent from the Quetta Shura and frequently called the "Miranshah Shura." Here, insurgent operations in Paktia, Paktika, and Khost and the Haqqani network's activities in the Kabul area are coordinated.[12] At the same time, however, the network's leadership is integrated into the Quetta Shura, with Jalaluddin Haqqani holding a post in this council and his son Sirajuddin serving as the Taliban's military leader for the three Afghan provinces.[13] And although there seems to be no Taliban interference in the actual course of operations in the area dominated by the Haqqani network, both groups have to coordinate their respective activities in those provinces where they fight alongside each other—as in Kabul and in the Kunduz region in northern Afghanistan, where both organizations intensified their activities between 2007 and 2008 (on insurgent activities in Kunduz, see chapter 9).

By and large, the Haqqani network tries to avoid asserting its independence publicly, probably in order to avoid evoking the impression that the insurgency is divided. Perhaps most important, it publishes all of its declarations under the Taliban's official title, the Islamic Emirate of Afghanistan, and makes extensive use of the Taliban propaganda infrastructure, including its official spokesmen Zabiullah Mujahid and Qari Muhammad Yusuf Ahmadi. Whenever asked, representatives of the Haqqani network state that they are part of the Taliban.[14] In practice, however, the Haqqani network has managed to preserve a substantial amount of independence. In fact, it sometimes seems as if the Taliban profits more from Jalaluddin Haqqani's religious reputation[15] and enormous prestige as one of the most famous surviving veterans of the war against the Soviets than Haqqani does from his association with the Quetta Shura.

Shortly after the Haqqanis' flight from Afghanistan in late 2001, Jalaluddin seems to have delegated the military leadership of his organization to his son Sirajuddin (born in the 1970s), who is reputed to be an even more ruthless and brutal commander than his father. After the insurgency escalated in 2006, the extent to which the elder Haqqani still influences the strategies and manages the affairs of his organization was subject to debate. In 2012, Jalaluddin Haqqani apparently remained a figurehead, perhaps influencing overall strategic guidelines and serving as a sort of religious authority, whereas his son enjoyed considerable leeway on the battlefield. What is obvious is that since 2006 the Haqqani network has increasingly adopted tactics such as suicide bombings and attacks using improvised explosive devices (IEDs), a development that has sometimes been interpreted as an outcome of al-Qaeda's transfer of terrorist know-how from its Iraqi battlefield. Most commentators make a new generation of field commanders, including Sirajuddin Haqqani, responsible for this trend, arguing that these new commanders have built stronger ties to al-Qaeda and other foreign militants and not only have adopted their terrorist tactics but are also increasingly influenced by internationalist thought, transcending the Taliban's essentially nationalist goals. Although Sirajuddin himself contradicted this hypothesis in 2008, stating that the Taliban (including the Haqqani network) seeks exclusively to liberate Afghanistan, other Haqqani commanders have stressed the strong ties binding their organization and al-Qaeda.[16]

The Haqqanis' continuing dependency on the Pakistani military might be a factor influencing the network's public position on its relation to al-Qaeda. Since the 1980s, Haqqani has enjoyed the support of the Pakistani military, mainly through the military's powerful intelligence service, the Interservices Intelligence. The Pakistani military sees the Haqqani network (besides the Quetta Shura Taliban and Hekmatyar's Islamic Party) as one of its most important assets in the struggle over the future of Afghanistan. Although the Pakistani government in Islamabad has been a nominal US ally since late 2001, it nevertheless sees Afghanistan against the background of its larger conflict with India. The Taliban was a creation of the Pakistanis, and its Islamic Emirate served the interests of the Pakistani military, which aimed at securing its Afghan hinterland by supporting an Afghan Pashtun client. The downfall of the Taliban in 2001 was regarded as the downfall of an important Pakistani client, and the new government of Afghan president Hamid Karzai was seen as too pro-Indian. So the Pakistani military decided to follow an ambivalent policy. On the one hand, it supported the United States in the latter's fight against al-Qaeda, arresting important operatives and from time to time leading offensives against foreign militants in their hideouts in the Pashtun areas close to the Afghan border. On the other hand, in order to safeguard its interests in Afghanistan, it has tolerated the Taliban's safe havens on the Pakistani side of the border and continues to give tacit support to clients such as the Haqqani network.

Perhaps the most glaring example of the ongoing connection between the Pakistani military and the Haqqani network is the aforementioned attack on the Indian embassy in Kabul on July 7, 2008. US intelligence sources insisted that it was a joint operation of the Haqqani network and the Interservices Intelligence and that the latter did not even make an effort to hide its involvement.[17] Even more important, connections to the Pakistani military have saved the Haqqani network from Pakistani military offensives against its headquarters and stronghold in North Waziristan. As a consequence of the Haqqani network's being an instrument to help secure Pakistani interests in Afghanistan, the Pakistani military has only reluctantly taken on the organization in recent years. Although it started military offensives in other tribal areas to root out the Pakistani Taliban, which after 2007 was increasingly targeting the Pakistani state, and battered foreign militants allied to these Taliban groupings, government forces have not yet attacked North Waziristan.

Knowing full well that its survival depends on the Pakistani military's policy of toleration, the organization repeatedly stresses that it exclusively fights the Americans and their allies in neighboring Afghanistan. However, a side effect of this policy has been to give the foreign allies of the Haqqani network, such as the IJU and al-Qaeda, the opportunity to use the areas around Miranshah and Mir Ali as safe havens. After 2002, the IJU became part of this emerging North Waziristan scene of militants. There are even some unconfirmed reports that al-Qaeda offered Jalolov and his supporters financial assistance if they left the IMU and built a new, more internationalist organization.[18] If true, this report would be in line with a great deal of information about constantly and severely strained relations between al-Qaeda and the IMU (see chapter 8). The IJU became a junior partner of the Haqqani/al-Qaeda alliance in North Waziristan, supporting the Haqqani network in its operations in Paktia, Paktika, and Khost and simultaneously trying to carry the jihad back to its home countries in Central Asia, primarily Uzbekistan. After 2006, the German recruits formed a new part of this jihadist landscape in North Waziristan.

Going Global in Uzbekistan

In late March and early April 2004, the IJU executed its first terrorist attacks. On March 28, a bomb exploded in a private home in Bukhara, killing ten people. The explosive device apparently detonated while members of the group tried to assemble it for an attack in the city. Despite its accidental start, the event was the opening to a larger-scale campaign in Uzbekistan. Beginning in the early hours of March 29, IJU fighters attacked police checkpoints, killing three policemen and wounding one. Later that same day two female suicide bombers blew themselves up at the compound of the Khorsu Bazaar, killing several policemen. The assault was followed the next day when two cars with IJU fighters were stopped on the outskirts of Tashkent. A woman in one of the cars blew herself up, and the remaining fighters fled the vehicles and barricaded themselves in a nearby house. The ensuing standoff ended when one of the fighters set fire to the house, leading to the death of most of the IJU fighters and one policeman. There were also reports of an attempted car bomb attack on the Kharvak Dam in the Tashkent region.

Despite the IJU's efforts during the three-day onslaught, the damage it inflicted on what appears to have been its main target, the police, was limited—especially when compared to the loss of life the IJU itself suffered. To add insult to injury, an IJU militant accidently blew himself up in his own house on March 31. In total, forty-six people were killed in the IJU attacks launched March 28–31, 2004: ten policemen, thirty-three IJU fighters—including their leader Ahmad Bekmirzayev—and three civilians. Fifteen IJU members were arrested. Perhaps the most striking detail that emerged from the events was that these suicide attacks were the first in Central Asia, sending shockwaves throughout the region, which had scarcely recovered from several offensives by the IMU in 1999 and 2000. The attacks took the Uzbek authorities by surprise; indeed, their first reaction was to blame the Islamic Liberation Party (Hizb al-Tahrir). This party is an important transnational organization with headquarters in Lebanon and the United Kingdom and has become especially influential in Central Asia. It is the largest and most active Islamist organization in Uzbekistan, but it has always rejected violence. Therefore, many observers doubted the claims that it was responsible for the attacks in March 2004 and perceived them as an effort on the part of the Karimov regime to justify its brutal repression of every kind of Islamist tendencies in the country.[19]

Meanwhile, the IJU published its own claim of responsibility on an Arabic-language Web site. At that time, it still used its original name, "Islamic Jihad Group" (Jamaʿat al-Jihad al-Islami):

> The Group of Muslim Mojahed Islamic Jihad (Islomiy Jihod) claims responsibility for the attacks and explosions directed against the government of Uzbekistan and its servants, which pursue a policy of violence against the people of Uzbekistan[,] and considers that all these actions are proof of Allah's orders, written in the Koran and calling for jihad against the enemies of Islam, being carried out. Our aim in these actions is to attach great significance to the words of Allah and respond with vengeance to the enemies of Islam, the evil people behind the execution, arrest and torture of our brothers and sisters. We will fight to the last drop of blood to achieve our aims! According to our information, the arrests of Muslims have begun again. We demand that the government of the dictator Karimov stop these arrests forthwith and free our Muslim brothers and sisters from its prisons! Otherwise our attacks will be even crueller, even stronger and longer, since Allah allows us to act, Inshallah.[20]

In the following months, Central Asian authorities provided additional information about the plot. Ahmad Bekmirzajev seems to have stood in close contact with the IJU leadership in Waziristan.[21] Although the plot's grand design was apparently developed in Pakistan, the attackers' trail soon led the Uzbek authorities to Kazakhstan. Here, as in the February 1999 attacks in Tashkent, the plotters seem to have used Shimkent, a historically Uzbek city of some 650,000 about seventy-five miles from the Uzbek border, as a launching pad and rear base. This assessment was confirmed by the Kazakh government in November 2004, when it reported that it had broken up a terrorist group named Mujahedeen of Central Asia Group. The details provided made clear, however, that this group was nothing more than the Kazakh branch of the IJU. According to the Kazakh government, the Mujahedeen of Central Asia Group had been founded in 2002 and consisted of some fifty Uzbek and twenty Kazakh citizens. Its leader in Kazakhstan was a Kyrgysz citizen named Zhakshybek Bimurzajev, and its branch active in Uzbekistan had until March 2004 been led by Ahmad Bekmirzajev. Both Bimurzajev and Bekmirzajev were former members of the IMU. During interrogations, Bimurzajev confessed to having organized the attacks in Tashkent on behalf of an unnamed leader of the organization living outside of Central Asia, probably Jalolov. Among the perpetrators of the attacks in Tashkent in late March 2004 were three Kazakh citizens, and some of the attackers had been trained in Shimkent.[22]

Although the attacks in spring 2004 mainly targeted Uzbek security forces, and the claim of responsibility used the domestic policies of the Karimov regime as a justification, the IJU's next step made clear that it sought to combine the fight against the "near enemy" with attacks on the "far enemy." On July 30, 2004, a mere four months after the initial attacks, members of the organization perpetrated three suicide attacks: one each on the Israeli and American embassies in Tashkent and one on the office of the prosecutor general. Two local guards were killed in the explosions at the Israeli embassy, two more at the American embassy compound, and seven people were wounded in the blast at the prosecutor general's office. These attacks were the first on Western targets in Central Asia, and the choice of the American and Israeli embassies resembled al-Qaeda's and other Arab jihadist outfits' target selection. The message was clear: an organization had emerged in Central Asia that supported al-Qaeda's global agenda. The bombings, however, coincided with the much publicized trial against members of the group who presumably had taken part in the attacks in March and April, so that it could reasonably be assumed that they were perpetrated by the same Uzbek organization. And the Islamic Jihad Group again claimed responsibility in a statement published on the Arabic-language Web site Islamic Minbar (Islamic Pulpit or Forum):

> A group of young Muslims executed martyrdom operations that put fear in the apostate government and its infidel allies, the Americans and Jews. The mujahideen belonging to Islamic Jihad Group attacked both the American and Israeli embassies as well as the court building where the trials of a large number of the brothers from the Group had begun. These martyrdom operations that the group is executing will not stop, God willing. It is for the purpose of repelling the injustice of the apostate government and supporting the jihad of our Muslim brothers in Iraq, Palestine, Afghanistan, the Hijaz,[23] and in other Muslim countries ruled by infidels and apostates.[24]

As a consequence of the attacks, the US government put the Islamic Jihad Group on its list of terrorist organizations and quoted the statements of suspects whom the Uzbek authorities had arrested after the attacks in Bukhara and Tashkent in March and April 2004.[25] The United Nations followed suit and on June 1, 2005, put the group on its terrorist watch list. In the meantime, however, the organization changed its name. For unknown reasons, it began to use the name "Islamic Jihad Union" instead.[26] By then, it had clearly established itself as a prominent international terrorist organization.

Some commentators—especially the former British ambassador in Tashkent, Craig Murray—have cast doubts on whether the attacks in Uzbekistan were really perpetrated by Islamist terrorists. A fierce critic of the Karimov regime, Murray claims to have visited the sites right after the attacks and found no traces of the explosions. He believes, rather, that Uzbek security forces made up the attacks and executed oppositionists on the spots where the attacks were to take place as part of the aim to legitimize the regime's repressive policies toward the Islamist opposition in the country and to procure US and other Western states' support for its fight against Islamist terrorists.[27] Other reports even claim that the IJU was invented by or is run by Uzbek secret services, and such reports have gained some popularity in Germany, especially in the left-of-center political sphere. Rumors that the IJU did not exist persisted even after the Sauerland four testified that the IJU had recruited them and sent them to Germany to perpetrate their attacks on American and Uzbek targets. Furthermore, when appearing in court in Düsseldorf, Fritz Gelowicz affirmed that Jalolov and his aides had declared the IJU's responsibility for the attacks in Uzbekistan in 2004.[28]

An Internationalist Ideology

Although the IJU became a household name in specialized intelligence circles in the years after the attacks in Uzbekistan in 2004, virtually nothing was known about its inner workings or its worldview. This situation changed in May 2007, when IJU leader Najmiddin Jalolov gave his first interview detailing the group's ideology and strategy. The statement was the starting point for a public-relations campaign on Turkish Web sites that a small group of Turkish members and supporters of the IJU in Istanbul managed. In the following years until 2011, Turkish rather than Uzbek became the IJU's main propaganda language. In this first interview, Jalolov appeared under one of his aliases, "Ebu Yahya Muhammed Fatih," probably referring to the Ottoman sultan and conqueror of Constantinople in 1453, Mehmet (Muhammad) Fatih (1432–1481); *fatih* is the Arabic honorific for "conqueror."[29]

In the interview, Ebu Yahya stated that the IJU was founded in 2002 with the aim of toppling the regime of Islam Karimov in Uzbekistan and that it still stuck to that target: "We have been working on strategies against the infidel regime in Uzbekistan. This regime is one of our most important targets." In addition, Ebu Yahya explained that his organization not only consisted of Central Asians but also cooperated closely with "Caucasian mujahideen": "In religious terms, young people who have found the right path to God within the territory of the former Soviet Union and who are willing to fight wars in the name of faith, have acquired different skills and abilities in the training camps. . . . In military terms, we are currently developing our activities on Afghan soil. We are striving to establish a relationship with the Caucasian mujahedeen and aim to seek a consensus regarding our common goals."[30] Ebu Yahya's hint regarding the IJU's connections to fighters from the Caucasus provided further evidence of the Chechen dimension of Central Asian jihadism, as reported after the attacks in Uzbekistan in 1999. Ever since his stay in Chechnya, Jalolov had maintained contact with fighters from this Russian republic and their foreign volunteers from Turkey and Azerbaijan. Only later did concrete evidence become available that the IJU cooperated closely with Turks and Azeris who had previously fought in the Caucasus and that it had built a small Turkic network, of which the German Turks became the most visible part.

In this interview, Ebu Yahya also declared that the IJU sought to liberate oppressed Muslims worldwide: "One of the objectives of our Union is to conduct jihad in the way of the one God in order to call to the true religion of God in the whole world and to free our Muslim brothers in the countries we have listed from the tyranny of the unbelievers [*kafirler*], thereby leading our brothers to the freedom of Islam. Our jihad will continue until the religion of God is fully realized."[31] This vision of a perpetual holy war—that will end only when all Muslims live in Islamic states—made clear that the IJU's agenda was substantially more internationalist than the IMU's. The change had already been confirmed by the attacks on the Israeli and American embassies in Tashkent in 2004, but it gained additional credibility when the Sauerland group was arrested in September 2007. If their plot had been successful, it would have shown that even small jihadist organizations can plan, organize, and perpetrate attacks across continents.

The roots of this internationalist ideology had been laid by the IJU's mother organization, the IMU, before the split. In 2001, the IMU leadership had still insisted on exclusively fighting the "near enemy," in this case the regime of Uzbek president Islam Karimov. This issue was, however, a contentious one for many members of the organization, which at that time was based in Afghanistan and whose members had come into contact with more internationalist groups such as al-Qaeda. As a result, heated debates over the IMU's aims and strategies developed within its ranks. Although the Uzbek nationalists prevailed in the debates over the organization's strategies, an ideological vacuum was created that the IJU could fill after it had split from its mother organization (see chapter 8 for details on these debates). As a consequence, the IJU joined the Haqqani network and al-Qaeda in their fight in Afghanistan, whereas the IMU made an alliance with Baitullah Mehsud and his Pakistani Taliban and fought the Pakistani state. Thus, the IJU became an extremely attractive destination for Germans who wanted to join the anti-American jihad in Afghanistan.

Al-Qaeda's Ally

The IJU's geographical location in North Waziristan seems to have played a major role in this internationalization process. Internationalist ideology gained ground among Uzbeks and other Central Asians the farther and the longer they were living in exile—in Tajikistan until 1997, Afghanistan until 2001, and the Pakistani tribal areas thereafter. In the latter, the alliance with the Afghan and Pakistani Taliban and its Pakistani, Arab, and Caucasian supporters left a mental and ideological imprint on the Central Asians. Although the IJU never forgot that the Karimov regime in its home country remained an important if not primary enemy, close contacts with these groups reinforced the conviction among the Central Asians that there was more to jihad than just toppling this particular regime. As a result, they increasingly concentrated on the fight against the United States and its allies in Afghanistan. Furthermore, the IJU became an integral part of the jihadist scene in North Waziristan and, just like the Haqqani network and al-Qaeda, came under rising pressure beginning in late 2007 when the United States intensified its attacks using unmanned Predator and Reaper drones, killing dozens of jihadist leaders and hundreds of fighters. In general, the experience of constant American pressure on the jihadist organizations in Pakistan has served to deepen the anti-Americanism espoused by many of their key players and helped the organizations gain a new popularity, especially among Central Asians.

Al-Qaeda's relationship with the IJU is strongly conditioned by the former's enduring connection to the Haqqani network, its most important ally in Pakistan. North Waziristan has become the most important safe haven for the Arabs of al-Qaeda since 2002. Until Osama Bin Laden's death in May 2011, some analysts even suspected that the terrorist leader might have gone into hiding somewhere in this area, which he is said to have passed through after he and his followers were forced to leave Afghanistan in late 2001. Although there also is ample evidence of the presence of Arab fighters in South Waziristan, they seem to have preferred North Waziristan. Most important, their relationship with the Haqqani network has made this agency the safer place to stay, as evidenced by the fact that no major Pakistani offensive has yet taken place in the North, whereas South Waziristan—where anti-Pakistani Taliban and anti-Pakistani Uzbek militants of the IMU are far stronger than those in the North—has seen heavy, intermittent fighting since 2004. The culmination of this development was the big Pakistani offensive of October 2009 that forced many Pakistani, Central Asian, and Arab militants to flee.

Alliances between Haqqani and Arab jihadists have been close since the 1980s, when the mujahideen commander befriended Osama Bin Laden, who concentrated his activities on the areas in Paktia, Paktika, and especially Khost, where Haqqani was fighting the Soviet troops. At that time, Jalaluddin Haqqani built strong relationships with supporters in the Arab Gulf states. He speaks Arabic and is married to a woman from the United Arab Emirates. His son Nasiruddin, who according to some sources is a son of Haqqani's Arab wife, serves as the organization's fund-raiser in the gulf, where most of the finances for the Haqqanis seem to originate.[32] To this end, Nasiruddin is reported to travel frequently to Dubai, the Gulf's trade and finance hub. As a consequence of Haqqani's strong relations with the Arab world, most Arabs fleeing from Afghanistan in late 2001 and early 2002 ended up asking for his protection in North Waziristan, which the warlord and his local allies readily granted.

The extent of the al-Qaeda presence in North Waziristan became most obvious in 2007 when US drone strikes increasingly targeted foreign militants present in North Waziristan. Between 2007 and 2012, the overwhelming majority of strikes hit targets in North Waziristan, pointing to the presence of large contingents of foreign fighters and their leaders in the agency.[33] Although numbers are contested, around two dozen important al-Qaeda, IMU, and IJU leaders have been killed since the attacks escalated in October 2007. The first prominent loss was Libyan Ali Ammar al-Ruqayi (a.k.a. Abu Laith al-Libi, b. 1972), who had led the remnants of the LIFG into the merger with al-Qaeda in November 2007 and who served as a kind of Central Asia representative for the organization. Libi was killed in a village close to Mir Ali in January 2008. On August 27, 2009, the IMU leader Tahir Yoldashev was killed in a drone attack in South Waziristan. His death was followed by a strike against the IJU on September 14, 2009, which killed its leader Najmiddin Jalolov. Among those killed in North Waziristan were the Egyptian Mustafa Abu l-Yazid (a.k.a. Sheikh Said al-Masri), the longtime head of al-Qaeda's financial operations who in May 2007 was appointed the organization's commander for Afghanistan. Abu l-Yazid was killed in Datta Khel in May 2010. His replacement, the Libyan Jamal Ibrahim al-Misrati (Atiyatallah Abu Abd al-Rahman) was reportedly also killed by a drone strike in August 2011. By killing these leaders and significant numbers of al-Qaeda's medium-level commanders, the United States succeeded in substantially weakening the organization's capabilities.

Many of the drone strikes took place close to Mir Ali, where many Arabs have been based in recent years alongside the Uzbeks of the IJU, Germans, Turks, and Azeris. Al-Qaeda elements were also present in and around Miranshah and the Shawal Mountains in the southwestern part of the region, an area replete with foreign fighters. Moreover, testimonies by German volunteers returning from the tribal areas report that the Arabs of al-Qaeda are present in both North and South Waziristan and form the core of a still active cadre of foreign fighters, who have suffered from increased pressures exerted by the Pakistani offensive in October 2009 and frequent American drone strikes in North Waziristan.[34]

Nevertheless, al-Qaeda's contribution to the Afghan insurgency seems to have been marginal ever since the escalation of the fight in 2006. The organization only serves as a junior partner to the Haqqani network, acting mainly in support of the latter's operations. This subordinate position, in effect, holds true for all foreign organizations, which have to submit to Taliban command as soon as they cross the border into Afghanistan. Although al-Qaeda claims to have carried out a number of attacks, its role is apparently confined to providing the Haqqani network with terrorist expertise and volunteers rather than acting on its own. This configuration is in part due to the shrinking numbers of Arab fighters, who by all accounts do not seem to number more than four to five hundred men in Afghanistan and Pakistan.[35] Most of them operate under Haqqani control in the area called Loya Paktia (referring to the three provinces Paktia, Paktika, and Khost), with some reportedly taking part in Haqqani operations in Kabul.[36] Al-Qaeda fighters also have taken part in the insurgency in Kunar and its neighboring areas.[37] There, they might be connected to the Islamic Party of Gulbuddin Hekmatyar rather than to the Haqqani network. In all other Afghan provinces, there are only scattered reports about al-Qaeda activity.

Besides gaining a safe haven for its leaders, al-Qaeda profits from its alliance with the Haqqani network primarily via its propaganda work. Through its media wing, al-Sahab (the Clouds), al-Qaeda tries to convey the impression to the world that it plays a major role in the Afghan insurgency, preparing for the time when the United States and its allies withdraw from the country and it can claim its contribution to the victory. The situation resembles the Soviet–Afghanistan War of the 1980s, when Arabs played a scant role in the anti-Soviet insurgency but later used their "victory" in the fight against the Soviet Union as a powerful mobilizing tool. At the same time, al-Qaeda seems to focus its energies, together with allied Pakistani groups, on destabilizing the Pakistani state and using its sanctuary in order to plan and organize attacks abroad. And here the IJU comes into play.

Al-Qaeda seems to have built close relations with the Uzbeks of the IJU, but without accepting the small Uzbek organization as an equal partner. Its main liaison to the IJU was the Libyan Abu Laith al-Libi—the most prominent Arab field commander in Afghanistan in his day and chief suspect as the true mastermind of the Sauerland plot.[38] Even before October 2001, Libi cultivated especially close ties with the Taliban and the Uzbeks but had long retained a certain distance to al-Qaeda. Relations between the Arabs and Uzbeks in Afghanistan had been strained since the 1990s, before the fall of the Taliban emirate, in part because of al-Qaeda's efforts to recruit Central Asians and the increasing attractiveness of internationalist thinking among Central Asians. In at least one case, only the personal intervention by the Taliban leader Mullah Omar seems to have prevented the outbreak of hostilities between Arabs and Uzbeks. Relations remained strained after al-Qaeda's escape to Pakistan, and the Uzbeks of the IMU rejected any contact with the Arabs of al-Qaeda, except for Abu Laith al-Libi.[39] Some of the resentment seems to have stemmed from al-Qaeda's responsibility for the fall of the Islamic Emirate following the 9/11 attacks and the subsequent American intervention. Libi belonged to a not-so-small group of prominent jihadists who, like Mustafa Abu l-Yazid and the famous Syrian ideologist Abu Musab al-Suri, had become ardent supporters of the Taliban and Mullah Umar.

Abu Laith al-Libi is also reported to have fallen out—at least temporarily—with al-Qaeda because of the domination of Egyptians in al-Qaeda's upper ranks.[40] By late 2007, however, al-Qaeda managed to bring Libi back to the fold and convinced him to declare the merger of the remnants of the LIFG in Afghanistan with al-Qaeda in November of that year.[41] By integrating commanders such as Abu Laith al-Libi into the organization, al-Qaeda broadened its appeal not only among those Arabs who had been critical of the group's strategies in the past, but also among the Uzbeks for whom the Libyan seems to have been a prominent leader.

Soon after the arrest of the Sauerland cell in September 2007, German officials suspected that Libi was the possible mastermind but did not have any conclusive evidence. The depth of his involvement with the IJU became obvious, however, after he was killed in an American drone attack at his hideout near Mir Ali in January 2008.[42] Soon afterward, the IJU—not al-Qaeda—confirmed that Libi had been killed during the attack. Most important, however, six Central Asian IJU members are reported to have died together with Libi.[43] In the declaration, the IJU authors called the field commander "our Sheikh," a designation hinting at Libi's prominent function for IJU members. In certain contexts, the title *sheikh* can indicate a religious function as well, but because Libi was a man of action, a field commander as opposed to a preacher or strategist, he must have been seen as a military leader.[44]

The IJU from Heyday to Demise

Al-Qaeda's support might have been the main factor in the IJU's survival after 2002. But even with the aid of al-Qaeda, Jalolov and his followers faced problems building their organization and maintaining its presence in competition with their mother organization, the IMU.

THE ORGANIZATION AND ITS MEMBERS

The IJU was led by its founding emir Najmiddin Jalolov (a.k.a. Ahmet or Yahya or Ebu Yahya Muhammed Fatih) until his death in September 2009. Many of the organization's members do not seem to have known the IJU under its official name, but rather as "the Uzbek group" or "Ahmet group." Knowledge of the organization's full name, aims, strategies, structure, and history seems to have been restricted to those members who assumed leading positions and functions within it. Fritz Gelowicz, for instance, was the only member of the Sauerland group who knew the full name and other details.

In addition, the seemingly widespread designation "the Ahmet group" hints at Jalolov's central role in the organization and his personalized style of leadership. Until his death, he remained the uncontested leader of the IJU, although his personal charisma seems to have been limited. He never appeared on any of the organization's videos, leaving some of the rare public appearances of Uzbek personnel to the IJU's military leader and second in command, Abdallah Fatih (a.k.a. Raushan Eke). The only known photograph of Jalolov appeared on the Internet shortly after his death in September 2009, showing a guarded but not unfriendly looking man in his late thirties. Indeed, Fritz Gelowicz described Jalolov as an unpretentious, friendly, and caring personality, stressing that the IJU leader even prepared a meal for his German recruit when the latter was sick and unable to look after himself.[45]

Jalolov's right-hand man and the IJU's chief translator was Suhail Buranov (a.k.a. Sulaiman or Mansur Suhail or Abu Huzaifa, b. 1983), an ethnic Uzbek and a native of Tashkent.[46] Buranov had already been a member of the IMU before he became a founding member of the IJU in 2002 at the age of nineteen. In 2006, when the Sauerland group trained in Waziristan, Buranov seems to have acted as Jalolov's deputy. He was perhaps the most talented figure in the organization, speaking Uzbek, Turkish, Russian, Arabic, and Pashto, which might explain his rise to the highest ranks of an increasingly multinational organization in spite of his young age. Buranov acted as the main liaison to the Sauerland group before and after they left the training camp in Waziristan and seems to have had a hand in the IJU's public relations.

Abdallah Fatih was appointed IJU leader after Jalolov's death.[47] Until September 2009, the Uzbek Fatih commanded the IJU's military activities in Afghanistan, personally leading the fighters into battle while Jalolov and his aides remained in Mir Ali. Even before his appointment, Fatih had appeared on at least one video in which he was presented as an IJU leader, thereby establishing himself as the only visible personality in the organization. But he lacked even the slightest hint of charisma, the videos showing a middle-aged, moon-faced Central Asian addressing his viewers in Uzbek with a dull expression that offered no clue as to his emotions. As a consequence, not much was heard of Abdallah Fatih after Jalolov died.

In 2002, the IJU consisted of only around a dozen people who had joined Jalolov when he split from the IMU. In the wake of the 2004 attacks in Uzbekistan, though, the group grew quickly, and from 2006 to 2007 Jalolov commanded between one hundred and two hundred fighters. In October 2007, however, US drones increasingly began to attack IJU targets around Mir Ali, effectively decimating the organization's leadership as well as its rank and file. Although no exact numbers are available, the losses were apparently substantial for such a small group.[48] Most of the IJU's members come from Uzbekistan, but they also include Tajiks, Kyrgyzs, and Kazakhs, and the organization cooperates closely with Chechen and Uighur militants. Furthermore, the IJU maintains well-established contacts with Azeri and Turkish jihadists. With the arrival of the German group in 2006, the organization managed to broaden its recruitment base even further. This small internationalization process culminated in 2009, when the numbers of Germans, Turks, and Azeris rose to such an extent that the IJU leadership seems to have decided to unite the respective groups and found a Turkic international brigade of fighters affiliated with the IJU: the German Taliban Mujahideen and Taifetül Mansura (on this development, see chapter 7).

In spite of its recruitment and public-relations successes starting in 2004, the IJU only survived in competition with and under constant threat of its far stronger and better-known mother organization, the IMU. The latter organization is known to react aggressively to the desertion of its Central Asian members (see chapter 8 for details). During the trial of the Sauerland group in Düsseldorf in 2001, Daniel Schneider reported that the IMU had issued death threats to one of its former members who had joined the IJU and thereby confirmed the picture of an authoritarian organization not willing to accept the desertion of its members under any circumstances. In a different case, when a bomb exploded underneath the Jeep of the military leader Abdallah Fatih in Waziristan in 2006, IJU members suspected the IMU of having planted the device.[49] This suspicion might be considered sufficient evidence for tense relations between the two organizations. In all likelihood, Jalolov and his followers would not have been able to keep up their independent activities if it had not been for the support of the Haqqani network and al-Qaeda.

A PUBLIC-RELATIONS CAMPAIGN

In 2007, the IJU started a propaganda campaign with the goal of establishing itself on the jihadist world map. The Sauerland plot and the organization's subsequent claim of responsibility brought the IJU to the attention of Western governments and world media, which had positive as well as negative consequences. First, the IJU became a household name for potential German and Turkish recruits. Second, increased public visibility meant that the small IJU became a competitor for the much less media-savvy IMU in the quest for recruits from Central Asia and monetary donations from supporters in the Arab states of the Persian Gulf. Third, by ordering the Sauerland group to look for American targets and publicly challenging the superpower, the IJU moved into the US government's sights. As a consequence, the CIA would invest substantial energies in going after the IJU leadership in North Waziristan. The death of Abu Laith al-Libi and his Central Asian companions in January 2008 were most likely the first American countermove. In 2009, Jalolov and Buranov were killed by American drone attacks, which nearly led to the demise of the young Uzbek organization.

Until 2007, the Uzbek jihadists in general seem to have neglected public relations. In fact, neither the IMU nor the IJU had its own Web site but relied instead on more traditional ways of disseminating messages, in most cases sending them to radio and television stations in Iran, Pakistan, Russia, and the Central Asian states. The IJU first seems to have used the Internet in 2004 when its claims of responsibility for the attacks that year were published on the Islamic Minbar Web site in Switzerland.[50] The texts appeared in Arabic, though, leaving serious doubts as to the authenticity of the claims at that time. It is paradigmatic for the IJU's weakness in public relations that from 2006 it had to employ a group of Turks to start its Internet propaganda activities in Turkish rather than in the IJU members' native tongue Uzbek.

In late 2006, the picture changed because the IJU established its own Internet presence. On the Turkish Web site Time for Martyrdom (www.sehadetvakti.com, since July 2008 www.sehadetzamani.com), it published declarations, interviews, and videos of guerilla and terrorist training and attacks in Pakistan and Afghanistan, trying to present itself as a successful transnational organization that aimed mainly at the recruitment of young jihadists from Germany and Turkey. The Web site was first launched in November 2006 and was administered by a small group of Internet jihadists in Istanbul who stayed in contact with the IJU and served as human traffickers for the organization. A German Turkish member of the group, Ahmet Manavbaşı (1977–2010, "the IJU's propaganda minister," according to a German intelligence official),[51] was the main liaison between the IJU and its Istanbul cell of public-relations specialists.

In the IJU's publications and videos, Manavbaşı was referred to as "Salahuddin Turki" (the Turk) and long remained an enigma to the German authorities. A Turkish citizen, Manavbaşı was born in the German town of Salzgitter in 1977 and had spent the years before the turn of the millennium in the Saarland close to the French border. He was well known to the local authorities as a notorious drug dealer, and the sheer number of his offenses led to his extradition to Turkey in 2000. Although he was considered to be completely nonreligious while in Germany, the next information that surfaced about him indicated that he had joined the jihadist movement and traveled to Pakistan at an unknown date before 2007. Most likely, he had met Fritz Gelowicz and come into contact with other members of the Sauerland cell.[52] After several months in a Pakistani jail in 2006–2007, he took over the IJU's propaganda work. His footprint could already be seen in the interview with the organization's emir, Najmiddin Jalolov, in May 2007. The interview was written in a very rudimentary Turkish, so it could be assumed that the text had been written by a diaspora Turk with only limited schooling and a limited knowledge of his mother tongue—typical for many Turks living in Germany.[53]

The IJU Web site represented the dominant themes of Turkish jihadism rather than functioning as an exclusive mouthpiece for the IJU. It contained news and videos of different jihadist organizations but concentrated on those theaters of war that mainly interested Turkish jihadists and their supporters and sympathizers—namely, Chechnya, Iraq, and Central Asia. In its header, the images of three charismatic jihadist leaders alternately popped up: the legendary Saudi Khattab (Samir al-Suwailim), who had led the Arab volunteers in Chechnya until he was killed in 2002; the famous Chechen Shamil Basayev (1965–2006), who had integrated the Chechen struggle into the jihadist movement and became Russia's enemy number one from the mid-1990s; and the Jordanian Abu Musab al-Zarqawi (1966–2006), who by ruthlessly attacking the Shiite majority in Iraq had provoked his adversaries there to start a bloody civil war in 2006. Nevertheless, most of the materials on Iraq and other jihad theaters on the IJU Web site were of secondhand origin. The Web site's only original contributions to the jihadist presence on the Internet were the IJU's videos and declarations.

After the IJU released its famous press statement on September 11, 2007, in which it claimed responsibility for the Sauerland plot, it began to publish an increasing amount of training videos and footage of attacks in Afghanistan and Pakistan. The propaganda campaign reached its first peak when photographs and later a video featuring Cüneyt Çiftçi, "the first German suicide bomber," appeared on the IJU Web site. In a press release dated March 6, 2008, the IJU announced this fighter's martyrdom, explaining that he had rammed an explosive-laden vehicle into the gate of an American–Afghan military camp in the Afghan province of Paktika (it was in fact Khost). Several pictures of the (still living) young man smiling at the camera and brandishing a pistol were attached to the statement.[54] In late March 2008, the IJU released a video showing Çiftçi during the preparations for the bombing, his farewell to his comrades, and the explosion at the American camp. In late April, the Taliban published another video in which Çiftçi is again shown preparing for the attack. Most important, however, Jalaluddin Haqqani in person is shown praising the attack by the young German Turk, which provided firsthand evidence for the strong connection between the Haqqani network and the IJU.[55]

Starting in April 2008, the IJU published an increasing number of videos, making use of a new recruit who had left Germany shortly before the Sauerland group was arrested. Between 2007 and 2009, Eric Breininger (1987–2010) became the public face of the IJU in Germany, frequently calling upon young Muslims living in Germany to join the Afghan jihad against the West. Within months, Breininger became a household name in Germany, the wider public wondering what had triggered his conversion not only to Islam, but to jihadism. He had been recruited by the Sauerland plotter Daniel Schneider, his close friend, and arrived in Waziristan in the winter of 2007–2008, where he joined the IJU (on Breininger's recruitment, see chapter 6).

In the videos, which seem to have been filmed (and sometimes translated into Turkish) by Ahmet Manavbaşı, Breininger always speaks less than basic German, a peculiar mixture of his native Saarland dialect and youth slang. In fact, this was the only language he knew, a fact that drew derisive commentaries from the German press because of his more than obvious linguistic and intellectual limitations. According to a police source, the police observation team named Breininger "idiot's assistant" when he first appeared in the company of known local radicals. "We did not know who he was, but he looked very stupid!"[56] As a consequence, segments of the German public and the security authorities did not take Breininger seriously. In spite of his limitations, he seems to have been a successful propaganda tool for the IJU. A growing number of young Muslims watched the videos attentively and heeded the call to join the fight in Afghanistan. This success became most obvious in 2009, when Breininger and other Germans demanded that German recruits bring their wives and children with them to Waziristan, stating that the IJU and its allies had built a family-friendly infrastructure with schools and hospitals a safe distance from the front. And in fact, in 2009 an increasing number of young couples from Berlin intended to join the IJU. In general, at least some of Breininger's German acquaintances seem to have seen him as a success story. One German returnee reported in 2010 that Breininger had made a reputation for himself by staying in North Waziristan for nearly three years, a feat that hardly any other German recruit could claim.[57]

The IJU profited from this propaganda campaign insofar as it conveyed the picture of a transnational organization with supporters in Pakistan, Afghanistan, Central Asia, and Europe. Although smaller than the IMU, the IJU became the more widely known organization.

RETURN TO UZBEKISTAN

After Cüneyt Çiftçi's suicide bombing in March 2008, the IJU claimed responsibility for a string of suicide attacks in the Haqqani network's area of operations, providing ample evidence of the IJU's dependence on its Afghan ally. At least one of these attacks was a public-relations disaster.

When a Turkish volunteer detonated a car bomb at a checkpoint close to the Mandozai District Center in Khost on December 28, 2008, he killed fourteen schoolchildren who were just passing by.[58] Such attacks show quite strikingly that the IJU, like al-Qaeda, was meant to provide Afghan insurgents with terrorist training and—more important—suicide bombers and that these bombers were to be drawn from among the ranks of the Germans and Turks who joined the IJU at this time.

Although the IJU's propaganda campaign ably demonstrated its international ambitions, its operations on the ground indicate that it had accepted its supporting role with respect to the Haqqani network in the struggle for Afghanistan. So it was surprising that the IJU claimed responsibility for a terrorist attack in the Fergana Valley in Uzbekistan in May 2009. On May 26, 2009, an IJU cell attacked an Uzbek post on the Uzbek-Kyrgysz border close to Khanabad with firearms and deployed a suicide bomber to Andijan. These attacks left a local police officer dead and several people injured.[59] The Uzbek government at first blamed the IMU, but on May 27 the IJU issued a press release and subsequently a video in which the military leader Abdallah Fatih claimed responsibility.[60] The claim went uncontested by the IMU, so we can assume that the IJU was indeed responsible. Most important, the attacks were the first in the Fergana Valley since 2000, and they made clear that the IJU commanded a network of members in that valley.

The IJU's rise to international prominence suffered a serious setback, however, when its leader, Najmiddin Jalolov, was killed in September 2009. Some three weeks later Suhail Buranov also was killed. Although the organization quickly announced the succession of Abdallah Fatih as its new leader, it seems to have been seriously weakened by the death of its founding leader, who had dominated the organization from 2002. Furthermore, an unknown, but substantial number of lower-ranking members were killed by subsequent aerial attacks. As a consequence, many observers considered the IJU a spent force in late 2009.

However, the picture was more complicated. During 2009, dozens of new recruits arrived in the IJU's Mir Ali headquarters, some of them experienced and battle-hardened Turkish and Azeri veterans of the Chechen jihad, others young volunteers from Germany. Their arrival led to the foundation of a kind of Turkic international brigade and the emergence of the first German jihadist group—the German Taliban Mujahideen.

5

The Turkish Dimension

The fourth member of the Sauerland group, Atilla Selek, left Germany in February 2007 for Istanbul in order to facilitate the group's escape after the attack and to support the logistics. With the help of other Turkish jihadists, Selek procured the detonators and sent them to Germany. After he was extradited to Germany, Selek told his interrogators a highly irritating story (because it revealed how secret information on a German counterterrorism operation that had been given to a Turkish intelligence service was passed on to a suspect) about his experiences with a jihadist operative in Istanbul in summer 2007. The operative was another German Turk, Mevlüt Kar, a well-connected logistics specialist, who also transported volunteers from Turkey to Chechnya and the northern Caucasus and was one of the central figures linking the German jihadists to the Turkish scene. While Selek was trying to procure the detonators, Kar informed him that the German authorities had contacted their Turkish colleagues and told them that Gelowicz and Yilmaz were suspected of planning terrorist attacks and that they believed Selek was part of that group.[1] Kar then explained to Selek that this inside information came to him by way of a contact in the Turkish National Intelligence Service (Milli İstihbarat Teşkileti). The contact kept Kar informed because he was related to Kar's wife and had Islamist leanings.[2]

Although it is much more likely that Kar himself was a National Intelligence Service informant and that he had been tasked with observing Selek's activities, he informed Selek because he was "carrying on two shoulders"—that is, working for the intelligence service but at the same time continuing his activities as a jihadist logistics facilitator. He seems to have continued funneling fighters to the Caucasus as part of a Chechnya support network that had been in place in Istanbul since the 1990s. The government must have known about his activities, and Kar—who had spent a few months in a Turkish jail in late 2002—seems to have been tasked with directly informing the Turkish authorities about those activities. But as is so often the case, his loyalties resided with his fellow jihadists rather than with the government.

The story hints at several peculiarities in Turkey's role in the development of the German jihadist scene. Perhaps most important, several people like Kar who were based in Turkey held central functions as recruiters, human traffickers, and propagandists, connecting the German scene first to Chechnya and then, between 2006 and 2007, to Waziristan. They built on alliances that had been established in the days of the Bosnian jihad in the first half of the 1990s and later intensified to support the Chechen struggle. Furthermore, they seem to have profited from a certain ambivalence on the part of the Turkish military and government, which until about 2005 turned a blind eye to the activities of jihadist recruiters as long as they recruited for Chechnya and not al-Qaeda. As a result, Istanbul became the logistics center for the German jihadists. In the early years, the country served mainly as a way station to Chechnya, but by 2006 most German recruits traveled via Istanbul to Iran and from there to Pakistan. In Istanbul, a small cell associated with the IJU transported Germans, Turks, and recruits from the Caucasus region to Waziristan, provided the organization with money collected in Turkey and Germany, and organized its propaganda (for more on this Istanbul cell, see chapter 7).

Mevlüt Kar and the Ambivalence of Turkish Policy

The most enigmatic and shadowy representative of German Turkish jihadism, Mevlüt Kar (b. 1979) had been living in the industrial city of Ludwigshafen in southwestern Germany until August 2002. Before that,

Kar had worked as a logistician for the Jordanian terrorist Abu Musab al-Zarqawi, providing his organization with forged passports and traveling to Iran and Georgia. His name had already come up in connection with the so-called Tawhid cell, whose members had been arrested by the German police in April 2002 (on this case, see chapter 2). The Tawhid activist Shadi Abdallah had contacted him in order to procure passports for Zarqawi in Iran. At around the same time, Kar himself seems to have started preparations for a terrorist attack on behalf of Zarqawi's organization. In Operation Schokolade (Chocolate), the German police monitored his activities. In conversations between Kar and contacts in Saudi Arabia and Azerbaijan, they frequently talked about "towers," prompting the German police to suspect a planned attack on the banking district of Frankfurt with its high concentration of high-rise buildings.[3] Along with trying to finance his operation with the help of these contacts, Kar made an effort to recruit personnel among his acquaintances in the criminal milieu in Germany.

In August 2002, Kar traveled to Istanbul, where he was arrested upon arrival and spent three months in jail for unknown reasons. After his release, he did not resurface until 2007, when he reappeared in connection with Selek and the plan to procure detonators for the Sauerland cell.[4] When the Sauerland four began confessing, however, it became clear that he had remained in contact with comrades in Germany and that since 2003 he had been working as a recruiter for Chechnya and possibly other jihadists from his new base in Istanbul. Fritz Gelowicz reported that he had visited Kar in Turkey when he tried to find a way to the northern Caucasus in 2004.[5]

From the confessions, it seems obvious that the Turkish government was informed about some of Kar's activities and that until around 2005 it had tolerated the funneling of Turkish, German, and other volunteers to Chechnya even while it at the same time continued to fight those jihadists who targeted Turkey and its allies. At the root of this Turkish ambivalence lie both an Ottomanist and a pan-Turkic vision of the world, significant aspects of which are shared by the government, military, and parts of the population. Such worldviews have more than once prompted these entities to look the other way when Turkish jihadists seemed to follow similar aims in regions formerly part of the Ottoman Empire, such as Bosnia, or aided former allies of the Ottomans, such as the Chechens.

In the early 1990s, pan-Turkism was revived in Turkey. Although originally a nationalist trend with only slight religious overtones, pan-Turkism encompasses both political and religious motives mixed with strong feelings of solidarity with the Turkic peoples living between the Balkans and Xinjiang in western China. Many Turks harbor strong sympathies for their brethren in Bosnia, the Caucasus, and Central Asia. In this pan-Turkic geopolitical vision, all the countries settled by Turks and all the territories formerly ruled by the Ottoman Empire deserve the special attention and—if need be—the solidarity of the Turks in modern-day Turkey. Ottomanism plays a role insofar as Turkey's ruling elites and the wider population showed a keen interest in the situation of Muslims in the Balkans, especially the Muslims in Bosnia, who were left behind by the Ottoman Empire when Austria-Hungary annexed this territory in 1908. Although the Bosnians are not a Turkic people, the shared past has led many Turks to see them as brethren worthy of their full support. According to estimates, between 2 and 4 million Turks are of Bosnian origin, and many more (up to 20 percent of the population) originated in the Balkans. After civil war broke out in the former Yugoslavia in 1992 (lasting until 1995), the Turkish government sided diplomatically with the Bosnian Muslims, organized a big humanitarian aid effort, and even provided the Bosnian army with weapons in spite of a United Nations arms embargo against all parties involved in the conflict.[6] Furthermore, the government and army seem to have turned a blind eye to the recruitment activities in Turkey that prompted a first wave of militant Islamists to fight for the cause of the historically related Muslim nation. The Bosnian experience proved to be radicalizing for many Turkish Islamists and helped them to establish relations with jihadists from the Arab world, who flocked to the Balkans in even higher numbers than the Turks.[7]

Ottomanism and pan-Turkism enter into a similar alliance with regard to the wars in Chechnya. Although the country was never part of the Ottoman Empire, many Turks show deep sympathies for the Chechens, whom they consider former brothers-in-arms from the days of the Ottoman Empire's wars with Russia in the nineteenth and early twentieth centuries. At that time, the Caucasus was the battlefield between the two powers, with the Muslim Chechens often siding with the Turkish Ottomans. The Turks remember fondly how the legendary Chechen rebel leader Imam Shamil succeeded in binding thousands of Russian troops during the

Crimean war in the early 1850s.[8] As a result of this decade-long struggle, a 100,000-strong Chechen diaspora lives in Turkey, providing the insurgents in the North Caucasus with support. Here, in the course of two wars (1994–1996 and 1999–c. 2006), Chechen rebels tried to shake off the yoke of Russian rule. They were assisted by foreign fighters who flocked to the North Caucasus after 1995 and increasingly influenced the insurgent movement's ideological outlook.[9] As a result, Chechen jihadists gained ground in their struggle for control of the insurgency. Their ambition to hijack the Chechen project was most strikingly embodied by the late jihadist leader Shamil Basayev (1965–2006), who became an increasingly influential figure among the Chechen rebels and one of the most notorious terrorist leaders worldwide. He was responsible for most of the high-profile terrorist attacks in this conflict until his death in 2006.

The Turkish government by and large tolerated the logistical activities of the Chechen rebels and their diaspora supporters beginning with the first Chechen war, which at times provoked tense political crises with the Russian government. Equally important, the Turkish government turned a blind eye to the recruitment of young Turks to join the fight on the Chechens' side.[10] As a consequence, an unknown but substantial number of Turks took part in the wars in Chechnya. In fact, Turks composed the majority of foreign fighters who were killed in Chechnya from the mid-1990s until 2005, which indicates that they were one of the biggest—if not the biggest—contingent of foreign fighters in Chechnya.[11] For Turkish jihadists, the North Caucasus remained the most popular destination until the end of the second Chechen war, and most of them had some connection to networks from the Caucasus. It was only around 2005 that Turkish–Russian relations improved, and the Turkish government began to stop the flow of volunteers from Turkey to Chechnya.[12] It might have been these new restrictions imposed by Ankara that hindered the Sauerland group from joining the fight in Chechnya as they had originally planned and forced them to go to Pakistan instead. More important, the change also dealt a heavy blow to many young Turkish jihadists' aspirations. Now they head increasingly to Pakistan and establish contacts with the Uzbek groups and al-Qaeda there.

This pan-Turkish vision shared by many Turks extends to Central Asia and Afghanistan as well. The region between Xinjiang in the East, Kazakhstan in the north, Turkmenistan in the west, and Afghanistan in the south is commemorated as the land of the early migrations of Turks from their ancestral home farther northeast toward Iran and Anatolia. Many Turks have deep sympathies for the Turkic peoples of Central Asia—the Uighurs, Kazakhs, Kyrgyzs, Turkmen, and Uzbeks. Some Turks are also sympathetic to the Islamist oppositionists in Central Asia, and it is no coincidence that the Uzbek organizations IMU and IJU receive considerable financial support from Turkey—the IMU since the 1990s. Turkey has also been home to a small but visible Central Asian diaspora community since the nineteenth century. As a result of the Russian and later Soviet expansion into Central Asia, some of that region's inhabitants fled to the Ottoman Empire and later Turkey. Since the 1990s, a new wave of oppositionists has found asylum in Turkey. It is not known, however, to what extent the Uzbek diaspora supports the Central Asian jihadist organizations.

Afghanistan plays a role in this context, too. In fact, the Afghan provinces north of the Hindu Kush are geographically a part of the Central Asian steppe and are inhabited by ethnic Tadjiks, Uzbeks, and some Turks. In part as a consequence of the presence of Turkic peoples in Afghanistan, relations between the two countries were quite strong in the nineteenth and twentieth centuries.[13] The invasion of Afghanistan by the United States and its allies in 2001 thus provoked severe hostility in Turkey, where some two-thirds of the population opposed the American campaign and rejected any Turkish support for the United States, including the use of military facilities on Turkish soil.[14] Large numbers of Turks joined the jihadists in Pakistan in order to support the insurgents. As members of the Sauerland group reported, there was a sizable Turkish group training in Waziristan in 2006. In subsequent years, the numbers of Turks in Pakistan rose substantially due to the difficulties of the fight in Chechnya (on the group Taifetül Mansura, see chapter 6).

The area stretching from the old Ottoman dominions in the Balkans to Turkey, passing along the Caucasus and Azerbaijan to Central Asia and Afghanistan, is much dearer to Turks than the Arab world. This outlook also affected the geopolitical worldview of the Turkish jihadists, who shared the same geographic frame of reference, which a thorough perusal of the Turkish jihadist Web demonstrates. Ever since Turkish jihadist Internet sites appeared in greater numbers after 2001, they have been dominated by the events in Chechnya. Furthermore, special attention has been given to the activities of Uzbek organizations in Afghanistan and

Pakistan. The only Arab country to play a role in Turkish circles was Iraq after 2003, which might simply have been due to Iraq's geographic proximity and thus a resulting stronger Turkish interest in the events there. Nevertheless, since the 1990s the Turkish jihadists have typically focused their attention on the events in Bosnia, Chechnya, Central Asia, and Afghanistan and have shown little interest in the Arabs of al-Qaeda or their struggles in the Arab world.

This Turkic jihad worldview has strongly affected the German scene, large parts of which have adopted exactly the same frame of reference. Bosnia was a big issue in the first half of the 1990s, and Chechnya gained special attention beginning in 1994. Three of the most prominent Salafist and jihadist personalities in Germany after 2001, the preachers Yahia Yusuf and Muhammad Çiftçi and the recruiter Aleem Nasir, were deeply involved in supporting the Bosnian struggle from the southwestern town of Freiburg between 1992 and 1995. During the Bosnian jihad, the organizational basis was laid for later supporting the Chechen cause after 1999 and the travels of many Germans to Pakistan after 2006. It is no coincidence that the first German jihadists who died in battle did so in Chechnya. It seems as if the Germans were heavily influenced by the Turks, which should not come as a surprise considering the presence of a large Turkish diaspora in Germany. As was the case for many Turks, it was only the difficulties of joining the jihad in Chechnya that then led German jihadists to try their luck in Afghanistan.

So it makes sense that a small group of Turkish supporters of the IJU in Istanbul served as the logistics center for the German jihadists and that this city emerged as the center of gravity of the German–Turkic jihad (for more details on the Turkish supporters of the IJU in Istanbul, see chapter 6). The former capital of the Ottoman Empire, Istanbul remains Turkey's biggest city and has developed into the most important cultural and economic center of the Turkic world, attracting ever more people from the Balkans, the Caucasus, and other parts of the Russian Federation and Central Asia.

Istanbul's status is due in part to Turkey's and especially the city's central geographical location at the crossroads between Europe, the Middle East, and Asia. Jihadist groups already recognized this centrality in the mid-1990s, when the city developed into an important logistics base for al-Qaeda, effectively serving as a meeting point that connected its home countries in the Middle East, the growing European scene, and its safe haven in Afghanistan. For some years, the Syrian Muhammad Bahaia (a.k.a. Abu Khalid al-Suri, b. 1963) served as a jihadist (not necessarily al-Qaeda's) point man in Istanbul, assisting volunteers traveling to and from the training camps in Afghanistan, and frequently traveled between London, and Madrid on the one end and Turkey and Afghanistan–Pakistan on the other.[15] He was greatly assisted by the indifference of the Turkish authorities, who, besides tolerating (if not encouraging) the travel of jihadists to Chechnya, were too preoccupied with the threat emanating from the activities of the Kurdish separatists of the Kurdistan Workers' Party (Partiya Karkerên Kurdistanê, PKK), which since 1984 had plunged the country into a civil war that cost the lives of some 40,000 people. Jihadist sources confirmed that they used Turkey as a way station and logistics base throughout the 1990s, unhindered by the Turkish authorities.

Only in 1999 did the Turkish government begin searching for Bahaia, who fled via Iran to Afghanistan. At the time Bahaia was present in Istanbul, however, connections between the Arabs of al-Qaeda and local Turks and Kurds remained rather limited, in part because the latter two were still more oriented toward Chechnya. In the late 1990s, however, al-Qaeda intensified its efforts to draw Turks closer to its organization. Bahaia's presence in Istanbul might have been one outcome of this effort. In general, al-Qaeda seems to have relied on Syrians in order to establish its relations to Turkey. Most important, the Syrian Turk Luayy Sakka (b. 1974) reportedly took over this task in the late 1990s. He also built his own network, establishing tentative links between his Turkish and Arab contacts and German jihadists (Sakka's career is discussed later in this chapter). Before effectively connecting the two scenes, however, the highly fragmented Turkish jihadist scene had to go through transformations that made it possible to link up with al-Qaeda and its German supporters.

The Emergence of a Turkish Jihadist Scene

Turkey is home to perhaps the most diverse, most fragmented, and arguably one of the most dangerous terrorist scenes worldwide. The structure of the jihadist movement reflects the division between ethnic Turks and ethnic Kurds, the latter forming a sizeable minority of 15 to 20 million in this country of some 70 million inhabitants. Militant Islamist thought first gained ground among the Kurdish population before its appeal grew among ethnic Turks beginning in the second half of the 1990s. This situation was until recently further complicated by the policies of the Turkish government and army, which prioritized the fight against the PKK, at times even tolerating militant Islamist organizations in order to counter the influence of the left-wing insurgents.

The two most important militant Islamist organizations to emerge since the 1980s, the Turkish Hizbullah (Party of God, which is not in any way affiliated to the Lebanese Hizbullah) and the Great East Islamic Raiders' Front (İslami Büyükdoğu Akıncılar Cephesi, IBDA-C), have been an outgrowth of Kurdish Islamism rather than Turkish Islamism. Both share the common goal to establish an Islamic state in Turkey, but whereas the Turkish Hizbullah has its roots in the predominantly Kurdish southeastern part of the country and only later moved to the big cities in the western part of the country, the IBDA-C has been a more urban phenomenon, recruiting most of its members from among the impoverished Kurdish migrants to the big cities Istanbul, Ankara, and Izmir.

THE TURKISH HIZBULLAH

The Turkish Hizbullah is primarily a Kurdish organization that has built its social base in the predominantly Kurdish eastern part of the country and among the Kurdish populations of the major cities in the western part, such as Istanbul and Izmir, which have grown enormously as a result of civil war and worsening economic living conditions in eastern Anatolia. It emerged in the early 1980s in Diyarbakir, the largest city in the Kurdish Southeast, under the leadership of Hüseyin Velioğlu (1952–2000).[16] It soon split into two factions, İlim (Knowledge, Science) and Menzil (Way Station), both of which operated under the same parent name and maintained contact with each other but gradually developed into distinct organizations.[17] The İlim branch was led by Velioğlu and was responsible for most of the organization's terrorist activity. Differences between the groups concerned strategy rather than ideology; both believed that only violence might bring about the creation of an Islamic state. However, whereas the İlim demanded immediate violent action, the Menzil argued for a step-by-step, propaganda-based strategy of winning over supporters before embarking on holy war.[18] These differences nevertheless led to a power struggle within the organization. The groups finally severed contact in 1987 and fought each other bitterly in the early 1990s. In 1994, the İlim faction gained ground and thereafter became the dominant branch.

İlim pursued a three-phase strategy. First, it aimed at defeating rival religious and secular Kurdish organizations by focusing on propaganda efforts, the education of its members, and the buildup of an effective organizational structure. In a second step, it tried to gather mass support for the creation of an Islamic state across the country before finally entering the *cihat* (Turkish for "jihad") phase and overthrowing the Turkish state.[19] From 1987, the Hizbullah stood as a competitor to the PKK among Turkish Kurds in eastern Anatolia and tried to win the loyalty of those who opposed the PKK's Marxist ideology on religious grounds. Hizbullah's growing influence among Kurds in eastern Turkey quickly brought it into conflict with the PKK, and from the early 1990s the group focused its assaults on pro-PKK intellectuals and politicians, kick-starting a bloody confrontation with the leftist guerrillas. In the second half of the 1990s, Hizbullah turned to kidnapping rich businessmen and often murdering them instead of releasing them for ransom. It has been proven that over time the organization gruesomely murdered almost five hundred people, but the real number of victims is estimated to be three times as high.[20]

The clashes between Hizbullah and the PKK prompted many observers to suspect the involvement of the Turkish security forces. They claimed that the Hizbullah was created to fight the PKK on behalf of the Turkish government and armed forces. In fact, the Turkish army does not seem to have developed any interest in fighting the Hizbullah at that time, and there is ample evidence that on a local level the security forces and Hizbullah cadres even cooperated in their fight against the PKK.[21] In this respect, the Turkish state, because of its preoccupation with the threat posed by the PKK, committed a grave mistake by cooperating with militant Islamists in order to weaken its secular and nationalist adversaries. Nevertheless, it is unlikely that the Turkish army founded the Hizbullah in order to use it as an instrument in the civil war. But the Hizbullah's role in the struggle against the PKK might explain the leniency with which the Turkish government dealt with Islamist militancy until 2000 and in some cases even later.

In any case, after PKK leader Abdullah Öcalan was arrested in 1999, and the PKK became severely weakened, the Turkish state decided to take on and crush the Hizbullah. Increasing the threat it posed, the Hizbullah had expanded its activities to the big cities in western Turkey, where it tried to attract Kurds who had migrated there. The shift of activities westward was reinforced by the PKK's weakened role in the southeastern provinces, which led to heightened government presence and the closing of Hizbullah's shelters. From 1995, the security forces increasingly targeted the Hizbullah. Its leader, Velioğlu, then prematurely called for the implementation of the second phase of the group's strategy, the creation of a mass movement in the Turkish West.[22] This goal was, however, illusory. The majority of Turkish citizens did not identify with the organization because it was a predominantly Kurdish phenomenon and associated with horrible crimes rather than with political goals.

In January 2000, Turkish police raided a house in Istanbul and killed Velioğlu. It then emerged that the group had kidnapped and executed several dozen businessmen, Islamist and secular intellectuals, and journalists. As a result, the organization quickly lost support even among its Kurdish sympathizers. When it tried to retaliate for the killing of Velioğlu by assassinating the chief of police in Diyarbakir, the government cracked down on it. Many of the top leaders were arrested, and others were forced to flee the country to western Europe, in particular Germany.[23] Between 1998 and 2001, Turkish police found large amounts of data on more than 1,000 members in safe houses and thus was able to arrest more than 7,000 suspects, which led to the dismantling of Hizbullah's cells. Despite these arrests, many members, supporters, and sympathizers in Turkey remained undetected in part because of the organization's highly secretive, cultlike structure. Every active member acted as an intelligence agent, with several identities and a code name. Members were recruited in semipublic places such as mosques and only on the basis of clan and family ties.[24] Hizbullah's major mistake was its obsession with storing data and filming its atrocities, which helped the government dismantle it temporarily.

In 2003, the Hizbullah reestablished itself mainly in southeastern Turkey and seems to have decided to return to phase one and embark on a proselytizing campaign among Kurds there.[25] Today the organization's ideology might be more widespread than ever among Kurds in Turkey. It has also left an imprint on Turkish Kurds in Germany.

THE GREAT EASTERN ISLAMIC RAIDERS' FRONT

The IBDA-C was founded in 1984 by Salih Mirzabeyoğlu (Salih İzzet Erdiş, b. 1950). As in the Hizbullah, most, if not all, IBDA-C members are ethnic Kurds like the organization's founding leader. Mirzabeyoğlu had first joined the mainstream Islamist National Salvation Party (Millî Selamet Partisi) of former prime minister Necmettin Erbakan, but he then left that party to build a more radical, militant group. He was deeply influenced by the writings and personality of the Islamonationalist poet Necip Fazıl Kısakürek (1904–1983), who in his book *The Ideological Network of the Great East* (*Büyük Doğu İdeolocya Örgüsü*, 1968) had propagated the idea of a supranational Islamic state. This state, called "the Great East," would comprise the territory of several Middle Eastern states and be ruled by a caliph from Istanbul. In essence, Kısakürek added a strong dose of Islamism to the quite peculiar mix of Ottomanism and pan-Turkism that is so widespread among Turks today. He thereby helped lay the ideological basis for the geopolitical worldview so deeply ingrained among the members of the Turkish (and German) jihadist movement.

In spite of this Ottomanist orientation, the IBDA-C stressed its own and Salih Mirzabeyoğlu's Kurdish roots and recruited most of its members in the big cities of western Turkey. From the IBDA-C's inception, Mirzabeyoğlu set out to fulfill Kısakürek's vision by violently fighting the Turkish state and Turkish secularism as the main obstacles on the path to an Islamic state. The IBDA-C is strongly anti-Shiite, anti-Alevite (the Alevites are members of a Shiite heretical sect and compose up to 30 percent of the Turkish population), anti-Christian, and anti-Jewish, and during the 1990s the group perpetrated numerous attacks on prominent secularists, but also on Jews, Alevites, and Christians. It frequently attacked banks and government installations as well as churches, bars, brothels, and nightclubs, but due to a lack of expertise, training, and logistical knowledge it avoided trying to carry out more sophisticated operations.

IBDA-C was and remains a relatively small organization with no more than a few hundred supporters. Its resources are limited, so its activities have never been very effective. It is also highly fragmented, but it has tried to turn this weakness into an advantage by following a strategy that Western authors later called "leaderless jihad."[26] The IBDA-C units normally consist of no more than three to five members, and the organization relies on cells forming independently after having been attracted to the IBDA-C by its propaganda activities.[27] Thus, arrests of individual members and the battering of cells have not damaged the organization as much as they have in cases of more centralized structures. As a result, the IBDA-C has relied heavily on the dissemination of its ideas. Mirzabeyoğlu himself wrote more than fifty books in which he expounds on his group's ideology. Even after he was arrested in late 1998, he continued his propaganda efforts in Turkish jails. His followers continued publishing his books on the outside. In 2001, they began publishing the journal *Awaited New Order* (*Beklenen Yeni Nizam*). And in 2005, the IBDA-C increasingly began to publish its materials on the Internet and started publishing a short-lived journal called *Kaide* (Al-Qaeda), in which the authors openly supported Osama Bin Laden's organization.[28]

The Istanbul Bombings, November 2003

Although the development of the Turkish Hizbullah and IBDA-C confirmed the continuing Kurdish domination of the Turkish jihadist scene, there was increasing evidence that a growing number of ethnic Turks were being integrated into the movement. The Kurds in Turkey apparently had no qualms about fighting the Turkish state, but far fewer ethnic Turks were ready to struggle against their own government. One of the most likely reasons for this reluctance is the staunchly nationalist character of Turkish Islamism. The ethnic Turks preferred to fight abroad, especially when pan-Turkist and Ottomanist motives could be combined with their desire to help their fellow Muslims in Bosnia, Chechnya, and Afghanistan. Thus, the jihadist scene in Turkey remained highly fragmented until the 1990s. The experience of the fight in the three countries triggered a slow rapprochement between Turkish jihadists and Kurdish jihadists. Having trained and fought together under the banner of jihadist internationalism contributed to an integration process in the divided jihadist scene within Turkey, which was then further internationalized by the influence of the 2003 Iraq War. The Istanbul bombings in November that year—when four

Turkish and Kurdish suicide bombers attacked Jewish and British targets, killing fifty-seven people and wounding more than seven hundred—provided the first notable example of successful cooperation between Turkish and Kurdish jihadists in the country, which became typical for the German scene in the mid-2000s.

THE PLOT

The attacks were carried out in two waves. On November 15, 2003, two suicide attackers detonated car bombs just outside the Neveh Shalom and Beit Yisrael synagogues in the Galata and Şişli quarters, respectively, in central Istanbul. They killed twenty-seven people and wounded more than three hundred. Five days later, on November 20, another two bombers targeted the local branch of the British HSBC bank in the Levant and the British consulate in the Beyoğlu quarters. They killed thirty, among them the British consul, and injured almost four hundred. But most of the victims were Turkish Muslims. The bombings were the most devastating terrorist attacks in Turkish history and were subsequently dubbed "Turkey's 9/11."[29] The events made clear that the authorities had for too long focused on the PKK threat and had grossly underestimated the danger posed by the Sunni jihadists returning from the Balkans, Chechnya, and Afghanistan.

The consulate, the bank, and the synagogues had originally not been the plotters' targets. The suicide bombers and other members of the group that planned the attacks had undergone training in al-Qaeda camps in Afghanistan prior to September 11, 2001. During the investigations, suspects stated that shortly before the attacks in New York and Washington, the Turkish cell had met with Osama Bin Laden and the organization's number three, its Egyptian military commander Muhammad Atif (a.k.a. Abu Hafs al-Masri, 1944–2001).[30] The al-Qaeda leadership wanted the Turks to attack Western and Israeli targets. The discussion centered on attacking Israeli cruise ships on the Mediterranean shore and Incirlik Airbase. Situated near Adana in southern Turkey, the base is used by the American and Turkish air forces and is the most important American installation in Turkey. The US military has used it since the early 1950s; in jihadist circles in Turkey and beyond, it has become a symbol for the close alliance between Ankara and Washington. In the 1990s, US planes used Incirlik to patrol the northern no-flight zone in Iraq, and in the first phase of the US invasion of Afghanistan and the aftermath of Operation Iraqi Freedom in 2003 Incirlik functioned as an important logistics hub for US forces.[31]

After returning to Turkey, however, the conspirators decided that because of the tight security around Incirlik Airbase, they would have to look for softer targets. In May 2003, the group set out to prepare the attacks. They opened a cell phone store in Istanbul, which enabled them to switch their communications equipment frequently and inconspicuously.[32] In addition, they rented a small workshop in Istanbul where they could prepare the explosives and assemble the homemade bombs based on hydrogen peroxide (just as the Sauerland group were to do later), which they had been trained to use in Afghanistan.[33]

The attackers apparently made the final decision to attack Jewish and British targets after the invasion of Iraq by US and British forces in the spring of 2003, an event that aroused considerable anger in Turkish jihadist circles. The war in the neighboring country provided the Turkish jihadists with an especially powerful motive to attack British targets. Although Great Britain has always been a prominent target for jihadist groups because of its strong alliance with the United States, the Iraq War strengthened al-Qaeda's resolve to hit British installations. Osama Bin Laden himself made this clear when in October 2003 he issued an audiotape in which he called upon his followers to attack countries that had provided troops to help the US stabilize Iraq, most prominently Great Britain, Spain, and Italy.[34] By that time, however, the Istanbul plot was already in the final stages of preparation.

It was also no surprise that al-Qaeda would try to hit Jewish targets. Although the organization had not shown any marked interest in the Israeli–Palestinian conflict before late 2001 and had therefore not attacked any Israeli or Jewish targets, the situation changed when al-Qaeda came under pressure by the invasion of Afghanistan in October 2001. Coinciding with the beginning of the American attacks, al-Qaeda published a video in which Osama Bin Laden concentrated on the Palestinian issue, trying to gain support from a wider Muslim public.[35] The organization has since then increasingly attacked Jewish and Israeli targets. The most striking examples of this trend were the attacks in Mombasa, Kenya, on November 28, 2002, when a suicide bomber crashed his bomb-laden vehicle into the lobby of an Israeli-owned hotel heavily frequented by Israelis and a second team fired surface-to-air missiles at an Israeli charter plane.[36] Attacks on Jewish targets in Turkey would thus ideally—as far as al-Qaeda is concerned—also affect the then close alliance between Turkey and Israel.

Finally, the attacks took place in Turkey primarily because the plotters were natives of the country and complied with suggestions by al-Qaeda to carry out attacks there. The decision, however, sparked a controversial debate in Turkish jihadist circles. Even before the November bombings, a debate had been raging about the legitimacy of attacks in Turkey. These widespread doubts were eventually reinforced by the high number of Turkish Muslim and civilian victims claimed by the attacks.[37] The criticism mirrored a still prevalent nationalist trend among Turkish jihadists, many of whom preferred not to extend the fight to their home country. As a result, the Istanbul bombings did not become the first in a series of terrorist attacks in the country but instead remained an isolated occurrence. Turkish jihadists preferred to join the fight against the "far enemy" in Iraq, Chechnya, and Afghanistan. The same holds true for the Germans of Turkish origin, who have not yet plotted any attacks in Turkey.

THE PLOTTERS

The Istanbul cell comprised a dozen young Turkish citizens, mostly ethnic Kurds, some of whom had a previous connection to the older organizations Hizbullah and IBDA-C. Although the Kurdish element seems to have played a major role in the early phase of the cell's formation and the radicalization of many of its members, the cell's final structure was much more diverse, crossing social classes and ethnic divisions.

The ringleader reportedly was Habib Akdaş (1973–2004), a known propagandist and recruiter for the jihadist causes in Bosnia and Chechnya throughout the 1990s. In 1990, Akdaş graduated from high school in his native Mardin close to the Syrian border and afterward went to Pakistan for the first time to attend "religious studies," following in the footsteps of many young Turks who were not able to enter a Turkish university. People from the more religiously devout Southeast went to Pakistani religious universities in high numbers.[38] During the 1990s, Akdaş took part in the struggles in Bosnia and Chechnya and seems to have traveled frequently to Pakistan and Afghanistan. There, he joined al-Qaeda, and while in Afghanistan around 2000 he was the emir of a close-knit Turkish group.

Azad Ekinci (b. 1978) became Habib Akdaş's senior lieutenant in the run-up to the attacks. A native of Bingöl, he reportedly was a member of the Turkish Hizbullah. He apparently also fought in Chechnya and completed terrorist training in an al-Qaeda camp in Afghanistan.[39] Ekinci's radicalization in Bingöl in the early 1990s was strongly influenced by Mesut Çabuk, one of the suicide bombers, who was connected to Hizbullah as well. Natives from Bingöl described the two as inseparable friends, both quiet and introverted. They went together to fight and train abroad in the northern Caucasus and Central Asia.[40] Yet not all of the Kurdish cell members sympathized with Hizbullah.[41]

Most of the members of the actual cell responsible for the bombings hailed from southeastern Turkey, and many of them were ethnic Kurds, thereby reflecting the strong Kurdish element in Turkish jihadism. The largest single group were Kurds from Bingöl, a remote and predominantly Kurdish town in eastern Anatolia, where unemployment rates are high and the devastating repercussions of the civil war of the 1980s and 1990s are all too visible.[42] Others came from Malatya, Mardin, Batman, and Van, all southeastern towns and cities with similarly miserable conditions as Bingöl and decades-old centers of Kurdish opposition to the Turkish state. Of the fifteen men accused of being directly involved in the plot—that is, planning, preparing for, and executing the attacks—at least ten came from southeastern Turkey. Three of the four suicide bombers were southeasterners, and the group's two senior leaders, Habib Akdaş and Azad Ekinci, were Kurds from that region.

The cell's mixed Kurdish and Turkish composition hints at a trend toward the integration of the Kurdish and Turkish jihadist scenes in Turkey. The initial circle around Akdaş quite possibly started recruiting in southeastern Turkey among friends and ethnic Kurds who belonged to the network of Hizbullah members, supporters, or sympathizers. When the cell grew and shifted its activity to western Turkey in preparation for the Istanbul attacks, it also integrated ethnic Turks, such as the fourth suicide bomber who attacked the HSBC Bank, İlyas Kuncak, forty-seven, an ethnic Turk and successful business owner.[43] The group's leaders may have decided that they needed ethnic Turks, but the suggestion to integrate may have been made by outsiders, either al-Qaeda central or Zarqawi's group, who pushed for integrating operatives from their own networks in Turkey.

DUAL RESPONSIBILITY

Shortly after the attacks, the Abu Hafs al-Masri Brigades (Kata'ib Abu Hafs al-Masri) and the IBDA-C claimed responsibility. The Abu Hafs al-Masri Brigades were named after al-Qaeda's Egyptian military chief Muhammad Atif, otherwise known as "Abu Hafs al-Masri," who had died as a result of an American airstrike in Afghanistan in November 2001, but it was apparently made up of a group of sympathizers active on jihadist Web sites who did not have any connection to an actual terrorist organization. It was active between July 2003 and August 2005 and took responsibility for terrorist attacks as well as for events unconnected to terrorism—for example, the blackout in the northeastern United States in August 2003.[44] Any involvement of al-Qaeda's military chief in the early planning of the attacks and the claim of responsibility by the virtual jihadist media group that adopted his name should therefore not be confused.

The IBDA-C's claim had to be taken more seriously because some of the plotters reportedly maintained a connection with this organization. Former jihadist and Afghanistan veteran Noman Benotman from Libya stated in a 2003 interview that he saw a clear operational connection between IBDA-C and al-Qaeda.[45] Moreover, he took IBDA-C's claim of responsibility more seriously on the grounds that it was made via telephone, not the Internet. Al-Qaeda's Internet statements were viewed with suspicion in Islamist circles in late 2003 because in November 2003 US intelligence services had shut down al-Neda (The Call), which was regarded as the quasi-official al-Qaeda Web site. After the shutdown, numerous jihadist Web sites issued conflicting claims of responsibility in the name of al-Qaeda for the Riyadh and Istanbul attacks in that same month.[46] Activists who frequented these sites said that these statements differed in tone and style from al-Qaeda's "originals."[47] Although the IBDA-C's claim of responsibility looks more authentic under these circumstances than the statement made by the Abu Hafs al-Masri Brigades, no concrete evidence was found for the former organization's involvement.

What is clear, however, is that al-Qaeda was the main organization responsible for the Istanbul bombings. During the plotters' stay in Afghanistan and shortly before September 11, 2001, Habib Akdaş approached the al-Qaeda number three and head of military operations, Muhammad Atif. Along with his lieutenants Baki Yiğit and Adnan Ersöz, Akdaş wanted to discuss with Atif the future training of Turkish jihadists. Atif is reported to have asked Akdaş whether he would be able to execute attacks on two Israeli ships in the Turkish port city of Mersin. Akdaş confirmed that he would but asked for support. Atif and the three Turks then met with Bin Laden, and all agreed upon a plan of assault. Atif apparently pushed for Israeli targets in Mersin, whereas Bin Laden preferred an attack against the US air base in Incirlik. Al-Qaeda provided the plotters with money for the attacks, which were at that time set for the end of 2002 but ended up being delayed due to the US invasion of Afghanistan.

In 2002–2003, al-Qaeda seemed unable to continue supervising the plot. Rather, the Zarqawi organization al-Tawhid came into play. Shortly before and after the bombings, the surviving senior group members Akdaş, Ekinci, and Gürcan Baç, the group's explosives expert, fled to Syria and joined Zarqawi supporters there, who later apparently took them to Iraq. The Istanbul plotters first found refuge in the Aleppo home of Luayy Sakka, the main link between Zarqawi and the Turkish jihadists and one of the central figures of the German–Turkish scene. The Turkish authorities probably correctly identified (and later convicted) Sakka as the mastermind of the Istanbul bombings. He is said to have financed the operation with up to US$160,000 and served as a courier between Iraq, Syria, and Istanbul. So the Istanbul plot was planned and organized by two jihadist organizations—al-Qaeda and the Zarqawi organization, which was later to become al-Qaeda in Iraq. Sakka was the most visible link between the Turkish and German jihadist scenes.

Luayy Sakka, Mevlüt Kar, and the German Jihad

Luayy Sakka was born in Aleppo in 1974 and began to take part in jihadist activity in his early twenties. His family—most likely of Kurdish descent—had lived in Diyarbakir in southeastern Turkey until 1960 but then immigrated to Aleppo, the most important Islamist stronghold in Syria. Sakka first joined al-Qaeda in Afghanistan in the mid-1990s and developed a close relationship with the Palestinian Zayn al-Abidin Muhammad Husain (a.k.a. Abu Zubaida, b. 1971) , an important logistics official based in Pakistan and a close associate of Osama Bin Laden. Abu Zubaida was arrested in Pakistan in 2002 and then transferred to Guantánamo and is widely considered to be the highest-ranking al-Qaeda leader captured after September 11, 2001. In 1997, he sent Sakka to the Khalden training camp in Afghanistan and later to Turkey in order to build structures for the organization there. Situated in the mountains near Khost close to the Pakistani border, Khalden seems to have been the al-Qaeda training camp most popular with Turkish volunteers until 2000; the plotters of the Istanbul attacks were trained here. Khalden's popularity with Turkish volunteers might have been because since the 1990s the camp—founded during the anti-Soviet jihad of the 1980s—had primarily trained fighters who sought to leave for the Balkans and the Caucasus. According to Abu Zubaida, most alumni had traveled from Khalden to Bosnia until the mid-1990s and then to Chechnya from 1995 to 2000.[48]

When Sakka returned to Afghanistan in 1999, however, he did not rejoin al-Qaeda but moved to Herat with Abu Musab al-Zarqawi and joined his organization, which at that time was called "al-Tawhid" (Monotheism).[49] As a Syrian, he might have been more attracted by an organization focusing on the Palestinian issue and attracting volunteers from Jordan and Syria. Sakka later became the Zarqawi organization's main contact person for Turkey. Furthermore, he established close links to Germany. In a letter describing Zarqawi's career, the Egyptian Saif al-Adl, al-Qaeda's former military chief, mentioned that among the five followers who joined Zarqawi in his Herat training camp in 2000, there was a Syrian with a Turkish and German connection.[50] This Syrian was Luayy Sakka, whose two sisters were married to two brothers who were converts to Islam living in southern Germany. Sakka's relationship with one of the brothers, Christian Kasprowicz, seems to have been established in Khalden in 1997, where the two men completed their terrorist training with al-Qaeda. In the following years, Germany seems to have become an important venue for Sakka, who reportedly set up base in the southwestern German town of Schramberg from September 2000 to July 2001. Seeking asylum for himself and his wife, he nonetheless kept traveling back and forth between the Middle East and Germany. Unfortunately, not much is known about his activities and contacts in Germany, perhaps because, as consistently rumored, he worked for several intelligence agencies, among them the German BND. If that was indeed the case, his case officers obviously did not succeed in controlling him. On the contrary, Sakka gained prominence in jihadist circles. From 2000, he became an important logistician for the Zarqawi organization and undertook several dozen journeys between Syria, Turkey, and Jordan, intermittently spending time in Afghanistan and Germany. In all of these countries, Sakka built an extensive network of jihadists, linking groups and individuals primarily in Turkey, Syria, and Germany.[51]

When the insurgency in Iraq broke out in 2003, Sakka joined Zarqawi in Iraq but kept up his networks in Syria and in particular Turkey. After his arrest in Diyarbakir in 2005, he claimed to have fought in Iraq and boasted that he had taken part in kidnappings and executions.[52] His activities do not seem to have kept him from serving as a logistician for the Istanbul plotters after al-Qaeda central had lost contact with the cell. He was finally arrested in August 2005 after he failed in the preparations for a suicide attack on Israeli cruise ships in the southern Turkish port city and tourist center Antalya. When parts of the explosives—again based on hydrogen peroxide—caught fire in an apartment in Antalya, Sakka and his accomplice fled. He was subsequently caught in the Kurdish metropolis Diyarbakir, carrying $120,000 in cash.[53]

Although not much is known about the exact nature of Sakka's activities in Germany, it is likely he was responsible for building the early contacts between the German and Turkish scenes. He probably was in contact with Mevlüt Kar during his stay in Germany as well because both were important logisticians for the Zarqawi organization, although this connection has not been confirmed. In any case, from 2003 Kar seems to have become the Germans' main contact point in Istanbul, facilitating their entry into the realm of the Turkic jihad. Unfortunately, not all questions with regard to Kar's role in the Sauerland plot have been answered. He played a role behind the scenes, perhaps even establishing his own connections to the IJU. It would not come as a surprise if Kar turned out to be a far more influential personality in German–Turkic networks than suggested by publicly available facts.

Kar's role has become somewhat exemplary for the German–Turkic jihad, which was deeply shaped by the focus on Chechnya until 2006. From that time, it became increasingly difficult even for those volunteers who had already mastered the necessary military skills to reach the battlefields of the northern Caucasus. Although the Chechen rebels and their allies in the neighboring republics Ingushetia and Dagestan were not beaten at that time, the insurgency lost momentum with the death of Shamil Basayev in 2006 and the consolidation of the rule of the Kremlin loyalist Ramazan

Kadyrov in Chechnya. Isolated terrorist attacks followed, and the level of violence in some of the republics, especially in Dagestan, remained high. Nevertheless, the foreign element lost importance when the Turkish government decided to prevent Turkish nationals and other volunteers passing through Turkey from continuing their travels to the Caucasus.

As a result, an increasing number of Turkish jihadists alongside an increasing number of Azeris reoriented and found their way to Pakistan, where they established strong links to the Uzbek organizations in Waziristan. Contacts established during the years of the Chechen struggle, closely related native languages, and strong sympathies among Turkish jihadists for the cause of their Central Asian brothers seem to have made these alliances possible. In 2009, a number of Turks connected with the Uzbek IJU founded the organization Taifetül Mansura (Victorious Group). It comprised Turkish and Azeri nationals returning from the Caucasus and became the first Turkish jihadist organization established abroad. Most important in the context of this book, it acted in concert with the first German jihadist organization, the German Taliban Mujahideen.

6

"Leaving Kuffaristan"

Radicalization and Recruitment in Germany

On February 14, 2008, the German police arrested Aleem Nasir, a German national of Pakistani origin and perhaps the most important financier and recruiter for al-Qaeda in Germany, in front of the Federal Court in Karlsruhe. Nasir had traveled back and forth between Pakistan and Germany for years and had been arrested in Pakistan in June 2007 after returning from Waziristan, where he injured his hand while apparently training in bomb-making techniques. In the custody of the Pakistani Interservices Intelligence, he confessed to being a member of al-Qaeda, so the agency informed the German authorities.[1] After Nasir was deported to Germany, though, he had to be released because it was suspected that he had been tortured while jailed in Pakistan, so the document the Pakistanis had submitted could not be used in court. Based on the information provided by the Pakistanis, however, German security authorities approached Nasir's stepson Yannick Nasir (b. 1987), whom Aleem had sent to a Lashkar-e Tayyiba training camp in Pakistani Kashmir in 2001. In late 2007, Yannick was serving in the German army, the Bundeswehr, and wished to keep open the option of a career in the military, so he readily provided German law enforcement with the information they needed to arrest his stepfather. The course of events was dramatic: Aleem Nasir was informed that his son was about to give evidence to a judge, and so he rushed to the Federal Court building in Karlsruhe where the interrogation was taking place. Just when Yannick provided the necessary information to arrest his stepfather, an observation team that had followed the latter was ordered to arrest him. To the delight of the law enforcement officials present, the al-Qaeda recruiter was pinned to the ground and handcuffed on the spot. Nasir's arrest was part of intensified measures against jihadist recruitment in Germany after the arrest of the Sauerland group in 2007. It came too late, though, to stop the tide of a "second generation" of German recruits to the Pakistani–Afghan war who followed in the footsteps of the Sauerland group. Most important, the number of German jihadists who left the country from 2007 rose considerably compared to previous years. This growth was the result of an increasing radicalization of young, German Salafists, an intensive propaganda campaign on jihadist Web sites, and increasingly effective, if still quite haphazard, recruitment efforts.

"Now Come the Real Professional Populists": Salafism in Germany

Salafism is an interpretation of Islam that puts a special emphasis on the emulation of a highly idealized vision of the life (and lifestyle) of the early Muslims in seventh-century Mecca and Medina, which the Salafists try to copy as closely as possible. Although Salafism should be seen as part of the wider Islamist movement, the Salafists—more than mainstream Islamists—try to revive a kind of "primeval" or "purist Islam" in their quest to purify modern Muslim societies and thereby find solutions to problems of modern life. In this way, they are following in the footsteps of older movements such as the Wahhabiya in Saudi Arabia, one of several purist reform movements that emerged in the Arab world and South Asia during the eighteenth and nineteenth centuries, such as the Deobandis and the Ahl-e Hadith in India, the Sanusiya in Libya, and the Uthman Dan Fodio movement in northern Nigeria. Yet the Wahhabis of Central Arabia are by far the most important predecessors of modern-day Salafists. Founded by the theologian Muhammad b. Abd al-Wahhab (1703/4–1792), this movement provided the nascent Saudi Arabian state with a powerful mobilizing tool that has remained the official religious doctrine in the kingdom. The first Wahhabis accepted as (true) Muslims only those who followed their doctrines and code of conduct to the letter and fought all non-Wahhabis in what they called a "jihad." The present Saudi Arabian government follows a much less militant variant of this ideology but still bases its legitimacy on the age-old alliance with the Wahhabi religious scholars. In part as a consequence of this alliance, the kingdom began to finance Islamist and especially Salafist groups worldwide starting in the 1960s. Saudi Arabian governmental and nongovernmental bodies to this day provide many Salafists worldwide with substantial financial means. In the same period, the Wahhabi-controlled Islamic University of Medina has become the most important educational center for Salafist movements worldwide.

Although it is difficult to make a clear-cut distinction between Islamists and Salafists in theoretical terms, Salafism can be distinguished from other strands of Islamism easily because most of its adherents try to draw a clear distinction between themselves and other Islamists. In recent years, Salafism has moved to the forefront of public debates because the phenomenon has grown in scope, with the Salafist movement becoming increasingly popular among young Muslims worldwide, and because it has become the most important recruitment pool for the jihadist movement.

For analytical purposes, the Salafist movement has generally been subdivided into three trends: purist Salafism, political Salafism, and jihadist Salafism.[2] The purists are Salafists who (in the first instance) are merely interested in reforming individuals and society, who reject political activism, and who thus do not pose an immediate security problem. In contrast, the political Salafists (who in Germany are also referred to as "mainstream Salafists") are heavily influenced by the more mundane ideology of the Muslim Brotherhood and sometimes by its militant and revolutionary wings as well. They show a marked ambivalence toward violence, often displaying sympathy for militant groups fighting for the liberation of what they consider to be occupied Muslim territory in Palestine, Iraq, and Afghanistan. And last but not least, the jihadist Salafists are fighting against the West and their own governments, and in doing so they do not hesitate to kill large numbers of fellow Muslims. Although these different categories are often blurred, the subdivision has remained influential, if not dominant, among students of Salafism.[3]

In Germany today, most Salafists belong to the second group and show a marked politicization while hotly debating their positions concerning the legitimacy and limits of violence. In fact, there are not many clearly identifiable "purists" in Germany, so the German security services have given up on using the categorization described here and instead differentiate between political and jihadist Salafists only. According to a manual of the German BfV, the political Salafists concentrate their efforts on intensive propaganda, spreading their ideology and gaining political and social influence, whereas the jihadist Salafists believe that they can realize their aims by employing violence.[4] However, the nonviolent mainstream Salafism has shown an increasing divergence in recent years, with a substantial growth of what might be called its "right wing," where supporters of violence are gaining ground. Furthermore, political Salafists propagate an ambivalent attitude toward violence and often refer to the same authorities as the jihadist Salafists, making a distinction difficult.[5]

The Salafist scene in Germany has developed in three phases.[6] In a first, formative phase from the mid-1990s to 2000–2001, Salafist thought and practice began to influence young Muslims. Two imams, the Syrian German Hasan Dabbagh (a.k.a. Abu l-Husain, b. 1972) in Leipzig and the Moroccan Muhammad Bin Husain (a.k.a. Abu Jamal, b. 1961) in Bonn began their preaching activities in the mid-1990s. Both were heavily influenced by like-minded scholars and preachers in neighboring countries such as the Netherlands, where Salafism had gained ground earlier. At that time, the local German milieu suffered from a lack of qualified preachers, so mosques and cultural centers often relied on religious authorities from other countries who went to Germany on proselytizing tours. In marked contrast to the situation ten years later, all these preachers were Arabs and taught in Arabic, restricting the Salafist recruitment base to Arabic speakers—that is, mainly Arabs and a few individuals of German and Turkish origin. The most prominent example of a visiting scholar was the Moroccan Muhammad al-Fazazi (b. 1949), who preached in the Hamburg al-Quds Mosque in the late 1990s, coming into contact with some members of the Hamburg cell of future 9/11 pilots there. An outspoken jihadist Salafist, Fazazi was later convicted and sentenced to thirty years in prison for inciting the Casablanca bombings in his home country in May 2003.[7]

The second phase lasted from 2001 to 2005. The Salafist scene in this period seems to have been dominated by three imams, all of them Arabs. Besides Hasan Dabbagh and Muhammad Bin Husain, who belonged to the Salafist mainstream and considerably broadened their proselytizing activities, Yahia Yusuf rose to prominence among more radical students but remained on the periphery of the Salafist scene. Both Dabbagh and

Bin Husain were "rather pragmatic" in their dealings with German society and the authorities and were "able to connect to non-Salafist trends of Islamist thoughts."[8] Rather poor theologians, they paved the way for a more propagandistically sophisticated generation of preachers that took over in phase three. The years from 2001 to 2005 were shaped by the emergence of the so-called Learn Islam (Lerne den Islam) seminars, which successfully spread the new school among young Muslims in the country and laid the basis for the emergence of translocal networks. These seminars were first organized by Bin Husain and Dabbagh in Bonn and Berlin from 2001–2002 and addressed young Muslims who came from various parts of Germany to attend them. They then spread to Cologne, Erfurt, Frankfurt, and many other cities. By lecturing to a multiethnic audience in German, these preachers were the first to combine transregional seminars with an extensive use of new media.[9]

In the third phase, starting in 2005, younger, more charismatic preachers of German and Turkish origin began to appear on the German scene, which has grown exponentially ever since. Because of their proficiency in their audience's native tongue, they seem to be more successful at capturing a German audience's attention than the "imported imams" had been before them. A police official who specializes in the analysis of the German Salafist scene said of the new scene, "Now come the real professional populists."[10] At the same time, the Salafist scene witnessed a growing differentiation among members of its mainstream. A prime example was a group that called itself "the True Religion" (die Wahre Religion) after a Web site (www.diewahrereligion.de) founded in 2005. Its most visible figurehead was Pierre "Hamza" Vogel (b. 1978), a former boxer and young preacher from a small town west of Cologne. Vogel converted to Islam in 2001 and received a scholarship to study religious sciences at the Islamic University in Mecca, Saudi Arabia, where he remained between 2004 and 2006. Speaking German with a strong Cologne accent, Vogel became a rising star, prompting many young Germans to convert to (Salafist) Islam and drawing several hundred followers to each of his public appearances.[11] Behind the scenes, however, Vogel's mentor, the German Palestinian businessman and Cologne resident Ibrahim Abu Nagie (b. 1964), seems to have been the more important personality.

In 2008, "the true religion" split into two groups when Abu Nagie distanced himself from Vogel. As is often the case, debates about the legitimate use of violence were only part of the reason for the split. Vogel and his followers have made an effort to denounce terrorism, at least rhetorically, and are in fact less radical than their former allies. The wing led by Abu Nagie openly demands the downfall of the ruling regimes in the Arab world and calls for jihad in Afghanistan and other Muslim territories that its members regard as occupied. In fact, this group shows a marked tendency toward classical internationalist thought. Although Abu Nagie and his followers continue to use the name "the True Religion," Vogel began to call his group "Invitation to Paradise" (Einladung zum Paradies).[12] Ironically, it was the less radical Invitation to Paradise that became known to the German public in summer 2010. Due to public pressure over Vogel's plan to open a Salafist center and mosque in the town of Mönchengladbach in western Germany, politicians all over the country developed an interest in the organization. Some demanded that Invitation to Paradise be outlawed. Ironically, Ibrahim Abu Nagie's True Religion, although more radical, was more successful in avoiding public scrutiny. Although he and others, such as Abdallatif Rouali and the Moroccan preacher Said al-Emrani (a.k.a. Abu Dujana), serve as figureheads for the group and are prominently featured in videos on the group's Web site, Arabic-speaking preachers such as Abu Dujana's father Sheikh al-Arabi might turn out to be more influential religious authorities in this network's informal hierarchy.[13]

In general, jihadist positions seem to have started gaining ground among German Salafists in 2005. Jamaluddin Qarar (a.k.a. Abu l-Khattab, b. 1971) and his younger brother, Farhad Qarar (a.k.a. Abu Hamza al-Afghani), Austrians of Afghan origin who live in Vienna, were the first to openly advocate Salafist jihadism and played an important role in the transfer of its ideology to Germany. Both brothers were closely connected to the like-minded Bosnian Imam Nedzad Balkan, who took over the Sahaba Mosque in Vienna in 2004,[14] where Abu l-Khattab also served as an imam. Beginning about the same time, Abu l-Khattab spread his message and published German-language jihadist ideological treatises, audios, and videos on a Web site called "Khutba" (www.khutba.net).[15] Perhaps most important, he inspired some of his followers to translate the writings of the Jordanian Palestinian Abu Muhammad al-Maqdisi—in particular *This Is Our Creed* (*Hadhihi ʿAqidatuna*)—and make them available to the German jihadist public.[16] German translations of Maqdisi's writings appeared on the bookshelves of many prominent German jihadists in the following years. For instance, Adem Yilmaz of the Sauerland group and Yusuf al-Hajj Dib, one of the suitcase bombers, are said to have been heavily influenced by his writings.[17]

Abu l-Khattab and Abu Hamza later joined the even more radical fringe of the Salafist movement, where a group referred to as *takfiri*s or *takfir* Salafists has gained ground. *Takfiri*s are Muslims who excommunicate fellow Muslims—that is, accuse them of unbelief and thereby legitimize killing them.[18] They have been a phenomenon in the development of Islamism since the 1970s, withdrawing even from Muslim societies because they deem these societies and their members to be "unbelievers." In most cases, their beliefs and practice have led to clashes with state authorities. The *takfiri*s acquired most of their notoriety in conflicts in Algeria during the 1990s, where the accusation of unbelief served as a convenient instrument to legitimize the killing of Muslim civilians. In Europe, *takfiri* Salafism was long thought to be especially pervasive among North Africans, but it has spread to other nationalities. After the charismatic Qarar brothers, Abu l-Khattab and Abu Hamza, adopted *takfiri* thought, arguing that Muslims were not yet ready to lead a jihad, Abu Hamza built a small network based in Vienna but extending into Germany. In 2009, supporters of Abu Hamza founded the Furqan Mosque in Bremen, the most important *takfiri* center in Germany today. Its most prominent member, Renée Marc Sepac (b. 1980), is reputed to be one of the most dangerous Salafists in Germany. Due to the Austrian origins of the *takfiri* scene in Germany, the movement tends to have good contacts with the Balkans. In a small town in eastern Bosnia, Gornja Maoca, *takfiri*s tried to build a Salafist model city until security forces raided the place in early February 2010.[19]

Referring to the differentiation between and radicalization of parts of the Salafist mainstream and the growth of jihadist and *takfiri* ideological influence, one German police official spoke of an "enormous dynamism in this field."[20] This dynamism is, in fact, demonstrated by the sheer number of adherents to Salafism. In 2001, the movement counted no more than a few hundred followers, but the number has increased yearly and in 2012 reached between 5,000 and 10,000.[21] Although there were only a handful of preachers and a very small number of mosques and cultural centers in 2001, since then the number of Salafist imams who command a following has risen to as many as fifty in about the same number of Salafist mosques all over the country.[22] Today, these preachers include a growing number of German converts and ethnic Turks, who have increasingly made use of their respective mother tongues, which has led to a broadening of the Salafist recruitment base. In general, instruction in German and, to a lesser extent, Turkish has become much more important for the German Salafist scene, mirroring the development of Salafist Web sites.

In 2012, the most prominent Salafist preachers in Germany included Pierre Vogel in the Cologne area, Hasan Dabbagh in Leipzig, Muhammad Bin Husain in Bonn, and Muhammad Çiftçi (a.k.a. Abu Anas or, in Turkish, Ebu Enes, b. 1973) in Brunswick. In most cases, these preachers' influence has spread to other regions of the country because of their teaching activities in Islam seminars, their presence on the Internet, their lecture tours to other cities, and their education of younger preachers. For instance, Çiftçi, a former student of the Islamic University in Medina, in 2007 established the Brunswick Islam School (Braunschweiger Islamschule) and gives online distance-learning courses in Salafist Islam, which have made him the most prominent Turkish Salafist preacher in Germany.[23] Supporters of jihadist positions, such as Ibrahim Abu Nagie and Said al-Emrani, act from behind the scenes in order to avoid prosecution. The best-known Salafist mosques and cultural centers in 2011 were the al-Nur Mosque in Berlin, the Muhsinin Mosque in Bonn, and the Bilal Mosque in Frankfurt. The Germany authorities closed two important Salafist mosques: the Multicultural House in Neu-Ulm in 2005 and al-Quds Mosque in Hamburg in August 2010.

Salafist mosques have become the preferred recruitment ground for the jihadist movement in Germany. Most jihadists who left the country in 2006 had established close links to like-minded people in other parts of the country. "They all know each other," commented one German police official.[24] In many cases, these contacts were made in Salafist centers, especially during the Learn Islam seminars, where the potential new recruits were given a first introduction to Salafist thinking. In the early years, Bonn was apparently the most popular destination for future fighters. Adem Yilmaz and Fritz Gelowicz, for example, met many of their jihadist acquaintances in the Muhsinin Mosque, where Muhammad Bin Husain organized the seminars,[25] but there are numerous other examples of future jihadists meeting and forming friendships while attending them.

"Al-Qaeda's German Loudspeakers": The Global Islamic Media Front

Just like the German Salafists, the German jihadist Internet activists were latecomers among their European comrades. The German jihadist Internet scene developed parallel to the growing attractiveness of Salafist thought in general and its jihadist variant in particular. Although there is no actual proof for this conclusion, there seems to be a causal relationship between the spread of all strands of Salafist ideology, the spread of its jihadist variant on the Internet, and the quick growth of the jihadist scene in Germany from 2006.

Before 2006, there was no major and organized German jihadist presence on the Internet. Isolated threats, discussions, and some videos with German subtitles notwithstanding, Arabic-language propagandists dominated jihadist Web sites, and then other languages such as English and French slowly began to be used in them. The first larger German presence was established by the German branch of the Global Islamic Media Front (GIMF, al-Jabha al-Iᶜlamiya al-Islamiya al-ᶜAlamiya). The international GIMF first came into existence in 2004 as a grouping formed by Arab Internet activists not connected to any major jihadist organization and had as its stated aim to support the jihadist movement on the Web by intensifying and coordinating its propaganda activities. It quickly developed into an unofficial news agency for al-Qaeda and other organizations. Although all of its publications were in Arabic at first, it soon began asking Muslims worldwide to translate these materials into their native languages. An English GIMF based in Canada was the first branch to emerge; a German one followed suit.[26]

The German GIMF came into being in late 2005 and remained a force until 2008, when most of its Internet activities were curtailed and the most important activists had been arrested. It was founded by a young Austrian of Egyptian origin, Mohamed Mahmoud (b. 1985), who was arrested in Vienna in September 2007 and later (March 2008) sentenced to four years in prison because of his Internet propaganda. Mahmoud's Egyptian father served as an imam in the notorious Sahaba Mosque in Vienna and is reported to have been a member of the militant Islamic Group (al-Gamaᶜa al-Islamiya) in his home country. Mohamed Mahmoud stayed in close contact with Abu l-Khattab, the pioneer of German jihadism, who—just like

Mahmoud—was connected to the Sahaba Mosque in Vienna, where Abu l-Khattab served as an imam. It was indeed the very same mosque where Mahmoud met his successor as head of the German GIMF, the Serbia-born Irfan Peci (b. 1989) from Weiden, a small city in northeastern Bavaria.[27]

In contrast to his German heirs, Mahmoud maintained close relations to active terrorists, especially in Iraq, and came to the German authorities' attention in connection with a kidnapping case in Baghdad. In February 2007, the sixty-one-year-old German national Hannelore Kadhim (Krause) and her adult German Iraqi son Sinan al-Tornachi were kidnapped by the jihadist group Battalions of the Arrows of Truth (Kata'ib Siham al-Haqq) in Baghdad, which demanded the withdrawal of German and Austrian troops from Afghanistan.[28] During the investigation into the case, Mohamed Mahmoud was noticed because on March 10, 2007, he was among the first Internet activists to post a video of the hostages on the GIMF site Jabha (www.jabha.info). Mahmoud was suspected of being closely associated with the hostage takers, so the German authorities intensified their scrutiny of him.[29]

But the case was not clear-cut. Some law enforcement officials describe Mahmoud as a "classical jihadist," much more dangerous than his German epigones. According to the Austrian indictment, in 2002 Mahmoud traveled to Iraq, where he was trained by the Iraqi Kurdish group Supporters of Islam (Ansar al-Islam, also called Supporters of the Sunna [Ansar al-Sunna]) and took part in combat. He was wounded and so left Iraq for Iran, where he was jailed for about six weeks. Other officials, in contrast, regard Mahmoud as an "armchair jihadist," "a loudmouth," and "a braggart" who despite doing his utmost to contact people whom he thought were real-world jihadists did not manage to enter this scene.[30]

Under Mahmoud's leadership, the GIMF quickly established an Internet presence in 2006 when it published materials on Jabha (the site was later moved to www.gimf5.extra.hu and to other addresses). Together with a small group of Austrian and German supporters, Mahmoud scoured the Internet for jihadist sites in Arabic and chose adequate materials for the German jihadist scene, produced mainly by al-Qaeda, al-Qaeda in Iraq, and Supporters of Islam. The materials included claims of responsibility; speeches and declarations by leading personalities such as Bin Laden, Zawahiri, and Zarqawi; ideological materials; and videos of the organizations' terrorist activities—including IED and suicide bomb attacks. The volunteers translated texts into German, produced subtitles for or dubbed audio materials, then uploaded the files on different Web sites. The war in Iraq was by far the dominating theme, providing ample evidence of the radicalizing effect of events in that country on the European jihadist scene. From 2007 to 2008, the GIMF apparently tried to build contacts with al-Qaeda in Iraq and become its mouthpiece in order to enhance its own standing in the jihadist online community.[31]

In March 2007, the group landed its biggest propaganda coup when it produced a video entitled *A Message to the Governments of Germany and Austria*, in which a speaker demanded a withdrawal of Austrian and German troops from Afghanistan. Since October 2005, the GIMF had produced an Internet TV news program called *The Voice of the Caliphate*, in which a hooded speaker in a studio setting tried to copy mainstream media news programs while presenting a jihadist view on world affairs. In *A Message*, the GIMF was using this format—a video in Arabic with German subtitles—to threaten Germany and Austria. Referring to the presence at that time of 2,750 German and 5 Austrian soldiers in Afghanistan, the speaker demanded their withdrawal, arguing that the buildup provoked the jihadists to fight back: "Isn't it stupid that you motivate the mujahideen to lead operations in your country?" As a consequence of the Afghanistan campaign, the GIMF argued, Germany and Austria had endangered the safety of their citizens.[32] Mahmoud was thrilled by the wide coverage the video found in German-language media in Austria and Germany. In a chat in August 2007, he wrote: "By God, the video has had an effect. The deeds will, Inshaallah, follow. By God, if you recommended the Sheikhs to attack Germany, this would be excellent."[33]

Less than a month later Mahmoud was arrested together with his Egyptian Austrian wife, Mona Salem Ahmad (b. 1986), who had supported his activities, and was sentenced to twenty-two months in jail. Astoundingly, Mahmoud had posted the video from his own computer. The Austrian security authorities only had to connect Mahmoud to his Internet provider address. Even if he was a dangerous jihadist fighter, he was rather inept at covering his tracks on the Internet.[34]

Upon Mahmoud's arrest, his assistant and deputy Irfan Peci (a.k.a. Muhammad Umar) and thereby the Germans took over the leadership of the GIMF. Peci was born in Novi Pazar, Serbia, and his family came to Germany in 1991, when he was only two years old. He failed in school and did not manage to find a decent job. Instead, he turned to Salafism, although the rest of his family were rather lax observers of Islam. In 2009, he and two friends were sentenced to one year and four months in jail for robbing a mobile phone shop and, armed with an iron rod, an iron chain, and a wooden bat, beating an employee and ransacking the shop. Because of his position in the GIMF, Peci was treated as a suspected terrorist in jail and therefore subjected to solitary confinement and other hardships. In part as a consequence of the harsh treatment, he was convinced to work as an informant for the BfV. In 2007, two years before he changed sides, however, he had managed to quickly reorganize the GIMF in Germany with the help of his new deputy, the Turk Emin Temiz. Born in 1992, Temiz was not even fifteen years old when he started his activities on behalf of the GIMF. He nevertheless seems to have acted with considerable criminal energy, serving as an administrator for a number of blogs and forums and posting hundreds of different jihadist contributions. Temiz's computer knowledge enabled him to quickly become the head of the GIMF's technology arm.[35]

With the arrest of Mohamed Mahmoud in Vienna in September 2007, the GIMF lost its geographical center, and its remaining members were spread all over Germany. The organization consisted of eight or more members of different social and ethnic backgrounds, thus resisting any effort by the authorities to profile the jihadist Internet activist in Germany. There were highly talented individuals among them, but also former drug addicts and second-generation immigrants unable to cope with the German educational system. Most of these young people held German passports, and all but Peci had been born in the country.[36]

Because the GIMF's history was closely connected to the jihadist trend established by Abu l-Khattab (Jamaluddin Qarar) in the Vienna Sahaba Mosque, the group was soon riddled with conflicts over the Austrian's ideological shift toward takfirism. In an interview with *Spiegel Online* in September 2007 shortly after the arrest of the GIMF leader Mahmoud in Vienna, Abu l-Khattab himself conceded that he knew Mohamed Mahmoud and his wife very well and that both had been longtime members of the mosque community. Referring to his own move toward takfirist Salafism, however, he stated that a conflict over ideology had emerged and that Mahmoud had stopped showing up at the mosque in early 2007.[37] Abu l-Khattab and those of his supporters who followed his ideological shift called themselves "People of the Sunna and the Community" (Ahl al-Sunna wa-l-Jamaᶜa), a self-designation popular with many Salafist Muslims. They created their own Web site at www.aswj.de and propagated their takfirist ideas among Austrian and German Muslims. Some GIMF supporters followed Abu l-Khattab's lead and promptly provoked heated debate and a split within the group. In July, the GIMF declared that a member calling herself "Ummu Hamza al-Muhajira" (*ummu* means "mother of") was taken off the GIMF membership list and her access to the forum was blocked because she had "exaggeratedly excommunicated Muslims" and allegedly distributed People of the Sunna texts in which Osama Bin Laden and other jihadist leaders were accused of being nonbelievers. Bin Laden, the accusation went, did not declare the Palestinian Hamas an infidel organization in spite of the fact that it had taken part in elections and entered a coalition with the secular Fatah. According to Abu l-Khattab's new creed, someone who does not identify an nonbeliever is himself an nonbeliever.[38]

The GIMF leadership's quick and indignant reaction to this posting went as follows: "We have already warned once that we will never tolerate such people here in our forum. These people who make *takfir* against our leaders and *shuyukh* [plural of *sheikh*], like, e.g., Sheikh Osama [Bin Laden], Sheikh Aiman [al-Zawahiri], Sheikh Abu Omar al-Baghdadi, Sheikh Abu Hamza al-Mujahir [leaders of al-Qaeda in Iraq], etc. . . . These people who prohibit the jihad and insult the Mujahidin."[39]

Besides Ummu Hamza, other GIMF members had adopted the *takfiri* creed wholly, among them Renée Marc Sepac. The ideological conflict might have played a role in an attack on the new GIMF leader, Irfan Peci, in late 2007. Less professional and less secretive than his former boss, Peci quickly became a controversial figure for some members of the GIMF. Under his alias "Muhammad Umar," he gave anonymous interviews to German and Austrian media in late 2007, provoking criticism especially by those activists who were particularly serious about their ideology and wanted to join the real-world jihad in Afghanistan.[40] After Peci posted an interview he had given the Austrian weekly *News*, Sepac reacted with a posting headed "What Is That?" in which he severely criticized Peci: "For me this is a show this is not the method of the brethren well this all looks very ridiculous, as I said previously I think not more than a braggart something we haven't seen with abu ussama [Mohamed Mahmoud] and besides you only produce problems for other people."[41]

Sepac further accused Peci of administering the GIMF forums in an authoritarian way in order to make it prominent in the media. He expressly wondered why Peci had not then been arrested after all the mistakes he made and demanded that Peci stop mentioning comrades' names and thereby putting them in danger. His remarks implicitly contained the suspicion that Peci might not be a jihadist at all, but a spy. As a consequence of the conflict, however, Sepac's access to the forum was closed off in early December 2007, effectively ending his career in the GIMF.[42]

During 2008, the German authorities shattered the GIMF infrastructure by searching its members' houses, confiscating their computers, arresting some of them, and subsequently putting them on trial for supporting terrorist organizations. This time the organization could not compensate for the losses and disappeared from the scene in the summer of 2008. It had nevertheless left its mark on the German scene by making an immense corpus of jihadist materials available to a new generation of German-speaking sympathizers and supporters.

Besides Mohamed Mahmoud, Sepac was apparently one of the few GIMF members to play a role in the jihadist scene outside of the virtual realm. Quite an unpleasant character, he was strongly influenced by events in Iraq, using "Abu Musab" (after Abu Musab al-Zarqawi) as one of his aliases in the GIMF forum. Born in 1980 in Bremen to a German mother and a Malay father, Sepac had converted to Islam in 1998. Security officials describe him as unpredictable and brutal; before being convicted to three years and six months in prison in the GIMF case in December 2011, he had already been sentenced to probation twice for obstruction of a police official in the performance of his duties. In March 2007, Sepac first tried to go to Pakistan in order to join one of the jihadist organizations there. He was, however, sent back when trying to enter Iran from Turkey. The setback made him realize that he needed a professional trafficker to bring him into contact with al-Qaeda or one of its allies. With the help of an acquaintance, Ömer Özdemir, he contacted Aleem Nasir, who provided him with a letter of recommendation and the contact data of Yassin al-Suri (a.k.a. Izz al-Din Abd al-Aziz Khalil, b. 1982), a prominent al-Qaeda human trafficker in Iran. For unknown reasons, Sepac was not able to meet al-Suri when he arrived in Teheran in May 2007, so he once again had to travel back to Germany.[43] Perhaps most important, the story of Renée Marc Sepac makes clear that in spite of the Internet's radicalizing function, it could not replace the recruitment activities of men on the spot. And even with logistical support, it was not easy at all to bring young Germans to Pakistan.

Recruitment

As a consequence of the German jihadists' increasing security consciousness, knowledge about their recruitment activities is still highly deficient in security circles. Nevertheless, several court cases have revealed increasingly detailed information about the careers of several individuals recruiting for al-Qaeda, the IJU, and the German Taliban Mujahideen in Germany and have made known the structures through which German volunteers are funneled to Pakistan. In general, recruiting can roughly be categorized as organized, independent, or hybrid. In this context, traditional recruitment through a local representative of a terrorist organization such as al-Qaeda seems to have given way to more independent, self-initiated forms of peer recruitment for the IJU and the German Taliban Mujahideen.

There are indications, however, that the recruiters have become more secretive in recent years. Although they still appear in Salafist mosques, they do not hold any official functions there but are known to the mosque officials and are more or less closely affiliated with the institution. They identify promising candidates whose thought has already been shaped by Salafist doctrine and then take them to private rooms where they instruct them in more militant variants of the Salafist creed. These recruiters are increasingly security conscious, in many cases avoiding the tools of modern communication for their business. As a German intelligence official described them, "We don't know a lot about the persons who recruit these young people, but they have become a lot more careful than before. They disappear for weeks if necessary [and] don't use mobile phones or telephones at all, and there is no way to track down their communications."[44] Increasingly aggressive intelligence operations, however, have led to some successes for the German authorities in recent years.

"ARABIC IS THE LANGUAGE OF THE MUJAHIDEEN"

Until his arrest in February 2008, Aleem Nasir, a German national born in 1962 in Lahore, seems to have been the most important recruiter for al-Qaeda in Germany. Nasir had come to Germany in 1987 and lived in Freiburg; he later moved to Karlsruhe and Germersheim in southwestern Germany. A manufacturing systems engineer by training, he seems to have had problems finding adequate work, especially after September 2001. At that time, he worked at Karlsruhe Institute for Technology but was fired after he commented approvingly on the 9/11 attacks in the United States. In the following years, he lived mainly on social benefits.

Nasir had befriended Yahia Yusuf in the late 1980s or early 1990s, when he—at that time studying German in Freiburg—visited the Islamic Center there. Nasir accepted Yusuf as his mentor and supported Yusuf's activities in Bosnia after the war there broke out in 1992. From 1994, the newly founded Ibad al-Rahman Mosque in Freiburg became the center of support for the Bosnian jihad in Germany. Nasir was one of its most active visitors. After undergoing military training in a camp in Afghanistan in September–October 1991, Nasir repeatedly traveled to Bosnia, accompanying aid convoys and joining the fight against the Serbs there.[45] In the following years, the first hints as to Nasir's recruitment activities appeared.

After the war in Bosnia ended, Nasir continued his friendship with Yusuf but also built close relations to the Pakistani group Lashkar-e Tayyiba (Army of the Pure). Founded in 1993, Lashkar-e Tayyiba had as its aim the liberation of Kashmir from Indian rule. From the early 1990s, the insurgency in Indian Kashmir had come under the control of the Pakistani military, which instrumentalized different jihadist groups for the fight against the big rival India but at the same time denied that it was playing any role in the struggle. From 1997, Lashkar-e Tayyiba became the weapon of choice for the Pakistani military because the latter broadened its strategy to Jammu, the southern part of the Indian province of Jammu and Kashmir. The inhabitants of this part of India are in the majority Punjabis, speaking the language of the same name. Because Lashkar-e Tayyiba recruited primarily from the neighboring Pakistani province of Punjab, its fighters were ideally suited to blend in with the local population and execute the new Pakistani strategy.[46] As a consequence of the Pakistani military's lavish support, the organization soon became possibly the strongest outfit among the insurgent groups operating in Kashmir.

Aleem Nasir entertained close associations with Lashkar-e Tayyiba's leadership and was named its "emir" in Europe.[47] He became a close friend of Sayyid Majed (or Sayyid Mir), an important personality in the department responsible for handling foreign recruits. Majed (who was born in the 1970s) gained notoriety after the terrorist attacks in Mumbai in November 2008, when investigations revealed that he seemed to be the commander of the operation, guiding the movements of the group by cell phone.[48] When in Pakistan, Nasir frequently met Majed and other leading personalities of the organization, including its leader Hafiz Muhammad Said and its influential head of military operations Zakiur Rahman Lakhvi, the person believed to be the mastermind of the Mumbai attacks.[49] From the late 1990s, Nasir provided Lashkar-e Tayyiba with financial donations and military equipment. Between 1995 (when the war in Bosnia ended) and 2007, Nasir traveled to Pakistan at least sixteen times.[50] In 2001, he recruited Yahia Yusuf's son Omar (born in 1983) for a training course in a Lashkar camp in the Pakistani part of Kashmir. At around the same time, as noted earlier, in summer 2001 he sent his own stepson, Yannick Nasir, who at that time was only fourteen years old, to undergo a basic-training course in a camp of the Lashkar-e Tayyiba in Pakistani Kashmir as well.[51]

Nasir's break with the Pakistani organization came in 2003 when conflicts around ideology and strategy surfaced. According to the verdict of a court in the western German city of Koblenz, Sayyid Majed, in a conversation with Nasir, had confirmed that Lashkar-e Tayyiba had given in to pressure by the Pakistani government and had stopped its support for the struggle of the Taliban and al-Qaeda in Afghanistan. According to Majed, another reason for Nasir's break with Lashkar involved an ideological conflict between the Taliban and Lashkar-e Tayyiba and the Taliban's lack of respect for the Pakistani fighters.[52] Aleem Nasir, for his part, wanted to continue his support for the Afghan cause and immediately ceased his associations with Lashkar-e Tayyiba, establishing contacts with al-Qaeda instead.[53] From summer 2004, Nasir acted on behalf of the Arab organization and—in subsequent years—met with several leading al-Qaeda functionaries in Waziristan, among them Mustafa Abu l-Yazid, its financial chief, who in May 2007 was named al-Qaeda's commander in Afghanistan. These contacts might serve as evidence of Aleem Nasir's prominence in these circles. Just as in his years with Lashkar-e Tayyiba, he continued to pose as a gem trader, a nearly perfect cover because of the large gem-trading networks in Afghanistan and Pakistan in general and in the border area in particular. His tasks included the collection of donations—which amounted to the large sum of at least 79,000 euro (US$100,000) between 2004 and 2007—and the procurement of military and other equipment such as night-vision goggles, range finders, scopes for rifles, directional microphones, Kevlar bulletproof vests, binoculars, and laptops. Furthermore, he was charged with spreading al-Qaeda's propaganda in Germany and recruiting new fighters.[54]

Back in Germany, Nasir made good on his promise and recruited a few young acquaintances for al-Qaeda by bringing them to his home and watching jihad videos with them. Nasir is known to have sent at least three young Germans to join al-Qaeda in Pakistan: the German Moroccan Bekkay Harrach (1977–2010), who later rose to prominence because of his role in al-Qaeda's propaganda activities; the Turkish citizen Ömer Özdemir (b. 1978); and Renée Marc Sepac. He employed Özdemir and the Turkish German Sermet Ilgen (b. 1978) primarily to assist him in his logistical capacity. Both lived in Sindelfingen close to Stuttgart in southwestern Germany, not far from Ulm and Neu-Ulm. After joining al-Qaeda, Nasir sent Özdemir to Waziristan, providing him with a letter of recommendation.

Ömer Özdemir's jihadist career is a prime example of the German jihad: the focus on Chechnya, the lack of Arabic language knowledge, and the disillusionment following the experience of the jihadist reality in the Pakistani tribal areas. After Özdemir finished school in Sindelfingen in 1994, he was trained as a screen printer but later worked in different short-term jobs, repeatedly living on unemployment benefits. Özdemir's radicalization began in 1999, when news of the impending second Chechen war aroused his desire to join his brethren in their fight against the Russians. During his interrogation in court, he stated that the fate of the Chechens especially affected him as a Turk.[55] In the ensuing years, the wish to fight in the Caucasus became the leitmotif of his jihadist life, and many conversations with like-minded friends centered on the events there. In 2001, Özdemir began to study Arabic and look for an opportunity to deepen his knowledge of Islam. He soon ended up in the Multicultural House in Neu-Ulm listening to Yahia Yusuf's sermons. Although he later reported that he was disappointed because the Egyptian preacher was not radical enough, the contacts he made shaped his future career. Özdemir is known to have been in contact with Fritz Gelowicz, the leader of the Sauerland group, as well as with other known jihadists and to have subscribed to *Think Islamic* magazine. Most important, it was in the Multicultural House that he met and befriended Aleem Nasir, whom he assisted by procuring money and equipment first for Lashkar-e Tayyiba and then for al-Qaeda, accepting Nasir as his "emir."[56]

Sympathy for the fight of the Chechen jihadists was the common denominator of the new scene that Özdemir entered. Nasir owned a large collection of jihadist videos of the fight in Afghanistan and Iraq, speeches by al-Qaeda leaders, and the executions of Western and Russian prisoners that he showed his young followers at home. When his apartment was searched after his arrest in February 2008, police were surprised by the special attention that the Pakistani had given to the Chechens' struggle. They found twenty copies of the German-language Chechen propaganda video *The Gate of Grief*, produced by young militants closely affiliated with Aleem Nasir.[57]

Nasir's young disciple, Özdemir, soon insisted that he wanted to join the fight, and it seems to have been understood that Nasir would recruit him for al-Qaeda in Pakistan. As a precondition, Özdemir had to prepare his friend Sermet Ilgen, who at that time already belonged to the small circle, to take over his procurement efforts. Furthermore, Nasir insisted that Özdemir's training with the Arabs of al-Qaeda would be successful only if he spoke Arabic. As he put it, "Arabic is the language of the Mujahideen."[58] As a result, Özdemir decided to study Arabic in Cairo, where he remained from December 2004 to April 2005, after which he returned to Germany. Finally, he left Germany in April 2006 with a letter of recommendation signed by Nasir and after having sworn an oath of loyalty to Bin Laden, Zawahiri, and Aleem Nasir.[59] Just like the members of the Sauerland group, he traveled first to Istanbul, then to Iran, where he contacted a jihadist human trafficker in Zahedan, who funneled him via Quetta and Bannu to North Waziristan.

Upon arrival, Özdemir entered an obligatory training course in North Waziristan in an al-Qaeda camp named after the second caliph, Umar "al-Faruq" (634–644). Although he caught malaria there, he remained and finished the course. Upon the trainers' request, he and other fighters were sent to the Swat Valley, where the Taliban offered an advanced, "harder" training that closely resembled real combat.[60] He then seems to have taken part in a Taliban operation in Afghanistan.[61] Although he would have liked to stay in Waziristan, he was sent back to Germany in August 2006 in order to continue his logistic tasks for al-Qaeda.

In spite of his illness and the difficult living conditions in Pakistan, Özdemir did not give up his original goal of fighting in Chechnya. In June 2007, he traveled to Turkey but did not manage to find a way into the Caucasus.[62] He decided instead to join al-Qaeda again and in April 2008 went to Istanbul and then to North Waziristan via Zahedan and Quetta. He later told the court in Germany that two events during this stay in Waziristan convinced him that he was psychically unfit for the fight in Afghanistan. In one case, he accompanied the doctor who had taken care of him in 2006 and who had been called to a site where four wounded mujahideen were dying. Özdemir, horrified by what he had seen, refused to talk about the second event, although he insisted that it ultimately led to his decision to return to Germany.[63] Upon his return in September 2008, he was arrested and later convicted and sentenced to six years in jail. By that time, Aleem Nasir had already spent seven months in jail, and his network was battered.

THE SAUERLAND FOUR RECRUITING FOR THE ISLAMIC JIHAD UNION

While plotting the attacks in Germany starting in late 2006, the Sauerland group recruited several of their friends to join the jihadists in Pakistan's tribal belt. As a consequence of their efforts and those of close acquaintances, the number of Germans joining the jihadists in Pakistan skyrocketed after 2007. Daniel Schneider and Adem Yilmaz apparently led this recruitment effort. Although Yilmaz recruited the larger number of young men, including Cüneyt Çiftçi, "the first German suicide bomber," Schneider's recruits left a more long-term imprint on the German jihadist scene in Pakistan and its propaganda activities. All young men who reached Pakistan joined the IJU there.

Adem Yilmaz had already built a small network of like-minded friends and acquaintances before leaving for Syria and Pakistan in 2006 by inviting them to his parents' garden in Langen, a town south of Frankfurt. Besides having barbecues and playing soccer, the young men discussed religious and political issues and traded jihadist videos and other materials. Together, the friends went to the Salafist Bilal Mosque in Frankfurt and the Tawhid Mosque in neighboring Dietzenbach. Most of the ten or so young men were Turks and Germans of Turkish or Turkish Kurdish origin; thus Yilmaz's activities more than that of any other recruiter led to the first travel movements by Turkish diaspora members to Pakistan. Pronounced anti-Americanism among its members was another characteristic of the Yilmaz group. For example, in May 2007 Yilmaz's little brother Burhan (b. 1987), Sadullah Kaplan (b. 1984), Hüseyin Özgün (b. 1981), and Turgay Türüt (b. 1985) procured, among other things, five knives, a carpenter's hammer, a crowbar, and a baseball bat, then drove to a discotheque frequented by Americans in Mainz, a city some twenty miles west of Langen. After identifying cars with American license plates, they scratched them, smashed the windows, and otherwise vandalized the cars.[64] During the Sauerland trial, members of the group stated that their comrades from Frankfurt had made a habit of looking for Americans at night so they could beat them up.[65]

When Yilmaz returned from Pakistan in late September 2006, he again took up the weekend meetings in the garden. He apparently did not have to make any special effort to convince his friends to join the IJU—which he called "the Uzbek group"—effectively showing that many young volunteers were sufficiently radicalized. On the contrary, the recruits had already nurtured the idea of joining the jihad for some time, but they had not seen an opportunity to reach the battlefield without help. Yilmaz recruited six people for the IJU, including the Turkish brothers Hüseyin and Bekir Özgün (b. 1990) from Langen, the German Afghan Omid Shirkhani (b. 1984 in Kabul) from neighboring Dietzenbach, Salih Seyhan (b. 1982) from Frankfurt, Sadullah Kaplan from Langen, and Cüneyt Çiftçi, who lived in Ansbach some one hundred miles from Langen but had befriended Yilmaz at a Salafist seminar in Brussels. The other members of the group preferred not to go to Pakistan, but they also supported Yilmaz's activities by helping to obtain equipment.[66]

The young men traveled in two groups—Seyhan, Shirkhani, and Çiftçi (who took his wife and children with him) in April 2007 and the three others in June. Hüseyin and Bekir Özgün were arrested while illegally trying to enter Pakistan from Iran and were extradited to Turkey and Germany. Seyhan and Shirkhani joined the IJU and were—like Hüseyin Özgün—convicted and sentenced to short jail terms after their return to Germany. Before sending the young men to Istanbul, Yilmaz gave them instructions on how to reach Zahedan in Iran, where they contacted Gofir Salimov, the IJU trafficker who had already funneled the Sauerland group across the Iran–Pakistan border. Most of the recruits carried money and equipment with them but left some of it with Salimov. The Uzbek then arranged for their passage into Pakistan and to Mir Ali in North Waziristan via Quetta and Bannu. In North Waziristan, the four remaining recruits were trained by the IJU. Sadullah Kaplan was the first German to die in the ranks of the Uzbek organization during a fight with the Pakistani army in October 2007. Cüneyt Çiftçi, however, became the most infamous member of the group by carrying out his suicide attack on an American–Afghan military camp in Khost in March 2008.

In his native Saarland, Daniel Schneider had been part of a small group of jihadists in Neunkirchen who remained in contact even when Schneider left for Egypt and later Pakistan in 2006. Members of this small group were the Turk Zafer Sari (b. 1985), the Lebanese Houssain Al Malla (b. 1984 in Beirut), the German convert Jan Pavel Schneider (b. 1982), and the German Eric Breininger (a.k.a. Abdul Ghaffar, 1987–2010), all of whom left Germany to join the jihad. Most of the young men had showed less than average intelligence during their school careers, had received only the most rudimentary education, and had spent their youth consuming alcohol and marijuana before they converted to Islam. All of them went through deep personal crises until jihadism gave their life a new orientation, a feeling of group security, and promised adventure.

In 2007, Breininger and Malla made their way to Pakistan, and Breininger describes their journey to the jihad in an autobiography that was published shortly after his death in April 2010.[67] Breininger had converted in January 2007 after he had come into contact with the group of young Salafists through a common friend, who introduced him to Daniel Schneider and Malla. He began to follow a Salafist lifestyle, which led to a breakup with his girlfriend. He subsequently moved into an apartment with Daniel Schneider, where they spent much time together and watched videos from the jihadist battlefields. These videos had a highly radicalizing influence on Breininger, as he himself relates: "We followed the events in the regions of the jihad and watched films showing how the mujahideen fight the Crusaders. We were especially horrified by the news from the prisons and how these Crusaders treat our brethren, how they torture and oppress them. Also the fact that these unbelievers put innocent women in jail, rape them day by day and that some of them [the women] have to carry their [the unbelievers'] children in their bellies and that these noble sisters are treated like shit fanned the rage against the *kuffar* [the unbelievers] in me."[68]

Listening to the conversations of his like-minded friends, Breininger decided that he could not stay idle in the face of these events: "I realized quickly that I have to undertake something against these Crusaders who defile[69] our brothers and sisters. . . . The decision was now clear to me that I have to leave on Allah's path in order to undertake the jihad against Allah's enemies and to die as a martyr for Allah's cause, namely that Allah's word will reign supreme."[70]

Before Daniel Schneider moved to Sauerland in early September 2007 to join in the group's final preparations, he advised Breininger to leave, too, most likely fearing a crackdown on the local scene after the attacks that he and his group were to perpetrate. Schneider informed Gelowicz: "I send my son to the kindergarten."[71] At that time, Malla was in jail after he had been arrested when trying to enter Pakistan illegally in June 2007 and then extradited to Germany, so Breininger had to act on his own.[72] His preparations to leave Germany and join the jihad show the young convert as an extremely naive country bumpkin who had no clue about the situation in the countries to which he was heading. He had in fact never previously left Germany or even his native Saarland. It was pure luck that he ever arrived in North Waziristan in late 2007.

Citing a lack of necessary contacts to organize his journey, Breininger writes that, together with two of his comrades, he decided that the best country to go to would be Algeria. He would study Arabic there and try to make contact with local jihadists in order to join them in their fight against the regime in Algiers. He found a friend who promised to bring him to the French Mediterranean port of Marseille, from where he would take a ferry to North Africa. Shortly before leaving, however, Breininger went to a mosque where he knew an Algerian who he hoped would help him find a place to stay in Algeria. Breininger's acquaintance advised against studying Arabic in Algeria, saying that Algeria had strayed from the path of religion.[73] More likely, the Algerian knew that Breininger would have stood little chance of joining the Algerian jihadists this way.

Breininger then went to a travel agency asking for flights to either Syria or Egypt; at the last minute, he decided to go to Hurghada, a Red Sea resort in Egypt. One of his friends in the mosque gave him a small piece of paper containing instructions to give to a taxi driver who would take Breininger from the airport to the bus station. Once Breininger arrived at the airport, he was shuttled to the bus station and taken to the bus to Cairo. Upon arrival in Cairo, he followed a similar plan to reach the language school, where he asked his teacher to call a friend in Germany, who then informed the teacher that Breininger wanted to enroll at his institute. After Breininger befriended some local Salafists and arranged his stay in the Egyptian capital, he learned that his friend Schneider and the rest of the Sauerland group had been arrested in Germany. Some days later he was joined by his Neunkirchen friend Malla, who had decided to try to go to the Pakistani tribal areas again. Although Malla also had a reputation for less-than-average intelligence, he seems to have had a much stronger personality than Breininger and immediately became a leader to the young convert.[74] As a police official acquainted with the cases said, "Breininger always seems to have looked for someone to tell him what to do."[75] Malla hardly had to convince Breininger to give up his Arabic studies and join him on his journey to Afghanistan via Iran and Pakistan. Although Breininger thought that he might become an "obstacle in the jihad" because of his lack of Arabic-language skills, after only four months in Egypt he decided to join Malla on the trip to Iran because he realized it would be difficult to travel without any help. Together the two young men traveled to Tehran and from there to Zahedan, where they contacted a human trafficker in the Makki Mosque. From Zahedan, they then took the already well-established route via Taftan to Quetta to Bannu, and finally to Mir Ali. In late 2007, they arrived at the headquarters of the IJU and were sent to train with some newly arrived Turks and Tadjiks.[76] Breininger remained with the IJU until his death in April 2010. Malla left Breininger at some point; his whereabouts were unknown until August 2011, when he was arrested in Turkey. The other members of the Saarland group—Jan Pavel Schneider and Zafer Sari—had for the time being disappeared.

THE PROPAGANDA MINISTER AS A RECRUITER: AHMET MANAVBAŞI

Ahmet Manavbaşı was the first German recruiter to make use of the Internet and the first to be based outside of Germany. Although his activities ended abruptly upon his death in April 2010 and therefore showed only limited success, they highlighted the potential of Internet-based recruitment if combined with more traditional peer recruitment. In the case of

Manavbaşı, his activities as an Internet recruiter only increased his central role in the development of the German scene, which included Internet propaganda, active recruitment efforts, and—from 2009—leadership in the first German jihadist organization.

As the IJU's most important propaganda official, Manavbaşı, together with a small group of like-minded Turks living in Istanbul, administered the Web site Time for Martyrdom between November 2006 and April 2010. There, Manavbaşı and his friends published IJU propaganda materials and, after September 2009, did the same for the German Taliban Mujahideen. The Web site also hosted a jihadist forum that served as a contact point for members, supporters, and sympathizers. In at least one case, it has been established that Ahmet Manavbaşı tried to recruit a German Turk, Ramazan Başçıvan, who had written to the official email address on the Web site. He was only partially successful. Başçıvan did travel to the Bosporus, where he spent some time with Manavbaşı, but he declined to join the fight in Afghanistan. Instead, he chose to support Manavbaşı financially, albeit with only very small amounts of money.[77]

More important, Ahmet Manavbaşı kept in close contact with a small group of supporters in Ulm and Berlin, in particular Fritz Gelowicz's wife, Filiz, and two other young Turks in Berlin, Alican Tufan (b. 1989) and Fatih Kahraman (b. 1978). They all supported the IJU and later the German Taliban Mujahideen with financial and material donations. It unfortunately has not been established how exactly Manavbaşı connected with the Berlin scene, but it is very likely that previous contact with the Sauerland group played a role. At this point, relations between different centers of jihadist activity in Germany were already quite well developed. Tufan and Kahraman were part of a larger group of young men, most of whom left the German capital for Pakistan in May and September 2009. Authorities suspect Kahraman of having been the human trafficker for the first part of the trip—to Turkey and to Iran—for some of the group members.[78] While the young men were in Germany, they, like Filiz Gelowicz, were responsible mainly for sending money to Istanbul and supporting Manavbaşı's propaganda activities.[79] At the same time, however, Manavbaşı tried to convince Tufan, who seems to have been his main local contact in Berlin, to perpetrate an undefined terrorist attack in Germany. At first, Tufan avoided a definitive answer until he was forced to confess that he was not ready for such a deed.[80]

Manavbaşı's activities were merely the first efforts to recruit via the Internet. Close to two dozen young people left Berlin in order to join the IJU and the German Taliban Mujahideen, but Manavbaşı reportedly played only a supporting role in this recruitment. Local recruiters apparently prepared the young men and women for the journey; Manavbaşı's network sprang into action only when the group arrived in Istanbul.[81] The events show the continuing importance of local networks based on personal knowledge.

A Growing German Jihadist Scene

The growth of the Salafist scene, the mounting popularity of jihadist preachers, the increasing spread of jihadist ideology, and intensified recruitment efforts—all led to a wave of young Germans "leaving Kuffaristan," the "Land of the Nonbelievers," as the al-Qaeda propagandist Bekkay Harrach would have it. The Sauerland four were not the first Germans to travel to Pakistan in 2006, but they paved the way for others. While they recruited friends and acquaintances for the IJU in 2007, Aleem Nasir served as a recruiter for al-Qaeda. Most of these recruits took the same route to Pakistan via Istanbul, Zahedan in Iran, Quetta, and then North Waziristan, making contacts with the respective traffickers stationed there. Although connections between the Sauerland and Nasir cases abound, with many of the recruits having known each other long before their travels to Pakistan, their recruitment efforts seem to have taken place separately. From 2008, the first German recruits joined a third organization, the IMU, but not much is known about the ways this organization recruited Germans.

Although the nucleus of the recruitment drive seems to have been the Multicultural House in Neu-Ulm, the network of the Sauerland group had other centers in the Frankfurt region and in the Saarland. In the following years, groups of young men and increasingly women assembled in Bonn, Hamburg, and Berlin. Whereas the members of the Sauerland network joined the IJU exclusively, volunteers from Bonn ended up in the camps of al-Qaeda or the IMU. Members of the Hamburg group also joined these two organizations, although all of those who first went to the IMU subsequently left it and were trained by al-Qaeda. All of the Berlin travel groups linked up with the IJU and its German offspring, the German Taliban Mujahideen.

As a result of these travel movements, in 2009 the Germans became the biggest Western contingent among the foreign fighters in the Pakistani tribal areas. All in all, according to the German BKA, up to February 2011 some 220 "sociological Germans" (people who were born in or grew up in Germany but might not have German nationality) had been trained in jihadist camps since 2001. By far the greatest number went to join the IJU in 2007. It was perhaps only a matter of time before a genuine German jihadist group emerged, something that happened in September 2009 with the founding of the German Taliban Mujahideen.

7

The German Taliban Mujahideen

On April 28, 2010, a small group of German and Uzbek fighters was traveling by car between the militant stronghold of Mir Ali and Miranshah, the capital of North Waziristan, when they were unexpectedly stopped by Pakistani military. A firefight ensued during which four jihadists were killed. News of the death of Eric Breininger (a.k.a. Abdul Ghaffar)—"the German Taliban," as he was called by the influential tabloid *Bild*, and perhaps the best-known face of German jihadism—quickly spread in his home country and the world.[1] Those who focused their attention on the intellectually and linguistically limited Breininger missed the importance of the simultaneous death of one of his comrades. The IJU's "propaganda minister" and emir of the German Taliban Mujahideen, Ahmet Manavbaşı (a.k.a. Abu Ishaaq al-Muhajir or Salahuddin Turki), also was killed. The other dead fighters were the Dutch citizen Danny Reinders (b. 1988) from Berlin and an unknown Uzbek curiously nicknamed "Hizbullah." In a single encounter, the German Taliban Mujahideen lost its founder and uncontested leader, its main public face, and about one-quarter of its fighting force. Yet it remained unclear whether the organization in fact survived this blow to its fortunes. The group totally stopped its public activities in subsequent months, so that when news about a new leadership emerged in December 2010, there were serious doubts as to whether the German Taliban Mujahideen really continued to exist.[2]

The Emergence of the German Taliban Mujahideen

The German Taliban Mujahideen emerged out of the IJU's group of propagandists around Ahmet Manavbaşı in North Waziristan. Since 2007, this Turkish criminal had been instrumental in raising the IJU's public profile by intensifying its propaganda drive. In February 2009, Manavbaşı founded the media group Elif Medya, named after the first letter of the Arabic alphabet, which subsequently published almost all video, audio, and other materials of the IJU, German Taliban Mujahideen, and the Taifetül Mansura.[3] The founding of such a media group made clear that its creators had developed the ambition to assert themselves in the jihadist scene. Since 2001, all jihadist organizations of significance have established similar media arms or departments in order to organize propaganda activity. Al-Qaeda's media group, for instance, is al-Sahab (the Clouds); al-Qaeda in Yemen relies on al-Malahim (the Battles); and the media wing for al-Qaeda in the Islamic Maghreb is al-Andalus (the Arabic name for Muslim Spain). The IMU later established the media office God's Army (Jundullah). At the time of its founding—still on behalf of the IJU—Elif Medya made clear that the organization sought a similar status. In the next two years, it primarily used the Turkish Web site Time for Martyrdom to distribute its materials. In addition, in May 2009 Elif Medya started its first Internet blog at the address http://elifmedya.wordpress.com and in January 2010 created the Web site Elif Medya. Just like its better-known forebears, Elif Medya developed its own logo, a globe with "Elif Medya" written on it. Videos and IJU declarations increasingly appeared on other Web sites as well.

Propaganda is so important to the German Taliban Mujahideen that some sources state that Elif Medya is identical to the group.[4] For one thing, Ahmet Manavbaşı played a dominant role in both groups; he and the administrators of the Web site Time for Martyrdom in Istanbul established Elif Medya. Furthermore, the German Taliban Mujahideen mainly seem to have been responsible for developing propaganda for a German audience. Although Ahmet Manavbaşı sought to build an effective German jihadist organization, his death rendered the group unable to consolidate its structure.

Eric Breininger describes the founding of the German Taliban Mujahideen in his autobiography, which the group published in late April 2010 shortly after his death.[5] Breininger had appeared in several IJU videos and played a prominent role in German Taliban Mujahideen propaganda. Although the text is authentic—that is, authored by Eric Breininger before his death—there must have been coauthors. Owing to linguistic deficits, the ill-educated Breininger would probably not have been able to write the book entirely on his known. The text also contains lengthy translations from Arabic texts into German that were beyond Breininger's capabilities. As a result, the so-called autobiography must be seen as a collective endeavor by several German Taliban Mujahideen members.

In the text, Breininger describes the emergence of the German Taliban Mujahideen (despite the multiple authors, the original text is written in poor German and full of mistakes; some errors are retained in my translation, but others are edited for clarity): "After three years with the Islamic Jihad Union, I still had problems communicating with the other Mujahidin. Although they were really all nice brothers, I missed conversations with a brother. I simply missed exchanging thoughts from time to time or that a brother spirits me up, when I had bad day. One realizes very quickly how much one needs encouragement and Nasiha [good advice] especially in times of war. . . . I started to make dua [prayer] to Allah. I have asked him to send German brothers to our Jamaa [group]."[6] Thus, it might be assumed that the Sauerland group's recruitment drive in 2007 had at first not led to a permanent German presence at the IJU camps. And Ahmet Manavbaşı apparently did not stay in Mir Ali permanently. In 2009, however, a new group of volunteers arrived and joined the IJU: "When we were back in Waziristan, the Amir [i.e. the IJU leader Jalolov] came up to me and related that at that time some German brothers were training with him. He allowed me to visit these brothers. In the beginning I thought they would stay with the IJU, but they told me that they wanted to join the Taliban. I then thought whether it would not be better for me as well to be in a Jamaa [group] in which I could communicate with the brothers."[7]

Breininger subsequently claims to have left the IJU together with his new friends and joined the Taliban: "Following the model of the prophet (s.), who brought together members of a tribe, I decided to go with the other brothers to Taliban. Already in the times of the prophet (s.), bringing together people of one tribe (today of one country) had advantages, because these have the same customs and habits and the same culture. Furthermore, one crosses the linguistic barriers, which exist among people, who do not stem from the same countries (tribes)."[8]

With the consent of "the Taliban"—no further specification is given in the text—six Germans (Ahmet Manavbaşı, Eric Breininger, Fatih Temelli [b. 1985], Yusuf Ocak [b. 1985], and probably Burhan Sauerland [b. 1987] and Danny Reinders [b. 1989]) founded the German Taliban Mujahideen: "The Taliban allowed [us] to form a subgroup. Initially, we were six brothers, founded the 'German Taliban Mujahideen' Jamaa and elected Abu Ishaaq al-Muhajir [Ahmet Manavbaşı] our Amir. This is how the worldwide first German jihad group emerged. This Jamaa shall become a home for all German-language Muslims, who can come here from all over the world in order to fulfill their duty towards Allah, to fight on the path of Allah, so that his word will reign supreme."[9]

This description of the German Taliban Mujahideen as an independent organization that left the IJU and joined the Taliban has led to heated debates about its status and the nature of its relations with the bigger Uzbek and Pashtun organizations dominating the jihadist scene in North Waziristan. Some observers believe that the German Taliban Mujahideen was founded after the Germans left the IJU because the IJU was severely weakened by the death of its leader Najmiddin Jalolov in September 2009. As a matter of fact, the German Taliban Mujahideen first appeared on September 24, 2009, with a video entitled *The Call to Truth*, in which the military training of German Taliban Mujahideen fighters is shown, and a speaker named "Ayyub Almani" (i.e., Yusuf Ocak) explains the organization's aims and program and threatens Germany with attacks on its soil.[10] However, the time span between Jalolov's death and the appearance of the video—ten days—is quite short for such an important decision and the production of the first video. It is more likely that discussions over the foundation of the German Taliban Mujahideen had already taken place before Jalolov was killed. In any case, it is inconceivable that the Germans were allowed to leave without the IJU leadership's consent. And it is questionable that a weakened IJU would simply let half a dozen propagandists and fighters leave, even if their military contributions were modest.

The most probable explanation for the founding of the German Taliban Mujahideen is that the IJU reacted to the sudden influx of Turkish, Azeri, and German fighters by founding a sort of international brigade that was tasked primarily with propaganda work geared toward the German and Turkish publics and that was given more leeway than usual for the non–Central Asian fighters. It speaks to a certain independence of the German

Taliban Mujahideen that the group reportedly established its main base in a village west of Miranshah at quite a distance from the IJU headquarters in Mir Ali.[11] At the same time, however, it is hardly conceivable that the German Taliban Mujahideen could have survived in the tribal areas without the IJU's continued support. Furthermore, the group maintained independent contacts with the Haqqani network. As the German returnee Thomas Usztics reported during his trial in Berlin in late 2012, Manavbaşi knew Sirajuddin Haqqani (a.k.a. Khalifa), the military leader of the network, well and had direct access to him.

Turks, Azeris, and Germans: The IJU's "International Brigades"

In its short history between September 2009 and April 2010, the activities of the German Taliban Mujahideen hinted at a close association with a Turkish–Azeri group Taifetül Mansura (Victorious Group), which apparently was the Turkic equivalent of the German Taliban Mujahideen but militarily much stronger. Its appearance on the scene in North Waziristan in spring 2009 was part of a trend insofar as the number of Turks in the tribal areas rose in parallel with the numerical rise of German recruits after 2007. Some Turks, although they would have preferred to fight in the North Caucasus, decided to go to Pakistan because it had become increasingly difficult to join the jihad in Chechnya.

In spring 2009, the Taifetül Mansura arrived in North Waziristan at about the same time as the first batch of Berlin volunteers for the IJU. On April 28, 2009, an interview with the Taifetül Mansura commander, Ebu Zer, by Elif Medya appeared on jihadist Web sites, explaining that the group had returned to Turkey in 2007 after it had taken part in the Chechen struggle for fifteen years. When its members tried to move back into the North Caucasus in summer 2008, the Russian–Georgian war hindered them from reaching their destination. It was at this point that the group, consisting of Turkish and Azeri nationals, decided to travel to Pakistan to join the Afghan insurgents operating in the tribal areas. There, reports Ebu Zer, they accepted the Taliban leader Mullah Omar as their commander in chief, and they were granted a base and the help of local supporters in return.[12]

The Taifetül Mansura evidently kept in close contact with the IJU and the Haqqani network and had its base in Mir Ali. It might be assumed that the contact was established through old networks built by the IJU leadership with foreign fighters in Chechnya. Most interesting in this regard is the mention of Azeri fighters in the ranks of the IJU. A group of Azeri jihadists had already made the first contact with the Sauerland group in Syria and had then sent them to the IJU in Waziristan, where they would be trained in order to join the struggle in Chechnya later (see chapter 3). These Azeris might have had something to do with the small group that now went to Pakistan with their Turkish brothers-in-arms.

Azeris have never played an important role in the jihadist movement, first and foremost because the Azerbaijan population is primarily Shiite. Of the approximately 9 million inhabitants of the country, only about 30–40 percent are Sunnis, the majority of whom live in the areas close to the Dagestani border in the northern and northwestern parts of the country. Furthermore, there is a substantial Sunni minority in the capital Baku. Although a staunchly secular state, beginning in the first half of the 1990s Azerbaijan developed into an important rear base for the struggle in Chechnya, which in the long run left its mark on some parts of the Sunni population and led to the radicalization of an increasing number of young Azeri Sunnis.

Independent Azerbaijan had already come into contact with modern jihadism in the early 1990s during its war with neighboring Armenia over the enclave Nagorno-Karabakh (1988–1994). Rooted in competing claims to the territory, the conflict erupted during the last days of the Soviet Union, escalating after its final breakup in December 1991. The Muslim Azeris—who finally lost the war and had to agree to a cease-fire in May 1994—were supported by volunteers from other parts of the Muslim world, mainly Afghans, but also by some fighters from neighboring Chechnya and a few from Turkey and Arab countries, their numbers ranging from 1,000 to 3,000.[13] The Chechnya connection in particular laid the basis for an intensified cooperation between groups from the North Caucasus, Arab countries, Turkey, and Azerbaijan in the following years. Many Chechen commanders regarded the conflict in Nagorno-Karabakh and the war in Abkhazia in 1992–1993 as useful training for the subsequent struggle for independence in their home country. For instance, the notorious Shamil Basayev is reported to have made his first experiences in irregular combat on the Azeri side in the conflict with Armenia in 1991–1992. Perhaps even more important, it was in Azerbaijan that the Chechens first came into contact with Arab and Turkish jihadists.[14]

Beginning in 1995, however, Azerbaijan had no use for the foreigners anymore. Although most of them—especially the Afghans—returned to their home country, many Arabs and Turks now used their newly established contacts with the Chechens to join the struggle against Russia. At the same time, Azerbaijan became an important logistics center for the Chechen rebels, with many recruits, weapons, and supplies arriving there via Dagestan. Although Georgia remained the more important rear base, with most of the actual smuggling taking place through the Pankisi Gorge and the mountain passes connecting northern Georgia with Chechnya, Azerbaijan hosted a large logistical infrastructure as well, which grew in importance with the beginning of the second Chechen war in late 1999.[15]

The events left a deep imprint on the local Islamist scene as well, a considerable number of young Sunni Azeris joining the fight of their Chechen brethren in 1995 and upholding especially strong contacts with the Turkish volunteers. Contacts with Chechens, Arabs, and Turks subsequently led to a radicalization among many Azeri young men, and the first indigenous jihadist group appeared in the second half of the 1990s—the Army of God (Jaishullah), which reportedly planned to attack the US embassy in Baku. After its leaders were apprehended and sentenced in 2000, though, nothing further was heard of the group. By and large, Sunni jihadist groups were long considered to be under control in Azerbaijan.[16]

Nonetheless, Azeris pop up at different points in the history of German jihadism. Already by 2002, an enigmatic "man from Baku" played a seemingly important role when Mevlüt Kar planned a terrorist attack in the Frankfurt region (on Operation Chocolate and Mevlüt Kar, see chapter 5). Kar maintained contact with personalities from Saudi Arabia and this man from Baku, the Azeri capital, and asked them to send personnel and money for the operation.[17] Seen in combination with Kar's prominent role in the preparations for the Sauerland attack, it might not have been pure coincidence that Adem Yilmaz came into contact with the group of Azeris in 2006 in Syria who later arranged the journey of the four young Germans to Waziristan (see chapter 3).

From the second Chechen war, Azeri jihadists became more visible on the transnational scene, apparently the result of an increasing radicalization of Sunnis within the country, partly under the influence of Salafists from neighboring Dagestan, which has traditionally been home to the most religiously conservative Muslim population in the area and where an increasing radicalization of many young Muslims could be witnessed from the second half of the 1990s. Besides, by 2000 it had become increasingly clear that the Chechen insurgents were beaten, and operating conditions for them and their foreign supporters became more and more difficult. Therefore, the Azeris and their Turkish allies looked for alternative fields of action, which some of them later found in Afghanistan. They withdrew from the North Caucasus and made their way to North Waziristan via Iran to join the IJU.

Upon arrival in North Waziristan, the various Turks, Azeris, and Germans seem to have closely coordinated their activities. During 2009 and 2010, Ahmet Manavbaşı's media group Elif Medya produced and distributed not only IJU and German Taliban Mujahideen material, but also their Turkish and Azeri allies' videos, interviews, and declarations.[18] German returnees report that Manavbaşı held meetings with Turkish jihadists in the market of Mir Ali and at least some of the Germans lived together with the Turks and Azeris in the same compounds in Mir Ali.[19] In some instances, though, it seems as if the Germans were subordinate to the Taifetül Mansura leadership, which was logical because the Turks and Azeris had long fighting experience on perhaps the most challenging jihadist battlefield (Chechnya), a factor that made them—and especially their (military) leader Ebu Zer—well-respected members of the jihadist community in Waziristan. The Germans, in contrast, could not present any jihadist credentials whatsoever because most of them had just joined the jihadist movement recently, in 2009, and had no military experience at all.

That the Germans were a subordinate group in what might be called the IJU's "international brigade" became quite obvious in a video published by Elif Medya in September 2009. In this video, Commander (Komutan) Ebu Zer sits in the middle and is the first to address the virtual audience, leaving the viewer with the impression that he is clearly the boss among the five. The mainly Turkish-language video is entitled *The Support Caravan Continues on Its Path* and was published in the name of the Islamic Emirate of Afghanistan (Afganistan Islam Emirliği), the Taliban's name for Afghanistan. Besides Ebu Zer, the speakers in the video include some unknown activists from the Pakistani province of Panjab calling themselves the

"Panjabi Taliban Movement" (Tehrik-e Taliban Pencab); the emir of the Azeri component in the Taifetül Mansura, Ebu Ömer; a second Azeri, Ilyas Azeri; and the German Taliban Mujahideen members Eric Breininger, Ayyub Almani (Yusuf Ocak), and Abdalfattah Almani (Fatih Temelli, a.k.a. Abdalfattah al-Muhajir).

In the video, shot on the occasion of the Muslim holy month of Ramadan and the feast of sacrifice (Id al-Adha), the speakers profess their loyalty to the Taliban and acknowledge financial support they claim to have received from Turkey and Europe, stressing that Turkey is their main source of donations. The two Azeri speakers emphasize the need for more support from Turkey, and Breininger expressly addresses the German Taliban Mujahideen's German audience by stating that it is compulsory to fight against the occupiers of Muslim lands and that those who do not join the jihad must support the active fighters by other means. After explicitly thanking his Turkish supporters for the money they have sent, Ebu Zer explains that his group had been based far from their home country for years and that in 2008 they had spent Ramadan in Chechnya.[20]

Structure of the German Taliban Mujahideen

The strong links of the Turks and Azeris to a German group should come as no surprise because German Turks and Kurds formed the group's backbone. Although in the beginning the group seems to have consisted of only six people, it grew to about a dozen members by April 2010. Approximately eight of the young men were Turks and Kurds from Germany; the rest were German converts and possibly one or two Arabs.

Not much is known about the inner structure of the German Taliban Mujahideen. Ahmet Manavbaşı seems to have been the uncontested leader, so that when the group "elected Abu Ishaaq al-Muhajir our Amir," as Breininger writes in his memoirs, the election must have resembled an acclamation, with the actual decision most likely taken by the IJU leadership. The choice of Manavbaşı as the new leader must have seemed the only option because the German Turk had the longest experience in the Pakistani tribal areas and was well connected with Sirajuddin Haqqani, many Turks, and other jihadists on the ground. With the exception of Eric Breininger, all the other Germans did not go to Pakistan until 2009.

The use of "Abu Ishaaq al-Muhajir" as a second alias (besides "Salahuddin Turki") is evidence of Manavbaşı's desire to protect himself and reminds the observer of the extreme secrecy surrounding the IJU leader Najmiddin Jalolov, who used several aliases and the only known photograph of whom was published shortly after his death on the IJU home page. And, in fact, Manavbaşı harbored wide-ranging ambitions. As Rami Makanesi, the German Syrian who was arrested in Pakistan in June 2010 and who met Manavbaşı in Mir Ali in April 2010, stated, "He wanted to have his own group independent of al-Qaeda, to build something powerful. One aim of the German group was to act against Germany."[21] Manavbaşı held a special grudge against Germany because of his extradition in 2000.

The German Taliban Mujahideen consisted of three distinct groups. The first was Manavbaşı's Istanbul group of propagandists and logistics specialists that handled the Turks, Azeris, and Germans who were on their way to Waziristan. This group was led by Emin "Mirza" Aydemir, the administrator of the German group's Web site who, according to one source, seemed to be Manavbaşı's superior, possibly his half-brother. Manavbaşı traveled back and forth between Pakistan and Turkey and brought videos with him, which were then published on sehadetvakti.com.[22] According to a police expert witness in a trial against German Taliban Mujahideen supporters in January 2011, Aydemir and other members of the group were still at large at that time.[23]

The second group comprised recruits from Neunkirchen in the Saarland. From Egypt, Breininger had traveled together with Houssain Al Malla, who was arrested in Turkey in August 2011 after nothing had been heard of him for four years. Another friend of the two, the German convert Jan Pavel Schneider might have joined the German Taliban Mujahideen as well because he joined the IJU in 2007 and was seen walking around Mir Ali in 2010.[24] Although Manavbaşı had lived near Neunkirchen until 2000, the contacts to the Saarland group of jihadists seem to have been made in Waziristan in 2007.[25]

The third group came from Berlin in 2009 and made the establishment of a German contingent possible. All the young men and women had been visiting the notorious al-Nur Mosque in Berlin, where they seem to have been recruited to join the IJU in Waziristan. The group consisted mainly of Turks, Turkish Kurds, and German converts and started traveling via Turkey and Iran to Pakistan in May 2009, when Yusuf Ocak, Fatih Temelli, and

Fatih Kahraman left Berlin. Five small groups altogether left the German capital between May 2009 and May 2010, numbering some fourteen young men and about twelve women. The biggest contingent left in September 2009, when five men and their wives and girlfriends traveled via Istanbul to Pakistan. After the first groups had left in 2009, the Berlin security authorities tried to keep an eye on potential travelers but did not properly monitor the suspects. As a result, in August 2010 a last group of five young men left under the leadership of Fatih Kahraman, but only two of them reached their destination.[26]

As a result of this influx of volunteers, the German Taliban Mujahideen grew from some six members in September–October 2009 to about a dozen members in April 2011. It is worth noting that an increasing number of young women in their late teens and early twenties accompanied the volunteers, most likely the result of IJU videos featuring Eric Breininger, in which the convert had called upon young Germans to bring their wives, arguing that there was a fully developed infrastructure in place in Waziristan, including schools and hospitals. Breininger himself mentions these women in his autobiography: "Thanks to Allah our group is growing steadily and not only single brothers arrive, but also families with children, who make great efforts here, far away from their birthplaces, for the sake of Allah."[27]

Not much is known about these women's role, but it is possible that some of them supported the German Taliban Mujahideen's propaganda activity. First and foremost, however, the presence of several women and girls with babies confronted the German authorities with a humanitarian problem, especially after some of their husbands were killed.

A Propaganda War

Although the German Taliban Mujahideen did not manage to perpetrate any terrorist attack, it unleashed a propaganda campaign that left an imprint on the German public. Its first and most influential video, *The Call to Truth*, published on September 24, 2009, shortly before the German parliamentary elections, was especially effective. In this video, the Berlin jihadist Yusuf Ocak warns of terrorist attacks in Germany and provides outsiders with a first look into the German Taliban Mujahideen's aims and strategies. Ocak names the group members' home country, Germany, as their most important enemy, aside from the United States, citing the presence of German troops in northern Afghanistan: "Only through your deployment here [in Afghanistan] against Islam, an attack on Germany becomes tempting for us Mujahideen. In order for you to taste the pain that the innocent Afghan people have to endure day by day. . . . It is only a matter of time until the jihad breaks down the German walls." As Ocak speaks, the video displays German landmarks, including the Brandenburg gate in Berlin, the skyline of Frankfurt, the Oktoberfest in Munich, the Hamburg main railway station, and the Dome of Cologne, which effectively declares these sites potential terrorist targets.

In 2009, following the arrival in Pakistan of a growing number of German volunteers, the IJU, IMU, al-Qaeda, and their allies tried to influence the debates in Germany by publishing propaganda videos featuring German jihadists living and operating in the Afghan–Pakistan border region. Although most of these videos were recruitment efforts trying to draw young Germans to the Pakistani training camps, some were part of a media offensive by the IJU, IMU, and al-Qaeda aimed at the wider German public. Never before had different jihadist organizations and individuals targeted a single country except the United States in such a large and sustained propaganda effort. Ever since the days of the Sauerland group, al-Qaeda and its allies identified Germany as the weakest link in the chain of large troop providers in Afghanistan and hoped to weaken the German government's resolve by all means. With the growing number of German recruits in Pakistan, these organizations were probably aware that public opposition to the German troop presence was mounting.

The culmination of this campaign was a video featuring Bekkay Harrach, a German of Moroccan descent who had been recruited by Aleem Nasir and had arrived in North Waziristan in spring 2007, when he joined al-Qaeda. In *Security—a Shared Destiny*, Harrach appears in a quite grotesque disguise: his chin-long black hair is neatly parted in the middle, and he is dressed in a dark suit, white shirt, and light-blue tie against a red background, mimicking US president Barack Obama's appearance during his famous speech to the Muslim world in Cairo in early June 2009. In contrast to two earlier videos featuring the young German, this one does not carry the official logo for the al-Qaeda media company al-Sahab, thereby failing to authenticate the material. Nevertheless, the video caused a great public stir in Germany because it contained the most direct threat to Germany ever. With the elections taking place on September 27, Harrach announced terrorist attacks within two weeks after the elections if the Germans voted for parties supporting the presence of German troops in Afghanistan:

> The parliamentary elections are the only opportunity for the people to shape the politics of the country. Therefore, before the elections is different to after the elections. In the elections, the people are in charge. And after the elections [Chancellor Andrea] Merkel will not find any other pitying words for the German people than those, which the German people have heard often enough.
>
> If the German people never want to hear those memorized words again, if the German people want to put an end to fear and violence once and for all, if the German people want to live in security again, then they have the opportunity now.
>
> Although Allah commands us in the Quran, sura 8, verse 60, to hold all our forces ready for our enemies, however, if the conflict partner gives in, and human lives can be saved through a peaceful resolution, then Allah the Generous commands us to be sensitive and lenient. . . .
>
> If the German people lean toward peace now, then the Mujahideen will also lean toward peace. And with the withdrawal of the last German soldier from Afghanistan, the last Mujahid will be withdrawn from Germany. Al-Qaeda vouches for that.
>
> This is the tolerance in Islam, which the West knows well and often praises, too. The German people can benefit from this tolerance now and seize the opportunity. Al-Qaeda is, pursuant to its constitution, the Holy Quran, ready to turn a blind eye regarding the German people. It is completely up to you.
>
> How would the German people like to withdraw its soldiers from Afghanistan, therefore giving peace and security in Germany a chance, and leaving Afghanistan to the Afghan people?
>
> However, if the majority of the German people do not want to convince the parties that are participating in the elections to withdraw the German soldiers from Afghanistan, then there will be a rude awakening after the elections.
>
> To the Muslims in Germany; may the peace, mercy, and blessings of Allah be upon you. My dear brothers and sisters in Islam. If the German

> people do not choose the withdrawal of its soldiers from Afghanistan, al-Qaeda asks you to stay away from everything that is not absolutely vital in the first two weeks after the elections. Please keep your children close to you during that time. May Allah protect you and your children and also all children.[28]

The threat was taken very seriously at that time because Harrach had already appeared on two al-Qaeda videos that carried the official al-Sahab logo, thus identifying the speaker on the September 2009 video as a member of that organization.[29] Furthermore, the German security authorities described Harrach as a prominent personality in the ranks of al-Qaeda and active in its Department of Foreign Operations.[30] Although in reality it is unlikely that Harrach was anything more than a foot soldier used and promoted for propaganda purposes, the video had to be taken seriously because Harrach had been a known al-Qaeda member for two and a half years. Furthermore, the leading al-Qaeda functionary Atiyatallah Abu Abd al-Rahman confirmed the threat to Germany by referring to Harrach's speech in the al-Qaeda video *The West and the Dark Tunnel*, which appeared September 22.[31]

As expected, German voters were not influenced by the threat and voted the conservative–liberal coalition led by Chancellor Angela Merkel into office, which did not indicate any intention to withdraw the German troops. After the ultimatum expired, al-Qaeda quickly lost credibility in Germany because it was apparently unable to carry out attacks.

The German Taliban Mujahideen was more prudent; it did not explicitly announce an attack. The September 24 video *The Call to Truth* was, rather, the first shot in a German Taliban Mujahidin propaganda offensive that had begun under the name "Elif Medya" some months earlier and lasted until the publication of Eric Breininger's autobiography in May 2010. The organization published several videos calling for supporters in Germany and Turkey to send recruits and money. As a matter of fact, from its inception, the German Taliban Mujahideen suffered from a severe shortage of funds, so that most of its videos and declarations contain calls for financial help. For instance, Eric Breininger in his autobiography urges his German sympathizers and supporters to send money:

> Here I would also like to address my German brothers and sisters directly and remind you that the jihad with property is equally obligatory

for every Muslim like the jihad with the own self. Currently we hardly receive any donations from Germany, although we are a German Jamaa [group] and although Germany is a very wealthy country. It is very sad that our brothers and sisters in Germany keep their hands that closed and do not perform their duty. If the brothers and sisters bought only one döner kebap[32] less per week, with this money one could buy 20 sniper bullets in order to fight the kuffar [unbelievers]. Just think what reward you would, inshaallah, receive if one of these sniper bullets would be a means for a kafir [unbeliever] to die.[33]

The same passage contains a hint that the German Taliban Mujahideen received "donations from different countries, but primarily from Turkey."[34] Different videos produced by Elif Medya contain similar evidence of the importance of Turkey as a logistics base for the German Taliban Mujahideen.[35] It was therefore only logical that Elif Medya began producing bilingual German–Turkish videos in which German Taliban Mujahideen and Taifetül Mansura members—both Turks and Azeris—mix. The Turkish-language parts are subtitled in German, the German-language parts in Turkish.

At the time Breininger's memoirs were published, Germany had lost most of its relevance as a financing hub because the most important supporters had been arrested in late 2009. Ahmet Manavbaşı had kept contact with Filiz Gelowicz, the wife of the Sauerland ringleader, and a small cell of supporters in Berlin. They collected money and sent it to Istanbul; the money was subsequently transferred to Pakistan. In turn, several videos mentioned the supporters' aliases. It is striking that the number of German supporters seems to have been low, and most of them traveled or attempted to travel to Pakistan instead of staying on in Germany and continuing their financing activities. The only one who did not try to leave the country was Filiz Gelowicz, who—with her husband in jail—could not expect to reach the Pakistani tribal areas and be accepted there as an unaccompanied woman.

Classical Internationalism Again: The German Taliban Mujahideen's Ideology

Although the German Taliban Mujahideen had no ideologists in their ranks, it did develop its own classical internationalist ideology by collecting fragments from jihadist publications and adding a characteristic focus on Germany and Uzbekistan, thus mirroring its members' strong connection to their home country and their close relations to the IJU. The base line of the group's publications was simple: the enemies of Islam—namely, the United States and its allies (most prominently Israel and Germany)—are waging a war against Islam. The only possible response to this aggression is the holy war of the Taliban, al-Qaeda, the IJU, and other jihadist organizations. Participation in this jihad is every Muslim's individual duty.

Although this motive might be discerned in most German Taliban Mujahideen declarations, it becomes especially clear in an audio tape titled *The Forgotten Duty*, released on February 25, 2010, in which an unknown speaker presents the group's jihad theory. Its title was taken from a book authored by the Egyptian Muhammad Abdassalam Farag (1952–1982), the ideological leader of the group that assassinated President Anwar al-Sadat on October 6, 1981. In this standard work of modern jihadism, Farag makes an effort to convince fellow Muslims that violent jihad against apostate rulers is one of their most solemn obligations, which had for too long been unjustly ignored.[36]

Members of the German Taliban Mujahideen were painfully aware that they were seen as terrorists in their country, but they protested the labeling of their "jihad" as terrorism. In an interview on January 24, 2010, the group's leader Ahmet Manavbaşı stated: "And today you can naturally trust the modern Romans [the United States] again and designate the German Taliban Mujahidin as terrorists. And nonetheless we will never be terrorists. Only if [the prophet] Muhammad (s.) was a terrorist, we are also terrorists. We are terrorists because we do not stand on the side of the occupying power America and its fascist servant Germany."[37]

CLASSICAL INTERNATIONALISM AND AFGHANISTAN

The German Taliban Mujahideen saw Afghanistan as the central battlefield of the fight between Islam and its enemies. This seems to be the main reason they pledged allegiance to the Taliban and even chose "Taliban" as part of their official name. In their declarations, members furthermore claimed to be a part of the "Islamic Emirates Afghanistan." As Ahmet Manavbaşı stated in the January 2010 interview, "Our movement works under the banner of the 'Islamic Emirates Afghanistan' and consists exclusively of German Mujahidin."[38] The use of the plural "Emirates" in the German translation might have been caused by a mistranslation.[39]

Just like the Taliban and al-Qaeda, the German Taliban Mujahideen repeated the well-known argument that foreign invaders had never yet had a chance to gain control of Afghanistan, and so the United States and its allies would also fail in their efforts. Ahmet Manavbaşı explained:

> As one can see, neither the Americans nor any other power could annihilate Communism, the biggest problem of the 20th century. It was the Mujahidin who destroyed the USSR and communism and together with excellent leaders such as Mullah Omar und Mullah Jalaluddin Haqqani affronted the occupying powers and dealt out blows to them already many times in history. We should remember how the British and Russian occupation powers in history on the territory of Khorasan [Afghanistan] had to take very hard punches and therefore had to flee. And exactly in this way the Christian occupiers and their Zionist alliance will have to accept a crushing defeat.[40]

The German Taliban Mujahideen's classical internationalist outlook became clear when Ahmet Manavbaşı declared: "and [we] hope that we will shoulder to shoulder fight against the occupational powers, who find themselves on Islamic territory in the whole world."[41] Although the group's leader did not name any concrete territory besides Afghanistan in this interview, other German Taliban Mujahideen publications name Palestine, Iraq, Somalia, the Caucasus, and Algeria as countries that need to be liberated.[42] Mentioning Algeria—a Muslim country ruled by people who at least claim to be Muslims—among these countries is an inconsistency that apparently did not bother the German Taliban Mujahideen.

UZBEKISTAN AND GERMANY

Algeria is not the only Muslim country that the German Taliban Mujahideen believed should be freed from its dictatorial regime by a jihadist revolution. The group focused special attention on Uzbekistan and its president Islam Karimov and thereby emphasized their continuously strong connection to the IJU even after the new German group had been founded. This anti-Uzbek orientation became obvious in the video *The Call to Truth* in

September 2009, in which Ayyub Almani vehemently criticizes the allegedly close relations between Germany and Uzbekistan: "Your [the German] government will stop at nothing. It even allies itself with the criminal state Uzbekistan, in order to realize its aims. A state on the same level as North Korea and Burma, outlawed for their cruel crimes against humanity." In this sermon, Ayyub Almani mentions the massacre in the Uzbek city of Andijan in the Fergana Valley on May 13, 2005, when Uzbek security forces killed hundreds of antigovernment protesters. Hinting at what he alleges is German collusion, Ayyub Almani relates that shortly after the incident the Schröder government allowed one of the Uzbek officials responsible for the brutal crackdown, then interior minister Zakirjon Almatov, to undergo medical treatment in a clinic in Hanover. "With actions like these," he warns the German government, "you go against your own principles." This was a convincing argument because many ordinary Germans also criticized this collusion with the Uzbek government.

The German Taliban Mujahideen more than once implicitly or explicitly threatened attacks on German troops in Afghanistan. As the group stated in a publication of October 2009, "We promise you that the German troops, which are the protectors of the Zionist Christian Union [i.e., the Christian Democratic Union of Chancellor Merkel], will return one by one in coffins from the occupied territories." The threat became more pronounced: "O you German Crusaders, you have proved your loyalty toward Merkel and the rest of the vermin, and did you obtain a good position as a result of your loyalty, how many heroes do you have in your ranks? Just like the terrorist Crusaders [the United States] were surprised and shocked, the unjust German Crusaders will be surprised and shocked."[43] Although the speaker is not explicit here, it seems obvious that he alludes to the 9/11 attacks. If one takes into account the German Taliban Mujahideen's limited resources and capabilities, this threat is rather exaggerated, although it might reflect the group's and especially its leader Ahmet Manavbaşı's long-term ambitions.

An Incomplete Terrorist Organization

During the nine months of its existence, the German Taliban Mujahideen not only was active on the propaganda front but tried to lay the foundation for an active terrorist organization. Nonetheless, most of what is known about the group's level of training and actual operations must be drawn from its propaganda videos. They offer the overall picture of a small group with limited financial, military, and terrorist capabilities, but with a strong determination to become a serious threat to the United States, Germany, and their allies in Afghanistan.

In the video *In the Name of Allah*, dated April 12, 2010, German Taliban Mujahideen members claim to show an attack by their forces on an Afghan military base in Paktika.[44] Under the heading "An Attack of the German Taliban Mujahideen, with Heavy Weapons, on a Military Base," the video shows fighters shooting a heavy machine gun and launching rockets at an unknown target. The video then shows an abandoned and partly burning camp and a certain "Abu Abdallah Almani" (possibly Danny Reinders) claiming that the camp had been the target of an attack and that the German Taliban Mujahideen had taken it over and killed many Afghan soldiers. Another part of the video presents German Taliban Mujahideen fighters in front of a pile of metal and one of them, Fatih Temelli (a.k.a. Abdalfattah al-Muhajir), claiming that these fragments are the remnants of a helicopter shot down by the group.

The video contains no other references to the presence of Afghan, Uzbek, or other fighting units in the Germans' company. It is nonetheless highly improbable that the German Taliban Mujahideen would be allowed to operate independently in Afghan territory. As a rule, as soon as foreign fighters arrive on Afghan soil, they operate under the command of local Afghan organizations. This rule holds true for much stronger organizations such as al-Qaeda and the IJU, who operate with the Haqqani network. In fact, Ahmet Manavbaşı confirmed the German Taliban Mujahideen's strong military dependency on the Taliban: "Of course we have Mujahideen who have good knowledge of arms and equipment. They are, however, not bound to me but act according to the orders of the Taliban."[45] As a consequence, even if the videos contain footage of actual fighting in Afghanistan, it most likely shows Afghan insurgents who were responsible for the takeover of the alleged army camp and the shooting down of the helicopter. Based on what is known about the German Taliban Mujahideen's numbers, arms capability, and training, it is impossible that its members alone would have been able to capture an army camp and highly unlikely that they would have been able to shoot down a helicopter. These videos are rather evidence of the group's propaganda function.

Nonetheless, the German Taliban Mujahideen recruits apparently received—at least in part—relatively decent military training, if not as sophisticated as their leader Manavbaşı claimed: "Of course we have mujahideen who have good knowledge of arms and equipment. . . . This training is given in a very substantial frame, i.e. lessons of chemical and explosive materials, knowledge of Hadith and Sharia, right up to weapons expertise of all weapons of our time. Furthermore we have knowledge in the realm of espionage and intelligence services or in using computers at our command. The German Taliban Mujahideen are currently a very modern fighting group. A military unit, which is light, effective, and capable of dealing its enemies severe blows."[46]

The videos of the German Taliban Mujahideen do not show any training with explosives but rather focus on training with firearms and light weapons. Nonetheless, other sources confirm that at least some members passed through a more specialized training course on explosives.[47] The training shown in the videos seems rather conventional, with the German recruits learning how to use light weapons such as the AK-47, rocket-propelled grenades, and machine guns. What is striking, though, is that the instructors try to meet military standards by, for example, standing behind each shooter in order to correct and control him. Furthermore, the recruits are required to fire only single shots. Although it is difficult to judge the fighters' quality because the targets and the distances between them and the shooters are not shown, many jihadist videos show less-sophisticated training efforts.

It remains unknown who the instructors in the videos are and whether they are German Taliban Mujahideen members or have been provided by other groups. Of all the known recruits, none of them seems to have undergone any sophisticated military training before going to Afghanistan that would have enabled that person to become a trainer for his comrades, so it can be assumed that the IJU or the Taifetül Mansura or both were responsible for the training.

The most important source in this regard is the training shown in the April 2010 video *In the Name of Allah*. Once again, the shooters fire single shots under their trainers' tight control. All the trainees wear clothes resembling uniforms and appear in formation. More important, though, they are shown training to use not only the usual light weapons customary in Waziristan, but also the Russian Dragunov sniper rifle. In addition, the video shows a German Taliban Mujahideen operation in Afghanistan during which mortars and BM 1 rocket launchers equipped with optical aiming devices are being used against unknown targets. These items rarely appeared on jihadist videos of this quality before this point and are evidence that the German Taliban Mujahideen had access to above-average weapons and possibly training, which was most likely due to their close relations to Uzbek and Chechen fighters, renowned for their military prowess in jihadist circles.

The German Taliban Mujahideen nonetheless did not pose a direct threat to Germany and its troops in Afghanistan. The group never managed to build a durable infrastructure in Germany because most of its supporters left for the battlefield in Pakistan and Afghanistan or were arrested for various reasons. Its bases of operations were in Paktia, Paktika, and Khost, far from the regions in northern Afghanistan where German troops were deployed. There is no evidence of German Taliban Mujahideen fighters taking part in operations in Kabul, where they would have had a chance to target German installations. The Haqqani network apparently did not rely on any Germans (or, for that matter, Uzbeks) to perpetrate attacks in the Afghan capital. Most important, at the time of the emergence of the German Taliban Mujahideen in 2009, the jihadists in the tribal areas were under constant pressure by the United States and Pakistan, with US drones killing substantial numbers of militant leaders and fighters and the Pakistanis aggressively taking on militant groups in some regions. Therefore, Ahmet Manavbaşı's plans to build an effective terrorist organization did not materialize, and the German Taliban Mujahideen never outgrew its original function as a mere propaganda tool.

The End of the German Taliban Mujahideen

The German Taliban Mujahideen's short existence effectively ended when Ahmet Manavbaşı, Eric Breininger, and Danny Reinders were killed in late April 2010. In the following months, the group dissolved and could not keep up even with its propaganda work. This problem was evident in the fact that the German Taliban Mujahideen did not announce Eric

Breininger's death; rather, that news was made public by the Turkish group Taifetül Mansura.[48] Although the Istanbul cell of propagandists continued its work on a limited scale, it could not compensate for the loss of Ahmet Manavbaşı, who had been the driving force in the preceding three years.

The remaining German Taliban Mujahideen fighters in North Waziristan dispersed, some of them leaving Pakistan in the direction of Germany. Thomas Usztics (a.k.a. Abu Hamza al-Majari, b. 1985), a German from Berlin of Hungarian origin who had appeared on German Taliban Mujahideen videos, was arrested in Istanbul in September 2010 and remained in a Turkish jail until May 2012, when he was extradited to Germany.[49] Another German Taliban Mujahidin operative, Fatih Temelli, went from Pakistan to Iran and seems to have tried to negotiate his surrender to the German authorities. When that failed, he traveled to Turkey, where he was arrested in June 2012 and extradited to Germany in July. Some members of the group who returned to Germany were most likely disillusioned with the situation in Pakistan, but German authorities were avowedly worried that these returnees might present a danger to national security.

Other members of the German Taliban Mujahideen decided to stay on in Waziristan, where Germans with unclear organizational affiliations were killed during American drone strikes, which increasingly took its toll on the German group. Bünyamin Erdoğan (b. 1991)—the brother of Emrah Erdoğan, who contacted the German authorities in November 2010 and provided them with information on the Europlot—and some German comrades were killed by an American drone strike in Mir Ali in October 2010. The case gained special attention because Bünyamin was a German citizen, and German media and politicians started asking whether information provided by German security authorities had helped the United States in tracking down the suspects.[50]

At least some of those who stayed on decided to join their mother organization, the IJU, and others asked to be accepted by al-Qaeda and the IMU. Nonetheless, it is not totally clear what happened to the remaining members of the German Taliban Mujahideen. In December 2010, a message was posted on a Turkish Web site declaring that the group continued to exist and that Abdalfattah Almani (Fatih Temelli) was its new emir. The short posting announced the publication of a longer declaration, but the fact that the latter never appeared, however, showed the extent to which the group had weakened.[51] It is therefore very likely that the German Taliban Mujahideen's history had effectively ended in April 2010. This hypothesis was supported by news of Yusuf Ocak's having been arrested in Austria in late May 2011 based on a German international arrest warrant because of membership in a foreign terrorist organization. After April 2010, Ocak, like other Germans, had joined al-Qaeda and was sent back to Europe together with the Austrian Afghan Maqsood Lodin to build new structures for the organization in Germany and Austria with the aim to perpetrate attacks.

Besides the German Taliban Mujahideen's propaganda activities, which left a deep imprint on the German scene, the group's main importance lay in the fact that it highlighted the potential of German jihadism. Combined with increased proselytizing of the German Salafists and intensifying Internet propaganda, the emergence of a German jihadist group became a powerful recruitment tool, attracting dozens of young Germans and making clear that substantial numbers of German jihadists were willing to risk their lives in Afghanistan. Furthermore, Manavbaşı's ambition to build a powerful German organization indicates the danger that one day a more sophisticated and successful German organization may emerge, taking on the fight against the German state at home.

Nonetheless, the German Taliban Mujahideen was too weak to survive under American and Pakistani pressure in North Waziristan, so it could not become a serious threat to Germany or to German forces in Afghanistan. Other organizations began to pose a much more serious danger. Most notably, the IMU began to internationalize its strategies after 2008 and increasingly attracted German volunteers. As a consequence, the organization began to aim at the German presence in northern Afghanistan.

8

"The Worst Enemy of Islam"

The Islamic Movement of Uzbekistan Against Germany

In a statement published on the IMU Web site in March 2009, its then leader Tahir Yoldashev (1968–2009) listed the group's most important enemies: "Rely neither on the organization called the United Nations, which is in fact an organization of Jews, nor on the worst enemy of Islam—the European Union, nor on countries such as the USA, Russia, France, China, and Britain that suck Muslims' blood, nor on the Security Council, nor on traitor and infidel governments that sold their religion, faith, values, peoples and history—Egypt, [word indistinct], Saudi Arabia, and Syria, which are traitor Arab countries."[1]

Yoldashev's list of states as such did not contain any surprises. Jihadist organizations have long identified the heavyweights of world policy as their most important enemies. Al-Qaeda has generally focused on the United States and Great Britain as its junior partner; the North Africans aim at France; the Chechens primarily target Russia; and the Central Asians hold a special grudge against the Russians and Chinese. What was peculiar about the IMU statement was the prominent naming of the European Union (EU) rather than any major world power as "the worst enemy of Islam." This statement was unprecedented and must have puzzled anyone familiar with the EU's less-than-effective foreign and security policies.

Only a month later, however, in April 2009, the IMU published a video featuring German jihadists calling on their comrades in Germany to join the jihad and seek martyrdom on the Afghan battlefield. The video ends with parts of a speech by Tahir Yoldashev in which the IMU leader directly addresses Germany by saying: "The German government is a criminal government that takes part in this war. Their grandfather Hitler killed the Jews, but today their sons stand in the service of the Jews."[2] Singling out the Germans among all European nations for his criticism might be seen as evidence that Yoldashev in fact meant the Germans when he designated the EU "the worst enemy of Islam."

Germany, the European Union, and Uzbekistan

It is highly probable that in this speech Yoldashev aimed at Germany rather than the whole EU because Germany rather than the EU had built close relations with the Uzbek government since 2001. Furthermore, German troops were deployed in the area where the IMU maintained its Afghan headquarters between 1998 and 2001 and from which it had tried to renew operations in Central Asia since 2008. As a result, Germany had become an increasingly important target for Uzbek groups.

After reunification in 1990 and regaining full sovereignty in March 1991, Germany became a more independent actor than it had been previously. This trend accelerated during the years of the government of Chancellor Gerhard Schröder (1998–2005). Outright rejection of the George W. Bush administration's plans to attack Iraq and topple the regime of Saddam Hussein in 2003 were the most visible evidence of the new German assertiveness in foreign affairs. From the early 2000s, this more independent approach made its presence felt in different aspects of foreign policy, although without exception less spectacularly than in the case of Iraq. Germany's strong relations with Uzbekistan were one instance of this trend. Since 2005, the two governments led by Chancellor Angela Merkel have made Germany the European nation with the closest relations to the regime of president Islam Karimov in Tashkent. This relationship has been built mainly out of necessity. In 2003, the first German troops were sent to northern Afghanistan, and in 2006 the majority of the German contingent was stationed there. In order to supply these troops, the German military used Termez Airbase in southern Uzbekistan. Because Berlin never looked for suitable alternatives, it became dependent on Uzbek goodwill and therefore turned an open ear to the Uzbek government. The case of the Sauerland group had also made clear that Uzbek jihadists were targeting Germany because of its presence in Afghanistan, so the German security authorities developed an increased interest in cooperating with their Uzbek counterparts and stepped up contact with them.[3]

This cooperation was problematic insofar as Germany became dependent on one of the most brutal dictatorships in the region and because the relationship prompted Uzbek opposition groups, including the jihadists, to single out Germany as their enemy. Just how brutal the Karimov regime was became obvious to a wider international public in May 2005 when Uzbek armed forces fired on protesters at a demonstration in the town of Andijan in the Fergana Valley, killing several hundred people.[4] The immediate cause of the protests was the trial of a group of some two dozen local businessmen who were accused of being members of the Islamist group Akramiya. Fanned by local grievances because of the dismal economic situation in the region, the protests turned into riots, which security forces brutally suppressed by opening fire on the protesters. The massacre prompted the EU to impose sanctions against the regime in Tashkent in November 2005. The sanctions included an entry ban against twelve leading Uzbek functionaries.[5] The German government was thus torn between its European allies' wish to sanction the Uzbek regime and its own dependency on Tashkent. It did not, therefore, hinder the EU from imposing sanctions, but it did allow interior minister Zakirjon Almatov to be treated at a cancer clinic in Hanover, citing "humanitarian reasons." There were unconfirmed reports, however, that the Uzbek government made threats regarding the German presence in Termez if Almatov were not allowed to enter Germany.[6] Berlin's marked ambivalence did not go unnoticed in Uzbek opposition circles.[7]

In the following years, Germany tried to normalize the EU's relations with Uzbekistan. Most important—and very likely influencing Yoldashev's argument—the EU lifted the visa ban for leading Uzbek politicians in October 2008 at the behest of the German government.[8] Only a few weeks after the ban was lifted, Rustam Inoiatov, the head of the Uzbek secret police and possibly one of the persons responsible for the Andijan massacre, traveled to Germany on an ostensibly private visit.[9]

Moreover, the presence of German troops in Afghanistan seems to have provoked the IMU as well. They increasingly came into the Uzbek jihadists' sights from 2008, when the organization started a new drive toward Central Asia. In order to return to Uzbekistan from its hideouts in the Pakistani tribal areas, the IMU had to pass through northern Afghanistan, most notably the Kunduz area, where German troops were stationed. The Uzbek jihadists had been based in this region until 2001 and had established strong links to local ethnic Uzbeks. In 2008, the IMU began using these ties to rebuild its structures in northern Afghanistan and at the same time began attacking the German troops, especially in Kunduz and Takhar provinces. It was only logical that Tahir Yoldashev and the IMU now singled out the Germans as enemy number one.

The IMU's transformation from an Uzbek Islamonationalist organization into an internationalist one was a long process. In fact, the group went through five distinct phases. In the first phase (until 1992), future IMU leaders Tahir Yoldashev and Juma Namangani (1969–2001) operated as part of the Islamist opposition in the Uzbek Fergana Valley against the regime of President Islam Karimov. In the second phase (1992–1997), the two leaders established the first structures of what became the IMU in 1998. Namangani, a charismatic military leader, operated in Tajikistan, where he and his followers took part in the civil war (1992–1997) on the side of the Islamists. Yoldashev spent these years mainly in Pakistan, building contacts with a wide array of movements and governments in the Middle East and South Asia.

During the third phase (1998–2001), the IMU had its heyday. It began with the official foundation of the group in Afghanistan, where Yoldashev and Namangani allied themselves with the Taliban and provided them with a disciplined and well-trained fighting force. From Afghanistan and Tajikistan, the IMU tried to destabilize Uzbekistan through military raids into the Fergana Valley and by means of the big terrorist attack in Tashkent in February 1999. With the downfall of the Taliban began the fourth phase (2001–2007), at the start of which the IMU withdrew to the Pakistani tribal areas, where it retains bases to this day. The group built strong relations with local Pashtun tribes, and when these tribes increasingly targeted Pakistani forces and formed the Pakistani Taliban Movement (Tehrik-i Taliban Pakistan) in 2007, the IMU began to take part in the tribes' fight against the government in Islamabad. In 2008, a new phase began in which the IMU clearly developed an internationalist agenda, aiming not only at Uzbekistan, the other Central Asian states, and Pakistan, but also increasingly at German forces and their allies in northern Afghanistan as well.

Early Opposition Against the Uzbek State (Until 1992)

The early history of the IMU began during the last years of the Soviet Empire in the Fergana Valley in Uzbekistan. Already in the 1970s and 1980s, the Soviet Union had begun to tolerate the Central Asian Muslims' increased religious activities, which led to the emergence of an Islamist underground movement. With the grip of the central government in Moscow fading in the late 1980s, more and more Islamists took over positions in mosques and private religious schools, and in 1990–1991 activists and preachers openly demanded the establishment of an Islamic state and the introduction of Islamic law as the only legal system.[10] The inhabitants of the Fergana Valley have been known for their piety and religious conservatism for ages, and it was thus no coincidence that they proved to be especially prone to Islamist thinking. As a consequence, this region became the center of Islamist activities in Central Asia from the end of the 1980s, with the cities of Namangan, Andijan, and Margelan serving as the strongholds of the first Islamist organizations, such as Adolat (Justice), Islam Lashkarlari (Soldiers of Islam), and Tauba (Repentance).[11] These groups protested the widespread corruption and social injustice in the newly emerging Uzbek state.

Adolat or Islom Adolat (Islamic Justice), as the group subsequently called itself, became the nucleus of what was later called the Islamic Movement of Uzbekistan. The small outfit was led by Tahir Yoldashev, a young firebrand local preacher, but other future leaders of the organization—including Juma Khojaev, who would later use the name "Namangani"—already played a role.[12] It was formed from small groups of local vigilantes that started patroling certain neighborhoods in Namangan, enforcing Islamist norms of behavior and dress codes, but also trying to establish themselves as an alternative to the security authorities. Due to their reputation for piety in a conservative local society and the widespread corruption and ineptness among government representatives, the young Islamists gained ground. They were supported by local Islamist scholars such as Abduvali Mirzaev (1952–1995) from Andijan, the most prominent teacher of many future IMU leaders.[13] As a result, in early 1992 Islom Adolat and its allies controlled most mosques in Namangan and had assumed greater influence in the religious infrastructure in Andijan, Margelan, and other cities of the Fergana Valley.

As might be expected, the Uzbek state fought back as soon as the regime of Islam Karimov began to consolidate its power after independence from the Soviet Union on August 31, 1991. Karimov had been named the Communist Party's first secretary in Uzbekistan in 1989, allowing him to seize power when the USSR dissolved. In December 1991, he was elected president of independent Uzbekistan. At about the same time, members of Adolat under Yoldashev's leadership attacked and occupied the headquarters of the Communist Party in Namangan because they had been refused a construction permit for a new mosque.[14] The preacher and his followers fiercely criticized the new government, calling for the establishment of an Islamic state and reportedly preparing for an armed uprising. As a result of these activities, the government began to crack down on the Islamist movement in the country in March 1992, banning and dissolving Islamist organizations and arresting their members. Leading personalities such as Yoldashev and Namangani as well as some of their followers managed to flee to neighboring Tajikistan.

Exile in Tajikistan, Afghanistan, and Pakistan (1992–1997)

Most of the young Uzbek Islamists who had to leave their home country found a refuge in Tajikistan, where they linked up with the local Islamic Renaissance Party (Hizbi Nahzati Islomi Tojikiston). In 1992, the party was preparing for violent conflict with the post-Communist government in Dushanbe.

When the war erupted, Tahir Yoldashev first went to Afghanistan and later to Pakistan, living in Peshawar from 1995 to 1998. He spent most of these years traveling to Saudi Arabia, the United Arab Emirates, Turkey, and Iran, laying the organizational and financial basis of the IMU.[15] Pakistan proved to be an ideal base for Yoldashev because since the 1980s young Uzbek students had flocked to the new religious schools established there during the rule of military dictator Zia ul-Haq (1977–1988), which were by and large controlled by the Assembly of the Scholars of Islam (Jamʿiyat-i ʿUlamaʾ-i Islam). In the schools of the Pashtun border areas, the Uzbeks came into contact with those students who later formed the Taliban movement. This contact was most obvious in the case of the assembly's Dar al-Ulum al-Haqqaniya in Akora Khattak close to Peshawar, which from 1989 became one of the most important training centers for the future leaders of the Taliban and the Haqqani network.[16] In the mid-1980s, several hundred of the roughly 3,000 students at this school were from Central Asia, and many of the alumni later joined the IMU.[17] Yoldashev himself established particularly close relations with the influential Assembly of the Scholars of Islam, which is reported to have financed his stay in Peshawar between 1995 and 1998.[18]

Most militant activists seem to have remained in Tajikistan, though, where Juma Namangani took the lead of a group of some two hundred Uzbeks and put them under the command of the United Tajik Opposition (Oppozisjuni muttahidi tojik), which was dominated by the Islamic Renaissance Party.[19] In 1993, Namangani and his fighters established their base in a small village in the Tavildara Valley in eastern Tajikistan. By that time, he had already been joined by fighters from other Central Asian states, most notably Tajiks. In addition, a small contingent of Arab fighters from Afghanistan joined the Uzbek militants, among them the notorious Saudi Samir al-Suwailim (a.k.a. Khattab), who in 1995 became a prominent field commander in Chechnya (on Khattab, see chapters 3 and 4). These Arabs were the Uzbeks' first contact with members of the transnational jihadist scene, and they deeply influenced the IMU's future path.

In the mid-1990s, Tajikistan became an ever more problematic rear base for the Uzbek militants. First, the Tajik Islamists began negotiations with the government that ended with an agreement in 1997; as a result, the Islamic Renaissance Party entered into a coalition government, effectively ending the civil war. Second, Yoldashev und Namangani had established links to the Taliban, but their Tajik allies cooperated closely with the Taliban's fiercest enemy in Afghanistan, the Northern Alliance (United Islamic Front for the Salvation of Afghanistan [Jabha-ye Muttahed-e Islami bara-ye Nejat-e Afghanistan]), led by the legendary Ahmad Shah Massoud (1953–2001), an ethnic Tajik. With the Taliban on the offensive in Afghanistan in 1994, and especially after it took the capital Kabul in September

1996, these competing alliances led to friction between the Uzbeks and their local allies in Tajikistan.

Although the pressure on Namangani quickly mounted, he first opposed giving up the jihad against the Tajik government until local allies convinced him that he had no alternative but to withdraw. Tahir Yoldashev is reported to have traveled to Tajikistan to get Namangani to help him establish the IMU, which was formally announced in the summer of 1998.[20] Namangani thus left Tajikistan for Afghanistan in November 1998, where he set up camp in the northern part of the country, acting as the new organization's military leader. Yoldashev for his part settled in Kabul and Kandahar, becoming the IMU's political head and overall leader.

The immediate causes prompting Yoldashev and Namangani to set up the organization remain unknown. One reason may have been a Taliban offer to host the Uzbeks in neighboring Afghanistan, where the movement had just established control over northern parts of the country, thereby providing the IMU with a launching pad for attacks on Central Asia. Another reason might have been that setting up such an organization was a reaction to increased repression of Islamist activities in Uzbekistan in 1997, which forced more young militants to leave the country and join Yoldashev and Namangani.[21] Yoldashev seems to have mulled over the establishment of a jihadist organization for several years and used every opportunity to strengthen its logistic, financial, and military capabilities. After 1995, most likely in 1997, he sent several groups of young Uzbeks to Chechnya, where they were trained in camps run by the Saudi Arabian field commander Khattab (al-Suwailim), who had arrived in the Caucasus in 1995.[22] Their stay paved the way for deepening relations between Central Asian and Chechen fighters, which shaped the future history of the IMU and especially the IJU. It is very likely that the future IJU leader Najmiddin Jalolov made his first contacts with Turks and Azeris during his training in Chechnya in the second half of the 1990s (see chapter 4).

The IMU had been in the works since 1991, and there is every indication that by 1997 the time was ripe to recalibrate the fight against Islam Karimov's regime. There was, moreover, a very practical reason for starting the new organization: in 1998, plans for the first major terrorist attack in Uzbekistan were in the making, and an established organization was needed to reap the profits of increased public attention for the jihadist cause in Central Asia.

The Islamic Movement of Uzbekistan During Its Heyday (1998–2001)

FIGHTING UZBEKISTAN

On February 16, 1999, four car bombs detonated in the Uzbek capital of Tashkent: close to a nightclub, at the National Bank, at the Interior Ministry, and at the Council of Ministers. Thirteen people died, and more than a hundred were wounded. The attacks in all likelihood were meant to kill President Karimov, who had been scheduled to meet the most important members of the cabinet at the Council of Ministers. The elimination of Karimov and his inner circle was designed to pave the way for an Islamist revolution in the country. The attacks, however, failed to kill the president or to have any effect on the regime's stability.

The IMU did not explicitly claim responsibility for the Tashkent bombings. This silence and widespread distrust of the official version espoused by the Uzbek government have prompted observers to doubt whether the IMU was in fact responsible for the attacks; some have gone so far as to suspect that Uzbek secret services planned the attacks in order to justify their brutal campaign against Islamists in the country.[23] Nonetheless, the absence of a claim of responsibility should not come as a surprise; by February 1999, Yoldashev was staying in Afghanistan, and an open claim of responsibility might have embarrassed his Taliban hosts. Instead, in March 1999 the IMU indirectly indicated that it had organized the attacks by launching a public-relations campaign in which the attacks played a prominent role. In an IMU statement of March 1999, it declared that the Karimov regime's continued oppression of Muslims "may lead to unpleasant events similar to the recent explosions in Tashkent." In that case, the Karimov regime would bear the responsibility.[24] The following month Yoldashev confirmed this statement in an interview with the Iranian radio station Voice of the Islamic Republic of Iran: "The result of the policy of pleasing strangers [the US and Israel] were [*sic*] the powerful explosions which took place on 16th February in Tashkent, which were a logical response to it [Islam Karimov's policy]."[25]

Yoldashev further demanded that Karimov and his government resign from their posts because "otherwise the explosions of 16th February in Tashkent must continue."[26] These hints make it very likely that the IMU was indeed responsible for the bombings, and several jihadist insiders have corroborated this theory. One of the most important supporting voices has been that of the Syrian jihadist Mustafa as-Sitt Mariam Nassar (a.k.a. Abu Musab al-Suri), a prominent strategic thinker who until 2001 kept in close contact with the Taliban and the IMU.[27] In his book *The Call for a Global Islamic Resistance*, Suri confirms that the IMU was indeed responsible for the Tashkent bombings and that the perpetrators had been trained in Chechnya prior to the attacks and had cooperated with local groups.[28]

Fritz Gelowicz, the leader of the Sauerland group, also supported this version of the events, relating in court in 2009 that he was given an introduction to the history of the IMU and IJU by the latter's deputy leader Suhail Buranov, who confirmed that the IMU had been responsible for the attacks and that Jalolov had taken part in them.[29] This confirmation is in line with official Uzbek information that states that Jalolov and another IMU member planted an explosive-laden car in front of the National Bank in Tashkent and later fled to Kazakhstan.[30]

The public-relations campaign that the IMU launched in March 1999 culminated in a declaration of jihad—published on August 25 of the same year—against the regime of Islam Karimov. In the declaration, the organization's religious head explained that the IMU sought primarily to establish an Islamic state that would faithfully apply the sharia based on the Quran and Sunna: "The primary objective for this declaration of Jihad is the establishment of an Islamic state with the application of the Sharia, founded upon the noble Koran and Noble Prophetic Sunna." According to the document, the IMU's further aims were: "The defense of our religion of Islam in our land against those who oppose Islam. The defense of the Muslims in our land against those who humiliate them and spill their blood. The defense of the scholars and Muslim youth who are being assassinated, imprisoned, and tortured in extreme manners—with no rights given them at all. . . . Also to secure the release of the weak and oppressed who number some 5000 in prison, held by the transgressors. . . . And to reopen the thousands of mosques and Islamic schools that have been closed by the evil government."[31]

Most striking is that in this and other statements the IMU showed little inclination toward jihadist internationalism, instead focusing on its priority goal of establishing an Islamic state in Uzbekistan. In spite of nearly two decades in exile in Pakistan and Afghanistan, Tahir Yoldashev never gave up his nationalist inclinations and seems to have been driven in part by a strong personal hatred of Islam Karimov.[32] Yoldashev and the IMU described the Uzbek president as an "atheist," a member of the Soviet ancien régime who continued the Communist oppression of Muslims in a different disguise.[33] IMU members sometimes called Karimov "the son of a Jew," obviously considered a particularly serious insult, and argued that this family heritage was the true cause for the alliance between the Uzbek regime and the Americans and Jews, who allegedly had tried to enslave the peoples of Central Asia.[34]

As a consequence of its Islamonationalist orientation, the IMU made strenuous efforts to remain a force to be reckoned with in its home country. In the summers of 1999 and 2000, IMU fighters from Tajikistan infiltrated southern Kyrgyzstan and Uzbekistan and attacked government installations, especially border posts and police stations, with the goal of destabilizing the two states. The IMU profited from the complicated situation in the southern Fergana Valley, where the Soviet rulers had rearranged the borders in the 1920s, effectively dividing the area between the Uzbek, Tajik, and Kyrgyz republics. With the emergence of nation-states in 1991, local populations—the majority of whom were ethnic Uzbeks—found themselves isolated from related populations in neighboring territories that suddenly belonged to foreign states. The complicated entanglement of state borders, enclaves, and exclaves facilitated the IMU's operations and escalated conflicts between the three states, which blamed their neighbors for the violence and their inability to fence off the jihadist militants.

At the same time, the IMU became more prominent owing to a number of highly publicized kidnapping cases. In August 1999, an IMU unit took four Japanese geologists and their translator hostage in the mountains of southern Kyrgyzstan. After the Japanese government allegedly paid a $5 million ransom, they were released in October of the same year.[35] In the following year, again in August, the IMU kidnapped sixteen mountain climbers, among them four Americans, who were ultimately able to escape.[36] In all of these cases and in the even more numerous cases of Kyrgyz citizens being taken hostage by the jihadists, the IMU seems to have been interested primarily in the ransom paid by the victims, their relatives, or their governments.

ALLIANCE WITH THE TALIBAN

From 1998, the new organization established its headquarters in Afghanistan. Although the IMU first retained a base in Tajikistan, Namangani had to evacuate his force and resettle in Afghanistan in November 1999, where the Taliban welcomed its guests with open arms. Beyond a sense of solidarity with the Central Asian Islamists, the Taliban was driven by concrete motives: the Uzbek regime supported the Afghan Northern Alliance in the person of the ethnic Uzbek warlord Rashid Dostum, one of the fiercest opponents of the Pashtun movement, so it seemed only logical to Mullah Omar and his entourage to host the Uzbek jihadist opposition on Taliban territory.

Furthermore, the Taliban hoped to win support among the ethnic Uzbek population in the Afghan North. Settling in the northern provinces between Faryab to the west and Badakhshan to the east, ethnic Uzbeks numbered about 1.5 million of the approximately 28 million Afghans. In order to win the ethnic Uzbeks over to the Taliban's cause, Yoldashev designed a program in which several hundred Uzbek preachers and students of religious sciences close to the IMU would be trained as missionaries and subsequently sent to the Uzbek-populated areas, where they would spread the IMU–Taliban worldview. Such proselytizing would be followed by a recruitment drive to win over ethnic Uzbeks to fight with the Taliban and subsequently carry the fight to Uzbekistan. Mullah Omar is reported to have invested great hope in this campaign, but it had to be aborted due to the downfall of the Taliban in 2001.[37]

The IMU also became an important military asset for the Taliban. In 1999, when Namangani arrived in northern Afghanistan with several hundred well-trained, experienced, and battle-hardened fighters from Tajikistan, the IMU established bases in the northern provinces close to the Uzbek and Tajik borders, most notably in Balkh, Kunduz, and Takhar, from where they supported the Taliban's war against the Northern Alliance.[38] In its heyday in 2001, the IMU commanded between 2,000 and 3,000 fighters, most of whom took part in the battles between the Taliban and the Northern Alliance.[39] Although Uzbeks dominated the IMU units, they were joined by hundreds of Tajiks, Kyrgyz, Chechens, and even Uighurs from Xinjiang in China.[40] In 2001, Taliban leader Mullah Omar appointed Namangani commander of a large unit of foreign fighters, Brigade 21, which operated in northern Afghanistan and is reported to have recruited not only Central Asians, but also some Pakistanis and Arabs.[41] The unit is said to have consisted of more than 3,000 fighters, and its commander Namangani established himself as the most important non-Afghan military leader in Afghanistan.

Because of his prominence as a military leader and his considerable personal charisma, some sources describe Juma Namangani as the leader of the IMU during these years. This mistake might stem from his own and his Uzbek fighters' military reputation. Namangani is reported to have served as a conscript of the Red Army and to have been stationed with an airborne unit in Afghanistan in 1987. In fact, many first-generation IMU members did undergo the rigorous and often brutal training of the Soviet armed forces and so subsequently built a tradition of professional military training into the IMU, which was further improved through training missions in Chechnya in the second half of the 1990s. Moreover, many IMU volunteers had gained considerable battle experience during the Tajik civil war and subsequent IMU incursions into the Fergana Valley. Thus, from the late 1990s on, the Uzbeks gained the reputation of being extremely well trained, battle hardened, but also exceedingly brutal and cruel fighters even by Afghan standards. Together with some individual Chechen volunteers—who had the reputation of being the elite force of the jihadist movement—the IMU forces commanded by Namangani were apparently the best-trained troops on the Taliban's side.

Although Namangani seems to have enjoyed considerable independence in military affairs, he is reported to have sworn an oath of loyalty to Tahir Yoldashev in late 1999 or 2000, clearly subordinating himself to the IMU leader.[42] During Namangani's lifetime, Yoldashev stood in the military commander's shadow, but reports indicate that he had considerable charisma as well. Some hints as to his impact on his followers might be drawn from the videos that the IMU has released more recently, showing Yoldashev as a rhetorically gifted orator. As reported by a German jihadist who spent some time with the IMU in South Waziristan in 2009 and met the IMU leader, Yoldashev made a deep and sometimes frightening impression on people who met him: "And there was a very aggressive man, when he spoke, in the sense now gave a presentation, he screamed and cried and rolled eyes and the people all cried with him. It was like this, he cried, we cried, he stopped again, we stopped, he laughed, they laughed. That was really, I have really recalled the film from back then these Nazi times, when the Germans really this way, we build streets . . . like a, how do you call that . . . dictator. . . . Because this was really so hard and he was such a hard man."[43]

Yoldashev came from Namangan in the Fergana Valley and began his career as an underground preacher, claiming religious authority in addition to his function as the political leader of the IMU. He is said to have studied with Abduvali Mirzaev, who disappeared in 1995 and who seems to have had a decisive ideological influence on what was to become the IMU. Nonetheless, Yoldashev's charisma clearly exceeded his religious knowledge, which apparently was rudimentary.[44] In general, the Uzbek organizations suffered from a scarcity of qualified religious teachers, most of whom were no match for their better-trained Arab colleagues. Instead, Yoldashev excelled in languages—speaking his native Uzbek, the northern Afghan dialect Dari (i.e., Afghan Persian), good Arabic, some English, and probably Pashto—evidence of the nearly two decades he spent in exile networking with other Islamist personalities and organizations.[45]

Yoldashev is reported to have led the IMU in an authoritarian way, leaving hardly any space for ambitious commanders to make a name for themselves in the organization. The treatment of recruits was extremely tough as well, perhaps mirroring the instructors' background in the Soviet military. German volunteers reported that mistakes during training were severely punished and that they were bullied by the trainers, a claim corroborated by a scene in an IMU video in which a member is flogged in front of an assembly of leaders.[46] The IMU and its leader were known not to tolerate dissent and are reported to have reacted aggressively in several instances in which members tried to distance themselves from the organization. Perhaps the most striking instance of this approach occurred in Kabul sometime before September 2001. According to Noman Benotman, a former leader in the LIFG, when Yoldashev heard that a Central Asian member of the IMU had decided to leave the organization and join al-Qaeda and had already moved to an Arab guesthouse in the Afghan capital, he sent a group of Uzbeks to force the "deserter" at gunpoint to return to the IMU fold. The resulting conflict between al-Qaeda and the IMU could be solved only through intervention by Taliban leader Mullah Omar.[47]

German recruits returning from Pakistan in 2010 and 2011 reported that IMU members trying to leave the organization were killed if they were apprehended. Rami Makanesi explained that "the Uzbeks had a reputation for being really harsh with that kind of stuff. If someone just leaves the group without warning or anything, he is seen as a, what do you call it . . . a traitor, as someone who's an agent or something, and then they would kill him, too."[48]

MILITANCY DEBATES 2001

In spite (or perhaps because) of Yoldashev's authoritarian rule, in 2001 a debate over the group's future direction broke out in the ranks of the IMU. A growing current inside the organization demanded that the IMU's strategy move toward internationalization yet was confronted by a leadership that insisted on fighting the "near enemy" exclusively—the regime of Uzbek president Islam Karimov. As a result, heated debates over the IMU's aims and strategies developed within its ranks.

Early evidence for a growing trend toward internationalization within the IMU appeared in 1997, when Namangani and his followers initially refused to give up their struggle against the Tajik government. Pressure mounted inside the organization to expand the fight from Uzbekistan to the whole of Central Asia, in part due to an enlargement of the IMU's social base, now including an increasing number of non-Uzbek citizens from Tajikistan, Kyrgyzstan, and Kazakhstan. Moreover, by 1992 IMU members had begun to build relations with an increasing number of non-Uzbek jihadists during the fight in Tajikistan, during training in Chechnya and in exile in Afghanistan and Pakistan, bringing them into contact with the ambitions and projects of jihadists outside of Uzbekistan and Central Asia. It seems only logical that as a result of these trends, the internationalists inside the organization gained ground.

In May 2001, reports emerged that Namangani had founded an organization that would replace the IMU, the Islamic Party (or Movement) of Turkestan (Hizb-e Islami Turkestan).[49] It was apparently intended to serve as an umbrella organization for those Central Asian groups that operated under the leadership of Namangani and the IMU in Afghanistan and sought to carry the fight back to Central Asia, including the western Chinese province of Xinjiang.[50] Most commentators interpreted this step as a change in the IMU's name.

At the same time, reports about competing ideological-strategic camps within the IMU emerged.[51] In June 2001, Zubair Ibn Abd al-Rahim, a Saudi

Arabian citizen of Central Asian origin and a religious authority in the IMU leadership, denied the change of name in an interview with Radio Free Europe. He insisted that Islam Karimov's regime in Uzbekistan was still the IMU's main enemy and that the organization did not seek in any way to establish an Islamic state between western China and the Caspian Sea, as Russian, Kazakh, and Pakistani media had reported. According to Ibn Abd al-Rahim, the IMU "had no problems" with Uzbekistan's neighbors.[52] As a matter of fact, the IMU kept its original name in the following years, and only the Central Asian and Russian media used the label "Islamic Party of Turkestan" from time to time. This continued use of the original name might be evidence that the Uzbek nationalists had prevailed in the debates over the organization's overall strategy. Nevertheless, not all IMU members accepted the leadership's insistence on a nationalist strategy, and so these internationalists founded the IJU as a competing organization (for the IJU in detail, see chapter 4).

The Pakistanization of the Islamic Movement of Uzbekistan (2001–2007)

The US campaign in Afghanistan in late 2001 proved to be a catastrophe for the IMU. The IMU lost its military head Juma Namangani as well as several important leaders during US airstrikes targeting the organization's bases in northern Afghanistan. In addition to the loss of a quite well-developed infrastructure, hundreds of the group's fighters died while unsuccessfully resisting the advance of Northern Alliance troops. Under the leadership of Tahir Yoldashev, the remnants of the organization retreated to Pakistan—not, however, without offering pitched resistance in a battle in Shah-e Kot in March 2002, which has become famous as Operation Anaconda in American sources.[53] Shortly afterward, the Central Asians found a refuge in South Waziristan, where they were to remain until 2009, when a Pakistani army offensive forced them to retreat to other regions.

Upon arrival in its refuge in the tribal areas, the IMU came under pressure to give up its Islamonationalist agenda. On the one hand, its local Pashtun allies expected the Central Asians to assist them in their fights in Afghanistan and Pakistan. On the other, the emergence of the IJU presented Yoldashev with a competitor that gained fame in jihadist circles after the attacks in Uzbekistan in 2004. If the IMU leader wanted to safeguard the survival of his organization, he could not ignore these challenges. As a first measure, he decided to join his local allies' fight against the Pakistani state. Nonetheless, he made this decision only after several Pakistani army offensives targeting the Central Asians, so that overthrowing the government in Islamabad became a stated goal for the IMU in 2007, even though in previous years the group had focused mainly on surviving and preparing for a future move to Central Asia. Most important, there is no evidence that the IMU took part in insurgent activities in Afghanistan before 2007–2008 (on IMU activities in Kunduz from 2008, see chapter 9).

The IMU's move against the Pakistani state had two causes. First, in 2004, 2007, and 2009, Pakistani troops and local Pashtun tribes attempted to expel the IMU from its hideouts west of the South Waziristan capital Wana. It was only logical that the Uzbeks not only defend themselves but also subsequently go on the offensive. Second, from 2004 the Pashtun leader Baitullah Mehsud became the most important local ally and protector of the IMU, which was strongly dependent on the protection offered by him and later by his successor, Hakimullah Mehsud. When Baitullah Mehsud and his followers chose to confront the Pakistani army openly in 2007, Tahir Yoldashev was apparently pressured to join his allies in the fight against Islamabad.

By 2004, the Pakistani army started a first offensive in South Waziristan, targeting Pashtun tribes and their foreign allies. The move was reportedly triggered by American threats that the US military would attack the hideouts of al-Qaeda, IMU, and other groups if the Pakistani army itself did not confront them.[54] The army first demanded that the local tribes hand over all non-Pashtun fighters. When the Taliban rejected this demand, the army went on the offensive in March 2004 and concentrated its attack on the areas surrounding Wana. The heaviest fighting seems to have taken place in the villages of Kalosha and Shin Warsak west of the city, where the Uzbeks of the IMU offered pitched resistance. Yoldashev is reported to have been seriously wounded, and there were rumors that he had been killed during the fighting, but he managed to escape with the help of local tribesmen. After some initial successes, the Pakistani military agreed on a truce with local militants under the leadership of Nek Mohammed of the Ahmadzai Wazir, the Pashtun tribe dominating Wana and its surrounds and the IMU's main ally.[55] Whereas the government subsequently argued that the agreement was an attempt to stir up conflicts between the local tribes and foreign fighters, Nek Mohammed celebrated it as a victory. In any case, the IMU infrastructure in the villages west of Wana remained intact, and in spring 2004 the Uzbeks hardened their attitude toward the Pakistani military and began routinely to attack Pakistani government targets.[56]

In June 2004, Nek Mohammed was killed, forcing Yoldashev and the IMU to look for a new protector. They found one in Baitullah Mehsud, who until 2007 had been a relatively obscure militant leader and only later rose to prominence as head of the Pakistani Taliban. He belonged to the (Pashtun) Mehsud tribe, which settles in the central and eastern parts of South Waziristan, but not in its capital Wana. Mehsud was part of a new generation in the Afghan and Pakistani Taliban strongly influenced by al-Qaeda's internationalist ideology, which increasingly adopted terrorist tactics from their foreign guests. When the Pakistani Taliban Movement was founded as an umbrella organization in December 2007, Mehsud was appointed its leader. The Pakistani Taliban come from the Pakistani side of the Afghan–Pakistan border region but are Pashtuns like their namesakes, the Afghan Taliban.

Ever since government forces had stormed the Red Mosque in Islamabad in July 2007, the Pakistani Taliban had increasingly targeted the Pakistani state. In the months before the attack on the mosque, the mosque and the affiliated Quranic school had become a center of protest against the Pakistani government under the leadership of a militant scholar named Abdalaziz Ghazi.[57] During the storming of the complex, at least sixty students were killed, which caused nationwide protests by Islamists and a wave of terrorist attacks starting in December 2007. The Pakistani and US governments stated that Baitullah Mehsud was responsible for the killing of the former Pakistani prime minister Benazir Bhutto in the same month and for numerous other terrorist attacks in Pakistan.[58] An ambitious personality, Mehsud tried to establish himself as a leader of the Pakistani Taliban just like Mullah Omar for the Afghan Taliban and granted shelter to Afghan Taliban, some Arabs, and especially the Central Asians of the IMU.[59] Yoldashev remained in close contact with Mehsud, and the IMU headquarters reportedly moved from the Wana area to Sararogha in Mehsud territory in 2007.

This move was triggered by a series of events in the Wana area in March 2007, when heavy fighting broke out between local Pashtun tribes and the Uzbeks in South Waziristan. In early 2002, Yoldashev and his Uzbeks had been given a hero's welcome by the Ahmadzai Wazir after their fight alongside the Taliban and the courageous resistance they had offered the Americans in Shah-e Kot during Operation Anaconda.[60] In the following years, "Tahir Jan[61] [became] a well-known figure in the region, held in high esteem for his chivalry and love for Islam."[62] This attitude changed after March 2004, however, when the Uzbeks increasingly turned against the Pakistani army and tensions between the IMU and their local hosts mounted.

One important cause of the confrontation seems to have been a shift in the local balance of power. Between 2004 and 2007, the Uzbeks in the Wana region were protected mainly by Maulvi Omar, a leader of the Ahmadzai Wazir and a close ally of Baitullah Mehsud.[63] Shortly before the outbreak of hostilities, however, another Ahmedzai Wazir leader named Maulvi Nazir asserted himself and replaced Maulvi Omar as the leader of the local Taliban supporters in the Wana area. When the IMU supported Maulvi Omar, it became a party to the conflict and seems to have borne the brunt of the fighting, losing between fifty and one hundred fighters.

The conflict between Maulvi Omar and the IMU on one side and Maulvi Nazir—who is reported to have been supported by the Afghan Taliban—on the other was also a conflict over the legitimacy of the fight against the Pakistani state. Maulvi Nazir was the main local ally of Afghan insurgent groups using South Waziristan as a rear base for their fight in their own country and a close affiliate of the Haqqani network.[64] Relying on the Pakistani military to tolerate their presence, the Afghan Taliban rejected taking up the fight against Islamabad, at least until victory was achieved in Afghanistan. They opposed the anti-Pakistani activities of Baitullah Mehsud's local supporters, especially the Uzbeks, who from 2004 had seized every opportunity to attack the Pakistani army and thereby threatened to provoke Pakistani countermeasures. Pakistani press reports in 2007 indicated that the locals differentiated between "good Uzbeks," who, like the Haqqani-affiliated IJU, supported the fight of the insurgents in Afghanistan, and "bad Uzbeks"—namely, the IMU led by Tahir Yoldashev.[65] The events made clear that the IMU's and Mehsud's anti-Pakistani strategy had provoked resistance among many Pashtun tribes in the area.

The labeling of the IMU as "bad Uzbeks" hinted at a radical change in the attitudes of parts of the local population between 2004 and 2007. This change was in part due to the IMU's attacks on the Pakistani army, which provoked a wide array of countermeasures by the authorities, including small-scale military campaigns and an economic blockade of Wana that lasted from May 2004 well into summer 2005.[66] Furthermore, the Uzbeks had gambled away their local hosts' goodwill by not respecting local customs and traditions, where respect for tribal elders is a basic requirement for any guest. According to local sources, the Uzbeks from 2004 started behaving like occupiers by confiscating houses (instead of asking the owners and paying for their stay), setting up a private jail, and harassing and sometimes even killing local tribesmen suspected of cooperating with the Pakistani state.[67] Furthermore, the IMU was reported to have killed an al-Qaeda finance official, evidence of continuing tension between Central Asians and Arabs.[68]

As a consequence, the IMU seems to have suffered heavy losses during the fighting that broke out in March and lasted well into April 2007. After the fighting ended, the Uzbeks had to evacuate some of their former strongholds in the Wana area. In subsequent years, they are reported to have had a base in Sararogha in Mehsud territory in the eastern part of the agency and a strong presence in the mountainous areas of Makin north of Wana and in Ladha, a town between Makin and Wana.[69] By 2007 at the latest, the IMU's anti-Pakistani agenda became a standard feature of its publications. For instance, in early January 2008, the IMU published a video message in which Tahir Yoldashev called for intensifying the "holy war" against the Pakistani military, taking Islamabad, and applying sharia law in Pakistan. He argued that the jihad in Pakistan was a religious duty, as in Afghanistan, and Muslims were obliged to take revenge for the storming of the Red Mosque in Islamabad in 2007.[70] In spite of this martial rhetoric, the IMU did not figure prominently in reports on militant activity in Pakistan in the following years. It did become clear, however, that the Uzbeks were still ready to fight the Pakistani state with all available means. In a video recorded and published in July 2009, the organization claimed responsibility for a suicide attack in Miranshah, the capital of North Waziristan, which killed a Pakistani soldier and seven civilians.[71] Videos featuring German volunteers that expounded on the IMU ideology for a German public and reports by German volunteers who joined the organization in 2009 and 2010 confirm the IMU's continuing strong anti-Pakistani orientation.[72]

With the Pakistani Taliban developing into an increasingly serious threat, the Pakistani military decided to embark on a renewed effort to gain control of the situation in South Waziristan with a major offensive in October 2009. Earlier that year, on August 5, Baitullah Mehsud had been killed by an American drone strike and was succeeded by his relative Hakimullah Mehsud, who kept up his predecessor's anti-Pakistani government strategy as well as his close connections to the IMU. Only some three weeks later, on August 27, Yoldashev also was killed in a drone strike. By early November, the army had taken most Pakistani Taliban and IMU strongholds in Makin, Sararogha, and Ladha. The fighters dispersed—some of them doing so even before the beginning of the offensive—and fled to the north, especially North Waziristan, Orakzai, and Kurram, where they found shelter with other militant groups.[73] Together with the militants, most of the local population fled the fighting as well, up to half a million people leaving their homes.[74] In early 2010, however, the IMU was back in South Waziristan, waging a protracted guerrilla war against Pakistani positions.[75]

Internationalization

Although the IMU's new focus on Pakistan seems to have been a pragmatic response to the situation on the ground in South Waziristan, the organization was simultaneously undergoing a more profound internationalization process that first and foremost affected its ideology, but also its strategy and social base. The roots for the IMU's internationalization had already been laid in the 1990s, when the young organization was based in Tajikistan and Afghanistan. Although the IMU was strongly oriented toward Uzbekistan, it also targeted Kyrgyzstan and Tajikistan. Because most of its members came from the Fergana Valley, in the late 1990s it became more of a Fergana Valley liberation movement, fighting the three ruling regimes there.

IDEOLOGY

The IMU integrated internationalist ideas into its ideology in the 1990s, although there is no evidence that the group intended to put them into practice at that time. In spite of its pronounced Uzbek nationalism, as early as 1998–1999 the organization identified the United States and Israel (or Christians and Jews) as its enemies. In several publications, as noted earlier, the IMU argued that Islam Karimov's regime played stooge to the Americans and Jews. In a declaration published in April 1999, the IMU's Political Committee identified Karimov's goals as follows:

> 1. To give Jews and Christians a chance to secure a predominant economic, political, and military status in Uzbekistan;
> 2. To implement the policy of eliminating Islam in Uzbekistan as part of a general policy being pursued by America and Israel in the world;
> 3. To turn Uzbekistan into a country that is hostile to close neighboring states such as Russia and China, in particular against neighboring Islamic states such as Afghanistan and Iran.

According to the IMU, the United States and Israel had attempted "to enslave the peoples of Uzbekistan and Central Asia, to plunder their wealth by means of building military bases and occupying them by military means."[76] In spite of this familiar anti-Western rhetoric, there is hardly any evidence that the IMU actually intended to strike American and Israeli targets. Rather, until 2007 the IMU leadership was apparently paying lip service to jihadist internationalism, with the possible goal of attracting support from anti-American donors in Persian Gulf countries and Pakistan. This adherence to the rhetoric changed in 2008, when the organization increasingly took part in the Afghan insurgency, most notably in the Kunduz region in the northeastern part of the country. One of its goals seems to have been to regain access to Tajikistan and eventually the Fergana Valley, but the immediate outcome was increasing attacks on the Germans stationed in that part of Afghanistan (these changes in the IMU's strategy are dealt with in detail in chapter 9).

As most observers slowly recognized the IMU buildup in Afghanistan, there was public evidence for an increased internationalization of the IMU's ideology and social base, most notably in Tahir Yoldashev's declarations and the growing number of non–Central Asian fighters in the organization. A first hint of the growing importance of internationalist ideology might be found in an audio statement made by the IMU emir on the fifth anniversary of 9/11. The choice of the date itself might serve as evidence that Yoldashev intended to show solidarity with the overall jihadist movement. In the statement, he said that he expected the United States and its allies to be beaten soon and expressly mentioned the "martyrs" Shamil Basayev, Abu Musab al-Zarqawi, and Sheikh Ahmad Yassin, presenting the Chechen, the Jordanian, and the Palestinian as role models for the jihadist movement. Nonetheless, Yoldashev again made clear that the IMU remained a primarily Uzbek and Central Asian organization. He focused his argument—which he notably presented in Uzbek—on the governments of Uzbekistan, Tajikistan, and Kyrgyzstan and announced forthcoming attacks in all three countries.[77] In this way, he made clear that in spite of internationalist rhetoric he would stick to the IMU's Central Asian agenda.

It was only in 2008 that Yoldashev gave up his resistance to further internationalization of the IMU's ideology and strategy. This capitulation became most obvious in March of the following year, when he used the Gaza war between Israel and the Palestinian Hamas in December 2008 and January 2009 to call for a global jihad against all enemies of Islam. The argument follows the well-known style of Arab theorists of jihadist internationalism in that it explains that the conflict was more than a local war between Palestinians and Israelis, but rather the outgrowth of a perennial fight between Islam and the West: "However, in fact, it is not the local issue between Palestinians and Jews, who have invaded with 30,000 soldiers and 150 tanks, killing Muslims in every possible way—from the air, sea and land, but is the issue of faith and non-belief. It was the major part of the uncompromising eternal fight of the entire Islamic ummah against the Jews." It is in this document that Yoldashev lists the main enemies of Islam, including the EU, quoted at the beginning of this chapter: "Rely neither on the organization called the United Nations, which is in fact an organization of Jews, nor on the worst enemy of Islam—the European Union, nor on countries such as the USA, Russia, France, China, and Britain that suck Muslims' blood, nor on the Security Council, nor on traitor and infidel governments that sold their religion, faith, values, peoples and history—Egypt, [word indistinct], Saudi Arabia and Syria, which are traitor Arab countries." According to Yoldashev, the only solution for Muslims lies in the jihad against all their enemies, anytime and everywhere, including attacks on civilians: "Go back to your glorious history to establish an Islamic caliphate. Kill every citizen of the Zionist country wherever you find them, as well as citizens of the countries and nations taking part in the Crusades."[78]

These declarations sounded more and more like al-Qaeda's internationalist propaganda rather than the old nationalist IMU's arguments against the legitimacy of the regimes in Central Asia. Nevertheless, this ideological rapprochement did not lead to improved relations between the IMU and the Arab organization. There is ample evidence of a continued and deep-seated enmity between them that remained even after Yoldashev's death.[79]

SOCIAL BASE

As noted earlier, that Yoldashev mentioned the EU as "the main enemy of Islam" was probably a reaction to close German relations with the regime in Tashkent. This surprising declaration might also be connected, however, to the increasing influx of German fighters in the Pakistani tribal areas, some of whom joined the IMU. The first Germans reportedly to join the organization were two brothers of Moroccan origin: Monir Chouka (a.k.a. Abu Adam or Abu Yusuf, b. 1982) and Yassin Chouka (a.k.a. Abu Ibrahim, b. 1985) from Bonn, who arrived in Pakistan in summer 2008 and were still there in 2012, becoming two of the best-known faces of German jihadism and important and prolific propagandists.

It has not been established how the two brothers were recruited, except that their radicalization process seems to have been closely connected to the Muhsinin Mosque in Bonn, one of the main centers of German Salafism. In February 2007, they traveled to Yemen, most likely to study Arabic (which they seem not to have mastered while living in Germany) and subsequently joined a jihadist group. In a February 2011 report by Yassin Chouka detailing their travels, he states that their only goal was to join the jihadist caravan and that they did not care whether it was in Somalia, Palestine, Chechnya, Indonesia, or any other country.[80] What or who prompted them to try their luck in Yemen first has not been established, but there are scattered reports about other German Salafists heading to Yemen to study Arabic or join Salafist communities or both.[81]

Yassin Chouka does not specify where the brothers lived during the first months of their one-year stay in Yemen, but he notes that after some months they joined the jihadist group al-Murabitun, which was closely affiliated with al-Qaeda and active in the Hadramaut region in the southeastern part of the country. He further boasts that they met with the notorious American Yemeni preacher Anwar al-Aulaqi, who was hiding in the

Shabwa Province in southern Yemen until he was killed by an American drone strike in September 2011.[82] The only reason Chouka gives for the brothers' move to Pakistan is that one of Aulaqi's supporters allegedly told them that Yemen was not a safe country for foreign fighters and that they had a good chance of reaching Afghanistan instead. Why their comrade deemed the Pakistani hideouts of al-Qaeda and the IMU a safer place than Yemen will remain his secret, but the brothers followed his advice and traveled to Pakistan.

No itinerary is described in the document, but it might be assumed that the Choukas traveled via Iran to Pakistan. Only three days before their arrival—that is, probably shortly before or after crossing the Pakistani border—the two were informed that the IMU was organizing their journey and were given a short introduction to the group's ideology and history. Yassin Chouka claims that they had not been familiar with the organization and that their Yemeni comrades had not informed them that they would eventually end up with an Uzbek group. Their human trafficker belonged to the IMU but explicitly gave the two Germans the freedom to choose to join the IMU or any other group they wished, stressing that the organization brought volunteers to Pakistan in the service of the community of believers, not exclusively for its own good.[83] The news seems to have unsettled the two brothers, who debated the issue and came to the conclusion that God wanted to test their faith. As Yassin Chouka reports,

> Just before we reached our destination, we felt that Allah wanted to put our intentions to the test, whether we would now be picky or not. For it was we who had always asked Allah to lead us to the Mujahideen, no matter where and of which origin they would be. It was we who had been begging and pushing in our prayers for Allah to lead us to the Mujahideen, promising that we were ready to carry out any duties for them. Peeling potatoes, doing their laundry, anything, and the main thing was to belong to the Mujahideen, no matter where. And now we felt that Allah also wanted to put this promise to the test. Now that we had almost made it, we would not breach our vows. We had never heard anything about the IMU; nevertheless we saw, due to the films they showed us, and the little information that we were given, that it was one of the oldest and most well-recognized jihadist movements under the official Baya [oath of allegiance] of [the Taliban leader] Mullah

> Muhammad Omar. Although we could choose freely and in our hearts there was an inclination toward joining the brothers of al-Qaeda who were familiar to us, we feared that Allah would not pave the rest of the way for us if we chose anything other than "La ilaha illa ALLAH."[84] For we did not set out to meet Osama or to be able to say "I belong to Osama's al-Qaeda." And neither did we set out to join an Arabic or German Jamaa [group]. Our motivation to set out was to make our contribution to the purpose of the Ummah [community of believers] and to fight so that Allah's word should become supreme. Therefore, the reason for our expedition was "La ilaha illa ALLAH Muhammadan rassoulu Allah."[85] And thus it was the fear of the wrong intention that led us to the decision to fight under the IMU, which also serves the Ummah and fights for "La ilaha illa ALLAH."[86]

Although Yassin Chouka's short report cannot be trusted in every detail, it is unlikely that the brothers would admit their own lack of orientation and knowledge of jihadist organizations if that had not been the case. Thus, it seems as if the Chouka brothers—like their predecessors in the Sauerland group—joined their Uzbek organization by chance. Most German jihadists apparently did not care that much about which jihadist group they joined upon arrival in Waziristan.[87] Furthermore, it is striking that the Chouka brothers explicitly confessed that they would have rather joined al-Qaeda than an Uzbek organization about which they knew nothing. In general, in jihadist circles Arabs are expected to join al-Qaeda, and Central Asians, Caucasians, and Turks are considered more likely IMU and IJU recruits. Nonetheless, a German jihadist who first joined the IMU and then al-Qaeda in Waziristan in 2009 and 2010 reported that the Chouka brothers were highly regarded in the tribal areas because they remained with the IMU in spite of their Arab background.[88]

Although Yassin Chouka reportedly became a highly skilled mortar man during his years with the IMU and built himself a reputation as a dedicated fighter, the IMU saw the Chouka brothers primarily as a public-relations asset.[89] Beginning in January 2009, the two appeared in more than a dozen IMU videos, calling on their comrades in Germany to join the jihad in Pakistan. This move was part of a radically modernized public appearance for the IMU, which until 2007–2008 had relied on an extremely old-fashioned way of distributing its propaganda materials—simply sending its written declarations to audio or print media in Commonwealth of Independent States countries, Pakistan, or Iran. Audio or video messages by Tahir Yoldashev were extremely rare, and the Internet had hardly played a role in IMU propaganda. This approach changed during 2008, when the IMU substantially modernized and expanded its public-relations activities, mainly by publishing video messages and posting them on its own Uzbek-language Web site Furqon (www.furqon.com).

Like other major jihadist organizations, the IMU established a media office called Jundullah (God's Soldiers), which produced the videos featuring the Chouka brothers and other German volunteers. A former German comrade reported that Mounir Chouka worked in the Jundullah media office, which until late 2009 was located in Makin.[90] The Jundullah logo contains the yellow inscription of its name in Arabic, on which is posted a black flag with the Muslim confession of faith, "There is no God but God and Muhammad is His prophet," written on it.

The Chouka videos are first and foremost recruitment tools to win over Germans for the IMU's fight in Pakistan and to convince them of the virtues of jihad and martyrdom. Most important in this regard is the third video *Victory or Shahada (Martyrdom)*, which appeared in April 2009 and in which Yassin Chouka states that the jihadists are fighting a "fight without defeat" because the warrior of the faith either experiences the victory of Islam or dies a martyr and is recompensed with immediate entry into paradise.[91] Furthermore, the video makers tried to depict the IMU as an increasingly multinational organization and part of a larger movement operating from Pakistan. The video *Soldiers of God* from March 2009 shows comrades who are said to hail from Uzbekistan, Tajikistan, Xinjiang, and Russia.[92] Half a year later, in a video dated September 2009, *Glad Tidings from Afghanistan*, the filmmakers explain the history of the IMU as an organization founded by Uzbeks but consisting of ten different nationalities in 2009 and being part of a movement of more than twenty jihadist groups fighting in the Afghan–Pakistani border area, submitting to the command of Mullah Omar.[93]

Perhaps most important, the IMU managed to attract an increasing number of young Germans to its camps in South Waziristan, as is evident in videos in which three Germans—Shahab Dashti (a.k.a. Abu Askar, 1983–2010), Jawad Sediqi (a.k.a. Abu Safiya, d. 2009), and someone with the alias "Abu Abdallah"—appeared in September 2009.[94] Dashti became widely known in Germany because he is shown with a ridiculously oversize knife on one of the IMU videos.

Dashti was a member of the Hamburg group of volunteers who left Germany in March 2009, most of whom joined the Uzbek organization upon arrival in Pakistan. Altogether, about a dozen recruits from Germany joined the IMU.[95] Although in 2009 and 2010 it seemed as if Germans began to form a growing group within the IMU, it soon turned out that most recruits quickly decided to leave again, the Chouka brothers remaining the only permanent German members of the organization.

In some cases (Rami Makanesi, Naamen Meziche), language problems played a role in their decision to leave the IMU, especially for the Arab-origin Germans, most of whom soon decided to join al-Qaeda instead of an Uzbek organization. At least one of the German recruits (Ahmad Sidiqi) preferred to leave the IMU because of the harsh training methods and the allegedly brutal maltreatment of recruits. Lack of finances and the resulting harsh living conditions for IMU members affected others' decision to leave the IMU. As a matter of fact, all available sources agree that the IMU was short of funds and that al-Qaeda was offering its members and their families far more financial support and social services than the Uzbek organization. For instance, Ahmad Sidiqi reported that in 2009 and 2010 al-Qaeda had much more money at its disposal than the IMU and provided fighters with families approximately 8,000 rupees—compared to the less than 2,000 rupees that the IMU allegedly paid its followers. As a result, living conditions for the al-Qaeda members are reported to have been far better, with better and more food (including meat) at their disposal and relatively decent housing provided for the volunteers' families.[96] The German recruits also mentioned that the men in the IMU were isolated from their wives, which some of the fighters reportedly regarded as an additional hardship.[97]

Perhaps as a result of the difficulty of keeping German volunteers in the IMU's ranks, the Chouka brothers intensified their propaganda efforts and radicalized their rhetoric—now threatening attacks in Germany. In a video tape entitled *Evil Fatherland*, dated December 2011, Monir Chouka announces terrorist attacks in Germany, stating that "the Jihad in Germany is only a matter of time." He argues that it was not acceptable that Muslims die as a result of German policies while peace reigned in Germany. Even a

German withdrawal from Afghanistan would not keep the IMU from taking revenge, and the jihadists' advance would be halted only when they ruled the whole world.[98] Yassin Chouka added to the threats in a video entitled *Yes, We Are Terrorists*, which appeared on the Internet in March 2012 and in which he calls on Muslims in Germany to follow Arid Uka (see the prologue) and other "lone wolfs" and perpetrate attacks on trains, shopping centers, restaurants, and discotheques in Germany even without training by a larger organization.[99]

New Recruitment Pools?

As a consequence of recruited Germans' unwillingness to bear the considerable hardships connected to being an IMU member, the organization has not yet been able to attract a significant following of Germans for longer periods of time. Besides the Chouka brothers, no one from Germany seems to have remained with the IMU for more than a few months. Nevertheless, the organization might have tapped into an important recruitment pool in Germany: ethnic Turks and former members of the defunct Kaplan organization.

For years, the IMU had commanded a small logistics network in Europe that was dominated by Turks. This network became known when members of a group in eastern France and southwestern Germany were arrested in May 2008. Under the leadership of the Dutch citizen Irfan Demirtaş (b. 1959), the group had funneled substantial amounts of money—amounting to hundreds of thousands of Euro—via Turkey to the IMU in Pakistan.[100] In addition, in late February 2011 two members (from Cologne and Gelsenkirchen in western Germany) of a logistics group closely related to Demirtaş were arrested. One of the group's members, the German Turk Turgay Çibir (b. 1982), later pleaded guilty to having supported the IMU with 39,000 euro and was convicted to three years and nine months in jail. His younger brother, the German Turk Ömer Çibir (b. 1986), returned to Germany from a stay with the IMU in Pakistan from September 2009 to May 2010, where he had been injured in battle. After his wounded leg was treated in Turkey, his father drove him all the way to Germany by car. Most important, however, Ömer, his brother Turgay, and their father, Hasan, just like Irfan Demirtaş, were members of the outlawed Caliphate State (Hilafet Devleti) organization, a pioneer of militant Islamism in Germany, and—together with more than half a dozen like-minded friends—had financially supported the IMU.[101]

The Caliphate State was founded in Cologne by the late Cemalettin Kaplan (d. 1995)—nicknamed the "Cologne Khomeini" by the German media—who sought to found an Islamic state in Turkey and establish a caliphate. During its heyday in the late 1980s, the organization had some 7,000 members but could not keep this level after the death of its founder. In 1995, Kaplan's son Metin (b. 1952) took over but lacked his father's charisma, intelligence, and talent, so the organization slowly disintegrated. In 2000, Metin Kaplan was sentenced to four years in jail because he had called for the murder of a rival within the organization, which was then carried out by his followers. In December 2001, the German government banned the Caliphate State. In 2004, after having served his jail term, Metin Kaplan was extradited to Turkey because of his alleged involvement in a planned terrorist attack on the Atatürk mausoleum in Ankara in 1998.[102] The remnants of the organization survived but kept a very low profile in the following years under pressure from German security authorities.

Due to the closeness of the Caliphate State's ideology to jihadist thinking, some observers expect the Kaplan supporters' scene to become an important recruitment pool for years.[103] In fact, according to the former IMU representative in Turkey, Zayniddin Askarov, in the 1990s the IMU received regular support from the Kaplan group. During an interrogation with the German Federal Police in 2000, Askarov also stated that he visited Kaplan's headquarters in Cologne at least once.[104] This visit was reciprocated by a delegation of the Kaplan movement in winter 1996–1997, when a group led by the Çibir brothers' father, Hasan (b. 1950)—a prominent member in Caliphate State—visited Afghanistan, meeting Osama Bin Laden and staying in the IMU's Kabul headquarters for five days.[105] If the IMU has managed to maintain these networks currently or formerly connected with the Caliphate State organization, the scope of the problem for Germany might grow substantially.

Although IMU recruitment among German Turks is quite a long-term concern, its internationalization drive first and foremost affected the German presence in Afghanistan. In 2007, there were the first indications of an IMU buildup in the Kunduz region in northeastern Afghanistan, and in 2008 it became increasingly clear that the Uzbeks had begun to take part in the escalating insurgency in the German area of operations. With the rising number of German recruits in the IMU, it became more and more likely that at one point German jihadists would fight German troops in Afghanistan. This nightmare, shared by many a security official, became true in spring 2011.

9

Germans in the Taliban Stalingrad

Fighting the Kunduz Insurgency

In early June 2011, reports emerged that a German jihadist had died in the German area of operations in the Kunduz region in northeastern Afghanistan. A young Peshawar-born Afghan named Abdullah Hafizi (a.k.a. Miqdad) had just left his German hometown Essen in November 2010; he traveled to Pakistan undetected and joined the IMU, which quickly deployed him to the Afghan Northeast. On March 20, 2011, he was killed by US Special Forces in an operation in Baghlan Province south of Kunduz. The Americans were looking for a local IMU commander, when they discovered insurgents in an agricultural field, who started shooting and tried to escape. Hafizi was killed in the shootout.[1]

Hafizi was reportedly called the "Afghan Lightning (der afghanische Blitz)" by his comrades in Germany because after he completed his training with the IMU in January 2011, he was quickly deployed to northern Afghanistan at his request. In an IMU video produced in May, Yassin Chouka explained: "Our brother Miqdad arrived in Waziristan only a short while ago, and he said to us, 'Please send me to Kunduz quickly because I am dying to kill Germans.' Only a short while ago he lived in Germany and had to stand back and watch the Germans' crimes. But when Allah taala [God the sublime] paved his way and bestowed upon him the honor of carrying a weapon, he did not hesitate." Chouka continued, holding the German government responsible for Hafizi's desire to join the fight in Afghanistan: "The number of deaths in Afghanistan is a number that is robbing us of our sleep. And the Germans have taken a leading position in this huge crime. So no one should be surprised when the Afghan Miqdad says, I am dying to kill Germans."[2]

The news especially worried the German authorities because although they had known Hafizi, they considered him to be a marginal figure in the jihadist scene in Essen and therefore only learned of his departure after the video announcing his death appeared. Perhaps even more important, Hafizi's death at the hands of the German allies prevented a public-relations disaster for the German government, which was under pressure from a public increasingly hostile to the deployment of German troops in Afghanistan. A German jihadist volunteer fighting German troops or possibly perpetrating a terrorist attack on them would help to invalidate the often heard official dictum that "Germany defends its homeland security at the Hindu Kush" and would counter the argument that the presence in Afghanistan was an important part of German counterterrorism. But it also would strengthen the case of those who argued that the very presence of the German military serves as a powerful recruitment tool for jihadist organizations and prompts potential terrorists to travel to Pakistan and Afghanistan—aggravating the threat rather than reducing it. In general, the official point of view did not enjoy much public support in 2011 and 2012. According to opinion polls, about 54 percent of the German population rejected the presence of German troops in Afghanistan in 2010, putting pressure on the government to end the campaign or at least to reduce the German footprint there.[3]

As a consequence, any occurrence drawing the German public's attention to the situation in Afghanistan met with nervous reactions in Berlin in 2011. Beginning in 2007, the German troops were confronted with an escalating insurgency but—due to extremely restrictive rules of engagement and a serious lack of equipment, especially helicopters—were not able to adequately react and follow the American lead when the latter began to implement a counterinsurgency strategy in 2009 and 2010. Instead, the German government's refusal to send additional troops to northern Afghanistan and to adopt the new American strategy prompted the US military to send an extra 1,400 troops to the Kunduz region in order to fight the insurgents there in early 2010. The German troops were thereby reduced to a supporting role while their American comrades had to take on the insurgents—including Abdullah Hafizi and his Uzbek friends. Many observers now asked why Germany had sent troops to Afghanistan in the first place if it was not willing to fight an escalating insurgency.[4] The fact is that the German presence in the Kunduz region was based on a fatal miscalculation borne out of a lack of awareness of the area's recent history.

"Unconditional Solidarity": The Germans in Afghanistan

When the German government sent its troops to northern Afghanistan in October 2003, it had done so because this area was calmer than most other parts of the country, and Berlin had no desire to get involved in actual combat, least of all a counterinsurgency operation. In fact, sending troops to Afghanistan had already brought the government of Chancellor Gerhard Schröder (1998–2005) to the brink of collapse in 2001. This situation was due mainly to the peculiarities of German history before and after the reunification of the divided country in 1990, with a public immensely skeptical concerning the country's involvement in military conflicts and the stationing of German troops abroad. Because of still strong memories of World War II, when the Wehrmacht and the SS conquered major parts of Europe and North Africa, killed millions, and destroyed large swathes of territories, the idea of sending German troops abroad again was unbearable to many citizens, especially but not only among the left of center on the political spectrum.

Nonetheless, after attaining full sovereignty in March 1991, subsequent German governments assumed greater international responsibility by deploying German army troops in Africa (Somalia 1993 and Congo 2006) and in the Balkans (Croatia and Bosnia 1996 and Kosovo 1999) as well as navy units off the Lebanese coast (2006) to stabilize the environment and provide humanitarian help. These experiences created the paradigm of a German military deploying its forces in supervisory roles based on a strict impartiality to the conflict in question, which also heavily influenced the German campaign in Afghanistan.[5]

The only major exception to this rule was the Kosovo war in 1999, when the North Atlantic Treaty Organization (NATO) evicted Serbian forces involved in ethnic cleansing of local Kosovo Albanians. The government's decision to have the German air force take part in the campaign met with major resistance even inside the ruling Red–Green coalition of Social Democrats and Greens under Chancellor Gerhard Schröder, for some weeks threatening the young coalition with its instant demise. Ever since, the question of stationing German troops abroad—even more so of German involvement in military conflicts—remained subject to controversial and heated debates, which every government would try to avoid if possible.

This was the situation in Germany when the events of September 11 prompted Chancellor Schröder to promise the United States "unconditional solidarity" in dealing with the threat posed by al-Qaeda. After the beginning of the Afghanistan campaign, it quickly became obvious that this solidarity would mean sending troops to Afghanistan to help stabilize the country after the Taliban's downfall. Again, just as in 1999, Schröder and his foreign minister Joschka Fischer linked their political future to the decision regarding deployment of German troops in Afghanistan. When the German Bundestag voted on the Afghanistan mandate on November 16, 2001, Schröder simultaneously called for a vote of confidence. Although this call effectively forced most of his opponents in the ruling coalition to vote for the mandate, his government would have collapsed if the mandate had failed.[6]

These difficulties in convincing the German body politic and the public of the need to send troops to Afghanistan in support of US efforts provided the framework for Germany's engagement during the next eleven years. The government and the military were totally unprepared for the tasks with which they would be confronted at the Hindu Kush. It was telling that the first German troops arrived late in Kabul in early 2002 because of a lack of transport planes and only after the Netherlands air force had provided assistance in the form of C-130 Hercules aircraft.[7]

The German troops were initially stationed only in the Kabul region, but this status changed when the ISAF area of operations was extended to the provinces in 2003, and the Germans chose the northern part of Afghanistan. Here, they took over responsibility for the Kunduz, Takhar, und Badakhshan provinces in increments, hoping that the conflict would not reach them in this seemingly remote corner of the country. In late October 2003, Germany established a Provincial Reconstruction Team (PRT) in Kunduz and in the beginning provided about 250 soldiers for protection. The PRTs were designed to coordinate civilian and military efforts in its area of responsibility. About a year later, in September 2004, a branch of the Kunduz PRT was built in Faizabad, the capital of the Badakhshan Province, which was later to become an independent PRT. In October 2004, establishment of the Regional Command North was completed and put under German command, with its headquarters first in Kunduz and then later relocated in 2006 to Mazar-e Sharif, the biggest city of the Afghan North, which subsequently hosted most of the German troops. Mazar-e Sharif and its surrounding Balkh Province belonged to the Swedish area of operations, and the Germans focused on Kunduz, Takhar, and Badakhshan.

The Germans wanted to be given these provinces because they had been rather peaceful since the fall of the Taliban, and the government and military leadership believed that the dangers facing the German troops in northeastern Afghanistan would thus be calculable. The German press made a habit out of using the phrase "Bad Kunduz" (Kunduz Spa) when writing about the German presence in northeastern Afghanistan.[8] Until spring 2007, German military intelligence personnel deployed to the region were briefed that there were no Taliban in Kunduz. A Bundeswehr handbook introducing soldiers to the situation in Kunduz from April 2007 indicated that "the Kunduz province is one of the former centers of the anti-Taliban-movement. Therefore, the Taliban receive relatively little support from the population. This and other factors only enable the Taliban to sporadically become active."[9]

As it would turn out some weeks later, this statement was utterly wrong, but most of the German troops stationed in Kunduz shared the feeling of security. An officer recalled the atmosphere in the German camp in Kunduz in spring 2007:

> We still had this "Bad Kunduz" feeling, and we thought that the Afghans loved us. There was a gardener in the camp who took care of the roses, and our worst enemies were the voles because they served as host animals for the sand flies, which in turn transmitted skin leishmaniasis. As a consequence, we were busy digging trenches and filling them with concrete, so the voles couldn't move anymore. Even the perimeter wall surrounding the camp in Kunduz was not designed to deter the Taliban but was built in order to keep out these flies who can't fly higher than a foot and seven inches or so.[10]

It would be only a matter of months, however, before the insurgency escalated dramatically in the Kunduz region in autumn 2007, and it turned out that neither the German government nor its military leadership had read the writing on the wall. This unpreparedness was due mainly to a serious lack of knowledge about the history and politics of Afghanistan and a serious lack of intelligence about actual trends in the provinces where the Germans were operating.

The Taliban's Stalingrad

When choosing the Kunduz region as their area of operations, German policymakers and their military counselors had not paid attention to the province's recent history, especially the dramatic events before, during, and after the battle of Kunduz in November 2001. This confrontation pitted Northern Alliance forces and their American allies against the Taliban and their Central Asian allies of the IMU-controlled Brigade 21. The latter suffered a humiliating defeat, "experiencing their Stalingrad," as a German military officer formerly stationed in Kunduz described it, which left deep scars in the collective psyche of the Pashtun fighters and their allies.[11] From 2006, the desire to take revenge for the defeat in 2001 seems to have played a role in the Taliban leadership's decision to open a front in Kunduz.

When the Taliban had conquered most of Afghanistan in the mid-1990s, some of the northern provinces managed to avoid capture, mainly because the predominantly Pashtun Taliban were unable to convince the local Tajiks, Uzbeks, and Turkmen that it constituted a viable alternative to the Northern Alliance led by Ahmad Shah Massoud. With a population of some 800,000 (in 2009), Kunduz Province was an exception insofar as a sizeable Pashtun minority—between 30 and 40 percent—lived there among an ethnically divided population consisting of Tajiks (around 25 percent), Uzbeks (15–25 percent), Turks, and even some Arabs.[12] In the context of large irrigation schemes, Pashtuns from southern Afghanistan had settled on arable land in the province between the 1880s and the 1930s. Resettlement and irrigation had made the province the country's breadbasket but created a heritage of conflicts over land between the settlers and the indigenous population. When the Taliban advanced in northern Afghanistan, it was able to take advantage of these conflicts and in 1997 captured the capital of the province, a city of some 250,000, with the help of local Pashtun commanders who switched allegiances and, with militias, joined the Taliban.[13] At the same time, however, the Taliban was suffering major defeats in northern Afghanistan. For about a year, Kunduz was the only urban center over which the Taliban maintained control. The city was surrounded by Northern Alliance troops for about sixteen months and at times had to be provisioned by the Taliban via airlift. Only the support of the local Pashtuns, who had helped the Taliban to establish Kunduz as a bridgehead from which they conquered broad portions of northern Afghanistan, saved the Taliban from defeat.

The traumatic events of 2001 seemed to carry even greater importance for the Taliban. In November 2001, the Taliban was cornered in its last two urban strongholds in Afghanistan, Kandahar in the south and Kunduz in the north. In the latter city, in what was the bloodiest battle of the Afghan war, the Taliban, even though assisted by several thousand Pakistani, Central Asian, and Arab fighters, was surrounded by Northern Alliance troops, who were supported by US warplanes bombarding Taliban positions in and around the city. The Pakistani military, reportedly in order to avoid embarrassing revelations about the presence of Interservices Intelligence officials on the side of the Taliban and their Pakistani supporters, struck a deal with the United States that allowed Islamabad to evacuate its (military) citizens. The operation subsequently became known as the "airlift of evil" because the Pakistani air force saved up to a thousand fighters and thereby substantially more people than originally agreed upon—not only Pakistanis, but also Taliban and IMU members.[14] Other fighters managed to bribe Northern Alliance personnel and fled overland to Pakistan. The remaining garrison of about 3,600 men surrendered, and they were arrested by Tajik and Uzbek forces.

Troops commanded by the Northern Alliance Uzbek warlord Rashid Dostum initially transported the prisoners to a fortress outside Mazar-e Sharif in northwestern Afghanistan, where they staged a bloody rebellion against their captors. After the revolt had been put down, the surviving Taliban and some foreign fighters were packed into shipping containers and in what was later called "the convoy of death" driven to a jail in Dostum's home town, Shiberghan. On the way, most of the prisoners died of suffocation and were buried in mass graves in the desert.[15]

These events left deep scars in the collective psyche of the Taliban and the IMU, and it should have been clear that these organizations would return to northern Afghanistan as soon as the insurgency gained momentum. It was to be expected especially because prominent Taliban military personnel—including Mullah Dadullah, a commander with close relations to foreign fighters who was killed in May 2007; Mullah Baradar, the military head of the Taliban at the time of his capture in February 2010; and Baradar's successor in this post, the former Guantánamo inmate Abdulqayyum Zakir—had participated in the fighting in Kunduz in 2001 and had never lost sight of the city.[16] It is no coincidence that Mullah Baradar was one of the commanders who bore the greatest responsibility for the escalation of the insurgency in northeastern Afghanistan that started in 2007. The Germans were utterly unaware of the importance of Kunduz for the Taliban. A former German military officer stationed in Kunduz remembered when the insurgency first made itself felt in the spring of 2007: "The Bundeswehr had no clue about the recent history of the place. We first heard about the 'convoy of death' in 2007, and the 'airlift of evil' was unknown to us. Some informants in Takhar were the first to tell us about the events. This is when we realized that 'Bad Kunduz' never existed."[17]

There was another aspect of recent history that the German government and military leaders had not paid attention to when they demanded that their troops be sent to the Northeast. The downfall of the Taliban and the massacre in Shiberghan had been followed by a wave of ethnic persecution in the Kunduz area, whence at least 20,000 Pashtuns were evicted to the south. Those Pashtuns remaining in the province were politically marginalized, thus offering the insurgents a large recruitment pool.[18]

In part as a consequence of these developments, the North has more insurgent factions with vested interests than any other region in Afghanistan. The Taliban wanted to take revenge for the catastrophic defeat it suffered here in 2001 and make use of the strong support base among disgruntled local Pashtuns. The Islamic Party (Hezb-e Islami) of warlord Gulbuddin Hekmatyar also has strong ties to the local population because he hails from the insurgent stronghold Imamsahib in the northern region of this province and because the party had been one of the most popular organizations among the Pashtun before the ascent of the Taliban in the 1990s. The IMU had also established a well-developed infrastructure in Kunduz during its stay there until 2001. When it returned to the region in 2007, it profited from close contacts to the local ethnic Uzbeks that had not been severed in the years of the group's Pakistani exile. And even the Haqqani network entertained relations with local Pashtuns from the Zadran tribe, to which its leader Jalaluddin Haqqani belongs.[19]

If the German government and military leaders had informed themselves about the recent past and the province's ethnic and social makeup, they could have prepared for the storm they would face starting in 2008. But they obviously did not, and so both were unprepared when confronted with an escalating insurgency in 2007.

Establishing the Insurgency in 2007

In 2006, the insurgency erupted full force in Afghanistan's southern and eastern provinces. Through that year and into 2007, the Taliban—led by the so-called Quetta Shura, the Haqqani network, and the Islamic Party of Gulbuddin Hekmatyar—managed to solidify its structures in these groups' respective areas of operation and succeeded in causing ever greater problems for Afghan security forces and ISAF troops. This success created the necessary conditions for expanding the insurgency to the Afghan North, which until then had been comparatively quiet, but, with a one- to two-year delay, ended up equaling the tactical and technical level of operations in the South. In contrast with the rest of the country, where the Taliban, the Islamic Party, and the Haqqani network dominated, the strongest groups in the Northeast were the Taliban, the Islamic Party, and the Uzbek IMU, who were able to fall back on structures and networks that had already existed for them prior to the downfall of the Islamic Emirate of Afghanistan in 2001. Most important, the potential for recruitment proved to be considerably higher in the Kunduz region (i.e., Kunduz Province as well as parts of the neighboring Takhar and Baghlan provinces) than in other regions in the North.

As a consequence, starting in 2007 the Kunduz region quickly became the most important battleground in northern Afghanistan. From 2006 until well into 2007, local Taliban and Islamic Party elements reorganized themselves in Kunduz and Baghlan, and somewhat later the first IMU groups followed suit (in Kunduz and Takhar). This period was characterized by a slow increase in attacks using still quite primitive but steadily improving IEDs and hit-and-run tactics. Due to their relative weakness, the insurgents in this phase attacked mostly from a distance, using missiles, rocket-propelled grenades, and mortars and thus avoiding direct confrontation. Starting in 2007, suicide bombers were increasingly employed—an indication that the local insurgency in the Northeast had become closely linked to the insurgents in Afghanistan's southern and eastern regions. Beginning in 2007, most of the suicide bombers were recruited, trained, and financed in the border region between Afghanistan and Pakistan and then transported by smuggler networks from this region to the location of their planned attack.[20]

In May 2007, the Germans' "Bad Kunduz feeling" was shattered by the first successful suicide attack on its personnel in the Kunduz city center. A group of Germans had taken a ride to the city from the plateau above it, where the German military base was located, to buy refrigerators. They took a walk through the city, passed a police station, and entered the market, where a suicide attacker approached them and detonated his suicide vest, killing two procurement officers and a German police official. The suicide bomber seems to have passed the rear security detail in order to target higher-ranking people. The Germans were possibly not the bomber's original targets. It was the second in a series of three attacks, all of which were perpetrated by professionally prepared suicide bombers equipped with high-quality explosive vests, two of whom sought Afghan police and their instructors. It is most likely the case that the three men were part of a group that had been sent from Pakistan and had chosen the Germans because they were passing the Afghan police station shortly before they were targeted or because the suicide bomber had missed an Afghan police convoy that had just passed through central Kunduz.[21]

In the first attack, which took place on April 16, 2007, and was the first quality suicide attack in the province, the attacker killed some twelve Afghan policemen who were training for a parade in the courtyard of the police headquarters in Kunduz.[22] The second attack killed the Germans in the Kunduz market, and the third one on May 28, 2007, targeted Dyncorp, a security services company tasked with training the Afghan police in the province. This time the suicide bomber sought to attack a Dyncorp convoy in Kunduz city but detonated himself without causing major damage. Nonetheless, two Afghan civilians were killed when the company mercenaries opened fire in response.[23]

In spite of the attack on the Germans in May, it seems as if the insurgents were aiming primarily at the Afghan police with their attacks—perhaps evidence of the still localized character of the insurgency in the Kunduz region, which was only gradually being incorporated into the command-and-control structures of the insurgents' headquarters in Pakistan. In any case, the May events became a turning point for the German engagement in Afghanistan. Most important, the German troops withdrew to their base after the attack and did not enter the city during the following weeks. Many military officials who served in Kunduz in these years are convinced that the withdrawal to the base gave the impression that the Germans could be intimidated by insurgent attacks. As one German officer explained, "The Germans only belatedly began to show strength, and our Afghan counterparts never understood why. We showed the Afghans time and again that when they smash in our faces, we will disappear again and leave them alone. This only served as an invitation for them to attack us."[24]

Some politicians subscribe to this view as well and describe the German withdrawals to the base as one of the most serious mistakes made by the German leadership in Afghanistan.[25] As a result, by autumn 2007 the Germans were increasingly attacked by insurgents. Missile attacks targeting the Bundeswehr camp in Kunduz escalated. By that time, the insurgent organizations had rebuilt parts of their structures, and the fight quickly intensified.

Escalating the Insurgency in 2008 and 2009

In 2008, it became increasingly obvious that the major insurgent organizations were showing a special interest in the Kunduz region. They started funneling markedly greater numbers of fighters and quantities of equipment and financial resources into northeastern Afghanistan. The IMU became more visible, and the Taliban incorporated local Pashtun groups into its structures, subject to their military leadership councils in Quetta and Peshawar. As a result, the security situation in the Kunduz region dramatically worsened in 2008 and 2009. Starting in the second half of 2008, the insurgents began executing complex IED attacks in addition to hit-and-runs, suicide bombings, and rocket attacks. During 2009, the insurgents gradually abandoned their tactic of avoiding open combat with ISAF forces. They showed in several engagements that they were continuously developing their technical, tactical, and logistical abilities. At this point, they began executing coordinated operations (albeit with temporal and spatial limitations) and making use of the elements of infantry warfare, employing early-stage and ongoing enemy reconnaissance, fighting from prepared locations, and deploying reserve forces and logistical support during ongoing engagements.[26]

Nonetheless, the most striking characteristic of the northeastern insurgency and its great strength were its highly diversified leadership and logistical structures. Quite unlike the situation in the South and Southeast, the insurgency in the Northeast consisted of several groups that followed different strategic objectives but maintained close tactical cooperation. The main groups were the Afghan Taliban, the Islamic Party of Gulbuddin Hekmatyar, and the IMU. Additional groups included the Haqqani network and al-Qaeda. Whereas the Afghan groups followed an exclusively Afghan agenda, the IMU had a more internationalist view of the situation, aiming at reestablishing a launching pad for attacks in Central Asia and possibly attacking German targets because of Germany's support for the Karimov regime in Uzbekistan (see chapter 8).[27]

THE TALIBAN IN KUNDUZ

In the winter of 2001–2002, after the crushing defeat at the hands of the Northern Alliance, most of the remaining local Taliban groups had disbanded, but the existing networks remained intact, which enabled the Taliban to regain a foothold starting in 2005 at the latest with the help of local followers. The German troops in Kunduz and the BND—which is Germany's military as well as foreign intelligence service—failed to appreciate the reestablishment of these structures.[28]

The Taliban quickly began establishing statelike structures in Kunduz and in other provinces in line with its goal to rebuild the Islamic Emirate, which existed from 1996 to 2001. Sharia law as interpreted by the Taliban would form the basis for the administration of justice and for social life in this state. For this reason, the Taliban sought to establish parallel structures in the contested provinces. These structures would also be led by so-called shadow governors in the northeastern provinces and districts. The Taliban's institutions were often more effective than those of the Afghan state. In early 2009, the Taliban temporarily controlled several districts in Kunduz, where they administered justice and collected taxes and tariffs.[29]

When the insurgency escalated in 2008, the Taliban constituted the strongest insurgent group in the Kunduz region, especially in Kunduz Province, where many local Pashtuns supported the movement. Besides its historic significance, Kunduz has gained strategic importance for the Taliban because of its location at the intersection of major highways running between Badakhshan in the East and Mazar-e Sharif in the West and between the Tajik border in the North and Kabul in the South. Since 2009, one of the most important NATO/ISAF supply lines ran from the northern border through Kunduz Province to Baghlan and Kabul. It has been one of the Taliban's main objectives to disrupt transportation along this road.[30] By expanding the insurgency to areas beyond the Pashtun heartland, the Taliban was also able to demonstrate clearly the weakness of the Karzai government in Kabul and gain a foothold in the northern part of the country.

THE ISLAMIC PARTY

The Islamic Party of Gulbuddin Hekmatyar is the third-strongest insurgent organization in Afghanistan and one of the three strongest in Kunduz. It has had a presence in northeastern Afghanistan since the late 1980s and is a largely Pashtun organization, although, unlike the Taliban with its rural and tribal character, the party's main social base comprises urban and non-tribal Pashtuns. Since the late 1980s, the Islamic Party has played an important role in Kunduz politics and has controlled, for instance, the district of Chahar Dara, an insurgent stronghold plagued by turmoil since 2008.

It was not until 1997, when the Taliban advanced in northern Afghanistan and Hekmatyar fled to Iran, that the party's importance began to recede rapidly. The majority of the party's leaders and fighters in Kunduz joined the Taliban. The old networks nevertheless remained intact, and many party functionaries retained their offices under Taliban rule. When Hekmatyar returned from exile to Afghanistan and Pakistan in 2002, this situation made it easier for him to reestablish an independent and powerful group, which cooperated with the Taliban but followed its own agenda with distinct objectives.

Most important, Hekmatyar advocates a modern Islamic state and views the Taliban's Islamic Emirate as too backward looking. Furthermore, he has followed a two-pronged policy, with the political wing of his Islamic Party becoming one of the main supporters of the Karzai government in Kabul. Although this wing denies any form of cooperation with Hekmatyar, it is probable that he exercises control over it and all other elements of the organization. The fact that the Taliban and the Islamic Party ultimately stand in competition with one another has been repeatedly demonstrated by local disputes, including bloody battles in Baghlan in March 2010.[31]

THE ISLAMIC MOVEMENT OF UZBEKISTAN

The IMU is among the most powerful groups in the Kunduz area alongside the Taliban and the Islamic Party. In many cases, it is hard to identify the exact affiliation of groups or individuals in the region because they cooperate on a tactical level, and many Western sources tend not to make too much of an effort to differentiate properly.[32] The IMU profits from the support of local Uzbeks, who make up between 15 and 25 percent of the population in Kunduz and around 40 percent in neighboring Takhar. The IMU also seems to profit from friction between Uzbeks and Tajiks in the Kunduz region, especially in Takhar, where the Uzbeks claim that they are politically marginalized by the dominating Tajiks.[33] Nevertheless, the IMU also commands a small following among local Tajiks, so that the area has always been an ideal base of operations for the IMU. It is no coincidence that the IMU built a relatively well-developed infrastructure in Kunduz and Takhar before 2001, including its own hospital, military bases, and training camps. There are even reports that relatives of Tahir Yoldashev live in the Imamsahib District in Kunduz and that he and more frequently his brother Sami visited the region after 2001.[34] When the insurgency escalated in 2008, it became increasingly clear that the IMU had its strongholds in the Takhar Province, on the one hand, and in the Imamsahib, Kunduz, and Chahar Dara districts of Kunduz Province, on the other, and could count on the support of many local Uzbeks and Tajiks. Until 2010, intelligence reports pointed to at least one IMU training camp in Imamsahib.[35]

Although the IMU closely cooperated with the Taliban and the Islamic Party, its strategy seems to have been based on its aim to return to Central Asia in general and to Uzbekistan in particular. Indeed, the Kunduz area and the Afghan North in general constitute a part of Central Asia geographically and ethnically, and commercial and cultural relations between the local Uzbeks and Tajiks and their relatives in Central Asia are very strong. The border with Tajikistan is extremely porous, so much so that all kinds of licit and illicit goods cross it in both directions. An important route for the export of Afghan opium and heroin runs through Kunduz to Tajikistan, and all insurgent organizations including the IMU profit heavily from controlling the smuggling routes. According to German military sources, the taxation of the drug trade constitutes the main source of income for the insurgents in the Kunduz area.[36]

Parallel to its buildup in northeastern Afghanistan, the IMU managed to assert its presence in Tajikistan again. In 2009 and 2010, news of renewed IMU activities emerged in Tajikistan, especially the areas where Namangani had established his bases in the 1990s. Most important, there were reports about gunfights in the Tavildara area, where government troops engaged units commanded by Abdallah Rakhimov (a.k.a. Mullah Abdallah), who had been a member of the Islamist opposition during the civil war, had rejected the peace agreement of 1997, and had subsequently retreated to Taliban Afghanistan, most likely in order to join the IMU.[37] Mullah Abdallah returned to Tajikistan in May 2009, but his forces were soon forced to retreat to the mountains, where he was killed in April 2011.[38] Nonetheless, during 2009 and 2010 reports emerged about intensified IMU activity in the country, including a daring and highly publicized jailbreak of prisoners sentenced because of their alleged involvement in Mullah Abdallah's incursion. Tajikistan's first suicide bomber attacked a police station in the northern city of Khojand at the entry point to the Fergana Valley in September 2010, killing at least two people. A previously unknown organization, Group of the Helpers of God (Jamaat Ansarallah), claimed responsibility, but the IMU was widely believed to be behind the attack.[39]

By 2007, the first reports surfaced about the presence of IMU personnel in the Kunduz area, and in 2008 the German military realized that the Uzbek organization took an increasingly active part in the insurgency. All available sources pointed to strong local support for the IMU among Uzbeks and Tajiks. Over the course of the year, the IMU sent experienced instructors from Pakistan and established a new underground infrastructure in Kunduz and Takhar. The lines of communication ran either directly from the Pakistani tribal areas to Kabul (and from there on the major road north to Kunduz) or via the northern Pakistani Chitral region, where the IMU is reported to have run a training camp at Shah Salim, close to the pass over the Hindu Kush range separating Chitral and Badakhshan, at which point the path continues to Takhar and Kunduz.[40] By 2009, numerous IMU forces were active in these three provinces and in northern Baghlan.

The German public did not become aware of the IMU's presence in the Kunduz region until the spring of 2010, when IMU fighters were heavily involved in a spectacular attack on a Bundeswehr patrol on April 2, Good Friday, resulting in the deaths of three paratroopers. The patrol was tasked with clearing the road of IEDs close to the Isa Khel village in the notorious Chahar Dara District, about three miles west of the German camp, when they were ambushed by about eighty insurgents. In the ensuing firefight, which lasted for several hours, three Germans were killed. Five other soldiers were severely wounded when they tried to come to the aid of their comrades, and their Dingo (an armored infantry transport vehicle) was destroyed by an IED.[41]

In addition to the Taliban, the IMU claimed responsibility for this attack in a declaration published on its Web site. The group also published a propaganda video in May 2010 showing pictures of the still-burning Dingo surrounded by IMU fighters and other materials depicting its operations in Kunduz. Tahir Yoldashev (who at that time was already dead) is shown giving a speech in Uzbek, claiming that the IMU had extended its operations to Kunduz and other parts of northern Afghanistan.[42] Military sources later confirmed that they had evidence of Central Asians and perhaps even Chechens taking part in the ambush, so it became evident to a wider public that the Uzbek organization had become an important part of the insurgency and had begun to target the German troops.[43]

With the move to Kunduz, the IMU had effectively internationalized its strategy in addition to its ideology and social base. There were three causes of this change. First among these causes was the mounting pressure from the Pakistani military and American drone attacks on the IMU in 2007. The situation became especially serious for the IMU after the beginning of the Pakistani offensive in South Waziristan in October 2009, when it lost its bases in that area. Although it started a guerilla campaign there in the following months, it was not able to rebuild its infrastructure in the agency, perhaps prompting it to send some of its fighters to northern Afghanistan.

Second, the IMU hoped to establish a launching pad in northern Afghanistan from which it could access the Central Asian states again. Increased activities of Islamist fighters in Tajikistan in 2009 and 2010 might be interpreted as evidence of this strategy. The move might have been connected to the organization's financial problems because in northern Afghanistan it would profit from intensive smuggling of heroin and opium to neighboring Tajikistan, which had reportedly been an important source of income for the organization until 2001.[44]

Third, the presence of the Germans in the Kunduz region might have been another motive for the IMU to join the insurgents in this part of Afghanistan. As described in chapter 8, the IMU developed a clearly anti-German agenda and might have aimed at putting its rhetorical internationalization into practice by attacking "the worst enemy of Islam." Whatever the reasons for the IMU's shift in strategy, it is very likely that the main cause for the return to northern Afghanistan was opportunity. When the Afghan insurgents returned to the area, it was only logical for the IMU to join them because it had never relinquished its bonds to the local population and had never given up its goal to return to Central Asia. It was thus only natural that the organization not let slip an opportunity to return to its former stronghold.

The German Reaction

Confronted with an escalating insurgency in 2008, the German government and military found it impossible to stick to their customary view of the German troops as an impartial stabilization force and accept that Germany was party to a conflict over life and death. The German government had long refused, however, to confront the realities on the ground, and military commanders in Afghanistan had to press for changes in the German war effort. Even then, Berlin only reluctantly accepted that more leeway for the troops on the ground was necessary to have even the slightest chance of success. As one military officer formerly stationed in Kunduz stated, "The military in Afghanistan was pointing out the necessity to adjust the German strategy, but politicians in Berlin refused to listen."[45]

The problem had already become clear in the vocabulary used in Berlin, where politicians until 2009 refused to speak of a "war" but preferred terms such as *stabilization operation* and, later, *combat mission*, effectively showing how detached they were from the realities of the insurgency in Afghanistan. Only in November 2009 did Minister of Defense Karl Theodor zu Guttenberg begin to use the term *warlike circumstances*, but even then without totally giving up his predecessor's cautiousness:

> To be sure, international law is unambiguous on this matter: War can only take place between states. But do you think that even a single soldier understands these necessary legal, academic, and semantic subtleties? . . . Personally, I understand every soldier who says: "What is taking place in Afghanistan is war, regardless of whether it is foreign military forces or Taliban terrorists that attack, injure, or kill me." The campaign in Afghanistan has also been a combat mission for years. At least in the minds of not only our soldiers, the Taliban are waging a war against the soldiers of the international community.[46]

Finally, in 2010, Foreign Minister Guido Westerwelle announced that the German government now considered the conflict in northeastern Afghanistan "armed conflict within the meaning of international humanitarian law."[47] The continuing hesitation to call the war a war was due mainly to the government's desire not to provoke even stronger resistance from a public increasingly hostile to the Afghanistan adventure. By 2010 at the latest, it became obvious that Berlin had no other desire than to leave the Afghan quagmire and withdraw the German military as early as possible.

On the ground in the Kunduz area, German forces by 2008 slowly adapted their strategies to the new situation. By September 2007, they had clearly become a target for the insurgents, who attacked the German camp with rockets and mortars from nearby villages. As a consequence, two hundred additional paratroopers were sent to Kunduz, without, however, changing the restrictive rules of engagement for them, thus effectively ruling out any offensive action.[48] In general, in 2007 the German troops were reinforced with specialized infantry (paratroopers and mountain rangers) and Special Forces and tried to show more force presence among the Afghan population, especially in the Kunduz and Chahar Dara districts.[49] For the German military, which had focused on force protection over the preceding years, these steps were far-reaching, but they proved to be too little too late. As a military officer formerly stationed in Kunduz argued,

"From 2008, we acted more aggressively, but we tried to deter the insurgents in a conventional way by showing presence in parts of the Kunduz area without any result. We did not adopt a counterinsurgency strategy, so the Taliban could dodge us whenever we arrived in their strongholds. Since we did not hold on to any territory or positions that we took, they trickled back in as soon as we left."[50]

Although the situation deteriorated during 2008 and 2009, the German government, military, and public did not debate the change to a new counterinsurgency strategy that US forces began to implement in 2009 and that many German officers thought of as the only viable way to at least partial success in Afghanistan. It was clear to decision makers in Berlin that any strategy focusing on the protection of the local population rather than on the protection of German forces would carry immense political risks, especially because it would require a substantial rise in the number of German troops stationed in the area—something with which German politicians were not prepared to confront their electorate. Commanders on the ground were nevertheless given more leeway in 2009 with new rules of engagement adapted to the realities on the ground and allowing for a more aggressive course of action in combat against insurgents.[51]

Nevertheless, other problems in the German war effort were largely ignored. One such problem was the lack of adequate air transport facilities, with only six transport helicopters serving the needs of some 5,000 German troops in northern Afghanistan.[52] Due to the presence of a relatively low number of German troops in an enormous territory, the ability to deploy the troops rapidly in different parts of the Afghan Northeast was essential for the mission's success. Nevertheless, in the eleven years between late 2001 and summer 2012, the German government did not address this requirement. Aside from this lack of attention to the issue, the Bundeswehr does not have any combat helicopters because it is waiting for the production of the German version of the German–French "Tiger." Although these helicopters were ordered some twenty-five years ago, only prototypes designed to combat tanks have been delivered to the German army. Confronted with the same problems as the Germans, the French military decided to accept a less sophisticated and refitted version and were thereby able to begin using the helicopters in summer 2009, effectively providing air cover to their patrols on the ground.[53] Another problem was the lack of actionable intelligence, with the BND unable to provide the troops with tactical intelligence because its representatives in Kunduz were liaising exclusively with their Afghan counterparts. According to military officials, the BND lacked qualified personnel with any knowledge whatsoever of the country, its languages, and the development of the insurgency in the Kunduz region. In order to cope with the most basic military needs on the ground, the Bundeswehr increasingly relied on field human intelligence teams, who suffered from a lack of specialized intelligence training, severe restrictions on their activities and finances, and a total absence of an analytical branch that would provide operatives with orientation. Military officials more than once complained that the German political and military leadership had not grasped the central importance of intelligence for a counterinsurgency operation.[54]

Although the German troops acted more aggressively in 2008 and 2009, they again retreated to their base in late October 2008 in reaction to an escalation of attacks and a rise in losses that had started in August. The most important cause of the renewed withdrawal from the battlefield was an attack on October 20, 2008, when a suicide bomber detonated his device next to a Mungo, a light infantry transport vehicle used by the German paratroopers. The paratroopers were blocking the entrance to the notorious Hajji Amanullah village (inhabited by Zadran Pashtuns), where their comrades were conducting a search operation, when a cyclist approached them and detonated his suicide vest. Two German soldiers and seven Afghan children who were playing right next to them were killed. The Germans had informed the Afghan police of the impending operation, and Taliban informers inside the police had told the insurgents so that the latter could prepare the suicide attack in advance.[55] After the incident, the commander of the Kunduz PRT made the decision to cease patroling the area until his contingent was replaced the following month.[56] Just as in the summer of 2007, the insurgents were again left with the impression that the Germans withdrew whenever they were hit hard.

It is not by chance that the escalation of the insurgency in Kunduz in 2009 coincided with the wave of threats against Germany in the same year (see chapter 7). The German government's hesitation and the German military's cautious mode of action in Kunduz created the impression among the Taliban, al-Qaeda, and other groups that they could possibly force a withdrawal of the Germans from Afghanistan by attacking German troops in the Northeast and simultaneously aiming at targets in Germany as well.

It was obvious that the jihadists considered Germany to be the weakest link in the chain of big troop providers. This view had already prompted the Sauerland group to plot attacks in Germany in 2006–2007, and the same strategy was still being followed in 2009. Although the insurgents did not manage to force Berlin to withdraw its troops, the escalation of their activities and the rising losses in German troops created an immense pressure both on the politicians in the capital and on the troops on the ground.[57]

This pressure became obvious after an incident in early September 2009, the so-called Kunduz affair. Caught between a government and military leadership not willing to create the necessary conditions for a more aggressive mode of action in Afghanistan, the German military focused on force protection, reacted nervously, and made mistakes. On the evening of September 3, 2009, insurgents hijacked two fuel tanker trucks close to the German camp while they were en route to Kunduz. Shortly afterward, an American warplane spotted the trucks stuck on a sandbank of the Kunduz River surrounded by insurgents. Fearing an imminent terrorist attack using the fuel trucks or smaller pickups as bombs and trusting the report of an Afghan informant insisting that there were no civilians close to the vehicles, the German PRT commander, Colonel Georg Klein, ordered that two five-hundred-pound bombs be dropped on the trucks, which destroyed the vehicles and killed between 50 and 140 bystanders.[58] Unfortunately, the trucks were surrounded not only by Taliban insurgents, but also by local civilians filling the gasoline into canisters. Although the exact number of civilian victims remains unknown, estimates range between 30 and 140.[59]

The German colonel's action was severely criticized by the commander of the NATO mission in Afghanistan, Stanley McChrystal, who perceived that a directive to reduce civilian casualties—based on the new American counterinsurgency strategy—had been violated. McChrystal apparently did not see any imminent threat emerging from the tanker trucks and believed that Klein had based his orders on the information presented by a sole informant.[60] Even more important, the incident was highly publicized worldwide and thereby foiled the German government's efforts to keep the Afghanistan mission out of domestic debates in the run-up to the German parliamentary elections on September 27, 2009. The ensuing crisis led to the resignation of the minister of defense, Franz-Josef Jung, who was confronted with devastating criticism from large sectors of the public.[61]

The Bundeswehr chief of staff Wolfgang Schneiderhan and Vice Minister of Defense Peter Wichert had to leave office as well. The government was soon confronted with a cumbersome parliamentary investigation commission looking into the case. More than ever, public emotions ran high, and rejection of the German presence in Afghanistan skyrocketed among the German population.

Furthermore, the jihadist propaganda machine began to exploit the pictures of the wrecked tanker trucks and of dead and wounded Afghans in their efforts to decry the German effort as a war against the Afghan Muslim people. In the most prominent example, the German Taliban Mujahideen referred to the events in the video *The Call to Truth*, which they published shortly before the German parliamentary elections on September 24, 2009. Here the speaker Yusuf Ocak refers to the events as evidence of Germany's leading "a war against Islam" and strongly attacks the minister of defense:

> The recent events in Kunduz have again clearly demonstrated the attempts to cover up the whole thing with [indistinct word] and lies. We seized two trucks and shared its content with the people—our brothers and sisters. Because of your false sense of pride and your suspicion and under the pretext of terrorism, you caused an enormous massacre of the civilian population with an airstrike. Your claim that more than fifty Mujahideen drove two tank trucks is simply ridiculous. Just think about it! How many persons are required to drive two vehicles? The participants can be counted on the fingers of one hand. How many innocent people died because of this? The dismembered bodies of more than 120 women, children, and civilians lay on the streets. The blood is on the hands, the dirty hands, of your troops and on those of Franz-Josef Jung, a man without backbone, a criminal, a liar, a case for the gallows.
>
> Why do you speculate about the number of victims and make presumptions when it is us who bury the dead? We know exactly how the Muslims that you have killed are merely numbers to you. You walk all over human dignity because for you a Muslim does not have the same value as one of you. Besides, to say that the two trucks were loaded with explosives is a huge lie. How can that be the case if its content had just been shared with the people? How can you try to use this as justification for this massacre? Because of your unfounded paranoia, you are now killing the people you supposedly want to protect. And this would not

> be the first case. It is naive to assume every time that it was merely an accident. Who are the terrorists in the eyes of the Afghans? Is it us, their sons, fathers, and friends, or is it you who kill and butcher them? You have irrevocably lost the support of the people a long time ago. And with each additional day on the front, you lose your money and your lives.[62]

The attack on the tanker trucks thus became a powerful propaganda and recruitment tool for the German jihadists and was frequently cited on jihadist Web sites in the months that followed.

The American Phase, 2010–2011

With the events of September 2009, the German mission had reached a political and military dead end. While public pressure kept the German government from rethinking its strategy in order to allow the military to adopt a more sophisticated counterinsurgency approach and follow the American lead in raising the number of troops, the German military remained under immense pressure in Kunduz, unable to fulfill its task of stabilizing the region. According to Winfried Nachtwei, a Green Party parliamentarian specializing in defense issues at that time, "Without the American reinforcement, Kunduz would have become a disaster for us. We were unable to control the situation in the province."[63]

From December 2009, the US government attempted to convince the German government to send at least 2,000 more troops to Afghanistan in order to make the new counterinsurgency strategy work—a strategy that among other things foresaw a more offensive approach following a massive increase in troop levels.[64] Although McChrystal had initially demanded a minimum reinforcement of 40,000 troops, the Obama administration sent only 30,000. When several NATO allies, among them Germany, refused to substantially increase their troop levels, the United States was forced to send 5,000 of its reinforcements to northern Afghanistan to combat the insurgency there instead of focusing on the South. Of these 5,000 new soldiers, approximately 1,400 were permanently stationed in the Kunduz region.[65]

Since March 2009, the United States had already deployed Special Forces to Kunduz, which succeeded in inflicting painful losses on the insurgency.

In part on the basis of German information collected in the previous years, these Special Forces began to liquidate leading insurgents. With the arrival of the new troops in the first months of 2010, the Americans took the lead in the Kunduz region and over the course of the same year captured or killed several of the Taliban's "shadow governors" in Kunduz and Baghlan; hundreds of fighters were killed, arrested, or changed sides, and several districts were cleared of the insurgents. As a result, the security situation greatly improved.[66] According to a German military source, the American buildup quickly and fundamentally changed the equation in Kunduz: "When I arrived in Kunduz in 2010, the American activities had created a new reality on the ground. From late April and May, the US forces began to strike against the insurgents by killing the leaders and midlevel commanders. They severed the head from the insurgency and broke its backbone. The targeted killings and arrests made the Taliban leaderless and impeded their coordination efforts. And uncoordinated activities are easier to suppress."[67]

The US troops showed a special interest in the IMU and became active whenever they gained information about the Uzbek organization's activities. The same source explained: "The United States knows about the potential of these foreign groupings that are well financed and whose fighters are better trained than the usual Afghan insurgents. Whenever they hear about foreign fighters, they try to hunt them down immediately. As a consequence, the IMU massively ducked its head in 2010."[68] There is ample evidence of US forces attacking IMU structures in the province. For instance, in late September 2010, Mohammed Amin, the Taliban's deputy governor and commander of an IMU group, was killed in Takhar.[69]

Reassured by the Americans' presence, the German troops began to act more aggressively as well. With a new approach the German military started implementing in July 2010, it partially abandoned its previous restraint in combating the insurgency. The Bundeswehr increasingly operated using mixed German–Afghan units and concentrated more than ever on the training of Afghan security forces. The mixed units primarily executed infantry operations in critical regions, such as the restive Chahar Dara District southwest of the city of Kunduz.

Although the insurgents were severely weakened by these strikes and the loss of many able commanders, they changed their strategies and were thereby able to achieve some successes. They imitated the American mode of action, targeting their adversaries' leading personnel—most notably important Afghan security officials—not only in Kunduz, but also in Kandahar in the South. In October 2010, the governor of Kunduz was killed, as was the head of the provincial police in March 2011.[70] In one of the most prominent cases, the insurgents killed the commander of the northern police, Mohammed Daud Daud, a leading Tajik security official, when he visited the compound of the provincial governor in Taloqan, the capital of Takhar Province, for a meeting between German military and Afghan officials. Daud was of special significance for the Taliban because he had been the commander of the Tajik forces in the battle of Kunduz in 2001. According to some reports, a suicide bomber dressed in a police uniform detonated his device close to the officials in the meeting. Others state that the bomb was hidden in a wall in the building and detonated via remote control.[71] In any case, the explosion left six people dead, among them Daud, the head of the Takhar police, and two German soldiers. The governor of Takhar was severely wounded, and the German commander of Regional Command North, General Markus Kneip, escaped with an injury. Although under pressure on the battlefield, the insurgents made clear that they were still able to execute high-quality terrorist attacks.

Withdrawal 2014

Although the situation substantially improved in 2010 and 2011, largely due to the presence of US forces, and the insurgents were forced on the defensive, Germany's Afghanistan mission remained a liability for German counterterrorism. The German troops' mode of action had contributed to the impression that a German withdrawal from Afghanistan might be brought about if high numbers of casualties could be inflicted on the German troops or an attack perpetrated in Germany. In the German case, political and military fickleness had arguably contributed to the jihadists choosing Germany as an attractive target.

Second, the German presence in Afghanistan in general and in the Kunduz region in particular had by 2011 become an important recruitment tool for the jihadist scene in Germany. The case of Abdullah Hafizi from Essen made clear that at least some of the Germans heading to join the IMU, IJU, and al-Qaeda in Pakistan especially aimed at fighting the German troops, in contrast to many of their predecessors, who were apparently motivated primarily by a diffuse desire to join the jihad in Afghanistan on the side of any jihadist organization that they might be able to join.[72] Perhaps most worrying, Hafizi was not an isolated case. In March 2011, the IMU published a video in which Yassin Chouka announced the martyrdom of "Faruq the German" in a suicide attack on an alleged CIA base in Kunduz city in July 2010. Faruq was later identified as the Moroccan citizen Said Ballout (b. 1987) from Bochum in the German Ruhr region, and there actually had been an attack that fit the information given by the IMU. On July 2, 2010, an IMU group attacked the Kunduz city office of the American company Organization Development Alternatives, Inc., killing the former German navy soldier Rouven Beinecke.[73]

Prospects for the future of the German mission in Afghanistan were bleak. In July 2011, the US government began to withdraw the first of those troop reinforcements it had sent to Afghanistan in 2010, thus reducing the pressure on the insurgents, who, according to jihadist sources, at that time were only waiting for the NATO troops to begin their withdrawal in order to escalate their activities again.[74] Furthermore, the conflict constellation in Afghanistan increasingly began to resemble the situation before the fall of the Taliban. Confronted with the coming withdrawal of NATO forces in 2014, President Hamid Karzai began to distance himself from his allies, preparing for a negotiated solution with the Taliban. His Tajik allies, who had dominated the former Northern Alliance, opposed this policy, leading many analysts to believe that after the American withdrawal, Afghanistan might move back to square one—that is, a conflict between a Pashtun-dominated alliance, including the Taliban, on the one side, and a remake of the Northern Alliance composed mainly of Tajik, Uzbek, and Hazara groups on the other. Be that as it may, the aim of stabilizing Afghanistan and preventing it from becoming a safe haven for international terrorists was perhaps farther than ever from being realized in 2012.

10

"This Is the Last Year America"

Threats and Prospects

When Arid Uka killed two American soldiers and perilously injured two others at Frankfurt airport on March 2, 2011, many commentators were perplexed. Although most specialists in Germany had long expected or at least feared a jihadist terrorist attack, the discussion in the previous months had centered on the threat posed by "new internationalist" jihadists—those who radicalized independently in Germany and then traveled in order to gain access to training and logistical support by larger organizations—returning from the training camps of al-Qaeda, IJU, and the IMU in Pakistan. Even if a successful lone-wolf attack had been seen as a possibility, especially after the failed plot of the two suitcase bombers in 2006, the travels of more than two hundred young Germans to Pakistan had led many specialists to focus on the threat they posed. Some argued that, in any case, not much could be done to prevent independent jihadists from perpetrating attacks. The Arid Uka case now seemed to indicate that those who had long argued that the future belonged to a "leaderless jihad" instead of to big organizations such as al-Qaeda had been right. Nevertheless, although the Frankfurt airport attack effectively pointed to the danger posed by independent jihadists and the difficulties of thwarting their plots, the leaderless and the "leader-led" forms of structures and activities will exist in parallel for some time.

Even though the American victims in Frankfurt were not protected, attacking military personnel arguably required much more determination and courage than an attack on a truly soft target. Therefore, the Arid Uka case showed that a single attack by a determined amateur can have grave repercussions. Most important, Uka would have likely killed more persons if his gun had not jammed when he tried to shoot the fifth American airman. Nevertheless, Uka, like all German jihadists except the members of the Hamburg cell that had perpetrated the 9/11 attacks, remained an amateur with limited capabilities. This assessment becomes especially obvious when one compares the numerous plots and attacks mentioned in this book with the one perpetrated by the Norwegian right-wing extremist and self-appointed crusader Anders Breivik. On July 22, 2011, Breivik detonated a car bomb in the government quarter of Oslo, killing eight people. He then went on a shooting rampage on the Utoya Island close to the capital, killing sixty-nine people, most of them teenage participants in a youth camp of the ruling Labour Party. Although a lone wolf like Uka and many others, Breivik committed attacks that were by far more devastating than most jihadist plots after 9/11, and his mode of action was much more professional than that of any German jihadist ever since the days of the first Hamburg cell. The reason for this decline in professionalism probably lies in the social base of the German jihadist movement, which after 9/11 shifted from Arab students of the sciences and technical disciplines to petty criminals, former drug addicts, and, in general, members of the primarily Turkish migrant lower classes. With few exceptions, the German jihadists had severe problems during their years in school, many of them because of language problems. The converts' social and educational profiles were not particularly terrible, but they were often similar: many had dropped out of school early, reducing their chances at becoming successful members of German society. Even those jihadists who graduated from high school and started university sometimes realized that their expectations (and those of their families) did not necessarily correlate with their limited talents. As a consequence, most of their terrorist activities were of limited sophistication as well.

This assessment does not necessarily minimize the threat to Germany. Many jihadists might be painfully aware of their own shortcomings when analyzing the Breivik case and might be able to improve their performance by trying to mimic his attacks. After all, not all German jihadists were inept fools, and plotters such as the suitcase bombers were reasonably knowledgeable and talented.

The Threat to Germany and Its Allies

The threat to Germany posed by al-Qaeda and other jihadist organizations is high and will remain high for the foreseeable future mainly because of two developments. First, al-Qaeda and its allies have decided to attack German targets wherever possible in order to force the German government to withdraw its troops from Afghanistan. Although this motive might lose some importance with the withdrawal of Western troops starting in 2011, the jihadists will want to give the impression that NATO forces are retreating under fire and as a result of strong jihadist pressure. And because Germany remains a weak link in the chain of big troop providers owing to strong public opposition to the presence of German troops in Afghanistan, it is very likely that attacks there and efforts to perpetrate attacks in Germany itself will continue until the last German soldier has left the bases at the Hindu Kush. Moreover, contrary to the widespread belief in Germany that a withdrawal from Afghanistan will eradicate the motive for al-Qaeda and its allies to attack Germany, most evidence suggests that the jihadists will continue their fight against the West in general and against Germany in particular. This became obvious shortly after the Madrid bombings on March 11, 2004. Although the jihadists responsible for the attack had reached their stated goal when the Spanish government announced the quick withdrawal of its troops from Iraq, they did not abandon their efforts to kill Spanish civilians. As noted earlier, the German jihadist Monir Chouka made clear in the IMU video *Evil Fatherland* in December 2012 that he and his superiors thought along similar lines. He said, "The Jihad in Germany is only a matter of time," and announced that the jihadists would continue plotting attacks in Germany, even after a withdrawal of the country's troops from Afghanistan. They would take revenge for the German military's wrongdoings and continue the fight until they ruled the whole world.[1] Foreign intervention in Afghanistan and Iraq quite obviously represents an important motive prompting jihadists to attack the West, but it is not the only one. Most of them are also driven by an intense hatred of Western civilization.

Second, the influx of substantial numbers of German recruits in 2006 has provided al-Qaeda, the IJU, the IMU, the Afghan Taliban, and the Pakistani Taliban with a critical mass of potential terrorists, enabling them to choose and train able and willing candidates for the fight in Afghanistan and Pakistan and for attacks in Germany. The actual threat has been somewhat reduced because many young recruits have been killed or captured or have returned home disillusioned by the state of the jihadist movement in Pakistan. The high losses as a result of the relentless American drone attacks seem to have contributed especially to the demoralization of many young fighters. Nevertheless, continued plotting in recent years has made clear that the remaining operatives are still a threat. In the worst case, a single well-trained, battle-hardened, and experienced returnee might be able to build a terrorist cell in Germany by recruiting from among the numerous supporters and sympathizers of the jihadist cause there. In addition, some legally convicted jihadists have already left or will leave jail in the coming years and might make efforts to restart their jihadist careers.[2] Prominent representatives of the German jihadist scene have indeed reappeared after years of apparent inactivity and became preachers, recruiters, or logistic facilitators again.

Although not all threats to Germany in recent years have been authorized by the organizations for which the authors claimed to speak, this does not mean that these organizations pose less of a threat to Germany than previously thought. Bekkay Harrach might have acted without the approval of al-Qaeda when he made his famous threat to Germany before the parliamentary elections in September 2009, but it was nevertheless confirmed by Atiyatallah in the same month. The organization attentively followed the debates that arose in Germany and elsewhere when it was apparently not able to perpetrate an attack after Harrach's ultimatum expired in the first half of October 2009. It is therefore very likely that if there is any chance at all, al-Qaeda will make a sustained effort to redress the loss of credibility it suffered because of this perceived failure. Furthermore, recent terror plots still provide a reason to assume that al-Qaeda has taken a strategic decision to target Germany if it has the personnel and capabilities to do so and that the jihadist movement will consider any attack in Germany in the coming years a major success.

The continuing threat to Germany became most palpable in late April 2011 when a foiled plot served as evidence that al-Qaeda was planning attacks on Germany from North Waziristan and that at least some of the information about the Europlot from 2010 remained relevant. At that time, the members of the "Düsseldorf cell"—consisting of the Moroccan Abdeladim el-Kebir (b. 1982), the German Moroccan Jamil Seddiki (b. 1980), and the German Iranian Amid Chaabi (b. 1992)—were arrested in Düsseldorf and Bochum in the western Germany.[3] Kebir, a former mechanical engineering student at Bochum University, had traveled to Pakistan in early 2010 and remained there for several months, undergoing training with al-Qaeda. He is reported to have kept in contact with the al-Qaeda operations commander Yunus al-Muritani (Abd al-Rahman Wuld Muhammad al-Husain), and the general orders for the attack are said to have come from the Libyan Atiyatallah Abu Abd al-Rahman (Jamal Ibrahim al-Misrati). Atiyatallah functioned as the head of al-Qaeda in North Waziristan from the summer of 2010 until his death as a result of a drone strike in August 2011.[4] In fact, information derived from the interrogations of Ahmad Wali Sidiqi and Rami Makanesi in 2010 prompted the American and German security authorities to step up their efforts to find individuals or cells already operating in Germany. Nevertheless, as in the case of the Sauerland group, the decisive intelligence seems to have come from the US National Security Agency, which intercepted an Internet communication between Kebir and Atiyatallah.[5]

The three men were arrested in the early stages of their plot, when they had started procuring chemicals to build bombs. According to information provided by the chief prosecutor, they had planned to detonate an explosive device in a place with a large crowd of civilians, possibly a bus or a bus station. A second reason to arrest Kebir and his comrades had been the attacks on a tourist restaurant in Marrakech, Morocco, on April 28, in which sixteen people were killed and which the police feared might serve as further encouragement to the plotters. In phone conversations, Kebir and his comrades had celebrated the attacks in Marrakech.[6] With the arrests, the danger had still not been averted because German authorities suspected that at least one other group tasked with executing attacks in Germany had not yet been discovered.

It may be that the last group of jihadists that had been sent from Pakistan to Germany in the context of the Europlot was the one formed by Yusuf Ocak—who had become known as a leading member of the German Taliban Mujahideen in 2009 and 2010—and the Austrian Afghan Maqsood Lodin (b. 1989). Both apparently joined al-Qaeda after the demise of the German Taliban Mujahideen in 2010 and were trained so that they could return to Germany, build a local cell, and perpetrate attacks. They were arrested in May when trying to establish contacts with like-minded friends in Berlin and Vienna and were subsequently put on trial in Berlin. Most spectacularly, Lodin had a USB stick in his possession containing an al-Qaeda strategy paper; a report on al-Qaeda's role in the preparation of the London bombings on July 7, 2005, and July 21, 2005, and the transatlantic airliner plot that British authorities had thwarted in August 2006; and another paper detailing the lessons learned from these operations. The three documents were internal al-Qaeda papers authored by people deeply involved in the events and seem to have been provided to the two recruits in order to prepare them for cell building in Germany. One of the two had also taken notes during training in Pakistan detailing practical aspects of their future terrorist activity in Europe, including communication with the al-Qaeda headquarters in Pakistan.[7]

In spite of these spectacular police and intelligence successes, events highlighted the German security authorities' shortcomings in monitoring militants and their radicalization processes in Germany and in tracking their movements abroad. According to all available information, the German police and intelligence services had not noticed Abdeladim el-Kebir leaving the country, an especially grave oversight because the security authorities for years argued that they had improved their technical ability to address such intelligence deficiencies. Nevertheless, the cases of the IMU operatives Abdullah Hafizi and Said Ballout, who were killed in the German area of operations in northern Afghanistan in 2010 and who some months earlier had left the country unnoticed, made clear that Kebir's was not an isolated case. The young militants had successfully hidden their intentions while in Germany.[8]

A Consolidated Jihadist Scene in Germany

The increasing sophistication of activists leaving the country for Pakistan and Afghanistan was only one indication among many of the growing maturity and consolidation of the German jihadist scene. Other indications include the establishment of the first German jihadist group, the integration of Germans into transnational Turkish–Central Asian networks, and the growth of the Salafist movement in Germany as a central recruitment pool.

Perhaps the most important indicator for the consolidation of the German scene and the most worrying development from German domestic security officials' point of view was the establishment of the German Taliban Mujahideen as the first German jihadist group. Ahmet Manavbaşı's belief that he could establish an independent German terrorist organization in Pakistan and thereby become a terrorist force to be reckoned with pointed to a well-developed self-confidence. There is, furthermore, evidence that Monir Chouka harbored similar ambitions regarding the Germans in the IMU, perhaps indicating that the number of Germans in Pakistan had reached critical mass at some point in 2009 and 2010—an event that prompted several German jihadists to consider founding an independent German group. For the time being, Manavbaşı's project was aborted by his death and the subsequent dissolution of the German Taliban Mujahideen. It cannot be ruled out, however, that other jihadists will take up the project and try to establish a similar organization in the future because the number of jihadists, their supporters, and sympathizers has substantially grown in Germany in recent years.

Another indicator of the consolidation of German jihadism was the gradual integration of many German recruits and groups into existing Turkic networks. These networks had been in the making since the 1990s in and around the conflicts in Bosnia, Chechnya, and Afghanistan. By 2011, the Germans had built a well-established travel route from their hometowns to Istanbul, then to Iran, passing by Mashhad and Zahedan, and going overland to Pakistan via Taftan, Quetta, and Bannu and from there to Waziristan. In Waziristan, they joined al-Qaeda, the IMU, the IJU, and the German Taliban Mujahideen. Istanbul has developed into the hub of this network, where logisticians for different organizations channel the flow of recruits and donations to Pakistan. It is there that fighters from Turkey, Azerbaijan, the Caucasus, and Germany are sent to Iran to begin their journey.

Perhaps most worrying are scattered reports about especially high numbers of Turkish volunteers who have joined the jihadists in the tribal areas and have even formed their own groups in recent years.[9] Reports about several large-scale arrests in Turkey between 2009 and 2011 also point to a growth of the jihadist scene there and to the fact that the

Turkish government now takes this problem more seriously than it did in the past. To what extent these Turkey-centered networks will become an even bigger threat in the future depends primarily on the effectiveness of the Turkish response. If the Turkish government's fight against jihadist terrorism is judged by its previous record, some skepticism might be justified. The Turkish security authorities still seem to be so preoccupied with the threat posed by the Kurdish PKK that they have not yet managed to address the jihadist threat with the same determination as some of their allies. In particular, the government still does not seem to consider those Turkish citizens who have decided to fight abroad a priority target. As a result, many indicators point to a growth of the Turkish jihadist scene, which might pose an increasing problem for Turkish and European security in the coming years. For the time being, the Turkish government is not decisively curtailing jihadist logisticians' freedom of action in Istanbul, so one might suspect that Ankara still avoids direct confrontation as long as the jihadists do not target the Turkish state itself. This strategy might backfire in the long-run, as the examples of Egypt and Saudi Arabia have already shown.

It remains difficult to diagnose to what extent the German–Turkish–Central Asian nexus in Waziristan has developed in recent years. On the one hand, the growing number of Turkish German recruits joining Uzbek organizations and the IJU's foundation of an "international brigade" comprising Turks, Azeris, and German Turks are evidence of a growing and more systematic cooperation among Turkic groups in Afghanistan. But this cooperation is apparently far from unproblematic, as, for instance, reports by former members of the IMU suggest. The German young men had difficulties adjusting to the harsh living conditions and the rigorous discipline in the Uzbek organization, prompting many of them to leave after a short time. The experienced, well-trained, and battle-hardened Central Asians did not cherish their new recruits, who mostly came without any experience and could only be used as propaganda instruments for the European audience. It is, furthermore, unclear why the IJU decided to allow for the creation of the German Taliban Mujahideen. Although the move was most likely due to the influx of larger numbers of Germans and their leader Ahmet Manavbaşı's desire to establish the first German jihadist organization, it is possible that disillusionment with the German recruits also played a role. Just like the Chouka brothers in the IMU, the

German Taliban Mujahideen were tasked mainly with propaganda activities targeting Europe, which might hint at the Germans' limited usefulness as actual fighters. In any case, relations between the German recruits and their hosts in Waziristan always remained highly asymmetrical, with the Germans offering little in return for the training they received.

A third indicator pointing to the continuing relevance of the jihadist phenomenon in Germany has been the growth of the Salafist movement in Germany. With the possible exception of Arid Uka, nearly all jihadists mentioned in this book were radicalized in Salafist mosques or cultural centers and developed their first contacts with the militant scene there. This does not necessarily mean that the recent growth of the German Salafist community will inevitably lead to an increase in jihadist recruitment in Germany, but it is likely that the dynamism in this field will translate itself into a continuing radicalization of young German Muslims. This radicalization will take place not only in the Salafist meeting places, but also via the Internet. If Arid Uka's case points to current developments on the jihadists' use of the Internet, independent forms of radicalization and self-recruitment will gain ground in Germany as well. To what extent these trends will have repercussions on the security situation highly depends on the development of al-Qaeda and the jihadist scene in general.

Political Irrelevance but Enhanced Operational Opportunities for al-Qaeda

With the death of Osama Bin Laden in May 2011, al-Qaeda received a heavy blow when it was already on the defensive. Since 1998, the Saudi had been al-Qaeda's world-famous figurehead, and there was every indication that the organization could not adequately replace him. His successor and al-Qaeda's long-time number two, the Egyptian Aiman al-Zawahiri, who had been the organization's chief strategist since its inception, does not even come close to Bin Laden's substantial charisma. Moreover, Zawahiri was the head of al-Qaeda's Egyptian contingent, which had long been criticized for monopolizing the leading positions to the detriment of North Africans and other nationalities. One might have expected that, as a consequence of these shortcomings, responsibilities among the leadership of al-Qaeda will rest on more shoulders than Zawahiri's and that the group might choose a collective leadership model. However, after the death of the Libyan Abu Yahia al-Libi (Hasan Muhammad Qaid), an influential internationalist religious authority and the highest-ranking al-Qaeda-leader after Zawahiri, in June 2012, not many candidates were left. Possible choices were the Egyptian Saif al-Adl, al-Qaeda's former military head, possibly residing in Iran, and probably less well-known functionaries who will rise to prominence beside Zawahiri.

The most important weakness of the new leadership appears to be the lack of a Saudi citizen or any other person from the Arabian Peninsula in its ranks. As elaborated in chapter 1, al-Qaeda had long been a predominantly Egyptian–Saudi Arabian organization and had immensely profited from financing through its logistics networks in Saudi Arabia and the smaller Gulf states as well as from the large number of recruits from these states and from Yemen. Without the money donated in the Gulf countries, al-Qaeda would probably not have been able to perpetrate the 9/11 attacks and would not have become the global threat it is today. Although it remains to be seen to what extent Bin Laden as a personality attracted these donations, al-Qaeda will nevertheless have to find a Saudi or at least a Yemeni member to represent the Arabian Peninsula in the new leadership circle. Bin Laden's son Saad (b. 1979) was sometimes mentioned as a possible candidate, but he never had any standing within the organization and in any event was killed in a drone strike in Pakistan in July 2009. Besides him, there do not seem to have been any convincing alternatives. The problem is an urgent one for Zawahiri and his followers. If al-Qaeda does not soon find a Gulf Arab for a leadership position, it risks losing support in the Gulf and thereby access to money and recruits. This loss will not necessarily lead to its demise, but it might prompt affiliates such as the Yemeni al-Qaeda to assert their increasingly important position or might reduce al-Qaeda's position in relation to competing organizations such as the IMU or Lashkar-e Tayyiba. Al-Qaeda central might thereby become just one jihadist organization among several.

If al-Qaeda is seriously weakened today, this status is not primarily the result of Bin Laden's death, but rather the result of the Arab revolutions in 2011, which constituted a strategic defeat for the jihadists. In January, protesters in Tunisia ousted President Zaynalabidin Ben Ali after he had ruled the country for nearly twenty-four years. He was followed by Egyptian president Hosni Mubarak in February after peaceful demonstrators forced the end of his near thirty-year rule. In late August, Muammar al-Gaddafi of Libya followed suit after rebels shattered his troops all over the country with air support provided by NATO allies, including the United States, France, and Britain. Regimes in Bahrain and Yemen are under pressure, and Syrian president Bashar al-Asad's regime has proved unable to stop widespread protests in the country in spite of brutal countermeasures, which by the end of 2012 had already led to the death of more than 60,000 people.

These events were a devastating defeat for al-Qaeda as well because neither the leadership of the organization in Pakistan nor its affiliates in Yemen, Iraq, and Algeria played any role in them. Since al-Qaeda's inception and even before then, its leaders had aimed at toppling the authoritarian regimes in Egypt, Saudi Arabia, and other Arab countries and had even begun to attack these regimes' allies in the West after they had found out that their adversaries were too powerful to be attacked head on. And suddenly the worst enemies of al-Qaeda in their home countries—liberal democrats, modern women, moderate Islamists, and many other citizens who would not want to have anything to do with al-Qaeda—swept away these regimes, in some cases without even having to employ violence on any major scale. Thereby, the Arab revolutions more than any other event have showed how irrelevant al-Qaeda's ideology has become in the eleven years after September 11, 2001. Al-Qaeda never commanded a mass following in any of its countries of origin, but now it has been reduced to political insignificance in large parts of the Arab world.

This does not mean, however, that al-Qaeda will not remain a militant organization to be reckoned with. Rather, widespread turmoil will provide the jihadist movement with new options for terrorist activity in places where strict government countermeasures have battered or at least weakened terrorist organizations in recent years. The revolts have already led to a substantial weakening of several states in the Arab world, and weak and failed states provide exactly the surroundings in which al-Qaeda has flourished since its inception. The history of jihadist terrorism in Algeria, Iraq, and Yemen provides ample evidence for this argument.

Furthermore, the Arab revolutions are at least a short-term setback also for al-Qaeda's Western enemies and their counterterrorism strategies. From 2001, the United States and its allies increasingly relied on cooperation with pro-Western regimes, among them Jordan, Morocco, Tunisia,

Egypt, and others. Without these partners, police and intelligence services in the United States and Europe will find it increasingly difficult to fight al-Qaeda and its allies. This difficulty is especially serious because after 2001 al-Qaeda's survival was in part rooted in its ability to convey the impression that it was an organization of global reach, which in reality it had ceased to be with the downfall of the Taliban and the loss of its base in Afghanistan that year. In 2003, however, the organization was assisted in its propaganda efforts by the emergence of powerful "affiliates" in its home countries in the Arab world. These groups will try their utmost to utilize the security vacuums resulting from the weakening of Arab regimes.

The most dangerous of these affiliates is the Yemeni branch of al-Qaeda, which was founded in 2009 and quickly established itself as the vanguard of the jihadist movement in the Arab world. Most important, it planned and organized the first plot by a regional al-Qaeda affiliate on US soil. On December 25, 2009, a young Nigerian on a Northwest Airlines flight arriving in Detroit from Amsterdam attempted to detonate a bomb hidden in his underwear but was overwhelmed by fellow passengers. This plot was followed by an attempt to detonate bombs hidden in printer cartridges on two cargo planes headed toward Chicago in late October 2010. Yemen has already proven to be a near-ideal rear base for al-Qaeda, so the end of Ali Abdallah Salih's regime and widespread disturbances in the country will bolster al-Qaeda's terrorist options in the near future. By spring 2011, the Yemeni government gave up its fight against al-Qaeda in order to ensure its own survival in Sanaa, so the organization was able spread its influence in the southern part of the country. Because Yemen is not likely to stabilize in the coming years, al-Qaeda will be a significant force there.

Al-Qaeda in Iraq will not be able to threaten the existence of the Iraqi state, but it will persist in executing a limited amount of large-scale terrorist attacks in the coming years. If large-scale and prolonged sectarian or ethnic violence were to break out again, the insurgency might again flare up and provide al-Qaeda with the near-ideal operating theater that it enjoyed until 2006. This scenario is not likely, however, because the Shiites have won the civil war, and their former Sunni adversaries have given up the fight. The situation is, however, more dangerous in northern Iraq, where basic questions about the future borders of the Kurdish region have not been resolved and ethnic tensions are running high, threatening the eruption of a Kurdish–Arab civil war in the coming years. Al-Qaeda would likely profit from such a development, just as it benefits from the escalation of the unrest in Syria into a civil war in 2012—where Syrian and foreign jihadists form a growing force among the insurgents.

Among the Arab affiliates, the Algerian al-Qaeda is considered the gravest threat to European security, especially in France and Spain. The process of "pan-Maghrebization" and a more general internationalization of its ideology, discussed in chapter 1, hinted at an increasing danger to Western targets. Although its newfound internationalist fervor seems to have died down slowly after 2007, the revolutions in North Africa might prove to be especially important. Tough security measures in Morocco, Tunisia, and Libya have until now prevented the expansion of the organization's activities to these countries. But specifically the downfall of the Gaddafi regime in Libya opened up new opportunities for local and regional jihadist groups, especially in the Sahel, where the influx of arms and trained fighters became a destabilizing factor in 2011 and 2012 and led to the takeover of northern Mali by jihadist groups connected to Al-Qaeda in the Islamic Maghreb. Al-Qaeda will try its utmost to profit from the revolutions in Algeria's neighboring countries and use North Africa as a springboard to threaten Europe as well.

For the future of German jihadism, however, the situations in Pakistan and Afghanistan as well as in Europe itself will be decisive.

Prospects for al-Qaeda and the German Jihad

As a consequence of these sometimes contradictory developments, prospects for the future of al-Qaeda and the jihadist movement are mixed and differ according to each of the geographical areas where al-Qaeda has established a presence in the roughly sixteen years of its existence as a truly transnational terrorist organization in South Asia and Europe.

PAKISTAN AND AFGHANISTAN

In Pakistan and Afghanistan, al-Qaeda has been under intense pressure ever since the US government intensified its drone campaign in late 2007. Although hundreds of its members and several important leaders have died, the organization's prospects are not completely bleak. Perhaps most important, the Arab jihadists have built lasting alliances in the tribal areas, which are effectively providing them protection against their numerous enemies without which al-Qaeda would arguably not have survived until now and would not have been able to establish the epicenter of international terrorism there. Its most important allies during all these years have been Jalaluddin Haqqani and his supporters, who have steadfastly backed up al-Qaeda in spite of the American wrath this drew upon them, so it is surprising how little scrutiny the Haqqani network drew until 2011.[10] The Haqqanis have masterfully managed to offer themselves as a weapon of choice to the Pakistani military in the latter's bid to retain influence in neighboring Afghanistan once the Americans and their allies leave, so they were able to offer al-Qaeda asylum in North Waziristan and adjacent areas. There are no signs that there are any cracks in this long-standing alliance between the Pashtun warriors and their Arab guests, so al-Qaeda will probably be able to stay on in its Pakistani safe haven. Although drone strikes have proven to be an effective weapon to weaken the organization and hamper any more sophisticated planning that might be in the making, expelling al-Qaeda from Waziristan will be possible only with a full-scale offensive by the Pakistani army—which in turn would risk a protracted guerilla war.

The future of al-Qaeda in Pakistan and Afghanistan hinges on the role that the Taliban, the Haqqani network, and the Islamic Party will be able to play in Afghanistan. Here, the beginning of the 2011 withdrawal of troop reinforcements that the Obama administration sent to Afghanistan in early 2010 has clearly encouraged the insurgents to continue their fight. The announcement of the partial withdrawal gave the impression that they would only have to wait for a year before American pressure would be reduced and merely a few years more before all foreign troops would finally withdraw and thereby open the path to Kabul for the Taliban again. The German jihadist Rami Makanesi, for example, reported how in 2010 his acquaintances in North Waziristan told him, "This is the last year America," referring to the beginning of the American withdrawal in 2011. Moreover, such was the mood that every able male in North Waziristan wanted to seize the allegedly last opportunity to join the jihad against the Americans in Afghanistan.[11] The insurgents were evidently confident of victory in spite of the brutal losses they had suffered at the hands of the Americans and their allies during 2010.

Although it is too early to tell what the situation might be in 2014, there is reason to believe that the Taliban will be able to have yet more impact on the history of Afghanistan in the years to come. Already in 2011, evidence abounded that the country might approach a new civil war along the lines of the conflict in the 1990s—with Pashtuns, Tajiks, Uzbeks, and the Shiite Hazara fighting in different constellations—after the withdrawal of Western forces. In a situation in which the Taliban might claim that it had won a victory against the invaders, al-Qaeda would not only improve its chances to survive but would probably make an effort to present the Taliban victory as its own. This situation would parallel events after the Soviet withdrawal from Afghanistan in 1989. Although the war was won by Afghans and the Arab military role was negligible, the emerging jihadist movement claimed victory and thereby recruited thousands of young Arabs for its cause in the next decades. Whatever the case, any NATO withdrawal in the coming years will take place under heavy Taliban fire; the Taliban will try its utmost to present the events as a direct result of its struggle, and al-Qaeda and other organizations will try to accompany these events with terrorist attacks in Afghanistan, Pakistan, Europe, and the United States.

The dramatic situation in Afghanistan notwithstanding, events in Pakistan hint at the more fundamental changes in the structure of the jihadist movement and the nature of the jihadist threat. Under the immense American pressure exerted primarily through the constant drone attacks, jihadists in the Pakistani tribal areas have increasingly closed their ranks. Although it is still possible to identify al-Qaeda as a primarily Arab organization, and the IJU, the IMU, and the different Afghan and Pakistani insurgent groups have remained independent of each other, they are more closely linked to each other than they were in 2002. Reports abound of fighters of widely varying ethnic and national backgrounds training together in al-Qaeda or IMU camps and fighting together under the command of their Afghan and Pakistani brethren.[12] Strong personal bonds between members of different organizations and joint terrorist operations point in a similar direction. Perhaps most important, al-Qaeda has managed to establish close ties to non-Pashtun organizations and individuals from the Pakistani heartlands, which has allowed it to perpetrate big attacks in the Pakistani cities since 2002. This convergence process, however, has remained incomplete. The best evidence for the continuing relevance of former dividing lines is the conflict between al-Qaeda and the

Uzbek IMU, which has shaped the history of the jihadist scene in the past decade. It remains to be seen whether the IMU's loss of bases in South Waziristan and its need for support by groups other than the Pakistani Taliban will have any impact on the relations between the organizations.

What is obvious, though, is that the dominant ideological trend among all these groups has been internationalization. It has affected even a hitherto staunchly nationalist organization such as the IMU and has increasingly shaped the views of Pakistani organizations, most notably the Lashkar-e Tayyiba, which has come a long way since its inception in the 1990s, when it aimed at the "liberation" of Kashmir, then broadened its goals to include the "liberation" of all Indian Muslims, until it increasingly aimed at the West in general. The Mumbai attacks of November 2008 might have been a harbinger of the future threat posed by this and other South Asian groups. The Indian subcontinent will remain a hotspot of Islamist terrorism, even after the possible demise of al-Qaeda.

EUROPE

Although jihadist organizations continue to dominate the scene in South Asia and the Middle East, their influence has dwindled in the Western diaspora. But Europeans and, since 2010, Americans have possibly become the most dynamic element of the jihadist movement, serving as standard bearers of jihadist internationalism and testing more independent variations of jihadist organization. Al-Qaeda's ideology has spread among young Muslims in Europe. Through an increasing amount of propaganda materials on the Internet and translations into more and more languages, al-Qaeda has managed to broaden the social base of the jihadist movement in Europe. Whereas in 2001 the movement was clearly dominated by Arabs, in 2011 Pakistanis, Afghans, Turks, Kurds, and even European converts to Islam have been drawn into the fold.

As a consequence, al-Qaeda has lost organizational influence but gained ideological impact in some areas, especially among young Muslims in Europe. In the first years after 9/11, the organized jihadists dominated the scene in Europe. The protagonists were mainly Arabs who remained closely connected to al-Qaeda, its affiliates, or other jihadist organizations operating in the Middle East and South Asia. Because they were forced to communicate with each other and travel across continents in order to sustain their structures, however, they proved extremely vulnerable to counterterrorism measures, which European governments substantially intensified in late 2001. In part as a response to the crushing of the organized jihadists in Europe, young volunteers increasingly operated independently of larger organizations in 2003. However, most of their plots were carried out rather amateurishly and failed, so European jihadists soon realized that they needed the training, logistics, and financing provided by al-Qaeda and its allies.

As a result, a hybrid form of organization developed in 2005. In this formation, the recruits radicalized in their European home countries without coming into contact with larger organizations. They then set out to join al-Qaeda and its affiliates in the Middle East or South Asia, where they would gain access to specialized training and logistics to carry out attacks either on the spot or in their home countries. One of the most striking examples of this trend is the Sauerland group.

In recent years, al-Qaeda's call to join the jihad against the United States and its allies in Afghanistan has enjoyed undaunted attractiveness in Europe. Not even the difficult living conditions and the dangers of being attacked by American drones has deterred young Europeans from joining al-Qaeda and other jihadist organizations in the Pakistani tribal areas.

The reasons for this attraction are manifold, but Western intervention and an appealing internationalist ideology seem to be paramount. Western intervention in the Muslim world has served as a powerful propaganda tool for al-Qaeda. The wars in Afghanistan, Iraq, and Somalia have convinced many young Muslims that the West is indeed fighting a war against Islam, as Osama Bin Laden and his followers argued. This motive is reinforced by the continuing attractiveness of classical internationalist thought. It is a standard tenet of the classical Islamic law of nations that Muslim territory occupied by a non-Muslim country must be liberated in a jihad. This is clearly the case in Afghanistan and Iraq, so that many young Muslims, numerous Europeans among them, have answered al-Qaeda's call to join the fight.

By 2011 at the latest, al-Qaeda decided to make use of these European recruits as part of a new strategy. Based on its observation that it had not been able to perpetrate larger-scale attacks in the Western world since the attacks in the United States on September 11, 2001, it decided to promote small-scale attacks in Europe in order to bridge the time until it regained strength. New recruits would have to be sent back to Europe as soon as possible and carry out individual attacks according to their capabilities, with the goal of proving that al-Qaeda was still able fight its enemies in the West. This was the gist of the strategy paper that Maqsood Lodin carried on a USB stick with him when he was arrested in Berlin in May 2011. The same message was transported in a spectacular propaganda video released by al-Qaeda in June 2011, featuring leaders such as Zawahiri, Atiyatallah, and Abu Yahia al-Libi and celebrating the virtue of "individual jihad."[13]

The context of this shift in strategies became clearer when a letter by Yunus al-Muritani to Osama Bin Laden apparently found during the Abbottabad raid in May 2011 was provided by the US government for the trial against the Düsseldorf cell in summer 2012. The letter seems to have been part of a broader exchange of ideas between Muritani and Bin Laden and gives a deep if somewhat unsystematic insight into al-Qaeda's strategic planning. Muritani apparently aimed primarily at attacks in Europe and America and wanted the Düsseldorf cell to perpetrate attacks as soon as possible. New groups worldwide, he stated, should focus on building cells and training members for air- and seaborne terrorist attacks—especially the latter, which seem to have been Muritani's passion. He focused on energy infrastructure such as on- and offshore gas pipelines and Qatari and Iranian gas tankers, but he also mentioned tunnels, dams, bridges, and all kinds of energy installations. He also referred to assassinations of political, economic, and intellectual leaders, giving possible hints as to what the Europlot mastermind had in mind when he sent operatives back to Europe.[14]

At least some of the German jihadists arrested in 2010 and 2011 had been sent back to Europe to put parts of this strategy into practice. The first major success based on the "individual jihad" part of this strategy most likely was twenty-three-year-old Mohammed Merah's attack on French soldiers and Jewish civilians in southern France in March 2011, killing seven. Although it could not be established whether Merah, a French citizen of Algerian origin, maintained contact with al-Qaeda, he had been to Pakistan in 2010 and executed the attacks as if he were following the organization's strategy paper. The grand design of reviving al-Qaeda by building new structures in Africa and Europe failed, however, because of its inability to keep its structures in Pakistan intact. In his letter to Bin Laden, Muritani stressed the importance of protecting al-Qaeda's three most important leaders in Waziristan—Atiyatallah Abu Abd al-Rahman, Abu Yahia al-Libi, and Mustafa Abu l-Yazid—to keep the organization intact.[15] But all three were killed in drone strikes between 2010 and 2012, and Muritani and most Germans who were sent to Europe and Africa were arrested, so that the plans could not be implemented. As a consequence, the grand new strategy as envisioned by Bin Laden, Muritani, and others in the al-Qaeda leadership utterly failed.

New Strategies?

Perhaps the most effective instruments in the fight against the epicenter of jihadism in Pakistan have been the controversial American drone strikes. They were part of a major shift in US strategy that took place in 2008 and 2009. In the last year of the Bush administration and increasingly in the Obama presidency beginning in 2009, the United States reshifted its focus from Iraq to Afghanistan and Pakistan. It thereby corrected its major strategic mistake after 9/11, when it gave up its focus on fighting al-Qaeda in South Asia and concentrated on the war against Saddam Hussein's Iraq. With the withdrawal of Special Forces and intelligence resources from Afghanistan and Pakistan in 2002, the United States arguably gave al-Qaeda and Taliban the chance to reorganize and thereby allowed for the Afghan insurgency to gain strength and escalate beginning in 2006. It was only in late 2007 and early 2008 that the United States intensified the drone campaign against targets in the Pakistani tribal areas and managed to substantially weaken al-Qaeda and other jihadist organizations. As long as the Pakistani military refuses to fight the militants in the tribal areas, the drone strikes remain the best weapon against al-Qaeda, IMU, IJU, and their Pashtun allies, reducing the threat posed by the German jihadists as well. Nevertheless, air strikes alone will not end the jihadist presence in this area.

Most important to note is that the drone strikes—as with most other measures—do not provide the West with an instrument to deal with an increasingly internationalist scene. Instead, the immense pressure on the jihadists in Pakistan seems on the contrary to have fostered their move toward internationalist ideologies. In general, internationalization has in part been a reaction to Western intervention in Afghanistan, Iraq, and

Somalia as well as to Western cooperation with authoritarian regimes in the Muslim world. Its attractiveness is due to a combination of these factors and an ideological predisposition toward classical internationalist thought. Although the West cannot influence these ideological predispositions, it can rethink its strategies toward conflicts in the Muslim world. Most important, the United States and its allies should avoid overreactions such as the Iraq War.

In general, direct intervention will have to be avoided if possible. For several years after 2003, the Iraq War was the single most important motive for terrorist activities in Europe and remains the most catastrophic mistake of US foreign policy in the past decade. If there is no alternative to intervention, as in Afghanistan in 2001, all the necessary resources to beat the insurgents and rebuild the country should be employed at once. The aim should be to leave the country in question as soon as possible. After the current fiasco in Afghanistan, Germany will probably not take part in similar campaigns in future. Public opposition and the domestic problems associated with the Afghanistan mission will convince German policymakers that most out-of-area missions are too dangerous.

Further, Western countries will have to rethink their security cooperation with dictatorships in the Muslim world. Al-Qaeda is targeting the United States because of its alliance with Saudi Arabia, Egypt, Jordan, and many other countries. In the case of Germany, the country's cooperation with the Uzbek regime made it a target for the Uzbek jihadists. What is needed is a mode of action stressing that the United States and Europe have an interest in stability and an equally important interest in incremental change toward the rule of law and greater popular participation in government. Authoritarian regimes that refuse to reform themselves are doomed, as the situations in Egypt, Tunisia, and Libya have shown, and should therefore be pressured to change. Otherwise, not only the jihadists but also other oppositionists might come to see the United States and its allies as continued accomplices of the authoritarian governments in their countries.

In addition, Germany will have to rethink its domestic counterterrorism strategy. The German security authorities have had significant problems identifying and monitoring the radicalization processes in Salafist circles in recent years. Legal and political restrictions have played a role in curbing police and intelligence services' freedom of action, but these services also suffer from a severe weakness in human intelligence, including a lack of qualified personnel. Although they claim to have addressed this problem, recent cases of Germans leaving for Pakistan without these services' taking notice indicate that the new measures have not been adequate to resolve the problem. The Salafist scene will have to be monitored much more aggressively than it has until now in order to control the situation.

Notes

In all cases where police interrogations have been quoted in the notes, the information has been corroborated by the defendants during the public main trial.

Prologue: Lone-Wolf Attacks and the Europlot

All translations are mine unless otherwise noted.

1. Matthias Bartsch, Matthias Gebauer, and Yassin Musharbash, "Im Turbotempo zum radikalen Islamisten" (Fast-Track to Radical Islamism), *Spiegel Online*, March 3, 2011.
2. David Crawford, Laura Stevens, and Marcus Walker, "Frankfurt Shooting Suspects Had Links to Radical Islamists," *Wall Street Journal*, March 4, 2011.
3. In fact, the day after the attack, a short notice appeared on a Turkish-language jihadist forum stating that Uka had made efforts to join the jihad in Afghanistan, but that he had not managed to leave Germany.
4. The composer of this song is unknown, but it is very likely that one of the two brothers or both of them were responsible. The translation of the song given here is mine.
5. Arabic for "Palestine."
6. Arabic for "Chechnya."
7. Arabic term that the jihadists use for Afghanistan.
8. Matthias Gebauer and Yassin Musharbash, "De Maizière warnt vor Anschlag in Deutschland" (De Maizière Warns of Attack in Germany), *Spiegel Online*, November 17, 2010.
9. Marcel Rosenbach and Holger Stark, "Eine Bombe für Deutschland" (A Bomb for Germany), *Der Spiegel* 19 (2011), 33.

10. Matthias Bartsch, Matthias Gebauer, and Yassin Musharbash, "Vorbild Mumbai" (The Mumbai Model), *Der Spiegel* 47 (2010): 20–23.
11. "Alarm in Deutschland—Bundespolizei-Chef warnt vor extremer Terror-Gefahr" (Alarm in Germany-Head of the Federal Police Warns of Extreme Danger of Terror Attacks), *Spiegel Online*, November 20, 2010.
12. As of 2012, Erdoğan was reported to have moved to Somalia, where he joined al-Shabab. In June 2012, he was arrested in the Tansanian capital Daressalam and extradited to Germany.
13. Author's interview with German intelligence official, Berlin, May 18, 2011.

1. Unlikely Internationalists: Putting German Jihadism into Perspective

1. For this view, see, for example, Bernard Lewis, *The Crisis of Islam: Holy War and Unholy Terror* (New York: Random House, 2004); Michael Ignatieff, "It's War—but It Doesn't Have to Be Dirty," *The Guardian*, October 1, 2001; Paul Bremer, "A New Strategy for the New Face of Terrorism," *The National Interest*, "Thanks Giving 9-11" special Issue (November 1, 2001).
2. Along this line of argumentation, see, for example, Guido Steinberg, *Der nahe und der ferne Feind: Die Netzwerke des islamistischen Terrorismus* (The Near and the Far Enemy: Networks of Islamist Terrorism) (Munich: Beck, 2005), and Fawaz A. Gerges, *The Far Enemy: Why Jihad Went Global* (New York: Cambridge University Press, 2005).
3. On KSM's biography in detail, see Terry McDermott, Josh Meyer, and Patrick J. McDonnell , "The Plots and Designs of al Qaeda's Engineer Khalid Shaikh Mohammed," *Los Angeles Times*, December 22, 2002.
4. On the development of jihadism in Saudi Arabia, see Thomas Hegghammer, *Jihad in Saudi Arabia: Violence and Pan-Islamism since 1979* (Cambridge: Cambridge University Press, 2010).
5. The Egyptian Jihad Organization or Group is known under different names, among them "Egyptian Islamic Jihad" and "Islamic Jihad/Gihad." In Egyptian Arabic, the letter *jim* is pronounced as a hard *g* (as in "Gideon") instead of a soft *j*.
6. Aiman al-Zawahiri, *Fursan taht rayat al-nabi* (Knights Under the Prophet's Banner) (n.p: n.p., July 2001), passim.
7. On Ramírez's biography, see John Follain, *Jackal: The Complete Story of the Legendary Terrorist, Carlos the Jackal* (New York: Arcade, 1998).
8. See the course of events as detailed in National Commission on Terrorist Attacks upon the United States, *The 9/11 Commission Report* (Washington, DC: U.S. Government Printing Office, 2004), 148. The commission quite fittingly called KSM a "terrorist entrepreneur."
9. Prominent examples include the Libyan ideologist Abu l-Mundhir as-Saidi and the leader of the LIFG, Abdallah Sadiq (a.k.a. Abdalhakim Belhaj).
10. Peter Bergen and Paul Cruickshank, "The Unraveling: The Jihadist Revolt Against Bin Laden," *The New Republic*, June 11, 2008.

11. Author's interview with former LIFG leader Noman Benotman, London, July 21, 2008.
12. On this ideological aspect of building a jihadist organization in a slightly different context, see Brian Fishman, *Dysfunction and Decline: Lessons Learned from Inside al Qaida in Iraq* (West Point, NY: Combating Terrorism Center, March 16, 2009), 28.
13. Libi has published numerous writings in recent years. See, for example, Abu Yahia al-Libi, *Al-Mu*ʿ*lim fi hukm al-jasus al-Muslim* (Guidance on the Ruling on the Muslim Spy) (n.p.: Markaz al-Fajr, 1430/2010).
14. The other three were the Iraqi Omar al-Faruq (1969–2006), formerly al-Qaeda's senior representative in Southeast Asia until he was captured in Indonesia in June 2002; the Saudi Muhammad al-Qahtani; and the Syrian Abdullah Hashimi.
15. Hasan Muhammad Qaid, *Haqiqat ma yajri wara*ʾ*a l-qudban fi sujun al-Amrikan* (The Truth of What Happens Behind the Bars in the Prisons of the Americans) (n.p.: Shaban 1426/September 2005).
16. The video first appeared in a report that aired in Arabic on al-Arabiya TV, Dubai, December 18, 2005.
17. The video was published on the IJU Web site at http://www.sehadetzamani.com.
18. Sudarsan Raghavan, "In Libya, Ex-militants Fight Extremism: Former Radicals Work to Discredit al Qaeda fighters," *Washington Post*, June 20, 2010.
19. Author's interview with former LIFG leader Noman Benotman, London, July 21, 2008.
20. On the merger, see Andrew Black, "Al-Qaeda, the Libyan Islamic Fighting Group, and Jihad in North Africa," *Jamestown Foundation: Terrorism Focus* 4, no. 39 (29 November 2007), at http://www.jamestown.org/single/?no_cache=1&tx_ttnews%5Btt_news%5D=4571.
21. This number is a rough estimate. Author's interview with former LIFG leader Noman Benotman, London, June 6, 2011.
22. Jonathan Schanzer, *Countering Algerian Terror: Increased U.S. Involvement?* Policy Watch no. 801 (Washington, DC: Washington Institute for Near East Policy, October 28, 2003).
23. Borzou Daragahi, "Algeria: Another Sad Morning," *Los Angeles Times*, January 29, 2008.
24. Guido Steinberg and Isabelle Werenfels, "Between the 'Near' and the 'Far' Enemy: Al-Qaeda in the Islamic Maghreb," *Mediterranean Politics* 12, no. 3 (November 2007), 411–412.
25. These figures constitute rough estimates based on birth rates, so the real figures may well be higher. The total number of Muslims of all ethnic backgrounds in France is likely to be close to 5 million. See Pew Forum on Religion and Public Life, *Mapping the Global Muslim Population* (Washington, DC: Pew Research Center, October 2009).
26. Francis Cornu and Philippe Bernard, "Les trois jours de terreur du vol AF 8969," *Le Monde*, December 27, 1994.
27. These North African immigrants in Germany include Moroccans, Algerians, Tunisians, and Libyans but exclude Egyptians. Moroccans are the biggest single group, composing about 60 percent of the whole. Sonja Haug, Stephanie Müssig, and Anja Stichs, *Muslimisches Leben in Deutschland* (Muslim Life in Germany) (Nuremberg: Bundesamt für Migration und Flüchtlinge/Deutsche Islamkonferenz, 2009), 311.

28. Frank Jansen, "Terror aus Nordafrika" (Terror from North Africa), *Der Tagesspiegel*, October 24, 2008. The author quotes a statement by the former head of the German BND, Ernst Uhrlau.
29. According to (unreliable) statistics by the Brookings Institution, Algerians made up as much as 20 percent of the foreign fighters in Iraq. Brookings Institution, *Iraq Index: Tracking Variables of Reconstruction and Security in Post-Saddam Iraq* (Washington, DC: Brookings Institution Press, September 21, 2006), 19.
30. "An Interview with Abdelmalek Droukdal," *New York Times*, July 1, 2008.
31. See Guido Steinberg, *The Iraqi Insurgency. Actors, Strategies, and Structures*, SWP-Research Paper 13/06 (Berlin: Stiftung Wissenschaft und Politik, December 2006), 26–27.
32. Camille al-Tawil, "Al-Zarqawi: Hukuma islamiya fi l-ʿIraq wa l-intilaq minhu li-qalb anzima duwal al-jiwar" (Al-Zarqawi: An Islamic Government in Iraq and the Start from There to Overthrow the Regimes in the Neighbouring Countries), *al-Hayat*, September 10, 2004.
33. Between 500,000 and 800,000 of these 2.5 million Turks in Germany are of Kurdish origin.
34. See, for example, a German-language video by the IMU: Islamische Bewegung Usbekistans, *Mutter bleibe standhaft* (Mother, Remain Steadfast) (Studio Jundullah, September 2010). In it, IMU member Yassin Chouka cites the (perceived) crimes of the West in Muslim countries as a reason to join the jihadist movement.
35. Marcel Rosenbach and Holger Stark, "Der Hass des Abdullah" (Abdullah's Hatred), *Der Spiegel* 36 (2008), 50.
36. On the Ansar al-Islam, see Brynjar Lia, "The Ansar al-Islam Group Revisited," paper presented at the seminar "Islamism and the European Security," Aarhus University, June 2006.
37. Among the four was Naamen Meziche, a French Algerian born in Paris in 1970. In 2009, Meziche left Germany with other members of the Hamburg group to travel to Pakistan and join the jihadists in the tribal areas. Interview with Dr. Manfred Murck, deputy head, state BfV, Landesverfassungsschutz, Hamburg, September 7, 2010.
38. Nir Rosen, "Iraq's Jordanian Jihadis," *New York Times Magazine*, February 19, 2006. On the structure of the Iraqi insurgency until 2006, see Steinberg, *The Iraqi Insurgency*.

2. Two Hamburg Cells: A History of Jihadist Terrorism in Germany

1. The *ansar*, or followers, were those people of Medina who supported the Prophet Muhammad after his flight (*hijra*) from Mecca in 622 CE.
2. On Bahaji's role in the 9/11 attacks, see National Commission on Terrorist Attacks upon the United States, *The 9/11 Commission Report* (Washington, DC: US Government Printing Office, 2004), 167.

3. The first evidence of Bahaji's involvement in al-Qaeda media production appeared in April 2004, when an audio message by Osama Bin Laden addressing the Europeans appeared in three versions: one in the original Arabic, one with German subtitles, and one with English subtitles. The German translation contains a few mistakes, and the German BND at that time concluded that Said Bahaji must have been responsible for the translation. Author's interview with German intelligence official, Berlin, May 23, 2011. Sidiqi corroborated Bahaji's function as a propagandist in the al-Sahab office in an interrogation while in detention in Bagram. Interrogation of Ahmad Wali Sidiqi in Bagram, October 2010, unreleased intelligence report.
4. Matthias Gebauer and Holger Stark, "Freunde des 11. September" (Friends of September 11), *Der Spiegel* 41 (2010), 112.
5. The German term for this category of potential terrorists is *Gefährder*, a person who puts something or someone in danger. In early 2011, the BKA had 130 people on this list. The second category of people with established connections to jihadist terrorists were called *relevante Personen* (relevant persons), a list that included 285 jihadists.
6. Hans Leyendecker, "Das Rätsel der Giftspur (The Riddle of the Poison Track)," *Süddeutsche Zeitung*, September 21, 1998.
7. Author's interview with German government official, Berlin, February 17, 2011.
8. Ibid.
9. Lawrence Wright, *The Looming Tower: Al-Qaeda and the Road to 9/11* (New York: Random House, 2006), 170.
10. Ibid., 131–133.
11. National Commission on Terrorist Attacks, *The 9/11 Commission Report*, 57–58.
12. Ibid., 127.
13. Steven Erlanger, "Traces of Terror: Berlin. Germans Press Investigation of Qaeda-Tied Businessman," *New York Times*, June 19, 2002.
14. For the Abu Dahdah network, see Brynjar Lia, *Architect of Global Jihad: The Life of Al-Qaida Strategist Abu Musʿab al-Suri* (New York: Columbia University Press, 2008), 137–147.
15. Dominik Cziesche, Georg Mascolo, and Holger Stark, "Das Puzzle lag auf dem Tisch" (The Puzzle Was on the Table), *Der Spiegel* 6 (2003): 96–98.
16. Essabar's whereabouts are unknown.
17. "Federal Criminal Police Report About Jihadist Travel Groups," April 1, 2009, unreleased BKA internal document.
18. Gebauer and Stark, "Freunde des 11. September," 112.
19. National Commission on Terrorist Attacks, *The 9/11 Commission Report*, 160–162.
20. James Risen, "Traces of Terror: The Investigation; 9/11 Suspect May Have Been with Plotters Abroad in 1999," *New York Times*, June 8, 2002.
21. Author's interview with German police official, Berlin, January 27, 2011.
22. For an earlier version of this categorization, see Guido Steinberg, *The Threat of Jihadist Terrorism in Germany* (Madrid: Real Instituto Elcano, 2008). A similar

categorization appeared around the same time in Peter R. Neumann, *Joining al-Qaeda: Jihadist Recruitment in Europe* (London: International Institute for Strategic Studies, 2008), 17–18.

23. *Urteil in der Strafsache gegen Mohamed Ghassan Ali Saud Abu Dhess (et al.)* (Verdict in the Case Against Mohamed Ghassan Ali Saud Abu Dhess [et al.]), Oberlandesgericht Düsseldorf, 2 StE 9/03-3 (March 2006), 56–61.
24. Phone conversation given in evidence in ibid., 44; see also Dominik Cziesche et al., "Als wäret ihr im Krieg" (As If You Were at War), *Spiegel*, special edition, 2 (2004), 28.
25. See Georg Bönisch, Dominik Cziesche, Georg Mascolo, and Holger Stark, "Ziele in Deutschland" (Targets in Germany), *Der Spiegel* 18 (2002), 95–96; Holger Stark, "Die Hunde hören mit" (The Dogs Listen In), *Der Spiegel* 48 (2002), 46–47.
26. *Urteil in der Strafsache gegen Mohamed Ghassan Ali Saud Abu Dhess*, 43.
27. Ibid., 44–45.
28. The Jewish community center is based in Fasanenstraße in the former West Berlin city center. The nightclub targeted in Düsseldorf was the Oberbayern, and the bar targeted was Le Clou. Ibid., 50–51.
29. Quoted in "Verurteilter Islamist stürmt aus dem Gerichtssaal" (Convicted Islamist Rushes out of the Court Room), Associated Press, October 26, 2005.
30. *Urteil in der Strafsache gegen Mohamed Ghassan Ali Saud Abu Dhess*, 7–10.
31. On the Tablighi Jamaat movement, see Muhammad Khalid Masud, ed., *Travelers In Faith: Studies of the Tablighi Jamaat as a Transnational Islamic Movement for Faith Renewal* (Leiden: Brill, 2000). For the case of the American jihadist John Walker Lindh, see Matthew Engel, "US Taliban Fighter Admits Guilt," *The Guardian*, July 16, 2002.
32. *Urteil in der Strafsache gegen Mohamed Ghassan Ali Saud Abu Dhess*, 27–37.
33. Ibid., 10–13.
34. Ibid., 13–15.
35. Quoted in "German Papers—Terrorists with German Visas," *Spiegel Online*, October 27, 2005.
36. Matthias Gebauer, "Fall Amer Cheema—Alptraum Einzeltäter" (The Case of Amer Cheema—Lone-Wolf Nightmare), *Spiegel Online*, May 11, 2006.
37. Ibid.
38. *United States v. Ilyas Kashmiri et al.*, US District Court, Northern District of Illinois, Eastern Division (January 2009), 19–21. For more detail on Kashmiri, see Seth Nye, "Al-Qaʾida's Key Operative: A Profile of Mohammed Ilyas Kashmiri," CTC Sentinel 3, no. 9 (September 2010): 15–18.
39. Jochen Bölsche, "Alberichs Tarnkappe" (Alberich's Cloak of Invisibility), Spiegel, special edition, 2 (2008), 113; Mark Landler and Souad Mekhennet, "Wider Network May Be Linked to Bomb Plot, Germans Say," *New York Times*, August 23, 2006.
40. Andreas Ulrich, "Fahrkarte in den Irak" (Ticket to Iraq), *Spiegel Online*, April 7, 2007.
41. Bölsche, "Alberichs Tarnkappe," 114.
42. For an overview of the Dib family members, see Muhammad Ali Ibrahim Dib, "Rihlat ʿaʾilat Saddam Dib baina tuhma fi ʿAkkar . . . wa-ukhra fi Almaniya" (The

Journey of Saddam Dib's Family Between a Suspicion in Akkar . . . and Another One in Germany), *al-Hayat*, June 10, 2007.

43. On the events in Nahr al-Barid in 2007, see Nadia Bakri, "Militants Are Driven from Refugee Camp," *New York Times*, September 3, 2007.
44. Johannes Nitschmann, "Geständnis im Kofferbomber-Prozess" (Confession in Suitcase Bomber Trial), *Süddeutsche Zeitung*, February 8, 2008.
45. Annette Ramelsberger, "BKA liest auf gelöschter Festplatte" (BKA Reads Deleted Hard Drive)," *Süddeutsche Zeitung*, March 8, 2007.
46. Frank Pergande, "Lange Haftstrafe für Redouane E. H. (Long Jail Term for Redouane E. H.)," *Frankfurter Allgemeine Zeitung*, January 24, 2008.
47. Meziche is reported to have stayed in Afghanistan in the late 1980s and again in 1996–1997. Interrogation of Rami Makanesi, Weiterstadt, October 27, 2010, unreleased BKA report, 12. He was reported to have been killed in a drone strike in October 2010, but it later turned out that he had survived and stayed on in Pakistan, where he was arrested in May–June 2012.
48. The statistical information is drawn from a powerpoint presentation by the LfV Hamburg, "Islamists in Hamburg," November 2009, copy of presentation in author's possession. Information on the names and biographies is drawn from an unreleased BKA report about jihadist travel groups, April 1, 2009.
49. From the interrogation of Ahmad Wali Sidiqi in Bagram.
50. Ibid.
51. Ibid.
52. Author's interview with German police official, Berlin, January 27, 2011.

3. "A Second 9/11": The Sauerland Plot

1. Rolf Clement and Paul Elmar Jöris, *Die Terroristen von Nebenan: Gotteskrieger aus Deutschland* (The Terrorists From Next Door: God's Warriors from Germany) (Munich: Piper, 2010), 52.
2. Fritz Gelowicz's wife, Filiz, is a German citizen of Turkish Kurdish origin and shares his jihadist beliefs. A Berlin court convicted her of supporting the IJU in March 2011. On Gelowicz's early years, see *Urteil gegen Fritz Martin Gelowicz et al.* (Verdict Against Fritz Martin Gelowicz et al.), Oberlandesgericht Düsseldorf, 2 StE 7/08-4 u. 2 StE 9/08-4 (June 24, 2010), 6–8. For more on Filiz Gelowicz, see chapter 6.
3. *Urteil gegen Fritz Martin Gelowicz et al.*, 11–13.
4. "Sauerland-Prozess: Anwälte fordern milde Strafe für jüngsten Angeklagten" (Sauerland Trial: Lawyers Demand Mild Verdict for the Youngest Defendant), *Spiegel Online*, February 17, 2010.
5. The details of Daniel Schneider's evolution from school dropout to terrorist are depicted in *Urteil gegen Fritz Martin Gelowicz et al.*, 14–17.
6. For the details of Selek's early life, see ibid., 22–25.

7. On Aleem Nasir, see chapter 6. Reda Seyam's exwife has written an account of their stay in Bosnia from 1994 to 1999, giving some insights into the group's activities. See Doris Glück, *Mundtot: Ich war die Frau eines Gotteskriegers* (Gagged: I was the Wife of a Warrior of God) (Berlin: Ullstein, 2005).
8. Author's interview with Herbert L. Müller, head of the Department of International Extremism and Terrorism at the state intelligence service, Landesverfassungsschutz, Baden-Württemberg, Stuttgart, May 11, 2011.
9. I received the first hint of this development from Ahmet Şenyurt, a television journalist and specialist on German Islamism. In early 2002, Şenyurt told me that the Multicultural House became an internationalist meeting point quite unlike other Islamist centers in Germany.
10. Author's interview with Herbert L. Müller, May 11, 2011.
11. Marcel Rosenbach and Holger Stark, "Der Hass des Abdullah" (Abdallah's Hatred), *Der Spiegel* 36 (2008), 48. Interrogation of Atilla Selek, Bochum, June 17, 2009, BKA report, 6.
12. Author's interview with Herbert L. Müller, May 11, 2011.
13. Ibid.
14. Author's interview with state police official, Berlin, March 14, 2011.
15. Dominik Cziesche, "Der schwäbische Krieger (The Swabian Warrior)," *Der Spiegel* 41 (2004): 66–71.
16. National Commission on Terrorist Attacks upon the United States, *The 9/11 Commission Report* (Washington, DC: US Government Printing Office, 2004), 165–166.
17. No information is available on exactly when *Das Tor der Trauer* was produced.
18. See, for example, the report about the radicalization and career of the former Guantánamo inmate Jabir al-Fifi: Nasir al-Haqbani, "Al-Fifi halima bi-kurat al-qadam fala'iba bi-l-qanabil wa-l-mutafajjirat" (Al-Fifi Dreamed of Football, but Then Played with Bombs and Explosives), *al-Hayat*, December 22, 2010. He dreamed of joining the jihad in Chechnya because he saw videos of the Chechen struggle in his home mosque in Taif. In Afghanistan, he was put up in a guesthouse reserved for those who wanted to go to Chechnya, most of whom were Arab.
19. *Urteil gegen Fritz Martin Gelowicz et al.*, 10 and 25.
20. When Thomas Fischer's father contacted members of the Multicultural House after the death of his son in late 2003, he was shown an obituary in a Muslim publication stating that his son had become a "martyr." Cziesche, "Der schwäbische Krieger," 71.
21. Interrogation of Fritz Gelowicz, Düsseldorf, June 16, 2009, BKA report, 8.
22. Ibid., June 29, 11; *Urteil gegen Fritz Martin Gelowicz et al.*, 64.
23. *Urteil gegen Fritz Martin Gelowicz et al.*, 29.
24. The friends studied at the Abu l-Nur Mosque complex in the Kurdish Rukn al-Din quarter in Damascus. It is a huge educational and cultural center with a mosque founded by the former Syrian grand mufti Sheikh Ahmad Kuftaru (c. 1911/1915–2004) in the 1970s. Kuftaru belonged to the Naqshbandiya Sufi order and upheld

close relations with the Syrian regime (see his biography at http://www.kuftaro.org). Although the Abu l-Nur center is not a university, up to 8,000 students were reported to study religious disciplines there in 2010. Besides the Sauerland cell, there have been no other known cases of jihadists studying here.

25. *Urteil gegen Fritz Martin Gelowicz et al.*, 44–45.
26. Yassin Musharbash and Holger Stark, "A German Jihad Colony: Islamists in Pakistan Recruit Entire Families from Europe," *Spiegel Online*, September 21, 2009.
27. Although Salimov is a central figure in the Sauerland plot, not much is known about him other than that he is an Uzbek citizen and was probably born in 1978 in Tashkent.
28. *Urteil gegen Fritz Martin Gelowicz et al.*, 45–46.
29. Ibid., 46. News of the group's activities first reached the German public in the form of an article in *Spiegel Online*. See "Terrordrohung—CIA warnt deutsche Behörden vor Islamisten" (Terror Threat—CIA Warns German Government of Islamists), *Spiegel Online*, April 21, 2007.
30. Clement and Jöris, *Die Terroristen von nebenan*, 80–81.
31. *Urteil gegen Fritz Martin Gelowicz et al.*, 47.
32. Ibid., 55 and 61.
33. Ibid., 46–48.
34. Ibid., 49, 52–53, 93.
35. Yassin Musharbash, "Phantom IJU wird greifbar" (The Phantom IJU becomes palpable), *Spiegel Online*, September 2, 2009; *Urteil gegen Fritz Martin Gelowicz et al.*, 62–63.
36. *Urteil gegen Fritz Martin Gelowicz et al.*, 62.
37. Author's notes from observations in court in 2009, Düsseldorf.
38. Gelowicz and Yilmaz were in Waziristan from April to September 2006. Schneider and Selek arrived in Waziristan in early July, but Selek left the IJU after only a month. Schneider was arrested in Iran in November 2006 because he had no passport and deported to Pakistan, where he was jailed for two months before he was deported to Germany in February. *Urteil gegen Fritz Martin Gelowicz et al.*, 43 and 65.
39. Various explosive devices using hydrogen peroxide have become popular with jihadist groups since 2001 and have featured in a number of attacks, such as those in Djerba 2002, Casablanca 2003, and London 2005, in all of which triacetone triperoxide (TATP), the most popular hydrogen peroxide–based explosive, was used.
40. *Urteil gegen Fritz Martin Gelowicz et al.*, 74.
41. Ibid., 81.
42. Yassin Musharbash, Marcel Rosenbach, and Holger Stark, "Der fünfte Mann" (The Fifth Man), *Der Spiegel* 17 (2009), 46.
43. *Urteil gegen Fritz Martin Gelowicz et al.*, 84–85. Taieb's brother-in-law, Muammar C., was extradited from Turkey to his native Libya in 2007 after the detonators were delivered. Marcel Rosenbach and Holger Stark, "Aladins Erzählungen" (Aladin's Stories), *Der Spiegel* 41 (2007), 68.

44. Rosenbach and Stark, "Aladins Erzählungen"; Simone Kaiser, Marcel Rosenbach, and Holger Stark, "Operation Alberich" (Operation Alberich), *Der Spiegel* 37 (2007): 20–26.
45. "Sauerland-Gruppe wollte mit Anschlag ISAF-Mandat torpedieren" (Sauerland Group Wanted to Torpedo ISAF Mandate with Attack), *Spiegel Online*, August 30, 2008. The mandates have to be extended by the Bundestag every year.
46. Ibid., 85.
47. Rosenbach and Stark, "Der Hass des Abdullah," 44.
48. *Urteil gegen Fritz Martin Gelowicz et al.*, 87.
49. Rosenbach and Stark, "Der Hass des Abdullah," 45.
50. On the details of this operation, see Kaiser, Rosenbach, and Stark, "Operation Alberich."
51. "Terrordrohung."
52. Josef Hufelschulte, "Total abgebrüht" (Totally Hard-Nosed), *Focus*, May 7, 2007; Josef Hufelschulte, "Abschied per Video" (Farewell by Video), *Focus*, May 14, 2007.
53. "Terrorismus—Warnung aus Washington" (Terrorism Warning from Washington), *Der Spiegel* 26 (2007), 15.
54. Holger Stark, "Der innerste Ring" (The Innermost Circle), *Der Spiegel* 46 (2007), 58.

4. The Islamic Jihad Union

1. For the Turkish original, see "İslami Cihad İttehadi Basın Açıklaması" (IJU Press Declaration), September 11, 2007, at http://sehadetvakti.com/haber_detay.php?haber_id=1587, accessed September 17, 2007.
2. Oleg Yakubov, *The Pack of Wolves: The Blood Trail of Terror* (Moscow: Veche, 2000), 254. Jalolov confirmed his own role in the Tashkent bombings in a conversation with Fritz Gelowicz in 2006, which Gelowicz reported during interrogation in 2009 (see chapter 8).
3. Zahid Hussain, *Frontline Pakistan: The Struggle with Militant Islam* (New York: Columbia University Press, 2007), 144.
4. On Haqqani's age, see Thomas Ruttig, "Loya Paktia's Insurgency: The Haqqani Network as an Autonomous Entity," in Antonio Giustozzi, ed., *Decoding the New Taliban: Insights from the Afghan Field* (London: Hurst, 2009), 63 n. 22.
5. There are reports that members of the Quetta Shura left Quetta for Karachi in autumn 2009 because they did not feel safe anymore.
6. According to sources in Kabul, Mullah Omar was based in Karachi or Peshawar after 2010.
7. Daniela Deane, "D.C. Man Killed in Suicide Attack at Hotel," *Washington Post*, January 16, 2008.
8. Jeremy Binnie and Joanna Wright, "Network Warriors: Al-Qaeda and the Haqqani Network," *IHS Jane's Security and Military Intelligence Consulting: Relationships and Rivalries* (October 2010), 16.

9. Joby Warrick, *The Triple Agent: The al-Qaeda Mole Who Infiltrated the CIA* (New York: Vintage, 2012). Although Warrick describes the plot as one hatched by al-Qaeda, a German jihadist who met Balawi tells a different story. According to this source, Humam al-Balawi was a medical doctor and an al-Qaeda member in North Waziristan, but the Libyan al-Qaeda commander Atiyatallah Abu Abd al-Rahman refused him as a volunteer for a suicide attack because his medical skills were needed. This is why Balawi approached the Pakistani Taliban Movement. Interrogation of Ahmad Wali Sidiqi in Bagram, October 2010, unreleased intelligence report.
10. Steve Coll, *Ghost Wars: The Secret History of the CIA, Afghanistan, and Bin Laden from the Soviet Invasion to September 10, 2001* (New York: Penguin, 2004), 157, 202–203.
11. Anand Gopal, Mansur Khan Mahsud, and Brian Fishman, *The Battle for Pakistan: Militancy and Conflict in North Waziristan* (Washington, DC: New America Foundation, 2010), 7.
12. Ibid., 8.
13. Ibid.
14. Binnie and Wright, "Network Warriors," 13.
15. On Haqqani's religious credentials, see Ruttig, "Loya Paktia's Insurgency," 73.
16. Gopal, Mahsud, and Fishman, *The Battle for Pakistan*, 11.
17. Mark Mazetti and Eric Schmitt, "Pakistanis Aided Attack in Kabul, U.S. Officials Say," *New York Times*, August 1, 2008.
18. Author's interview with the Uzbek author and IJU expert Victor Michailov, Cadenabbia, Italy, March 22, 2011.
19. Kathleen Knox and Daniel Kimmage, "Uzbekistan: Sifting for Clues," *Asia Times Online*, April 2, 2004.
20. Translation given in "Unknown Group Pledges to Fight to 'the Last Drop of Blood' in Uzbekistan," Centrasia Web site, Moscow, *BBC Monitoring Newsfile*, April 3, 2004.
21. "Religious Fanaticism Fuels Uzbek Blasts," *Washington Times*, July 31, 2004.
22. Daniel Kimmage, "Kazakh Breakthrough on Uzbek Terror Case," Radio Free Europe/Radio Liberty, November 15, 2004; "Suspect in Uzbek Terror Trial Says Group Leader Was Follower of Taliban Fugitive Mullah Omar," America's Intelligence Wire, July 27, 2004.
23. "Hijaz" is the Arabic appellation for the western part of Saudi Arabia, with the holy cities Mecca and Medina and the port city Jidda. What is meant here, though, is the whole of Saudi Arabia. Many jihadists refrain from using the official name "Saudi Arabia" because they deny that the Saudi family's rule in the country is legitimate. Al-Qaeda, for instance, normally uses the names "Arabian Peninsula" and "Land of the Two Holy Sites" instead.
24. Quoted in MIPT Terrorism Knowledge Base, "Islamic Jihad Group (Uzbekistan)," last updated November 28, 2007, no longer online, but copy in author's files.
25. US Department of State, "U.S. Department of State Designates the Islamic Jihad Group Under Executive Order 13224," press release, May 26, 2005, at http://2001-2009.state.gov/r/pa/prs/ps/2005/46838.htm.

26. US Department of State, Office of the Coordinator for Counterterrorism, *Country Reports on Terrorism 2005* (Washington, DC: US Department of State, April 2006), 107 and 199.
27. See, for example, Murray's interview with the German TV magazine *Monitor*, October 4, 2007, at http://www.wdr.de/tv/monitor/beitrag.phtml?bid=915&sid=170, accessed March 2, 2008. For Murray's depiction of the events in detail, see Craig Murray, *Murder in Samarkand: A British Ambassador's Controversial Defiance of Tyranny in the War on Terror* (Edinburgh: Mainstream, 2006), 325–339.
28. From the author's notes of Fritz Gelowicz's testimony in court, Düsseldorf, September 2009.
29. *Ebu* is the turkified equivalent of the Arabic *abu* (father of). So "Ebu Yahya" means "father of Yahya." Most jihadists use aliases of this kind, taking the name of their eldest sons. For example, Bin Laden was also known as "Abu Abdallah."
30. Author's translation from the original Turkish, "Islami Cihad Ittehadi Emiri Ebu Yahya Muhammed Fatih ile Röportaj" (Interview with the IJU Emir Ebu Yahya Muhammed Fatih), May 31, 2007, on the Turkish jihadi Web site Soldiers of Islam at http://www.cihaderi.net/haber.php?item_id=770.html, accessed March 6, 2008. The interview also appeared at http://www.sehadetvakti.com.
31. Ibid.
32. Gopal, Mahsud, and Fishman, *The Battle for Pakistan*, 10. Other sources state that Sirajuddin is the son of Jalaluddin's Arab wife. See Ruttig, "Loya Paktia's Insurgency," 62; and Binnie and Wright, "Network Warriors," 14. According to some reports, the Pakistanis jailed Nasiruddin in December 2010. As of August 2012, his whereabouts were unknown.
33. Between 2007 and 2011, out of a total of 255 drone strikes, 176 took place in North Waziristan. See Bill Roggio and Alexander Mayer, "Charting the Data for US Airstrikes in Pakistan, 2004–2011," *The Long War Journal*, August 3, 2011.
34. On the situation in Waziristan in 2009 and 2010, see Interrogation of Rami Makanesi, Weiterstadt, September 9 and 29, October 11 and 12, November 17, and December 9, 20, 2010, as well as February 3, 2011, and Darmstadt, October 27, 2010, unreleased BKA reports. Drone strikes in South Waziristan were substantially reduced in the run-up to the Pakistani military offensive in October 2009. Marcel Rosenbach and Holger Stark, "Homegrown Terror Takes on New Dimensions," *Spiegel Online*, May 9, 2011.
35. Frank J. Ciluffo, Jeffrey B. Cozzens, and Magnus Ranstorp, *Foreign Fighters: Trends, Trajectories, & Conflict Zones* (Washington, DC: Homeland Security Policy Institute, October 1, 2010), 17.
36. Gopal, Mahsud, and Fishman, *The Battle for Pakistan*, 12.
37. Binnie and Wright, "Network Warriors," 17.
38. In a discussion with me while in court in December 2009, Fritz Gelowicz ruled out Libi's possible involvement in planning the attacks in Germany.
39. Author's interview with Noman Benotman, former LIFG leader, London, July 21, 2008.

40. Hazim al-Amin, "Inshiqaqat iqlimiya fi al-Qaʿida . . . wa-l-Zarqawi tahadda al-Maqdisi bi-tafjirat ʿAmman" (Regional Fissures Within al-Qaeda . . . and Zarqawi Challenged al-Maqdisi with the Amman Bombings), *al-Hayat*, April 5, 2006.
41. Camille al-Tawil, "Al-Qaʿida tatawassaʿ maghribian baʿda dhammiha al-Muqatila" (Al-Qaeda Extends Its Influence Direction in the Maghreb After It Included the Muqatila [LIFG]), *al-Hayat*, November 4, 2007.
42. The attack targeted a house in the village of Khushali Torikhel, some eight miles south of Mir Ali. Samar al-Muqrin and Camille al-Tawil, "Abu Laith al-Libi wa-l-Darnawi qutila fi tariqihima li-liqaʾ al-muttahim bi-ghtiyal Bhutto" (Abu Laith al-Libi and al-Darnawi Were Killed on Their Way to a Meeting with the Prime Suspect in the Bhutto Assassination), *al-Hayat*, February 2, 2008.
43. "Maqtal Abu Laith al-Libi maʿa 11 akharin fi Bakistan" (Abu Laith al-Libi's Death Together with Eleven Others in Pakistan), *al-Hayat*, February 1, 2008.
44. In this declaration, the IJU sent the first report about the suicide attack perpetrated by Cüneyt Çiftçi: "Our operation was in retaliation for our Sheikh, the Mujahid Abu Laith al-Libi, who was killed a short while ago and in retaliation for our killed Mujahideen." From "İslami Cihad İttehadi Basın Açıklaması" (IJU Press Declaration), at http://www.sehadetvakti.com/haber_detay.php?haber_id=1889, accessed March 7, 2008.
45. From author's notes of Fritz Gelowicz's testimony in court, Düsseldorf, December 1, 2009.
46. US Department of the Treasury, "Treasury Designates Leadership of the IJU Terrorist Group," press statement, June 18, 2008, at http://www.treasury.gov/press-center/press-releases/Pages/hp1035.aspx; Ismail Khan, "Rocket Attack Plan Was Approved by Al Qaeda," *Dawn*, online edition, November 4, 2006.
47. See the respective press declaration "İslami Cihad İttehadi Basın Açıklaması" (IJU Press Declaration), at http://www.sehadetzamani.com/haber_detay.php?haber_id=2246, accessed October 16, 2009.
48. When Abu Laith al-Libi was killed by a drone attack in January 2008, six members of the IJU are said to have been killed with him. Al-Muqrin and al-Tawil, "Abu Laith al-Libi wa-l-Darnawi."
49. Interrogation of Daniel Martin Schneider, Cologne, June 18, 2006, unreleased BKA report, 6–8.
50. The Web site was at http://www.islamicminbar.com/forum/viewtopic.php?t=338 and could be accessed on September 7, 2004, but it was shut down sometime later.
51. Author's interview with a German intelligence official, Berlin, September 13, 2010.
52. In testimony on January 20, 2011, during the trial of Fritz Gelowicz's wife, Filiz, a BKA official mentioned that Manavbaşı had told Filiz that he had met her husband.
53. "Islami Cihad Ittehadi Emiri Ebu Yahya Muhammed Fatih ile Röportaj."
54. "İslami Cihad İttehadi Basın Açıklaması" (the statement cited in note 44).
55. Matthias Gebauer, "Top-Taliban kommandieren deutsche Gotteskrieger ("Top Taliban Command German Warriors of God")," *Spiegel Online*, April 5, 2008.
56. Author's interview with German police official, Tübingen, September 8, 2010.

57. Interrogation of Rami Makanesi," Weiterstadt, February 3, 2011, unreleased BKA report.
58. Binnie and Wright, "Network Warriors," 14.
59. Farangis Najibullah, "Uzbek Attacks Trip Alarm Bells in Ferghana," Radio Free Europe/Radio Liberty, May 27, 2009.
60. The video can be found on the IJU Web site: *Komutan Abdullah Fatihin Açıklaması* (Declaration of Commander Abdullah Fatih), at http://www.sehadetzamani.com/haber_detay.php?haber_id=2115, accessed July 16, 2009. The press declaration can be found at http://www.sehadetzamani.com/haber_detay.php?haber_id=2105, accessed July 16, 2009.

5. The Turkish Dimension

1. *Urteil gegen Fritz Martin Gelowicz et al. (Verdict against Fritz Martin Gelowicz et al.)*, Oberlandesgericht Düsseldorf (2 StE 7/08-4 u. 2 StE 9/08-4) (June 24, 2010), 82.
2. "Terrorismus: Suche nach dem Leck" (Terrorism: Search for the Leak), *Der Spiegel* 32 (2009), 15; Interrogation of Atilla Selek, Bochum, June 25, 2009, unreleased BKA report, 11.
3. Author's interview with German law enforcement official, Berlin, May 10, 2011.
4. Yassin Musharbash, Marcel Rosenbach, and Holger Stark, "Der fünfte Mann" (The Fifth Man), *Der Spiegel* 17 (2009), 46.
5. "Terrorismus," 15.
6. Philip Robins, *Suits and Uniforms: Turkish Foreign Policy Since the Cold War* (Seattle: University of Washington Press, 2003), 346–348.
7. On the jihadist scene in Bosnia in the 1990s, see Evan Kohlmann, *Al-Qaida's Jihad in Europe: The Afghan Bosnian Network* (Oxford: Berg, 2004).
8. Yossef Bodansky, *Chechen Jihad: Al Qaeda's Training Ground and the Next Wave of Terror* (New York: HarperCollins, 2007), 8–9.
9. On these foreign fighters in detail, see Brian Glyn Williams, "Allah's Foot Soldiers: An Assessment of the Role of Foreign Fighters and al-Qaʿida in the Chechen Insurgency," in Moshe Gammer, ed., *Ethno-Nationalism, Islam, and the State in the Caucasus: Post- Soviet Disorder*, 157–178 (London: Routledge, 2007).
10. On the Turkish authorities' attitude toward the issue, see Gareth Jenkins, *Political Islam in Turkey: Running West, Heading East?* (New York: Palgrave Macmillan, 2008), 205.
11. Brian Glyn Williams, "Turkish Volunteers in Chechnya," *Jamestown Foundation: Terrorism Monitor* 3, no. 7 (May 5, 2005), at http://www.jamestown.org/single/?no_cache=1&tx_ttnews%5Btt_news%5D=300.
12. Graham E. Fuller, *The New Turkish Republic: Turkey as a Pivotal State in the Muslim World* (Washington, DC: United States Institute of Peace Press, 2008), 130.
13. Ibid., 126–127.
14. Ibid.

15. On Bahaia's career, see Brynjar Lia, *Architect of Global Jihad: The Life of al-Qaida Strategist Abu Musʿab al-Suri* (London: Hurst, 2007), 189–193.
16. On Velioğlu's biography, see Jenkins, *Political Islam in Turkey*, 186.
17. Both factions were named after bookshops that the respective leaders of the two factions had opened in Diyarbakir in the early 1980s and where radical discussion groups were formed: Fidan Güngör (1949–1994) opened the Menzil bookshop in 1981, and Hüseyin Velioğlu opened the İlim shop in 1982. Ibid.
18. Rusen Cakir, *The Reemergence of Hizballah in Turkey*, Policy Focus no. 74 (Washington, DC: Washington Institute for Near East Policy, September 2007), 8.
19. Jenkins, *Political Islam in Turkey*, 186.
20. Dieter Bednarz, Ralf Beste, Siegesmund von Ilsemann, Georg Mascolo, Günter Seufert, Gerhard Spörl, Holger Stark, and Erich Wiedemann, "Der fromme Weltkrieg" (The Pious World War), *Der Spiegel* 48 (2003): 128–142.
21. Jenkins, *Political Islam in Turkey*, 191.
22. John T. Nugent Jr., "The Defeat of Turkish Hizballah as a Model for Counter-Terrorism Strategy," *Middle East Review of International Affairs* 8, no. 1 (March 2004), 63–70; Asli Aydintasbas, "Murder on the Bosporus," *Middle East Quarterly* 7, no. 2 (June 2000): 15–22.
23. Cakir, *The Reemergence of Hizballah in Turkey*, 13.
24. Nugent, "The Defeat of Turkish Hizballah," 71–73.
25. Cakir, *The Reemergence of Hizballah in Turkey*, 13–15.
26. Marc Sageman, *Leaderless Jihad: Terror Networks in the Twenty-First Century* (Philadelphia: University of Pennsylvania Press, 2008).
27. Lawrence E. Cline, "From Ocalan to al Qaida: The Continuing Terrorist Threat in Turkey," *Studies in Conflict and Terrorism* 27 (2004), 325; Gareth Jenkins, "Turkey's Islamic Raiders of the Greater East Seeking Ties with al-Qaeda?" *Jamestown Terrorism Focus* 4, no. 40 (December 5, 2007), 6.
28. "*Kaide* (*al-Qaeda*) Magazine Published Openly in Turkey," *Memri Special Dispatch Series*, no. 951, August 7, 2005, at http://www.memri.org/report/en/0/0/0/0/0/0/1432.htm#_ednref3, accessed August 18, 2011.
29. Haldun Gülalp, "Turkey's 9/11," Project Syndicate, December 22, 2003, at http://www.project-syndicate.org/commentary/turkey-s-9-11.
30. Karl Vick, "Al-Qaeda's Hand in Istanbul Plot," *Washington Post*, February 13, 2007.
31. Dieter Bednarz, "Anatolischer Alptraum" (Anatolian Nightmare), *Der Spiegel* 13 (2003): 38–41; Frank Hyland, "U.S. Air Base at Incirlik Faces Political and Security Threats," *Jamestown Terrorism Focus* 4, no. 42 (December 19, 2007), at http://www.jamestown.org/single/?no_cache=1&tx_ttnews%5Btt_news%5D=4619.
32. "Eşler, El Kaide'nin bomba kuryesi çıktı" (The Wives Acted as Bomb Couriers for al-Qaeda), February 28, 2003, at http://www.milliyet.com.tr/2004/02/28/guncel/agun.html, accessed August 29, 2012.
33. Vick, "Al-Qaeda's Hand in Istanbul Plot."
34. "We reserve the right to retaliate . . . against all countries that take part in this unjust war [the Iraq War], namely Britain, Spain, Australia, Poland, Japan, and Italy." Bin

Laden on October 18, 2003, broadcast on *Timeline: Messages from Bin Laden*, al Jazeera, at http://english.aljazeera.net/news/middleeast/2010/01/2010124123232335456.html, accessed February 11, 2010.

35. See Guido Steinberg, *Der nahe und der ferne Feind: Die Netzwerke des islamistischen Terrorismus* (The Near and the Far Enemy: Networks of Islamist Terrorism) (Munich: Beck, 2005), 83–84.
36. David Ignatius, "The Mombasa Attacks: Al-Qaeda's New Weapon," *New York Times*, November 30, 2002.
37. Jenkins, *Political Islam in Turkey*, 210.
38. Ibid., 205.
39. After the attacks, Ekinci is reported to have fled to Dubai or Syria. Bernhard Zand, "Codename Abu Nidal," *Der Spiegel* 50 (2003), 141–142. He was later on suspected to have gone to Iraq. As of 2010, his whereabouts were unknown.
40. Helena Smith, "Suicide Bombers Are Buried in Turkey's Breeding Ground of Extremism," *The Guardian*, November 27, 2003.
41. The family of Gökhan Elaltuntaş, who attacked one of the synagogues on November 16, had trouble with extortionists from Hizbullah. Zand, "Codename Abu Nidal," 142.
42. Frank Bruni, "Turkish Town's Despair Breeds Terrorists, Residents Fear," *New York Times*, November 27, 2003.
43. Zand, "Codename Abu Nidal," 142.
44. Craig S. Smith, "Group Tied to al Qaeda Warns Europe of Attacks in Near Future," *New York Times*, July 3, 2004.
45. "Usuliyu Lundun: Al-Qaᶜida khasirat mu'ayyidiha baᶜd tafjirat al-Riyadh wa-Istanbul" (London Fundamentalists: Al-Qaeda Has Lost Her Supporters After the Riyadh and Istanbul Bombings), *al-Sharq al-Awsat*, November 19, 2003, at http://www.aawsat.com/details.asp?section=4&article=203846&issueno=9122, accessed February 11, 2010.
46. On November 8, 2003, al-Qaeda attacked the Muhayya residential compound in Riyadh and detonated a truck bomb. Seventeen people were killed, among them five children.
47. "Usuliyu Lundun: Al-Qaᶜida khasirat mu'ayyidiha baᶜd tafjirat al-Riyadh wa-Istanbul" (London Fundamentalists: Al-Qaeda Has Lost Her Supporters After the Riyadh and Istanbul Bombings), *al-Sharq al-Awsat*, November 19, 2003.
48. Abu Zubaida gave an introduction to the Khalden camp's history and function during his combatant status review tribunal hearing at Guantánamo in March 2007. He sent volunteers from Pakistan to this camp from 1994 and stressed that only those fighters were trained here who aimed at fighting the classical internationalists' "defensive jihad." Although parts of the statement sound apologetic, there is no reason not to accept his comments on Bosnia and Chechnya. See "Verbatim Transcript of Combatant Status Review Tribunal Hearing for ISN 10016," March 27, 2007, 9, 13, available through the US Department of Defense at http://www.defense.gov/news/transcript_ISN10016.pdf.

49. Holger Stark, "Wein, Whisky und Waffen" (Wine, Whisky, and Guns), *Der Spiegel* 34 (2005), 114–115.
50. "After two years of work and setting things up in Herat, Abu Musab started to think about sending his good companions whom he trusted to regions outside of Afghanistan. There, they should recruit and finance. It started, as far as I remember, with Turkey and Germany because the Syrian brothers who had joined him had a good outreach to these two regions." Saif al-Adl, *Al-Sira al-jihadiya li-l-qa'id al-dhabbah Abi Mus'ab al-Zarqawi* (The Jihad Career of the Slaughterous Leader Abu Mus'ab al-Zarqawi), at http://alboraq.info/showthread.php?t=97685, accessed June 21, 2010.
51. Stark, "Wein, Whisky und Waffen."
52. Funda Keskin, "Sakka'dan çarpıcı itiraflar" (Spectacular Confessions by Sakka), *Hürriyet*, February 21, 2006.
53. Dominik Cziesche, Jürgen Dahlkamp, and Holger Stark, "Aladin aus dem Schwarzwald" (Aladin from the Black Forest), *Der Spiegel* 33 (2005), 108–109.

6. "Leaving Kuffaristan": Radicalization and Recruitment in Germany

1. Christoph Scheuermann and Holger Stark, "Unter Freunden (Among Friends)," *Der Spiegel* 15 (2009): 44–46.
2. On this categorization, see Quintan Wiktorowicz, "Anatomy of the Salafi Movement," *Studies in Conflict and Terrorism* 29, no. 3 (2006): 207–239.
3. The standard work on Salafism is Roel Meijer, ed., *Global Salafism: Islam's New Religious Movement* (London: Hurst, 2009).
4. Bundesamt für Verfassungsschutz, *Lagebild zur Verfassungsfeindlichkeit "salafistischer Bestrebungen"* (April 24, 2011), 12–13, at http://www.bundesrat.de/DE/gremien-konf/fachministerkonf/imk/Sitzungen/11-06-22/anlage14,templateId=raw,property=publicationFile.pdf/anlage14.pdf.
5. Ibid, 13.
6. This phase model is drawn from Klaus Hummel, *Salafismus in Deutschland: Eine Gefahrenperspektive* (Salafism in Germany: A Threat Persepective) ([Dresden]: n.p., June 2009).
7. Lorenzo Vidino, *Al Qaeda in Europe: The New Battleground of International Jihad* (Amherst, NY: Prometheus Books, 2006), 255–256. Fazazi was released in April 2011. See Souad Mekhennet, "Moroccan King Opens Door for Change," *New York Times*, April 27, 2011.
8. Author's interview with Klaus Hummel of the Saxonia State Police, a leading German specialist on Salafism, Dresden, January 18, 2011.
9. Klaus Hummel, "Informelle Islamische Milieus in Deutschland: Blackbox der Radikalisierungsforschung" (Informal Islamic Milieus in Germany: The Blackbox of Radicalization Studies), in Stefan Malthaner and Peter Waldmann, eds., *Radikale*

Milieus: Das soziale Umfeld terroristischer Gruppen (Radical Milieus. The Social Environment of Terrorist Groups) (Frankfurt: Campus, forthcoming).

10. Author's interview with Klaus Hummel, January 18, 2011.
11. On Vogel's career in detail, see Hella Schmidt, "Der Salafismus in Deutschland: Pierre Vogels 'Einladung zum Paradies'" (Salafism in Germany: Pierre Vogel's "Invitation to Paradise"), MA thesis, Johannes Gutenberg-Universität, Mainz, 2011, 31–32.
12. As of August 2012, the Web address www.einladungzumparadies.de was closed down and substituted by www.muslimtube.de, but www.diewahrereligion.de still functioned.
13. Author's interview with Klaus Hummel, January 18, 2011.
14. The Sahaba are the prophet Muhammad's companions.
15. *Khutba* is the Arabic word for "sermon." On the developments in Vienna, see Hummel, *Salafismus in Deutschland*, 13.
16. On Maqdisi's career and thought in detail, see Joas Wagemakers, "A Quietist Jihadi-Salafi: The Ideology and Influence of Abu Muhammad al-Maqdisi," PhD diss., Radboud University Nijmegen, 2010.
17. *Urteil gegen Fritz Martin Gelowicz et al.* (Verdict against Fritz Martin Gelowicz et al.), Oberlandesgericht Düsseldorf, 2 StE 7/08-4 u. 2, StE 9/08-4 (June 24, 2010), 14; *Urteil gegen Youssef Mohamad El Haj Dib* (Verdict against Youssef Mohamad El Haj Dib), Oberlandesgericht Düsseldorf, 2 StE 7/07-3 (December 9, 2008), 26–27.
18. The Arabic verbal noun *takfir* means "excommunication." Hummel hints at the emergence of a fourth wing among German Salafists in *Salafismus in Deutschland*, 6.
19. Erich Rathfelder, "Bosnien: Razzia in der Hochburg der Islamisten (Bosnia: Razzia in the Islamists' Stronghold) ," *Die Presse*, February 2, 2010. The *takfiris*' ideological mentor is the *takfiri* scholar Abu Mariam al-Mikhlif in Kuwait. Abu Hamza's writings are available on his Web site at http://www.risalatun.com.
20. Author's interview with Klaus Hummel, January 18, 2011.
21. Estimates of the number of Salafists in Germany greatly vary, reflecting methodological difficulties. In my interviews with different German police and intelligence officials, the lowest estimate mentioned was 2,500, the highest was "at least 20,000."
22. Author's interview with Klaus Hummel, January 18, 2011.
23. See Çiftçi's biography on his Web site at http://www.abuanes.com. Between 1992 and 1994, he worked for the Turkish Islamist charity Foundation for Human Rights and Freedoms and Humanitarian Relief (İnsan Hak ve Hürriyetleri İnsani Yardım Vakfı) in Bosnia, but the German authorities suspect him of having also taken part in combat. Between 1998 and 2006, he studied religious science at the Islamic University of Medina and then settled in Brunswick in 2007. For a short overview of his career, see Frank Horst, "Salafist Jihadism in Germany" (January 2011), at the International Institute for Counter-Terrorism Web site, http://www.ict.org.il/Articles/tabid/66/Articlsid/887/currentpage/1/Default.aspx, accessed August 29, 2012. His online Islam school was closed down by the German authorities in summer 2012.

24. Author's interview with German police official, Berlin, May 7, 2011.
25. On Adem Yilmaz and the seminar in Bonn, see *Urteil gegen Fritz Martin Gelowicz et al.*, 28.
26. Yassin Musharbash and Marion Kraske, "Dschihadisten in Österreich—E-Mails an al-Qaida" (Jihadists in Austria—E-Mails to al-Qaeda), *Spiegel Online*, September 13, 2007.
27. The first one to mention the Iraqi dimension of the group was the German journalist Yassin Musharbash, who closely followed GIMF activity on the web from its beginnnings. Yassin Musharbash, "Al-Qaidas deutsche Lautsprecher" (Al-Qaeda's German Loudspeakers), *Spiegel Online*, August 29, 2006.
28. Matthias Gebauer and Yassin Musharbash, "Hannelore Krause fleht um ihren Sohn" (Hannelore Krause Pleads for Her Son's Life), *Spiegel Online*, July 11, 2007.
29. Hannelore Kadhim was later released, but her son remains missing.
30. Yassin Musharbash, "Wiener Propaganda-Bande: Starthilfe aus Kanada für den Medien-Dschihad" (The Vienna Propaganda Gang: Start-Up Aid for the Media Jihad), *Spiegel Online*, September 14, 2007.
31. Judith Kubitschek, "Dschihad auf Deutsch: Die wachsende Bedeutung des Internets für Dschihadisten und deren gezielte Ansprache deutschsprachigen Publikums am Beispiel der 'Globalen Islamischen Medienfront' (GIMF) und der deutschen Internet-Seite der 'Ansar al-Mujahideen'" (Jihad in German: The Growing Importance of the Internet for Jihadists and Their Targetting of a German-Language Auditorium. The Examples of the Global Islamic Media Front and the German Web Site "Ansar al-Mujahideen"), MA thesis, Eberhard-Karls-Universität Tübingen, n.d., 92.
32. Ibid., 105–106. *Eine Nachricht an die Regierungen von Deutschland und Österreich* (A Message to the Governments of Germany and Austria), video (GIMF, March 2007).
33. Quote in Yassin Musharbash, "Globale Islamische Medienfront—Anklage gegen den Qaida-Lautsprecher in Wien" (Global Islamic Media Front—Indictment of the al-Qaida Loudspeakers in Vienna), *Spiegel Online*, February 12, 2008, my translation into English.
34. Yassin Musharbash, "Terror-Propaganda im Internet—Dschihadist und Dilettant" (Terror-Propaganda on the Internet—Jihadist and Amateur), *Spiegel Online*, March 2, 2008.
35. Interview with German law enforcement official, Berlin, May 18, 2011.
36. The group consisted of a Serb (Peci), a German Tunisian, a German convert, a converted German Malay (Sepac), a Turk, a Pakistani, a German Indonesian woman, a German of Syrian descent, and an Afghan.
37. Marion Kraske and Yassin Musharbash, "Terrorpropaganda—Wiener Propaganda-Zelle besuchte radikale Moschee" (Terror-Propaganda—Vienna Propaganda Cell Frequented Radical Mosque), *Spiegel Online*, September 26, 2007.
38. For the arguments in this case, see Yassin Musharbash, "Osama Bin Ungläubig" (Osama Bin Nonbeliever), *Spiegel Online*, July 4, 2007.
39. Quoted in ibid., my translation into English.

40. See, for example, Umar's interview in "Der Video-Terrorist spricht: 'Der Heilige Krieg ist eine Pflicht'" (The Video-Terrorist Says: "Holy War Is a Duty"), *News* 48 (November 28, 2007): 16.
41. Text of a posting by Abu Dujana (=Sepac) on www.german-gimf.com, no date [December 2007]. I thank Yassin Musharbash for providing me with a copy of the original German text.
42. Interview with German law enforcement official, Berlin, May 18, 2011.
43. *Urteil gegen Ömer Özdemir und Sermet Ilgen* (Verdict against Ömer Özdemir and Sermet Ilgen), Oberlandesgericht Koblenz, 2 StE 3/09-8 (November 22, 2010), 90.
44. Author's interview with German intelligence official, Berlin, January 4, 2010.
45. *Urteil gegen Aleem Nasir (Verdict against Aleem Nasir)*, Oberlandesgericht Koblenz (2 StE 6/08 - 8) (July 13, 2009), 41.
46. For an overview of Lashkar-e Tayyiba, see Stephen Tankel, *Storming the World Stage: The Story of Lashkar-e-Taiba* (London: Hurst, 2011).
47. *Urteil gegen Aleem Nasir*, 48.
48. See Sebastian Rotella, "The Man Behind Mumbai," *Propublica*, November 13, 2010. On Majed in more detail, see Tankel, *Storming the World Stage*, 145, 158, 215, 222, 224, 252.
49. On Lakhvi, see Tankel, *Storming the World Stage*, 2–3, 20, 68, 75, 115, 171, 221, 230. On Nasir's relations to Lakhvi, see *Urteil gegen Aleem Nasir*, 44, 48, 50.
50. *Urteil gegen Ömer Özdemir und Sermet Ilgen*, 143–144.
51. *Urteil gegen Aleem Nasir*, 47–48.
52. Ibid., 52. As a matter of fact, there are religious and ideological differences between the Taliban—which is part of the Deobandi movement—and Lashkar-e Tayyiba, which is an offshoot of the smaller Ahl-e Hadith movement, close to the Saudi Arabian Wahhabiya. On these differences, see Guido Steinberg and Jan-Peter Hartung, "Islamist Groups and Movements," in Werner Ende and Udo Steinbach, eds., *Islam in the World Today: A Handbook of Religion, Culture, and Society* (Ithaca, NY: Cornell University Press, 2010), 686–687, 692.
53. *Urteil gegen Aleem Nasir*, 52–54.
54. Ibid., 56–64. On Nasir's contacts with leading al-Qaeda personnel, see ibid., 67–68.
55. *Urteil gegen Ömer Özdemir und Sermet Ilgen*, 30.
56. Ibid., 32.
57. Another of Aleem Nasir's possible recruits, Tolga Dürbin, has been convicted of incitement of the people because he produced this video together with Omar Yusuf. Ibid., 227; *Urteil gegen Aleem Nasir*, 58–59. On the content of the video *Das Tor der Trauer* (The Gate of Grief), see chapter 3.
58. *Urteil gegen Ömer Özdemir und Sermet Ilgen*, 68.
59. Ibid., 75–76.
60. Ibid., 80–81.
61. "Koblenz: Anschlag gestanden" (Koblenz: Confessed to an Attack), *Frankfurter Allgemeine Zeitung*, April 13, 2010.
62. *Urteil gegen Ömer Özdemir und Sermet Ilgen*, 91.
63. Ibid., 92.

64. *Urteil gegen Burhan Yilmaz wegen Unterstützung einer terroristischen Vereinigung im Ausland ("Islamische Jihad Union")* (Verdict Against Burhan Yilmaz Because of Material Support for a Foreign Terrorist Organization ["Islamic Jihad Union"]), Oberlandesgericht Frankfurt am Main, 5–2 StE 1/09-5-2/09 (March 16, 2010), 8.
65. Rolf Clement and Paul Elmar Jöris, *Die Terroristen von nebenan: Gotteskrieger aus Deutschland* (The Terrorists from Next Door: Warriors of God from Germany) (Munich: Piper, 2010), 104.
66. For instance, Kadir Türüt helped Yilmaz to procure night vision goggles and a video camera, which were sent to the IJU. *Urteil gegen Kadir Türüt* (Verdict Against Kadir Türüt), Oberlandesgericht Frankfurt am Main, 5–2 StE 8/09-5-12/09 (February 4, 2010), 18–19.
67. Abdul Ghaffar El Almani [Eric Breininger], *Mein Weg nach Jannah* (My Way to Jannah), edited by Elif Medya (n.p.: n.p., April 2010).
68. Ibid., 52.
69. Breininger uses a word here, *schändigen*, that does not exist. He most likely meant to write *schänden* (to defile) or *schädigen* (to harm).
70. El Almani, *Mein Weg nach Jannah*, 53, 55–56.
71. Author's interview with German police official, Berlin, January 27, 2011.
72. Al Malla was arrested together with Tolga Dürbin from Ulm.
73. El Almani, *Mein Weg nach Jannah*, 76–77.
74. As a police official recounts, Malla walked around Neunkirchen like a religious scholar, telling everyone what is Islamic and what not, even though he had attended a "special school" (*Sonderschule*) that is reserved for the weakest pupils whose intelligence borders on intellectual disability. In Malla's case, insufficient knowledge of German seems to have been the main reason for sending him to such a school.
75. Author's interview with German police official, Berlin, May 8, 2011.
76. El Almani, *Mein Weg nach Jannah*, 85.
77. Interrogation of Ramazan Başçıvan, Waldshut-Tiengen, October 15–18, 2009, unreleased BKA report.
78. Kahraman joined the first group of volunteers but returned to Germany from Iran. He was later prohibited from leaving Germany pending his trial because of his support for a terrorist organization, but he managed to escape and travel from Warsaw to Istanbul in August 2010. He was subsequently caught by the Turkish authorities and extradited to Germany. In April 2011, he was sentenced to one year and ten months in prison.
79. *Urteil gegen Alican Tufan* (Verdict Against Alican Tufan), Kammergericht Berlin, (1) 2 StE 6/10-4 (6/10) (June 22, 2011), passim; *Urteil gegen Fatih Kahraman* (Verdict Against Fatih Kahraman), Kammergericht Berlin, (1) 2 StE 6/10-4 (8/10) (April 6, 2011), passim; *Urteil gegen Filiz Gelowicz* (Verdict Against Filiz Gelowicz), Kammergericht Berlin, (1) 2 StE 6/10-4 (1/11) (March 9, 2011), passim.
80. Urteil gegen Alican Tufan, 38. Several members of the Berlin group of recruits were militant in their propaganda activities but apparently not ready to perpetrate terrorist attacks.
81. Author's interview with German intelligence official, Berlin, January 8, 2011.

7. The German Taliban Mujahideen

1. The word *taliban* is the Persian/Pashto plural of *talib* (student) and therefore not used correctly by *Bild*. "Eric Breininger—der deutsche Taliban: Sein Weg in den Tod" (Eric Breininger—the German Taliban: His Path to Death), *Bild*, May 6, 2010.
2. On December 15, 2010, the German Taliban Mujahideen declared that Fatih Temelli (a.k.a. Abdalfattah Almani, b. 1983, from Berlin) had been appointed its new emir. The declaration is very short, containing no hints as to its authenticity, indicating only the place of publication, a known Turkish jihadist Web site. See "Elif Medya Çok Yakında Yayında Olacak" (Elif Media Will Soon Be Online), December 15, 2010, at http://www.cihadmedya.net/11_Elif-Medya-Cok-Yakinda-Yayinda_Olacak.html, accessed February 6, 2011.
3. The founding of the group was announced in an Internet statement. See "Elif Medya Enformasyon Grubu Kuruldu" (The Elif Media Information Group Was Founded), February 12, 2009, at http://www.sehadetzamani.com/haber_detay.php?haber_id=2059, accessed February 1, 2011.
4. Interrogation of Rami Makanesi, Weiterstadt, September 29, 2010, unreleased BKA report.
5. Abdul Ghaffar El Almani [Eric Breininger], *Mein Weg nach Jannah*, edited by Elif Medya (n.p: n.p., April 2010). For a short summary of the text, see Yassin Musharbash, "Getöteter Eric Breininger—die Memoiren des deutschen Dschihadisten" (The Killed Eric Breininger—Memoirs of a German Jihadist), *Spiegel Online*, May 5, 2010.
6. El Almani, *Mein Weg nach Jannah*, 101.
7. Ibid., 102.
8. Ibid.
9. Ibid.
10. Deutsche Taliban Mujahideen, *Der Ruf zur Wahrheit* (The Call to Truth), video (Elif Medya, September 24, 2009). The name "German Taliban Mujahideen" appeared in the subtitles to the training sequences.
11. According to Ahmad Sidiqi, the hamlet was called "Machet" or "Masjid." Interrogation of Ahmad Wali Sidiqi in Bagram, October 2010, unreleased intelligence report.
12. *Horasan'dan Sesleniş* (Call from Khorasan), video (Elif Medya, April 28, 2009).
13. Michael Taarnby, *The Mujahedin in Nagorno-Karabakh: A Case Study in the Evolution of Global Jihad*, Working Paper 20/2008 (Madrid: Real Instituto Elcano, 2008), 7.
14. Yossef Bodansky, *Chechen Jihad: Al Qaeda's Training Ground and the Next Wave of Terror* (New York: HarperCollins, 2007), 36.
15. Ibid., 169–170.
16. Zeyno Baran, S. Frederick Starr, and Svante E. Cornell, *Islamic Radicalism in Central Asia and the Caucasus: Implications for the EU* (Washington, DC: Central Asia-Caucasus Institute and Silk Road Studies Program, July 2006), 17.
17. Author's interview with German law enforcement official, Berlin, May 17, 2011.

18. Jane's Terrorism and Security Monitor, "Victorious Sect Turkish Jihadists Move to Afghanistan," July 3, 2009, at http://www.janes.com/articles/Janes-Terrorism-And-Security-Monitor-2009/Victorious-Sect-Turkish-jihadists-move-to-Afghanistan.html, accessed August 15, 2009.
19. The Turks of the Taifetül Mansura are reported to have been based close to Mir Ali, and Eric Breininger is reported to have lived with them.
20. *Yardım kervanı yoluna devam ediyor* (Die Hilfskarawane setzt ihren Weg fort; The Support Caravan Continues on Its Path), video (Elif Medya, September 8, 2009).
21. Interrogation of Rami Makanesi, Weiterstadt, February 3, 2011, unreleased BKA report, 7.
22. On the group in detail, see interrogation of Ramazan Başçıvan by BKA, Waldshut-Tiengen, October 15–18, 2009, unreleased BKA report.
23. Author's notes from his observations in court, Kammergericht Berlin, January 20, 2011. The "other members" were most likely Yakub Erdal and Taner Kasapoğlu.
24. Jan Pavel Schneider was the child of German resettlers and born in Alma-Ata. From 2004, he studied at the Islamic University of Medina in Saudi Arabia and had met Daniel Schneider of the Sauerland group in August 2007. Shortly afterward, he took a flight to Saudi Arabia and from there to Pakistan, finally arriving in Waziristan in October.
25. Author's interview with German police official, Berlin, May 4, 2011.
26. These two people were the Moroccan Mohammed Ali Abdellaoui and the German Florian Korring.
27. El Almani, *Mein Weg nach Jannah*, 102.
28. Al-Hafidh Abu Talha der Deutsche, *Sicherheit—ein geteiltes Schicksal* (Security—a Shared Destiny), video (September 18, 2009).
29. In January 2009, the video *A Bailout Plan for Germany* appeared on the Internet. See Antje Kraschinski, *Al-Qaida's "A Bailout Plan for Germany": A NEFA Analysis* (New York: NEFA Foundation, February 10, 2009).
30. Yassin Musharbash, Marcel Rosenbach, and Holger Stark, "Langsame Eskalation: Drohbotschaften von al-Qaida beunruhigen die deutschen Sicherheitsbehörden" (Slow Escalation: Al-Qaeda's Threat Messages Worry the German Security Authorities), *Der Spiegel* 40 (2009): 22–26.
31. Al-Gharb wa-l-nafaq al-muzlim (The West and the Dark Tunnel), video (al-Sahab, September 2009).
32. A very popular Turkish fast-food item simply called *Döner* in German, costing roughly between 2.5 and 3.5 euro each.
33. El Almani, *Mein Weg nach Jannah*, 102–103.
34. Ibid., 102.
35. *Kurban Kampanyasi 1430/2009* (Id al-Adha Campaign, 1430/2009), video (Elif Medya, 2010); *Yardım kervanı yoluna devam ediyor.*
36. On Farag and his book, see Fawaz A. Gerges, *The Far Enemy: Why Jihad Went Global* (New York: Cambridge University Press, 2005), 10–11.

37. "Der einzige Weg ist der Widerstand und die Verbundenheit mit dem Jihad" (The Only Way Is Resistance and Sticking to Jihad), interview with Abu Ishaaq al-Muhajir (Ahmet Manavbaşı), January 24, 2010, at http://kufrakbar.blogspot.de/2010_01_01_archive.html, accessed August 31, 2012. The interview was first published at http://www.sehadetzamani.com. The interviewer is not named, and it can safely be assumed that the piece is a self-interview.
38. Ibid.
39. The Turkish Taifetül Mansura uses the name in singular form, as in when it appears on videos together with the German Taliban Mujahideen. See, for instance, the introduction to the video *Yardım kervanı yoluna devam ediyor*, where the correct Turkish translation "Afganistan İslam Emirliği" is used.
40. "Der einzige Weg," interview with Abu Ishaq al-Muhajir.
41. Ibid.
42. See, for instance, the German Taliban Mujahideen declaration "Die einzige Alternative ist der Widerstand [*sic*] und die Verbundenheit mit dem Jihad" (The Only Alternative Is Resistance and Sticking to Jihad), Elif Medya, October 8, 2009, at http://www.sehadetzamani.com/haber_detay.php?haber_id=2260, accessed November 21, 2009.
43. Ibid.
44. Deutsche Taliban Mujahideen, *Im Namen Allahs* (In the Name of Allah), video (Elif Medya, April 12, 2010).
45. "Der einzige Weg."
46. Ibid.
47. A "sister" addressing Filiz Gelowicz mentioned a more specialized explosives training in a letter describing the living conditions and activities of the German Taliban Mujahideen in Waziristan. *Urteil gegen Alican Tufan* (Verdict Against Alican Tufan), Kammergericht Berlin, (1) 2 StE 6/10-4 (6/10) (June 22, 2011), 72.
48. The announcement appeared on Turkish forums—for instance, at http://www.alcihad.com—and was signed by an alleged German called "Ebu Esila Almani."
49. Usztics had left Berlin together with a group of friends and their partners, including Danny Reinders, in September 2009. In summer 2011, his wife and baby, who had been jailed with him, were extradited to Germany.
50. Holger Stark, "Feuer und Schwefel" (Fire and Sulfur), *Der Spiegel* 20 (2011): 20–28.
51. "Elif Medya Çok Yakında Yayında Olacak."

8. "The Worst Enemy of Islam": The Islamic Movement of Uzbekistan Against Germany

1. "Islamic Movement of Uzbekistan on Situation in Palestine" (in Uzbek, original untranslated title unknown), Islamic Movement of Uzbekistan Web site, at http://www.furqon.com, March 23, 2009. I thank Natasha Cohen for providing me with the translated statements from the IMU, including those from the Voice

of the Islamic Republic of Iran and the one by Zubair Ibn Abd al-Rahim, cited in this chapter.

2. Islamische Bewegung Usbekistans, *Sieg oder Shahada (Märtyrertum)* (Victory or Shahada [Martyrdom]), video (April 2009).
3. Jochen Bittner, Andrea Böhm, Helene Bubrowski, Christian Denso, and Michael Thumann, "Befleckte Freundschaft (Stained Friendship)," *Die Zeit*, December 4, 2008.
4. The number of victims is highly contested. Official Uzbek sources speak of 187 dead, whereas witnesses estimated that the numbers might have reached 500. Jeremy Page and Anthony Browne, "Minister Who 'Led Killings' Treated in EU Despite Ban," *London Times*, November 18, 2005.
5. Ibid.
6. "Usbekistan—Hilfe für einen Verfemten" (Uzbekistan—Help for the Ostracized), *Der Spiegel* 46 (2005): 175; Michael Steen, "EU Policy on Uzbekistan Hypocritical—Rights Group Says," Reuters News, May 19, 2006.
7. For the German Taliban Mujahideen's comment on the Almatov case, see chapter 7.
8. Günther Lachmann, "Was die usbekische Stasi in Deutschland zu suchen hat" (What the Uzbek Stasi Has to Do in Germany), *Die Welt*, October 31, 2008.
9. In spite of the alleged private nature of the visit, Inoiatov is said to have had dinner with the head of the German BND, Ernst Uhrlau. Author's interview with German government official, Berlin, November 23, 2010.
10. Vitaly V. Naumkin, *Militant Islam in Central Asia: The Case of the Islamic Movement of Uzbekistan* (Berkeley: Berkeley Program in Soviet and Post-Soviet Studies, University of California, 2003), 15.
11. The organizational and ideological relations between these three groups are not always clear. Whereas some authors state that Adolat was one of two wings of Islam Lashkarlari, others describe the two as independent organizations. Naumkin, *Militant Islam*, 21, esp. n. 24; Uwe Halbach, *Sicherheit in Zentralasien*, vol. 2: *Kleinkriege im Ferganatal und das Problem der "neuen Sicherheitsrisiken"* (Security in Central Asia, vol. 2: Small Wars in the Fergana Valley and the Problem of "New Security Risks") (Cologne: Bundesinstitut für Ostwissenschaftliche und Internationale Studien, 2000), 14.
12. Martha Brill Olcott, *The Roots of Radical Islam in Central Asia*, Carnegie Papers no. 77 (Washington, DC: Carnegie Endowment for International Peace, January 2007), 36.
13. Abduvali Mirzaev disappeared in 1995. The Islamist opposition and most independent observers believe that he was kidnapped and killed by the Karimov regime. Ahmed Rashid, Jihad: *The Rise of Militant Islam in Central Asia* (New Haven, CT: Yale University Press, 2002), 145–146 , 256–257 n. 11.
14. Naumkin, *Militant Islam*, 22.
15. Michael Fredholm, "From the Ferghana Valley to Waziristan and Beyond: The Role of Uzbek Islamic Extremists in the Civil Wars of Tajikistan, Afghanistan, and Pakistan," *Islam, Islamism, and Politics in Eurasia Report* no. 22 (August 25, 2010), 6–7.

16. Guido Steinberg and Jan-Peter Hartung, "Islamist Groups and Movements," in Werner Ende and Udo Steinbach, eds., *Islam in the World Today: A Handbook of Politics, Religion, Culture, and Society* (Ithaca, NY: Cornell University Press, 2010), 688, 692–693.
17. Zahid Hussain, *Frontline Pakistan: The Struggle with Militant Islam* (New York: Columbia University Press, 2007), 77, 81.
18. Rashid, *Jihad*, 140.
19. Fredholm, "From the Ferghana Valley to Waziristan and Beyond," 5.
20. Ibid., 6.
21. Halbach, *Kleinkriege im Ferganatal*, 17 and 29.
22. ʿUmar ʿAbd al-Hakim [Abu Musʿab as-Suri], *Daʿwat al-Muqawama al-Islamiya al-ʿAlamiya* (n.p.: n.p., 2004), 784. Among the recruits was the later leader of the IJU, Najmiddin Jalolov. Other IMU leaders also trained in the Khattab camps in Chechnya.
23. Craig Murray, "Her Majesty's Man in Tashkent," *Washington Post*, September 3, 2006.
24. "Uzbek Islamic Movement: Government Must Go" (in Persian, untranslated original title unknown), Voice of the Islamic Republic of Iran, Mashhad, March 19, 1999.
25. "Uzbek Islamic Head: Karimov Must Resign" (in Persian, original untranslated title unknown), Voice of the Islamic Republic of Iran, Mashhad, April 24, 1999, quote from translated document, including material in brackets.
26. Ibid.
27. For more on Nassar, see Brynjar Lia, *Architect of Global Jihad: The Life of al-Qaida Strategist Abu Musʿab al-Suri* (London: Hurst, 2007).
28. Abd al-Hakim, *Daʿwat al-Muqawama al-Islamiya*, 785.
29. Interrogation of Fritz Martin Gelowicz, Düsseldorf, June 23, 2009, 11, unreleased BKA report.
30. Oleg Yakubov, *The Pack of Wolves: The Blood Trail of Terror* (Moscow: Veche, 2000), 254.
31. Az Zubayr Ibn Abdur Raheem, "The Call to Jihad by the Islamic Movement of Usbekistan," August 25, 1999; Rashid, *Jihad*, 248.
32. Yoldashev and Karimov had met in person in April 1991 when Karimov went to Namangan and promised demonstrators that he would name Islam as a state religion in the constitution of independent Uzbekistan. A debate between Karimov and Yoldashev over the latter's demand that Uzbekistan be made an Islamic state soon turned into a heated argument, with a furious Karimov finally walking out on Yoldashev and his supporters. Ahmed Rashid, *Jihad*, 138.
33. See, for instance, an interview with Tahir Yoldashev: "Uzbek Opposition Talks of Islamic State" (in Uzbek, original untranslated title unknown), Voice of the Islamic Republic of Iran, Mashhad, May 17, 1999.
34. See the declaration of the IMU's Political Committee: "Uzbek Islamic Movement Issues Statement" (in Persian, original untranslated title unknown), Voice of the Islamic Republic of Iran, Mashhad, April 11, 1999.
35. Naumkin, *Militant Islam*, 42; Abd al-Hakim, *Daʿwat al-Muqawama al-Islamiya*, 784.
36. "U.S. Puts Uzbek Group on Its Terror List," *New York Times*, September 15, 2000.
37. Abd al-Hakim, *Daʿwat al-Muqawama al-Islamiya*, 784.

38. Rashid, *Jihad*, 174.
39. On the estimate of the number of IMU fighters in Afghanistan, see ibid., 174; Ahmed Rashid, *Descent Into Chaos: The United States and the Failure of Nation Building in Pakistan, Afghanistan, and Central Asia* (New York: Viking Penguin, 2008), 80–81; and Abd al-Hakim, *Daʿwat al-Muqawama al-Islamiya*, 785.
40. The presence of Uighurs in Juma Namangani's troops was confirmed by the later emir of the Uighur Islamic Party of Turkistan, Abdalhaqq at-Turkestani, in an interview in March 2009. "Liqaʾ maʿa Amir al-Hizb al-Islami al-Turkistani, al-Akh al-Mujahid ʿAbd al-Haqq" (Meeting with the Emir of the Islamic Party of Turkestan, the Brother and Mujahid Abd al-Haqq), *Turkistan al-Islamiya* 1, no. 3 (Rabiʿ al-Awwal 1430): 9–12.
41. Abd al-Hakim, *Daʿwat al-Muqawama al-Islamiya*, 785.
42. Ibid., 783.
43. Interrogation of Rami Makanesi, Weiterstadt, September 3, 2010, 52, unreleased BKA report.
44. Olcott, *The Roots of Radical Islam*, 56, 60–61.
45. On Yoldashev's knowledge of Arabic and English, see interrogation of Rami Makanesi, Weiterstadt, September 3, 2010, 51.
46. Interrogation of Ahmad Wali Sidiqi in Bagram, October 2010, unreleased intelligence report. For the video, see Islamische Bewegung Usbekistans, *Frohe Botschaft aus Pakistan* (Glad Tidings from Pakistan) video (December 2010). The video appeared on jihadist Web sites in February 2011.
47. Author's interview with Noman Benotman, former LIFG leader, London, July 21, 2008. Ahmad Sidiqi also related this anecdote (with minor changes made here) in court in Koblenz, March 26, 2012.
48. Interrogation of Rami Makanesi, Weiterstadt, September 3, 2010, 93. Ahmad Sidiqi gave a similar account during his interrogation by German intelligence agents in Bagram. See interrogation of Ahmad Wali Sidiqi in Bagram, October 2010.
49. "Turkestan" is a name that many Islamists use for the whole of Central Asia, stressing the shared Turkic origin of the majority of its inhabitants. It includes the Chinese province of Xinjiang, which is inhabited by the Turkic Uighurs.
50. "Uzbek Exile Forms Political Party," Associated Press, May 21, 2001.
51. Michael Fredholm, *Uzbekistan and the Threat from Islamic Extremism* (Camberley: Conflict Studies Research Centre, Defence Academy of the United Kingdom, 2003), 10–11.
52. For a short summary of the interview with Zubair Ibn Abd al-Rahim, go to the Hellenic Resources Network Web site, specifically http://www.hri.org/cgi-bin/brief?/news/balkans/rferl/2001/01-06-07.rferl.html, accessed August 31, 2012.
53. On the battle at Shah-e Kot, see Paul L. Haster, "Operation Anaconda: Perception Meets Reality in the Hills of Afghanistan," *Studies in Conflict and Terrorism* 28 (2005): 11–20. For the IMU's role, see Sean Naylor, "The Lessons of Anaconda," *New York Times*, March 2, 2003.
54. On the course of events, see Hussain, *Frontline Pakistan*, 140–152.

55. On Nek Mohammed, see M. Ilyas Khan, "Profile of Nek Mohammed," *Dawn*, June 19, 2004.
56. Imtiaz Gul, *The Most Dangerous Place: Pakistan's Lawless Frontier* (London: Penguin, 2009), 24.
57. Ghazi was killed and so has been celebrated as a martyr of the jihadist movement on IMU videos ever since.
58. Jane Perlez, "Pakistan to Talk with Militants, New Leader says," *New York Times*, March 22, 2008.
59. Rahimullah Yusufzai, "Hidden Hand," *Newsline* (Karachi), February 2008.
60. Gul, *The Most Dangerous Place*, 21.
61. According to many sources, Tahir Yoldashev is simply called "Tahir Jan." Interrogation of Rami Makanesi, Weiterstadt (Hessen), September 3, 2010, 49. *Jan* or *Can* (Uzbek and Turkish for "soul") is an honorific used after the first name and indicates high respect and sympathy.
62. Gul, *The Most Dangerous Place*, 22.
63. On Maulvi Omar, see Sohail Abdul Nasir, "South Waziristan's Veteran Jihadi Leader: A Profile of Haji Omar," *Jamestown Terrorism Focus* 3, no. 31 (August 8, 2006): 5–6.
64. Thomas Ruttig, "Loya Paktia's Insurgency," in Antonio Giustozzi, ed., *Decoding the New Taliban: Insights from the Afghan Field* (London: Hurst, 2009), 77.
65. Bahukutumbi Raman, "Why Is There so Much Anti-Uzbek Anger?" *Outlook India*, April 9, 2007.
66. Gul, *The Most Dangerous Place*, 30.
67. Ibid., 55–56.
68. Raman, "Why Is There so Much Anti-Uzbek Anger?"
69. Interrogation of Ahmad Wali Sidiqi in Bagram, October 2010.
70. Syed Saleem Shahzad, "Pakistan: Al-Qaeda Leaders Call for New Jihad Against Armed Forces," *Adnkronos International*, January 17, 2008.
71. Jeremy Binnie and Joanna Wright, "The Evolving Role of Uzbek-Led Fighters in Afghanistan and Pakistan," *CTC Sentinel* 2, no. 8 (August 2009), 7.
72. See, for instance, Islamische Bewegung Usbekistans, *Frohe Botschaft aus Pakistan*. Rami Makanesi claims that Yoldashev personally told him that the IMU fought against Pakistan but did not mention other enemies. Interrogation of Rami Makanesi, Weiterstadt, September 3, 2010, 52.
73. Gul, *The Most Dangerous Place*, xxii–xxiii.
74. Ibid., xxii.
75. For a video of guerrilla operations in South Waziristan during 2010, see Islamische Bewegung Usbekistans, *Frohe Botschaft aus Pakistan*.
76. "Uzbek Islamic Movement Issues Statement."
77. Excerpts of this text are to be found in "Islamist Leader Threatens Central Asian Presidents," *BBC Monitoring Former Soviet Union*, September 17, 2006.
78. "Islamic Movement of Uzbekistan on Situation in Palestine."
79. Rami Makanesi reported that when he met the al-Qaeda leader Abu Yahia al-Libi in 2010 and told him that he had first joined the IMU, Libi covered his ears with his

hands. He did not want to hear anything about the competing organization. Interrogation of Rami Makanesi, Weiterstadt, October 11, 2010, 10.

80. Abu Ibraheem al-Almani [Yassin Chouka], *Unser Weg zur IBU* (Our Way to the IMU) (n.p.: February 2011), 2.
81. In September 2009, German police searched the houses of the members of a group around the German convert "Alexander F." suspected of helping German recruits travel to Yemen and study in the Dar al-Hadith, a notorious Salafist school in Dammaj in the northern part of the country. See, for example, Sven Böll, "Polizei durchsucht 19 Wohnungen" (Police Searches 19 Apartments), *Spiegel Online*, September 26, 2009.
82. Al-Almani, *Unser Weg zur IBU*, 3.
83. Ibid., 3–4.
84. "There is no God but God," the first part of the Muslim profession of faith.
85. This is the full profession of faith: "There is no God but God, and Muhammad is his prophet."
86. Al-Almani, *Unser Weg zur IBU*, 4.
87. Ahmad Sidiqi confirmed this conclusion. Interrogation of Ahmad Wali Sidiqi in Bagram, October 2010.
88. Ibid.
89. Ibid.
90. Ibid.
91. Islamische Bewegung Usbekistans, *Sieg oder Shahada (Märtyrertum)*.
92. See, for instance, Islamische Bewegung Usbekistans, *Soldaten Gottes* (Soldiers of God), video (Jundullah, March 2009).
93. The video is an extended version of an earlier video of the same title published in September 2008: *Frohe Botschaft aus Afghanistan* (Glad Tidings from Afghanistan) (September 2009), copy of video in author's possession.
94. "Terrorverdächtige identifiziert" (Terror Suspects Identified), *Der Spiegel* 42 (2009), 18.
95. These recruits were Yassin and Monir Chouka, Ahmad Sidiqi (and his wife), Sulaiman Sidiqi, Rami Makanesi, Jawad Sediqi (and his wife, who was reportedly forced to marry Yassin Chouka after Sediqi's death), Shahab Dashti (and his wife), Ömer Çibir, Abdullah Hafizi, Said Ballout (Faruq the German), and Samir Hattour (Abu Laith). Two other Germans—given the names "Abu Abdallah" and "Imran" (possibly Bünyamin Erdoğan, 1990–2010)—appear in the videos, but I could not identify them. Another German named Abu Anas is reported to have joined the IMU as well but did not appear in any video. Interrogation of Rami Makanesi, Weiterstadt, October 11, 2010, 20.
96. Interrogation of Ahmad Wali Sidiqi in Bagram, October 2010.
97. The women apparently stayed in Makin while most of the men were stationed in eastern South Waziristan. Ibid.
98. Islamische Bewegung Usbekistans, *Böses Vaterland* (Evil Fatherland), video (December 2011).
99. Islamische Bewegung Usbekistans, *Ja, wir sind Terroristen* (Yes, We Are Terrorists), video (March 2012).

100. Author's interview with German law enforcement official, Berlin, May 10, 2011.
101. Axel Spilcker, "Spenden vom Kalifen" (Donations by the Caliph), *Focus Magazin*, no. 9 (February 28, 2011), 61. Turgay Çibir is the son-in-law of the former head of the organization, Metin Kaplan, who has been in jail in Turkey since October 2004 and sentenced to life imprisonment.
102. For a short overview of the history of the organization Caliphate State, see Guido Steinberg, "Germany," in Barry Rubin, ed., *Guide to Islamist Movements*, 2 vols. (Armonk, NY: M. E. Sharpe, 2010), 2:459–468, esp. 464–465. The standard reference on the Kaplan movement is Werner Schiffauer, *Die Gottesmänner: Türkische Islamisten in Deutschland: Eine Studie zur Herstellung religiöser Evidenz* (God's Men: Turkish Islamists in Germany: A Study to Create Religious Evidence) (Frankfurt: Suhrkamp, 2000).
103. Author's interview with Ahmet Senyurt, a German TV journalist who specializes in the Muslim and Islamist scene in Germany, Cologne, May 12, 2011.
104. Author's interview with German intelligence official, Berlin, August 24, 2011.
105. Hasan Çibir himself gave a lively description of his conversation with Osama Bin Laden and the stay in Kabul in a report that he published in the Kaplan organization's magazine *Muhammad's Umma*: Hasan Cundullah [Çibir], "Afganistan Dosyası" (Afghanistan Dossier), *Ümmet-i Muhammed*, February 13, 1997, 6.

9. Germans in the Taliban Stalingrad: Fighting the Kunduz Insurgency

1. Matthias Gebauer and Holger Stark, "Islamist aus Essen wollte deutsche Soldaten töten" (Islamist from Essen Wanted to Kill German Soldiers), *Spiegel Online*, June 10, 2011.
2. Islamische Bewegung Usbekistans, *Der afghanische Blitz* (The Afghan Lightning), video (May 2011).
3. Thomas Bulmahn, Rüdiger Fiebig, and Carolin Hilpert, *Sicherheits- und verteidigungspolitisches Meinungsklima in der Bundesrepublik Deutschland: Ergebnisse der Bevölkerungsbefragung 2010 des Sozialwissenschaftlichen Instituts der Bundeswehr, Forschungsbericht 94* (Opinion Climate Concerning Security and Defense Policies in the Federal Republic of Germany: Results of the Opinion Poll 2010 by the Social Sciences Institute of the Bundeswehr, Research Report 94) (Berlin: Sozialwissenschaftliches Institut der Bundeswehr, May 2011), 56–57.
4. Ulrike Demmer, Christoph Hickmann, Dirk Kurbjuweit, and Ralf Neukirch, "Fear of Rising Death Toll: Berlin Reluctant to Follow American Lead on Afghanistan," *Spiegel Online*, January 25, 2011.
5. Timo Noetzel, "Germany's Small War in Afghanistan: Military Learning Amid Politico-strategic Inertia," *Contemporary Security Policy* 31, no. 3 (December 2010), 486.
6. Joschka Fischer, *"I Am Not Convinced": Der Irak-Krieg und die rot-grünen Jahre* ("I Am Not Convinced": The Iraq War and the Red-Green Years) (Cologne: Kiepenheuer & Witsch, 2011), 48, 52, 57, 62.
7. Claus Christian von Malzahn, "Schnell Flagge zeigen" (Quickly Showing One's Colors), *Der Spiegel* 3 (2002): 120–122. On the German troops' delay in getting to

Afghanistan, see Philip Blenkinsop, "Germany Explains Troops' Delayed Arrival in Kabul," *Reuters News*, January 11, 2002.

8. Markus Feldenkirchen, Matthias Gebauer, and Susanne Koelbl, "Der Fall von Bad Kunduz: Wie die Taliban ihre Macht im Raum Kunduz ausbauen" (The Fall of Bad Kunduz: How the Taliban Expand Their Power in the Kunduz Area), *Der Spiegel* 34 (2009): 29–33.
9. Zentrum für Nachrichtenwesen der Bundeswehr, *Leitfaden für Bundeswehrkontingente Afghanistan* (Field Manual for Bundeswehr Contingents Afghanistan), Druckschrift Einsatz no. 29 (Bad Neuenahr, Germany: Zentrum für Nachrichtenwesen der Bundeswehr, April 2007), 137.
10. Author's interview with German military intelligence officer formerly stationed in Kunduz, Berlin, September 3, 2010.
11. Author's interview with Captain (ret.) Nils Wörmer, military intelligence officer formerly stationed in Kunduz, Berlin, August 15, 2010.
12. Laurence Devlin, Jacob Rink, Christian Dennys, and Idrees Zaman, *Conflict Analysis: Kunduz City, Kunduz Province* (Kabul: Cooperation for Peace and Unity, March 2009), 5.
13. Ibid., 6–7.
14. On the "airlift of evil" in detail, see Ahmed Rashid, *Descent into Chaos: The United States and the Failure of Nation Building in Pakistan, Afghanistan, and Central Asia* (New York: Viking Penguin, 2008), 91–94. On the evacuation of IMU members, see ibid., 93, 164.
15. On the massacre, see the film by Jamie Doran, *Afghan Massacre: The Convoy of Death* (Atlantic Celtic Films, 2002). In July 2009, the *New York Times* reported that the Bush administration had obstructed efforts to investigate the killings because Dostum was an important US ally. James Risen, "U.S. Inaction Seen After Taliban P.O.W.'s Died," *New York Times*, July 10, 2009.
16. On Mullah Baradar in detail, see Guido Steinberg, Christian Wagner, and Nils Wörmer, *Pakistan Against the Taliban: Wave of Arrests Weakens Afghan Insurgents, but Still Doesn't Signal Strategic Shift*, SWP-Comments 8/2010 (Berlin: Stiftung Wissenschaft und Politik, March 2010), 3–6.
17. Author's interview with German military intelligence officer formerly stationed in Kunduz, Berlin, September 3, 2009.
18. Devlin et al., *Conflict Analysis*, 7.
19. Guido Steinberg and Nils Wörmer, *Escalation in the Kunduz Region: Who Are the Insurgents in Northeastern Afghanistan?* SWP-Comments 33/2010 (Berlin: Stiftung Wissenschaft und Politik, December 2010), 4–7.
20. Author's interview with German military officer formerly stationed in Kunduz, Berlin, August 16, 2011.
21. Author's interview with German military officer formerly stationed in Kunduz, Berlin, September 3, 2010.
22. Carlotta Gall, "Bombing Kills 9 Police Officers in Northern Afghanistan," *New York Times*, April 17, 2007.
23. "Wieder Selbstmordanschlag in Kunduz—zwei Tote" (Again a Suicide Attack in Kunduz—Two Deaths), *Spiegel Online*, May 28, 2007.

24. Author's interview with German military intelligence officer formerly stationed in Kunduz, Berlin, September 3, 2010.
25. Author's interview with Winfried Nachtwei, former member of Parliament for the Green Party and member of the Defense Committee, Berlin, July 22, 2011.
26. Author's interview with German military officer formerly stationed in Kunduz, Berlin, August 16, 2011.
27. On these groupings and their roles in Kunduz in detail, see Steinberg and Wörmer, *Escalation in the Kunduz Region*, passim.
28. The BND is the German foreign and military intelligence service. It is supervised by the Federal Chancellor's Office, not by the Defense Ministry.
29. Antonio Giustozzi and Christoph Reuter, *The Insurgents of the Afghan North: The Rise of the Taleban, the Self-Abandonment of the Afghan Government, and the Effects of ISAF's Capture-and-Kill Campaign* (Kabul: Afghan Analysts Network, 2010), 35–36.
30. Bill Roggio, "Afghan, Coalition Forces Strike the Taliban in Kunduz," *The Long War Journal*, November 9, 2009.
31. Alissa J. Rubin, "Reports Say Afghan Official in Showcase City May Have Criminal Background," *New York Times*, March 7, 2010.
32. See, for instance, the texts on northern Afghanistan in *The Long War Journal* (http://www.longwarjournal.com), which are based mainly on official ISAF reports.
33. Matthias Gebauer, Susanne Koelbl, and Christoph Reuter, "Die Stimmung wird kippen" (The Mood Will Turn), *Der Spiegel* 23 (2011), 39. Takhar has a population of some 900,000.
34. Author's interview with German military officer stationed in Kunduz, Berlin, May 14, 2011.
35. Author's interview with German military officer stationed in Kunduz, Berlin, December 9, 2010.
36. Ibid. Also see Anthony Bell, David Witter, and Michael Whittaker, *Reversing the Northeastern Insurgency* (Washington, DC: Institute for the Study of War, 2011), 10, 14–16.
37. Reinhard Veser, "Tadschikistan: Wiederkehr eines blutigen Gespenstes" (Tajikistan: Return of a Bloody Phantom), *Frankfurter Allgemeine Zeitung*, July 15, 2009; Abdujalil Abdurasulov, "Afghan, Pakistani Conflicts Spilling Into Central Asian States?" *Christian Science Monitor*, July 30, 2009.
38. International Crisis Group, *Tajikistan: The Changing Insurgent Threats*, Asia Report no. 205 (Brussels: International Crisis Group, May 24, 2011), 3–5, 8.
39. Roman Kozhevnikov, "Islamist Group Claims Responsibility for Tajik Bomb," *Reuters News*, September 9, 2010; Michael Ludwig, "Viele Tote und Verletzte bei Anschlag in Tadschikistan" (Many Dead and Injured After Attack in Tajikistan), *Frankfurter Allgemeine Zeitung*, September 3, 2010.
40. Author's interview with German military officer stationed in Kunduz, Berlin, December 9, 2010.
41. "Blutiger April" (Bloody April), *loyal: Magazin für Sicherheitspolitik* 5 (2010), 9.
42. Islamische Bewegung Usbekistans, *Der Afghanische Jihad* (The Afghan Jihad), video (May 2010).

43. The Chechen/Central Asian participation was first reported by *Der Spiegel*. See Susanne Koelbl, "Das Gesicht des Feindes" (The Face of the Enemy), *Der Spiegel* 15 (2010): 90–91.
44. Svante E. Cornell, "Narcotics, Radicalism, and Armed Conflict in Central Asia: The Islamic Movement of Uzbekistan," *Terrorism and Political Violence* 17 (2005): 577–597.
45. Author's interview with German military officer formerly stationed in Kunduz, Berlin, August 16, 2010.
46. Quoted in Nikolaus Blome and Jan Meyer, "1. Interview mit Verteidigungsminister Guttenberg: 'Ich verstehe jeden, der sagt, in Afghanistan ist Krieg' " (Interview with Defense Minister Guttenberg: "I Understand Everyone Who Says That There Is War in Afghanistan"), *Bild*, November 13, 2009.
47. Quoted in Oliver Das Gupta, "Herr Westerwelle redet ein bisschen Tacheles" (Mister Westerwelle Talks a Little Bit Plain), *Süddeutsche Zeitung*, February 10, 2010.
48. Marco Seliger, "Kunduz: Was läuft falsch?" (Kunduz: What Goes Wrong?), *loyal: Magazin für Sicherheitspolitik* 1 (2010), 24.
49. Author's interview with German military officer formerly stationed in Kunduz, Berlin, August 16, 2010.
50. Author's interview with German military officer formerly stationed in Kunduz, Berlin, September 3, 2010.
51. Noetzel, "Germany's Small War in Afghanistan," 492.
52. In August 2011, approximately 5,000 German soldiers were based in Afghanistan. Around 1,400 of them were deployed in Kunduz.
53. Berthold Kohler, "Dem Krieg ganz nahe" (Close to War), *Frankfurter Allgemeine Zeitung*, November 16, 2009.
54. Author's interview with German military intelligence officer formerly stationed in Kunduz, Berlin, September 3, 2010.
55. Author's interview with German military officer formerly stationed in Kunduz, Berlin, August 16, 2010. Another military officer told me that this had become a general problem in 2011: "In the very moment that the Germans provide the Afghan security forces with information, it is already leaked to the insurgents." Interview with German military officer stationed in Kunduz in 2010, Berlin, December 9, 2010.
56. Marc Lindemann, *Unter Beschuss: Warum Deutschland in Afghanistan scheitert* (Under Fire: Why Germany Fails in Afghanistan) (Berlin: Econ, 2010), 44–45.
57. As of August 2012, the Bundeswehr had lost fifty-three soldiers in Kunduz, thirty-four of them fell in combat.
58. Rajiv Chandrasekaran, "Sole Informant Guided Decision on Afghan Strike," *Washington Post*, September 6, 2009.
59. For a summary of different estimates, see Generalbundesanwalt beim Bundesgerichtshof, *Ermittlungsverfahren gegen Oberst Klein und Hauptfeldwebel Wilhelm wegen des Verdachts einer Strafbarkeit nach dem VStGB und anderer Delikte: Einstellung des Verfahrens* (Preliminary Investigations Against Colonel Klein and Sergeant Wilhelm Because of the Suspicion of Criminal Liability According to the Code of Crimes

Against International Law [Völkerstrafgesetzbuch] and Other Offenses: Dismissal of the Investigations) (April 16, 2010), 36–39, at http://www.generalbundesanwalt.de/docs/einstellungsvermerk20100416offen.pdf, accessed September 12, 2012. In this report, the German chief prosecutor himself presents a very conservative estimate of fifty persons altogether killed and wounded.

60. Chandrasekaran, "Sole Informant Guided Decision on Afghan Strike."
61. See, for instance, Christoph Schwennicke, "Merkels Altlast" (Merkel's Burden of the Past), *Der Spiegel* 38 (2009), 78–79.
62. Deutsche Taliban Mujahideen, *Der Ruf zur Wahrheit* (The Call to Truth), video (Elif Medya, September 24, 2009).
63. Author's interview with Winfried Nachtwei, July 22, 2011.
64. Matthias Gebauer and Veit Medick, "Poker um Bundeswehr in Afghanistan: Obama lockt, Merkel zockt" (Poker Over Bundeswehr in Afghanistan: Obama Bluffs, Merkel Gambles), *Spiegel Online*, December 2, 2009.
65. Matthias Gebauer and Shoib Najafizada, "Karzai, McChrystal Declare German Deployment Area a Crisis Zone," *Spiegel Online*, December 12, 2009.
66. Bell, Witter, and Whittaker, *Reversing the Northeastern Insurgency*, 9 and passim.
67. Author's interview with German military officer stationed in Kunduz, Berlin, December 9, 2010.
68. Ibid.
69. Ibid.
70. On the new insurgent strategy, see Gebauer, Koelbl, and Reuter, "Die Stimmung wird kippen."
71. Ray Riviera, "Taliban Bomber Infiltrates Afghan–NATO Meeting, Killing Police Official and Others," *New York Times*, May 28, 2011; Matthias Gebauer and Shoib Najafizada, "Taliban-Sprengsatz war in Mauer versteckt" (Taliban Explosive Device Was Hidden in the Wall), *Spiegel Online*, May 30, 2011.
72. Gebauer and Stark, "Islamist aus Essen wollte deutsche Soldaten töten."
73. Faruq himself is shown in the video addressing his audience in accent-free German. Islamische Bewegung Usbekistans, *Der kompromisslose Bräutigam* (The Uncompromising Bridegroom), video (March 2011).
74. Interrogation of Rami Makanesi, Weiterstadt, September 3, 2010, 105, unreleased BKA report.

10. "This Is the Last Year America": Threats and Propects

1. Islamische Bewegung Usbekistans, *Böses Vaterland* (Evil Fatherland), video (December 2011).
2. For instance, Sauerland group member Atilla Selek was released in July 2011 after having served two-thirds of his sentence of five years.
3. In December 2011, they were joined by their German Turk comrade Halil Şimşek (b. 1984), who was accused of continuing to plan the attack after the others were arrested.

4. On the connection between Kebir and Atiyatallah, see Marcel Rosenbach and Holger Stark, "Eine Bombe für Deutschland" (A Bomb for Germany), *Der Spiegel* 19 (2011), 28. Ahmad Sidiqi described Atiyatallah as the successor to Mustafa Abu l-Yazid, who was killed by a drone strike in May 2010. Interrogation of Ahmad Wali Sidiqi in Bagram, October 2010, unreleased intelligence report. In August 2011, Atiyatallah was killed in a drone attack.
5. Author's interview with German intelligence official, Berlin, August 29, 2011.
6. Thorsten Dörting, "Auf der Spur des Lötkolbens" (On the Track of the Soldering Iron), *Spiegel Online*, May 1, 2011.
7. The strategy paper was entitled "Future Work," and the papers on activities in the United Kingdom "Report on Operations" and "Lessons Learned from Previous Operations." The BKA official testifying in the trial against Ocak and Lodin called the documents "a sensation."
8. The inability to monitor the militants' radicalization processes does not seem to be an exclusive German problem, but rather one that most Western intelligence services face. On the case of the American al-Qaeda member Bryant Neal Vinas, for instance, see Michael Powell, "U.S. Recruit Reveals How Qaeda Trains Foreigners," *New York Times*, July 24, 2009.
9. Interrogation of Rami Makanesi, Weiterstadt (Hessen), September 3, 2010, unreleased BKA report, 106, 109.
10. On the centrality of the Haqqani network, see Don Rassler and Vahid Brown, *The Haqqani Nexus and the Evolution of al-Qaʿida* (West Point, NY: Combating Terrorism Center at West Point Harmony Program, July 14, 2011), passim.
11. Interrogation of Rami Makanesi, Weiterstadt, September 3, 2010, 105.
12. For instance, the German Rami Makanesi reported that he took part in an al-Qaeda basic-training course in Waziristan in 2010 together with Tajiks, Turks, Kuwaitis, Saudi Arabians, Lebanese, Syrians, a South African, and a Russian. His instructor was Lebanese, and the latter's boss was Libyan. Interrogation of Rami Makanesi, Weiterstadt, November 17, 2010, 8.
13. *La tukallaf illa nafsak* (You Are Held Responsible Only for Thyself), part 1, video (As-Sahab Media, June 3, 2011).
14. Yunus al-Muritani to Zamaraʾi [Bin Laden], March 28, 2010, unfiled court documentin my possession.
15. Ibid.

Index